MASTERING WORDPERFECT

MASTERING WORDPERFECT®

Susan Baake Kelly

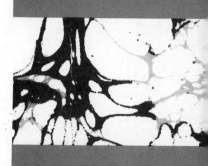

San Francisco • Paris • Düsseldorf • London

Cover Design by Thomas Ingalls + Associates
Photography by Casey Cartwright
Book Design by Lisa Amon
Layout and paste-up by Karin Lundstrom

To my wonderful husband Jim, with love

Personally I'm always ready to learn, although I do not always like being taught.

—Winston Churchill

ACKNOWLEDGMENTS

Special thanks to Mom, for everything.

Thanks also to Greg Harvey, for getting me started and being there when I needed to talk.

I am especially grateful to my patient and thoughtful editors David Kolodney, developmental editor, and Michael Wolk, copy editor, and all the others who were responsible for this book, including Joel Kroman, technical review; David Clark and Olivia Shinomoto, word processing; Lisa Amon, book design; Dawn Amsberry, typesetting; Laura Hurd, proofreading; Anne Leach, indexing; and to Karl Ray, managing editor, and Carole Alden, acquisitions editor.

For their work on the revised edition I wish to thank David Clark, editor, who did a marvelous job with the update and found many minor errors we had all overlooked previously; Barbara Gordon, acting managing editor; John Kadyk, word processing; Karin Lundstrom, layout and paste-up; Denise Hilton and Gladys Varon, typesetting; Michelle Hoffman, screen reproduction; and Stephanie Bower, proofreading.

Many thanks to Jeff Acerson and Dan Lunt of WordPerfect Corporation, and all the folks on WordPerfect Corporation's technical support line who have been so helpful, including Sherry, Lynn, Robin, Debbie, Stuart, Kelly, Becky, and Lisa.

Finally, thanks and much appreciation to Kathy and Manny Sotomayor; Pam Warriner and Elizabeth Chatham of Bay Area Business Services for their wonderful advice about word processing and legal terms; Suzanne Statler, who helped me understand and incorporate the learning process of a computer novice into Chapter 1; Sharon and Ron Bealle; the law firm of Varni, Fraser, Hartwell, and Rogers, for help with line numbering and table of authorities and for being such enthusiastic students; Patrick Corrigan of the Corrigan Group for his help with DOS and networking applications; Valerie Frank of Diablo Valley College for pertinent observations and suggestions about the book and her strong enthusiasm; and to the many outstanding professors at San Francisco State University's School of Business, who gave me a great education.

TABLE OF CONTENTS

Introduction   *xxii*

Why a Book about WordPerfect?   xxv

   How to Use This Book   xxvi

   Assumptions about Your Hardware and Software   xxvii

   A Final Word   xxviii

Part I   All the Fundamentals

1 *The Keyboard and Basic Editing*   1

Starting WordPerfect   2

   Starting WordPerfect on a Two Floppy Disk System   2

   Starting WordPerfect on a Hard Disk   3

The WordPerfect Editing Screen   4

   The Status Line   4

The WordPerfect Keyboard   6

   Shift   6

   Alt and Ctrl   6

   The Function Keys   7

   The Return Key   9

   Num Lock and Caps Lock   10

   The Delete, Backspace, and ← Keys   11

   Ins (Insert)   12

   Cancel and Undelete   13

Basic Cursor Movement   14

   Moving One Character at a Time   15

   Moving Word by Word   16

Moving to the Beginning or End of a Line   16
Page Up, Page Down, Screen Up, and Screen Down   16
Deleting Hidden Codes   17
Unwanted Page Breaks   18
Getting Help   18
Deleting Larger Segments   21
Exiting from WordPerfect   21
File Management and Overflow Files   22
Summary   23

2 *Creating a Short Letter*   **27**
A Word about Intimidation   28
Creating a Sample Letter   28
Inserting the Date   28
The Inside Address   29
The Salutation   30
Using Word Wrap   30
Inserting a New Sentence   30
Deleting a Sentence   32
The Complimentary Close   32
Saving the Letter to Disk   32
The Save Key   33
Save and Exit   34
Printing   35
The Print Key   35
If the Printer Does Not Work   36
Exiting from WordPerfect   36
Summary   37

3 *Formatting and Enhancing Text*   **41**
Formatting Your Text   43
Margins   43

Flush Right   44
Print Enhancements   45
Tabs   46
The Tab and Indent Keys   48
The Speller   49
Saving and Printing the Letter   51
Experimenting with the Margins   52
Spacing   53
Hyphenation   54
The Reveal Codes Key   55
Summary   59

4 *Block Operations*   63

The Block Key   64
Copy and Cut   65
Move   66
Delete   67
Using the Move Key Alone   68
Relocating a Sentence within a Paragraph   70
Printing a Block   70
Saving a Block   71
Converting between Uppercase and Lowercase   72
Block Underlining and Boldfacing   74
Summary   74

Part II   Advanced Word Processing Features

5 *Page Formatting*   81

The Page Format Key   82
Page Number Position   82

Page Number Column Positions   85
New Page Number   86
  Numbering Style   87
Center Page Top to Bottom   88
Page Length   90
  Calculating Customized Settings   91
Top Margin   92
Headers and Footers   93
  The Header/Footer Screen   93
  Viewing Headers in the Reveal Codes Screen   95
  Placing a Page Number in a Header or Footer   97
Suppress for Current Page Only   98
Soft Page   99
Conditional End of Page   100
Block Protect   100
Widows and Orphans   102
Summary   104

6 *Search and Replace*   *109*

Search   110
  Repeating the Search   111
  Reverse Search   112
  Restricting the Search   113
  Searching with Ctrl-X, the Wildcard Character   113
Search and Replace   115
  Finding and Deleting Codes with Search and Search and
    Replace   118
  Extended Search   120
Summary   120

7 *Advanced Formatting Features*   *123*

Hyphenation   124
    Soft Hyphens   126
    Other Hyphens   126
    Changing the Hyphenation Zone   127
Left, Center, Right, and Decimal Tabs   129
    Leader Characters   131
The Alignment Character   132
    Editing Text that Has Been Aligned   135
Hard Spaces   137
The Date Key   139
    Date Format   139
    Insert Function   141
Hanging Paragraphs   142
Superscript and Subscript   143
Advance   144
    Advance by Lines   146
Overstrike   147
Redline and Strikeout   148
Line Numbering   150
    The Line Numbering Options   151
Summary   154

8 *Printer Control and Options*   *159*

The Printing Methods   160
    The Full Text and Page Printing Options on the Print Key   160
    Two Methods of Printing a Document from Disk   161
    Printing by Block   164

The Print Screen Key   164

Typewriter Mode   164

Printer Control   168

Select Printers   169

Display Printers and Fonts   169

Select Print Options   169

Controlling Print Jobs   172

The Print Format Key   176

Pitch and Font   176

Lines Per Inch   179

Right Justification   179

Underline Style   180

Sheet Feeder Bin Number   180

Insert Printer Command   181

Print Preview   181

Summary   182

9 Reference Tools 187

Lists   188

Creating a List   189

A. Marking the Items To Be Included in the List   189

B. Defining the Style   190

C. Generating the List   193

Generating a List If Your Document Already Includes a List, Index, or Table of Contents   194

Changing the Page Number Position   195

Tables of Contents   196

Creating a Table of Contents   198

A. Marking the Items To Be Included in the Table of Contents   198

B. Defining the Style   198

C. Generating the Table of Contents   201

Indexes   201
Creating an Index   202
   A. Marking the Text to Be Included in the Index   202
   B. Using a Concordance File   204
   C. Defining the Style   206
   D. Generating the Index   208
Tables of Authorities   208
   A. Marking the Citations to Be Included in the
      Table of Authorities   209
   B. Defining the Style   214
   C. Generating the Table of Authorities   216
Paragraph Numbering and Outlines   216
Creating an Outline   216
   Numbering and Punctuation Styles   220
   Numbering Paragraphs   224
Summary   225

10 *Parallel and Newspaper Columns*   *229*
Newspaper Columns   230
   A. Defining Newspaper Columns   230
   B. Turning the Columns Feature On   236
   C. Entering Text in Columns   237
   Retrieving Data into a Column   239
   Erasing Column Formatting   239
   Column Display   241
Parallel Columns   241
Summary   244

11 *Footnotes and Endnotes*   *247*
Creating and Editing Footnotes   248
Creating and Editing Endnotes   249

Changing Footnote and Endnote Options   249

Deleting Footnotes and Endnotes   254

Renumbering Footnotes   254

How Margin Changes in the Document Affect Footnotes and
    Endnotes   255

Summary   255

Part III   Supplemental Features

12 File Management   261

The List Files Key   262

    Cursor Movement in the List Files Screen   263

    Selecting Multiple Files   263

    Narrowing the Display with Wildcards   264

    Retrieving Files   265

    Deleting Files   266

    Renaming Files   266

    Printing Files   266

    Importing ASCII Files   266

    Looking at Files   267

    Changing, Creating, or Deleting a Directory   267

    Copying Files   270

    Searching All Files for a Word or Phrase   270

Block File Commands   271

    Save   271

    Append   271

The Text In/Out Key   272

    Converting a WordPerfect File to ASCII   272

    Importing ASCII Files to WordPerfect   273

    Password Protection   273

Document Summary   275

Document Comments   277

Displaying the Summary and Comments   278

Deleting the Summary and/or Comments   279

Editing the Summary and/or Comments   280

Temporarily Exiting to DOS: The Shell Key   280

Working with Two Documents in RAM   281

Making Automatic Backups   284

Summary   285

13 *Merges*   *291*

Form Letters   292

The Primary File   292

The Secondary File   295

Merging the Primary and Secondary Files   297

Stopping a Merge   297

Updating the Screen   298

Merging to the Printer   298

Merging from the Keyboard   299

Inserting Reminders in the Primary File   301

Producing Mailing Labels and Envelopes from the Secondary
File   302

Printing Envelopes and Mailing Labels   305

Summary   306

14 *Math*   *309*

Totalling Numbers   310

Math Columns   314

Defining the Columns   315

Entering the Data   317

Changing the Math Definition   319

Using Total Columns   320
Copying, Deleting, and Moving Columns   321
Using Averages in Math Columns   324
Summary   326

15 *Sort and Select*   *329*

Line Sort   330
Select   334
Paragraph Sort   337
Secondary Merge Sort   340
Sorting a Block   343
Summary   344

16 *Macros*   *349*

Alt Macros   351
   A Line-Spacing Macro   352
Temporary Macros   353
   A Macro to Underline a Word   354
   A Macro to Convert a Character to Uppercase   354
Repeating a Macro   355
User Input in a Macro   355
Making Your Macros Visible   356
Macros with Search and Replace   357
Macro Chaining   359
Macros with Merges   360
   Starting a Macro from within a Merge   361
Summary   362

17 *Line Drawing*   *365*

Using Line Draw   366
   Using the Escape Key to Speed Up Drawing   367

Using Option 4 to Change the Character   368

Moving the Cursor   369

Erasing a Line   370

Cutting, Copying, or Moving a Line Drawing   370

Printing   371

Summary   372

18 *The Speller and Thesaurus*   *375*

The Speller   376

Checking a Word, Page, Block, or Document   376

The Speller Utility   383

The Thesaurus   385

Summary   388

A *Installation*   *391*

Program Installation   391

Floppy Drive System   391

Hard Disk System   393

The PC-DOS Tree Command   394

Options for Entering WordPerfect   395

Automatic Backup   395

Redirecting Overflow Files, Buffers, and Temporary Macros   396

Start Up with a Document File   396

Uninstalled or Copied Versions of the Original   396

Start Up with a Macro   396

Non-Flash Version   397

Non-Synch Version for Hyperion Machines and Color
Monitors   397

Speeding Up the Program   397

Starting WordPerfect with the Set-Up Menu   397

The WordPerfect Set-Up Menu   398

Printer Installation   400

B Commands, Functions, and Codes   405

Commands and Functions—Listed Alphabetically   405
Commands and Functions—Listed by Key   413
Cursor Movement   417
Codes   418

C WordPerfect Corporation's Other Products   423

WordPerfect Library   424
PlanPerfect   425
DataPerfect   426
   Repeat Performance   426
The WordPerfect Support Data   427

Index   428

Introduction

WordPerfect is one of the most powerful and comprehensive word processing programs available for the IBM PC and compatibles. The manufacturer, WordPerfect Corporation, has been making improvements in the program constantly since it was first released in 1982, demonstrating an admirable effort to satisfy user requests and to incorporate suggestions from reviewers. The latest version, 4.2, has earned lavish and well-deserved praise from the critics, and the program is now widely acclaimed as one of the best word processors on the market. Sales reflect the endorsements, for as of this writing, WordPerfect was the best seller in the word processing category, and one of the top three among all microcomputer programs on the market.

WordPerfect is an amazing package. It is fast, efficient, and a genuine pleasure to use. However, the program is better known for an abundance of helpful features and the fact that WordPerfect Corporation keeps adding more to each version. All of the fundamental word processing functions are available, such as *automatic word wrap,* which creates a new line when the cursor reaches the right margin, and moves both the cursor and any words that would have exceeded the right margin to the new line automatically; *search and replace,* which can locate and change a word or phrase; *block commands* to copy, move, and delete sections of text; and *automatic rewrite,* which automatically reformats your paragraphs after any editing changes such as additions or deletions.

WordPerfect's abilities extend way beyond the basics, though, to include such special features as *macros,* which can automate your most commonly used keystrokes and commands; the ability to *index* a document and create a *table of contents* for it; *outlining* and *paragraph numbering; mathematical functions* such as addition, subtraction, multiplication, division, and averaging; *document locking,* which protects confidential files with passwords; a *switch documents* feature to shift back and forth and even exchange data between two documents that are held in the computer's memory; and a built-in *spelling checker.*

Version 4.1 added more to this impressive collection, including *windows* to split the screen horizontally so that two documents can be viewed simultaneously; *newspaper columns,* in which text flows from one column to the next; the ability to create as many as five *parallel columns* of text that appear side by side on screen, and are edited independently of one another; a *thesaurus;* the ability to *sort* text or numbers in ascending or descending order, using up to nine sorting levels; the ability to *select* speci-fied kinds of items from a list; a *line draw* feature that can draw lines, boxes, and graphs; a *word search* feature that can check all documents on the data disk for a word or phrase; and an improved *undelete* command that can remember and restore the last three deletions.

WordPerfect 4.2 added even more features, including *line numbering* and *table of authorities* for law offices; nonprinting *document comments*; a *document summary* that can include the file name, date, author, typist, and up to 880 characters of comments; *left, right, center,* and *decimal tabs*; *document preview* so you can view margins, page numbers, headers, foot-ers, footnotes, and endnotes on screen; and a *concordance* feature to sim-plify the indexing process.

Why a Book about WordPerfect?

The manual that comes with WordPerfect is clear and well written, but it has a tendency to assume that you are already familiar with the word pro-cessing concepts being demonstrated, and it often lacks explanations that are detailed enough to help you master the many exceptional features. These weaknesses are especially noticeable when you read the chapters covering the more complex operations such as merges and sort and select, which are the hardest to understand and the least likely to be familiar to the typical user. Rather than providing the necessary background so that you will understand exactly what you are doing and why, the manual con-centrates on telling you the precise keystrokes necessary to use each fea-ture in one or more specific examples. In fact, you are often led through an exercise and never told or shown in an illustration what the outcome will be, so you can't even be sure if you've performed it correctly!

The manual can also be ineffective as a learning tool for those who have never used a word processor. Although the introductory lessons are easy to follow as they lead you through the proper sequence of keystrokes, it would have been helpful if the individual steps had included adjacent defi-nitions of the basic concepts being used. It doesn't do you much good to be told precisely how to flush a header at the right margin if you don't understand what a header is or what flush means.

Mastering WordPerfect is designed to fill this need, and will become indispensable as both a tutorial and a reference guide. Although it is not intended to replace your manual, which is still useful as a supplement, you'll find this book clearer and more comprehensive. The book's goal is to help you get an understanding of the concepts behind each function: that is, not just how they work, but when, where, and why they are used, so that you are better equipped to explore WordPerfect and expand your understanding of its powerful features on your own.

Mastering WordPerfect is excellent for the beginner, because it assumes no prior knowledge of word processing; it explains the purpose and significance of WordPerfect's basic operations as they are introduced, in a logical step-by-step approach. For users who have had some experience with the program, this book will fill in the gaps and make it easier to explore and utilize some of the more sophisticated features you have not been taking advantage of. For the skilled user, the book will explain the advanced features in greater depth, and provide many new examples and ideas to incorporate into your work.

How to Use This Book

Users of all levels of experience can benefit from this book, but not all readers will want to use it the same way. Part One is a basic tutorial that covers the fundamentals and helps new WordPerfect users to get acquainted with the basics of the program before being introduced to more complex topics. It will teach you how to create, edit, format, print, and save commonly used documents such as letters and memos, and then examine some of the fancier offerings that differentiate word processors from typewriters, their antiquated ancestors. If you follow the lessons in sequence, by the end of the fourth chapter you should be comfortable with all of WordPerfect's basic word processing operations, and you will be able to skip to any other chapter that interests you without feeling overwhelmed by the material.

The remaining chapters are designed to be comprehensive guides to specific topics. Readers who already have a solid foundation in the program's fundamentals can study these in any order without having to labor through the basics, but less experienced users should not attempt them until they have mastered the skills covered in Part One.

Part Two teaches advanced word processing operations, providing extensive examples and detailed explanations. It covers formatting features such as hyphenation assistance, hard spaces, justification, footnotes, and end-notes, as well as search and replace, the print queue, and much more. It also explores some of the more unusual ones that help distinguish WordPerfect from the majority of word processors on the market, including indexing, newspaper columns, parallel columns, outlines, and paragraph numbering.

Part Three covers WordPerfect's supplemental features and utilities such as math, macros, sort and select, line and box drawing, merges, the spelling checker and thesaurus, document locking, and the many file management functions.

Several appendixes complete the book, describing installation and system requirements, summarizing WordPerfect's commands, functions, and keyboard usage, and describing other programs available from WordPerfect Corporation.

Assumptions about Your Hardware and Software

This book was written for the IBM PC, XT, and AT, which use PC-DOS, as well as all highly compatible computers that use MS-DOS. Separate versions of the program are available for most of the less compatible computers such as the DEC Rainbow, Texas Instruments PC, Victor 9000, Data General, Apricot, Tandy 1000 and 2000, and IBM 3270. Readers using these computers may have to press a few different keystroke combinations from the ones shown in this book to implement the commands, but the functions will be the same.

Although there have been several versions of WordPerfect, this book assumes you are using version 4.2, (which requires DOS 2.0 or a later version of DOS). Earlier versions used different keystroke combinations for several functions, so if you are not using 4.2, you may need to check your manual or keyboard template for the correct ones. In addition, several features were introduced in 4.2, so many of the subjects covered in these chapters will be unavailable to you. It is strongly recommended that you upgrade to Version 4.2, because it contains major improvements and additions. WordPerfect Corporation has a very reasonable upgrade policy, charging only $35.00 for the new manual and diskettes if the upgrade is from version 4.1 to 4.2, and $60.00 if the upgrade is from version 4.0 to 4.2.

A Final Word

If you are familiar with the WordPerfect manual, you know that it assigns proper names to commonly used keystrokes. For example, the keystroke combination that is used to center text on a line is called the Center Key, and the keystroke combination that is used to insert the current date into your text is called the Date Key. These names will be used throughout this book and will always be capitalized including the word *Key*. When the physical key on the keyboard is referred to, the word *key* will be lowercase. For example, the Underline *Key* is invoked by pressing the F8 *key*. However, the manual frequently directs you to use these named Keys without telling you the corresponding physical keys to press, such as Shift-F6 for the Center Key, and Shift-F5 for the Date Key. In this book, both the Key name and the exact keystroke combinations required to execute it will be listed. This will help you learn the combinations and save you a lot of time flipping back through the pages. Also, this will save you some frustration if you don't read the chapters in the order they appear and thereby learn each combination as it is introduced.

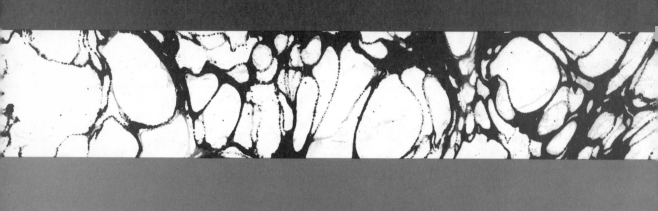

PART I

ALL THE
FUNDAMENTALS

CHAPTER 1 KEYSTROKE SUMMARY:

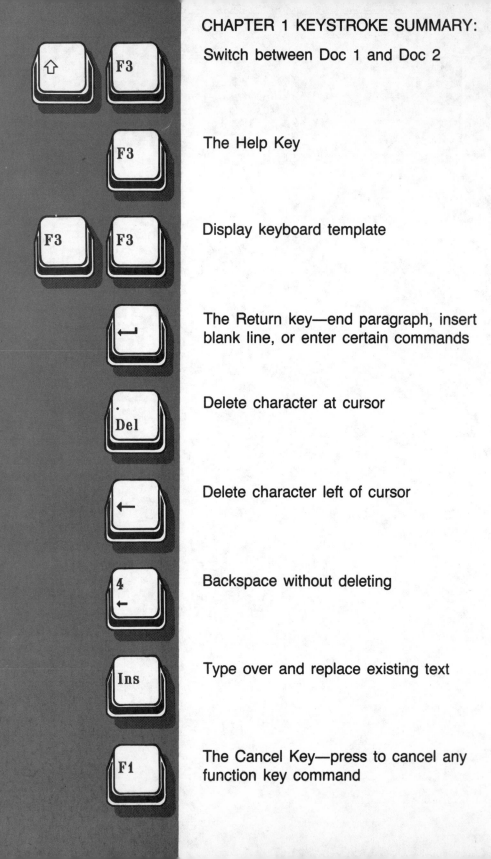

⇧ F3   Switch between Doc 1 and Doc 2

F3   The Help Key

F3 F3   Display keyboard template

↵   The Return key—end paragraph, insert blank line, or enter certain commands

Del   Delete character at cursor

←   Delete character left of cursor

4 ←   Backspace without deleting

Ins   Type over and replace existing text

F1   The Cancel Key—press to cancel any function key command

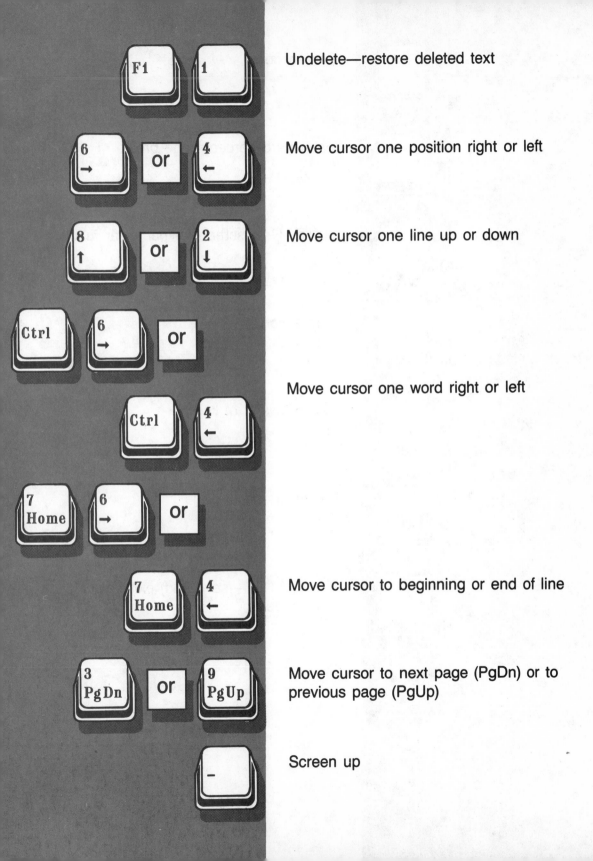

Undelete—restore deleted text

Move cursor one position right or left

Move cursor one line up or down

Move cursor one word right or left

Move cursor to beginning or end of line

Move cursor to next page (PgDn) or to previous page (PgUp)

Screen up

Screen down

Insert hard (forced) page break

Display Help screen for particular function key (F*n*)

Delete word

Delete to end of line

Delete to end of page

The Exit Key—(save and) exit from WordPerfect

THE KEYBOARD AND BASIC EDITING

BEFORE YOU CAN START USING WORD-Perfect, you must understand some fundamental aspects of the program such as how to load it into your computer, what you see on your screen when it is loaded, where to locate important keys, and how to use them to perform critical tasks such as cursor movement. You should spend the time to master these basics in order to avoid unnecessary frustration when using WordPerfect.

Learning the WordPerfect keyboard is especially important. In this chapter we will discuss several keys which are used constantly and are mentioned often in this book. To minimize confusion, read this chapter carefully and refer to it as often as necessary. If you are an experienced computer user, you will recognize all of these keys, but you still should skim the chapter to be sure you understand how they work in WordPerfect.

If you have already worked with the program and feel comfortable with the keyboard, you may want to skip this chapter and move right on to the next one in which you will learn how to create your first letter. Please be aware that there still may be some useful information in this chapter for you and that you may want to peruse it selectively. For instance, many users know how to move the cursor character by character but are unaware of the faster methods of moving word by word, page by page, or other handy techniques.

Starting WordPerfect

When it comes to learning a word processing program, actual practice is worth a million words. However, before proceeding to the exercises that teach you about the WordPerfect keyboard, you must learn how to start the program. If you already know how to do this, skip this section and proceed to the one titled "The WordPerfect Editing Screen."

Starting WordPerfect on a Two Floppy Disk System

The first step is to turn your computer on and load the operating system, PC-DOS or MS-DOS. To do this, insert your DOS system disk into drive A, turn on the power switch, and enter the correct date and time when asked (unless your system is set up to enter it automatically, in which case you will see a message which tells you the correct date and time).

If you have not yet installed your WordPerfect system disk and formatted a blank data disk, please turn to Appendix A for guidance.

After the operating system is loaded, the disk drives will be silent and the red lights on the front will be off. You will see the following symbol, the A prompt, on your screen:

A>

This is your signal that the operating system is loaded and that you can now start your applications software, WordPerfect. Insert the WordPerfect system disk into drive A and a blank formatted data disk into drive B.

The Default Drive

Since the WordPerfect system disk has very little free space left for new files, you will normally store letters, memos and other documents on the disk in drive B. By starting WordPerfect from this drive, you can save your-self a lot of trouble. The B drive becomes the default drive, meaning that the program will assume all data files belong there and will always go to that drive to save and retrieve them unless you tell it otherwise. The basic advantage is that you won't have to remember to type the drive designator *B:* every time you ask WordPerfect to save a file.

Log on to drive B (make it the default drive) by typing

B:

and pressing the Return key. (See Figure 1.4 below for its location.) Next, start WordPerfect by typing

A:WP

followed by a Return.

Starting WordPerfect on a Hard Disk

Turn on the computer and enter the time and date (unless your system is set up to enter them automatically, in which case you will see a message which tells you the correct time and date). You should then be logged onto the main (or *root*) directory of the C drive, and the following C prompt symbol should appear on your screen:

C>

It indicates that the operating system is loaded so you can start your applications program, WordPerfect. The next step is to change to the subdirectory that contains WordPerfect. If you followed the directions in Appendix A when setting up the program, the name of this subdirectory on your hard disk will be WP. So type

CD WP

and press Return. The screen will show a new C prompt:

C> CD WP
C>

You can then start the WordPerfect program by typing

WP

and pressing Return.

If in the course of starting up you see a message like this:

Invalid directory

or

Bad command or file name

this probably means that your WordPerfect program is located in a sub-directory other than WP or that the program has not been successfully copied onto your hard disk at all. To check this out, see the section of Appendix A titled "The PC-DOS Tree Command."

The WordPerfect Editing Screen

Congratulations! You are now logged on to WordPerfect. Initially, you will see a start up screen, but after a few seconds it will disappear and you will see the editing screen.

The Status Line

Now your screen will be blank except for a single line of information at the bottom of the page, and a cursor in the top left corner. The cursor is a small blinking underline that marks the position where the next character you type will appear. The line of information at the bottom of the page is called the Status line; it provides information about the cursor's current location. In addition, it often displays messages, warnings, and other prompts. Here's how it looks at the outset:

Doc 1 Pg 1 Ln 1   Pos 10

The Document Indicator

The purpose of the notation Doc 1 is to tell you which document you are currently working on. It will always be either a 1 or a 2 because WordPerfect can retain two files in the computer's memory simultaneously, an unusual and convenient feature. Although you can only work on one document at a time, you can easily switch back and forth between documents and even exchange blocks of information between them. If you're in the habit of making notes to yourself while writing, you'll find this feature invaluable since you can keep notes in one document while editing the other.

If you happen to be working on a document and it suddenly disappears, don't panic. Simply check the Status line to see if the document number has changed. If it has, your Status line will show Doc 2.

Doc 2 Pg 1 Ln 1   Pos 1

The Doc 2 message indicates that you have accidentally switched into the second area of the computer's memory. You got there by inadvertently pressing the Shift-F3 key combination, and can return to the first document by pressing the same two keys.

The Page Indicator

The Pg 1 represents the number of the page where the cursor is currently located. The pages indicated on the screen correspond to the actual pages where text will appear when it is printed out on paper.

The Line Indicator

The Ln 1 tells you the number of the line where the cursor is currently located. Unless you change the page length or other page format settings (which you will learn how to do when you reach Chapter 5), each page will have 54 lines of text.

The Position Indicator

Pos 10 shows the current position (column) of the cursor. Unless you change the margin settings, the WordPerfect editing screen will be divided into 65 columns per page, numbered from 10 to 74. You start at position 10 to leave 10 spaces (equal to 1 inch) for the left margin. Each time you type a character or press the Spacebar one column is filled. You will learn about margin settings in Chapter 3.

The WordPerfect Keyboard

Shift

There are two Shift keys on the IBM PC keyboard, which work exactly the same, one on the lower right just above the gray Caps Lock key and one on the lower left next to the F8 key. The Shift keys are gray and labelled with an outlined arrow pointing upward. (All of the other arrows on the keyboard are solid black ones.) Figure 1.1 shows the Shift keys along with two other special keys we will be discussing next, Alt and Ctrl.

The Shift keys are used as on a typewriter, to type letters in uppercase. They must also be used to type symbols such as the question mark and characters such as the percent sign that appear on the numeric keys on the top row of the keyboard. The Shift keys also have other functions that you will learn about a little later.

Alt and Ctrl

The Alt and Ctrl keys are easy to identify since they are actually labelled Alt and Ctrl (see Figure 1.1). They are both gray and are located at the left side of the keyboard. Although Alt stands for *alternate* and Ctrl stands for *control,* these full names are virtually never used and the keys are always written as Alt and Ctrl.

Figure 1.1: *The Shift, Alt, and Ctrl keys*

The Alt and Ctrl keys, like Shift, don't do anything by themselves. They are always used together with another key, giving that key a meaning it would not have by itself. In WordPerfect, the most important keys used in conjunction with Alt and Ctrl (and Shift) are the *function keys*.

The Function Keys

The function keys are the ten gray keys located in two vertical rows at the left edge of the IBM PC keyboard, or on the top row of the PC/AT keyboard. As illustrated in Figure 1.2, they are labelled F1 through F10.

Each of these keys has four different functions in WordPerfect depending on whether it is used by itself or in combination with Shift, Alt, or Ctrl. To use one of these combinations, you press the Shift, Alt, or Ctrl Key first, and continue holding it down while pressing the function key. We indicate such key combinations in this book with a hyphen as in Shift-F8.

Try pressing Shift-F8 right now. As you can see, the Status line at the bottom of the screen is replaced by a *prompt line* that offers six options pertaining to formatting features such as tabs, margins, and line spacing (see Figure 1.3). Press the Spacebar once, and the prompt line will disappear. (You will study each of these formatting options individually in later chapters.)

While many function-key combinations invoke prompts at the bottom of the screen such as the one you just saw, there are others that replace the entire screen with a menu and several that execute a command immediately with no special display of further choices. Try pressing the Alt-F8 combination, which brings up the full-screen Page Format menu. Again, pressing the Spacebar once will bring you back to the editing screen. The Shift-F6 combination

Figure 1.2: *The function keys*

is an example of one that executes a command as soon as you press it, automatically centering a line of text between the margins.

You will learn the WordPerfect names and uses of each of these combinations of the function keys with Shift, Alt, or Ctrl in the chapters that pertain to them and you'll find that it won't take long to remember the ones you use the most. Appendix B serves as a guide to the key combinations as well as all commands and functions.

The WordPerfect Template Color Scheme

The WordPerfect function-key template, supplied with the program, fits around the function keys and indicates what each one does. The template uses a color scheme to identify the four different features obtainable from each function key and its combinations with Shift, Ctrl, and Alt. When a feature is shown in green on the template, the function key is used with the Shift key. Red indicates the function key is used with Ctrl. Blue indicates the function key is used with Alt. A feature shown in black indicates the function key is used alone. In case you lose your keyboard template, you can display a copy of it on your screen by pressing F3 (the Help Key) twice.

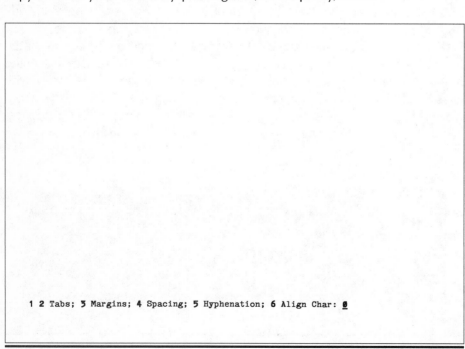

```
    1 2 Tabs; 3 Margins; 4 Spacing; 5 Hyphenation; 6 Align Char: 0
```

Figure 1.3: *The result of pressing Shift-F8*

The Return Key

The Return key is the large gray key labelled ⏎ and located between the numeric keypad and the letter keys. The Return key is shown in Figure 1.4, along with the Caps Lock and Num Lock keys, to be discussed below. The Return key is also known as the Enter key or the Carriage Return key. Throughout this book, it will be called the Return key, or simply Return. It has several important functions in word processing.

Like most word processors, WordPerfect has an *automatic* carriage return feature known as *word wrap*. It operates on its own in place of the Return key whenever the cursor reaches the right margin, creating a new line and automatically moving both the cursor and any words which would have exceeded the margin down to the new line. This feature also realigns paragraphs correctly after any additions, deletions, or other alterations are made. In order to use WordPerfect's word wrap feature, you must follow this important rule: *Never press the Return key to end a line which appears in the middle of a paragraph, but always press it to end a paragraph.*

If you want to see word wrap in action, type a few sentences without pressing the Return key at all. When your cursor reaches the right margin you will see it move down to the next line, and if the word you were typing would have extended past the margin, it will also be moved down. (Don't worry about the appearance of your screen since you will be discarding this work after you reach the end of this chapter.)

The Return key is also used to insert extra blank lines into your document. To test this function, press the Return key several times and watch the cursor move down and the line indicator on the Status line change.

Figure 1.4: *The Return, Caps Lock, and Num Lock keys*

Lastly, Return often works as an Enter key, which must be pressed after certain commands are issued. In these cases, it serves as a confirmation to the program that you want it to begin executing the command you typed. For instance, you can view a list of all the files stored on your data disk by pressing F5, which is the List Files Key. When you do, you see a message at the bottom of the screen which resembles the DOS command DIR. If you are using the B drive to store files, it will appear as follows:

Dir B:\ * . *

After you see this message, you must press the Return key, now functioning as an Enter key. As soon as you do this, the directory listing appears on your screen. If you do not press Return, nothing will happen and you'll be looking at the DIR message indefinitely.

In using WordPerfect you are frequently asked to type something such as a file name and then press Return. I will often refer to these two steps—typing the name and pressing Return—as a unit by saying "*Enter* the file name" without explicitly reminding you to press Return.

Num Lock and Caps Lock

The Num Lock (numeric lock) and Caps Lock (capital lock) keys are important because of the effects they have on other keys. The Caps Lock Key is the gray key to the immediate right of the Spacebar, as shown in Figure 1.4. When it is turned on, all alphabetical keys that you type will be entered in uppercase. Note that it only affects the A through Z keys and cannot completely substitute for the Shift key, which is still required for entering such symbols as the percent sign and dollar sign.

The Num Lock key, also shown in Figure 1.4, is located on the top row above the numeric keypad. This key serves to activate the numeric keypad so that when you press one of the keys on it a number will be entered. When Num Lock is off, many of these keys are used for cursor movement, as you will see in the next section.

The Shift keys reverse the action of either the Caps Lock or the Num Lock key. In other words, if the Caps Lock key is turned on and you hold down one of the Shift keys, any alphabetical characters you type will appear in lowercase. Likewise, if the Num Lock Key is on and you hold down Shift while pressing a key on the numeric keypad, you will not see a number on your screen. Instead, you may find yourself in some other section of the document because all of these keys except for the 5 are used for cursor movement. When you want to enter a few numbers, it is often easier to use the Shift key instead of turning on Num Lock.

The Caps Lock and Num Lock Indicators

The position indicator on the Status line you read about earlier in this chapter corrects a significant deficiency in the IBM PC keyboard by letting you know the current status of the Caps Lock and Num Lock Keys. When Caps Lock is on, the position indicator appears on the screen in uppercase.

POS 1

When you turn Caps Lock off again the position indicator switches back to its original appearance.

Pos 1

A flashing position indicator shows that the Num Lock key is on and the numeric keypad is activated.

The Delete, Backspace, and ← Keys

There are two keys that you can use to delete individual characters. The first one, Del, erases the character the cursor is positioned on and moves the text that follows it leftward to fill in the blank. Del is the white key at the lower right corner of the keyboard, labelled with a period and the word Del. To try it, type a few characters, move the cursor back over them using the ← key (number 4 on the numeric keypad), then press Del.

The second key used for deletion is the gray key with a bold left arrow symbol (←) located at the right on the top row of the keyboard. Although the WordPerfect manual refers to it by its common name, the Backspace key, it should never be used to move the cursor if there is any text in the way (to the left of it) because it will delete characters rather than simply backspace over them. However, it is safe to use the Backspace key to move the cursor to the left over blank space (if you want to delete the spaces).

To understand this better, type a few words and then press Backspace. As you see, the letters disappear. The ← key is the one that actually backspaces in WordPerfect. When you press this key, the cursor will move one position to the left without erasing anything. Figure 1.5 shows the Del, Backspace, and ← keys.

Figure 1.5: *The Del, Backspace, and ← keys*

Another problem you might face when using Backspace or Del is that they occasionally bump into the hidden codes that control formatting features and try to delete them also. When this happens, you'll see an unexpected message at the bottom of your screen, such as this one:

Delete [Undrline]? (Y/N) N

As you may guess, this prompt asks if you want to delete an underline code, and you must respond by pressing Y or N. Whenever you press the Underline Key (F8), a special hidden code is automatically inserted into your document so that the program will know where to begin and end the underlining. You will learn about underlining in the next chapter, and Chapters 3 and 6 further discuss the special codes. For now, you need only recognize the type of message and what it means: whenever you see a prompt with the word Delete followed by a code or symbol enclosed in brackets and then a (Y/N) prompt, you can be sure that you have bumped into a hidden code. If you do not want to delete it, press N so it will not be erased. However, it is quite possible that you placed it there accidentally by inadvertently pressing one of the keys or combinations that inserts a formatting code. If this is the case, press Y to go ahead and delete it.

Ins (Insert)

The Ins (Insert) key is located at the right of the bottom row of the keyboard. Figure 1.6 shows the Ins key along with the Cancel Key (F1) to be discussed next. Ins is a toggle key, which means you press it once to turn a

Figure 1.6: *The Ins (Insert) and Cancel Keys*

feature on and again to turn the feature off. When you press it, the following message appears in the lower left corner of the screen:

Typeover

This means you have gone into Typeover mode and new characters you enter will literally type over and replace existing text. If there is nothing but blank space there you won't notice it, but if there are existing characters they will disappear. When this key is off, which is the program's normal state, you do not see the Typeover message on the screen, and new text that you type will be inserted into the document, pushing any existing text to the right or down to the next line to make room without erasing anything.

To see how Ins works, type a few words and use the ← key to move the cursor back to the beginning of the first one. Press the Ins key, watching for the Typeover message, and start typing over your original words. Now, release the Ins key and try the same thing.

As you have seen, the Ins key can be confusing for it works in precisely the opposite manner from what you would expect. In fact, you should really think of it as a Typeover key. When it is *on,* you are typing over old text and replacing it with new text.

Cancel and Undelete

The Cancel Key (F1) is the one function key you should learn immediately because it can be a lifesaver. If you press F1 after having pressed one of the function keys (or combinations) that summons a prompt line or replaces the screen with a menu, that feature will be cancelled and you can return to your work. This function is especially helpful if you accidentally press the wrong key—which is easy to do—and see an unexpected prompt at the bottom of the screen, or if your work disappears entirely and an unfamiliar screen appears in its place.

To see how it works, press F10, which is called the Save Key, and you will see this prompt:

Document to be Saved:

When you press F1, the prompt disappears and you are returned to the editing screen.

You can also press F1 without having called up a feature you wish to cancel. This invokes the Undelete command which is one of WordPerfect's most useful features. Undelete instantly restores text that has been deleted. You can restore the text from any of the last three delete actions. So far, you have only studied a few of the methods used to delete text, but when you learn about others in later chapters, keep in mind that the Undelete command works equally well with all but those that use the Block and Move keys (and you will learn about these in Chapter 4).

To see how it works, type a word or two, and then use the Backspace key to erase them. Next, press F1 and you will see the characters you just erased reappear in a highlighted block (in reverse video). In addition, you will see a prompt line at the bottom of the screen:

Undelete 1 Restore; 2 Show Previous Deletion: 0

To restore the characters, press 1 for Restore. If you were to press 2, WordPerfect would highlight the most recent characters or words you had deleted prior to these, if there were any, and you could then restore them. This previous segment of deleted text is called level 2. If you wanted to undelete text that was deleted one level before that, you would press 2 once more and the third level of text would appear for you to restore. Note that the entire segment of text you erased with Backspace is grouped into one level because you deleted it all at once without doing any typing in between.

Basic Cursor Movement

When editing, you will find yourself constantly moving the cursor around within the document to add, change, or delete text, or just to review your work. WordPerfect has many different keys which can be used for cursor movement, and you will soon learn to move the cursor character by character, line by line, to the top or bottom of the page, all the way to the beginning or end of the document, to a specific character or word, to a specific page, and much more. All of these methods are summarized in Appendix B and you will be learning them as you progress through this book. To begin with, though, you should concentrate on learning the most basic and frequently used methods.

Moving One Character at a Time

To move the cursor one position at a time, use the four directional arrow keys on the numeric keypad, illustrated in Figure 1.7. As you've just learned, these keys are normally used for cursor movement, and do not function as numeric data entry keys unless the Num Lock key is turned on. You have also learned that the ← key is used to backspace, moving the cursor one position to the left. The → key (number 6) works the same way, moving the cursor one position to the right (without erasing any text) each time your press it. The ↑ and ↓ keys (numbers 8 and 2, respectively) move the cursor up and down one line at a time. Experiment with these keys until you feel comfortable with them.

Like most keys on the IBM PC keyboard, the arrow keys are affected by a feature known as auto repeat. When you press one, if you continue to hold it down after the cursor has moved one position, the cursor will keep on moving until you release the key. Try auto repeat by pressing the T key and holding it down until you fill the line with Ts.

Figure 1.7: *The arrow keys on the numeric keypad*

Moving Word by Word

Moving the cursor character by character can be slow, so WordPerfect has two key combinations, Word Left and Word Right, which you will come to appreciate. By pressing Ctrl along with the ← or → key, you can move the cursor a whole word to the left or to the right.

Moving to the Beginning or End of a Line

It is often necessary to move the cursor to the beginning or to the end of a line. To speed up this process, press the Home key, number 7 on the numeric keypad (shown in Figure 1.8), together with the ← key, and the cursor will jump left to the first position on the line. To move the cursor to the end of a line, press the Home-→ combination or the End key. The cursor will move just to the right of the last character in the line (or the last blank space that was placed using the Spacebar).

Page Up, Page Down, Screen Up, and Screen Down

If your documents exceed a page or two in length and you want to move the cursor up or down in large jumps WordPerfect has four commands to serve you: Page Up, Page Down, Screen Up, and Screen Down, as shown in Figure 1.8.

The Page Up and Page Down Keys are clearly marked PgUp and PgDn (numbers 9 and 3 on the numeric keyboard). As you would expect, Page

Figure 1.8: *The Home, Page Up, Page Down, Screen Up, Screen Down, and End Keys*

Up and Page Down are used to move the cursor page by page to the first line of the page, automatically bringing the new text into view. A page is usually 54 lines of text (unless you alter the page length settings, which you will learn about in Chapter 5).

You can try these keys, but if you haven't filled a whole page with text, they will only move your cursor as far as the text extends. To overcome this, you can insert enough blank lines to fill a page by pressing the Return key repeatedly until the line indicator shows that the cursor is on line 54.

Screen Up is the gray key marked with a minus sign (−), located at the right edge of the keyboard (see Figure 1.8). The Screen Down Key is the large gray key below it, marked with a plus sign (+). Pressing Screen Up will move the cursor to the top line currently visible on your screen. If you press it again, it will move the cursor up by one more screenful of text, bringing the new text into view with the cursor at the top. (The last screenful will have disappeared altogether.) Screen Down works exactly the same way, except in the opposite direction. A screen is defined as 24 lines. When Num Lock is on, these keys are converted into the minus and plus keys.

Deleting Hidden Codes

When you make formatting changes such as underlining, indenting, changing the spacing in your document from single to double, or centering a line, you are actually inserting special codes into your document which direct the program to make these modifications. These codes are not visible on the screen because they would clutter it up and make it hopelessly impossible to read (they will not be visible in the printed version either). Since you cannot see them, it's easy to bump into them by mistake when using the Backspace or Del key.

It is also easy to insert a formatting code accidentally, unless you are extremely agile and never make typing mistakes. When that happens, or when you simply change your mind, you will want to delete a code. For example, try pressing F8, which is called the Underline Key, then type the word Hello. Notice that it is underlined. To get rid of the underline code use the ← key on the numeric keypad to move the cursor back to the H in Hello, and then press it one more time. It will appear that the cursor has not moved, but in reality it is actually moving from the H onto the invisible code. If you press the Del key next, you will see a message asking if you wish to delete the code, as shown below:

Delete [Undrline]? (Y/N) N

As you can see, the name of the code, Undrline, appears in brackets, and the message is followed with a (Y/N) prompt. To delete the code you press Y, and the underlining will immediately disappear.

Formatting codes can actually be made visible and deleted on a special screen called the Reveal Codes screen, which you will learn about in Chapters 4 and 6. However, this screen can be confusing, if not totally intimidating, and it is not recommended that you try to understand it until you are reasonably comfortable with WordPerfect.

Unwanted Page Breaks

Pressing the Ctrl-Return combination produces a double line of dashes (equal signs) across the screen, which signals the beginning of a new page. This is called a *hard page break*. Under normal conditions, you would see a new page indicator only after typing line 54, at which point WordPerfect automatically inserts a page break. The page break WordPerfect creates is called a *soft page break,* and it appears on screen as a single line of dashes. If you see a hard page break that you wish to delete, move the cursor to the first line below the double dashes and press the Backspace key, or place your cursor above it and press the Del key. Soft page breaks cannot be deleted, but you will learn how to prevent them from appearing where you don't want them in Chapter 5.

Getting Help

The Help Key (F3) replaces your document with the screen shown in Figure 1.9. As the screen indicates, you must press the Enter key (which is the same as the Return key) or the Spacebar to exit from the Help menu. If you press any other key, you will keep seeing this screen or one of the subsidiary Help menus.

The Help Key can be very useful when you are lost or uncertain about a function. To try it, if you are using a hard disk, press the Help Key (F3), and then press the S key to view information about the features which begin with the letter S. The screen should resemble Figure 1.10.

```
Help                                        WP 4.2    10/28/86


   Press any letter to get an alphabetical list of features.

        The list will include the features that start with that letter, along
        with the name of the key where the feature is found.  You can then
        press that key to get a description of how the feature works.


   Press any function key to get information about the use of the key.

        Some keys may let you choose from a menu to get more information
        about various options.  Press HELP again to display the template.


   Press the Enter key or Space bar to exit Help._
```

Figure 1.9: *The Help screen*

Function Key	Feature	Key Name
F10	Save Text	Save
+(Num Pad)	Screen Down	Screen Down
-(Num Pad)	Screen Up	Screen Up
F2	Search	-> Search
Alt -F2	Search & Replace	Replace
F5	Search for Text in File(s)	List Files - 9
Shft-F7	Select Printers	Print - 4 Printer Control
Shft-F7	Send Printer a "GO"	Print - 4 Printer Control
Ctrl-F8	Sheet Feeder Bin #	Print Format - 9
Shft-F7	Sheet Feeder Y/N	Print - 4 then 5 Select Printers
Ctrl-F1	Shell	Shell
Ctrl "-"	Soft Hyphen	Soft Hyphen
Ctrl-F9	Sort	Merge/Sort
Shft-F8	Spacing	Line Format - 4
Ctrl-V	Special Characters	Ctrl-V then decimal ASCII code
Ctrl-F2	Speller	Spell
Ctrl-F3	Split Screen	Screen - 1
Alt -F5	Strikeout (Block On)	Mark Text - 4
Shft-F1	Subscript	Super/Subscript - 2
Ctrl-F5	Summary	Text In/Out - A
Shft-F1	Superscript	Super/Subscript - 5
Shft-F3	Switch Documents	Switch_

Figure 1.10: *The help screen for the letter S*

If you are using a computer with only floppy-disk drives, press the Help Key (F3) and you will see the following message:

WPHELP.FIL not found. Insert Learning diskette and press drive letter.

Next, remove your data disk from the B drive and replace it with the WordPerfect disk labelled Learning. Now type B (without a colon) and press the letter S. Your screen should resemble Figure 1.10.

Notice that the screen is organized alphabetically by the name of the feature (which is the middle column) such as *Save Text, Spacing,* and *Switch Documents.* This is useful when you know a certain feature exists but do not know how to implement it. The keys you must press in order to implement the feature are listed in the column **Function Key** to the left of the feature. The third column, **Key Name,** refers to the proper name which the authors of WordPerfect have assigned to those keystrokes.

Any time you are uncertain about how to use a particular function key, you can obtain a screenful of information about it by pressing the Help Key (F3) followed by the function key in question. Try this now, pressing F3 then the Exit Key (F7). The screen should look like Figure 1.11.

```
Exit

        Allows you to save your document and either clear your screen or exit.
        The first y/n answers the question if you want to save your document, the
        second y/n answers the question if you want to exit.

        Keystrokes                           Result

        [Exit] y (filename) n                Save the document and clear the screen.

        [Exit] y (filename) y                Save the document and exit WordPerfect.

        [Exit] n n                           Clear the screen.

        [Exit] n y                           Exit WordPerfect._
```

Figure 1.11: *The Exit Key Help screen*

As you can see, the main purpose of the Exit Key is explained, followed by details about each of the possible paths you can take and their outcomes.

Other function keys and combinations (such as Alt-F8, the Page Format Key), invoke menus or prompts, which offer several choices. When you call up their help screens you will see a list of these choices and brief explanations. To get more information about one of the options, you can then press the number which corresponds to it on the help screen and you will see another help screen devoted to that feature.

Deleting Larger Segments

If you make a mistake while typing and need to delete some text, you have several options. In earlier sections of this chapter you learned how to delete individual characters using the Backspace and Del keys. WordPerfect has many other useful methods, including deleting words, deleting to the end of a line, and deleting to the end of the page.

To delete a word, position the cursor on any character in the word or on the first space following it, then press the Ctrl-Backspace combination. To delete a word to the left of the cursor, place the cursor at the beginning of a word and press Home, then Backspace. Pressing Home and then Del deletes from the cursor position to the right until it reaches the end of a word.

To delete the text from the cursor to the end of a line, press the Ctrl-End combination.

To delete from the cursor to the end of the page press Ctrl-PgDn, the Delete To End Of Page Key. When you do this, WordPerfect double-checks to make sure you really want to delete the rest of the page:

Delete Remainder of Page? (Y/N) N

If you press any key other than a Y (or the lowercase y) the page will not be erased.

Exiting from WordPerfect

Since you have just covered so much material, it is likely that you're ready to turn the computer off and take a break. The only correct method of exiting from the WordPerfect program is to use the Exit Key. If you try to turn off the program using any other method, you will create unnecessary problems. To understand why, you need to know a little about how the program manages files.

File Management and Overflow Files

As you are working, WordPerfect constantly moves data back and forth between the disk drives and your computer's on-line *memory*. This on-line memory, also called RAM (random access memory), can be thought of as the computer's workspace. If your computer is equipped with a large amount of memory (512 or 640K), you probably won't notice this movement because there will be enough workspace for both the program's own instructions and the data (text) in the document you are editing. However, if you are working on a long document and your computer has a limited amount of memory, the program moves the parts of your document that you are not presently working on from the memory to the disk, while you are working on another section. Disk files temporarily created in this manner are called overflow files. Text that appears to the left and above the cursor is stored in an overflow file called {WP}.TV1 and text that follows the cursor is stored in a file called {WP}.BV1. (If you are also using document 2, you will have a {WP}.TV2 file and a {WP}.BV2 file as well.)

To close the overflow files when you finish work and guarantee that your entire document is properly assembled in its own permanent file, it is imperative that you use the Exit Key. If you do not, the next time you start the WordPerfect program you will see an error message asking if other copies of WordPerfect are running, and you will have to enter N to start the program, possibly losing some data (in the overflow files) in the process. You will explore this issue further in Chapter 12, and also learn how to set up the program to create simultaneous backup files, in case the computer is unexpectedly turned off due to a power failure or some other unpredictable cause.

Now that you understand why, use the Exit Key (F7) to turn the program off. You will see the following message in the lower left corner of the screen:

Save Document? (Y/N) Y

Notice that it is followed by a Y. WordPerfect inserts the Y because it initially assumes your answer will be yes, erring on the side of caution to ensure that you don't lose your work by accidentally exiting without saving it. Since in this case you do not want to save your work, press N.

Next, you will be asked if you wish to exit from WordPerfect, as illustrated below:

Exit WP? (Y/N) N

Once again, WordPerfect is double checking to make sure you really want to leave the program, so the default is N. You'll find that if you press any key other than Y or y you will remain in WordPerfect, ready to work on a new document, and the screen will be blank.

Press Y or y and you will find yourself back in the operating system, with a DOS prompt such as B> or C> on the screen.

Summary

To start WordPerfect, you must make sure the operating system, either PC-DOS or MS-DOS, is loaded into your computer. If you have a hard disk, you must also change to the subdirectory (WP) which contains your WordPerfect system files using the DOS CD command. If you are using a computer that has only floppy disks, you should log onto drive B before starting WordPerfect so that your work will automatically be saved on the disk in that drive.

When you start WordPerfect the screen is empty except for the cursor in the top left corner and a single line in the lower right called the Status line. This line tells you the page number, line number, and position at which the cursor is currently located, as well as which of two possible documents you are working on.

The function keys are used by themselves or in combination with the Shift, Alt, or Ctrl keys to implement various WordPerfect commands. Therefore, each function key has four different applications.

The Return key is used to signal the end of a paragraph, but never to end a line within a paragraph. It is also used to insert extra blank lines in text, or to enter a command.

The Caps Lock key converts all alphabetical keys to uppercase. The Num Lock key activates all of the numeric keys on the numeric keypad.

The position indicator on the Status line also informs you if the Caps Lock key is turned on, in which case the POS appears in uppercase, or if the Num Lock key is turned on, in which case Pos blinks on and off.

The Del key erases the character on which the cursor is positioned and pulls the text which follows it leftward to fill in the blank. The Backspace key deletes characters to the left of the cursor. Do not use the Backspace key to backspace over text, since it will delete instead. To backspace without erasing, use the ← key (number 4 on the numeric keypad).

Pressing the Insert key (Ins) before typing causes new text to be typed over old text, erasing it in the process.

The Cancel Key (F1) is used to activate WordPerfect's Undelete command. It restores text that was erased during any of your last three delete commands. F1 can also be used to back out of a menu, screen, or prompt which has been accidentally invoked.

The ← and → keys on the numeric keypad move the cursor one position to the right or left, and the ↑ and ↓ keys move it one line up or down. The Word Left (Ctrl-←) and Word Right (Ctrl-→) Keys move the cursor word by word. Pressing the Home key followed by either the ← key or the → key will move the cursor to the first or last position on the line.

The Page Up (PgUp) and Page Down (PgDn) Keys move the cursor up one page or down one page. The Screen Up and Screen Down Keys— the gray minus (−) and plus (+) keys on the numeric keypad—move the cursor up one screen or down one screen.

The Help Key (F3) is used to obtain a screenful of information about a particular function key (or key combination) or about any of the cursor-movement keys, or to get help with any WordPerfect feature that begins with a letter you specify.

You can delete whole words by pressing the Delete Word Key (Ctrl-Backspace). Home-Backspace deletes a whole word to the left and Home-Del deletes a whole word to the right when the cursor is positioned at the beginning of a word. You can delete to the end of a line by pressing the Delete To End Of Line Key (Ctrl-End). You can delete the entire page from the cursor downward by pressing the Delete To End Of Page Key (Ctrl-PgDn).

The only proper method of exiting from the WordPerfect program is to use the Exit Key (F7). If you do not use this key to turn the program off, you will see an error message the next time you start up meaning that the overflow files were not properly closed, and you will have to overwrite them. The Exit Key can also be used to leave the program without saving the document from the computer's memory (RAM) to the disk.

Armed with all this knowledge, you're all set to go! In the next chapter you'll learn much more about WordPerfect, and in the process you are going to create and revise a short letter, then save and print it.

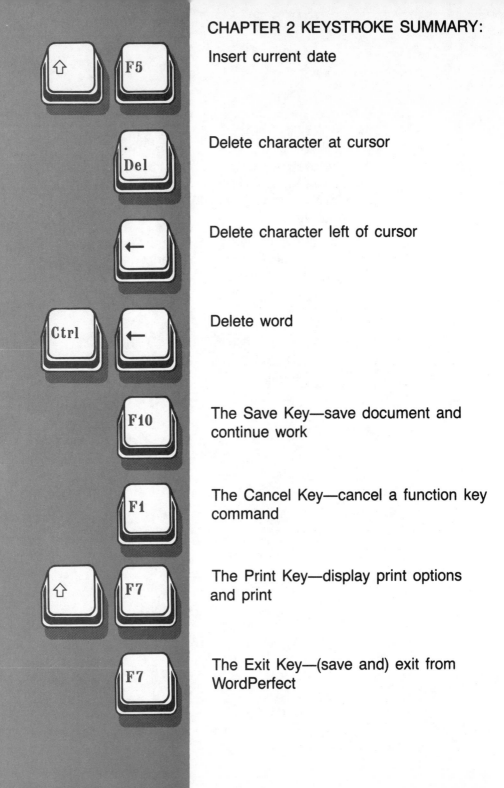

CHAPTER 2 KEYSTROKE SUMMARY:

Insert current date

Delete character at cursor

Delete character left of cursor

Delete word

The Save Key—save document and continue work

The Cancel Key—cancel a function key command

The Print Key—display print options and print

The Exit Key—(save and) exit from WordPerfect

CREATING
A SHORT
LETTER

WORDPERFECT IS A COMPLEX, SOPHISTI-
cated program, but that does not mean it
has to be hard to use. You already know that
it is loaded with helpful features, which is
probably the reason you purchased it in the
first place. However it isn't necessary to
learn every one of them in order to get
some work done.

The next five chapters are designed to
introduce WordPerfect's essential word processing operations, and if you study them
carefully you'll be producing meaningful
documents in no time. In fact, in less than
one hour you will have succeeded in creating, saving, and printing your very first letter!

A Word about Intimidation

Just don't make it hard on yourself. After all, Rome wasn't built in a day. If you try to memorize every single command and function the first time around, chances are you'll be overwhelmed. Indeed, it is infinitely more useful just to be aware of WordPerfect's many features than to memorize a bunch of keystrokes that may have no meaning to you. Then when you find yourself needing a particular function, you can easily go back and refresh your memory as to the exact steps needed to execute it.

So relax!

Creating a Sample Letter

Now that you have studied all the preliminaries such as loading the program and utilizing the various special keys, you are ready to create your first letter, which is illustrated in Figure 2.1. If you get lost or confused during the process of starting up and entering the letter or if you make a typing mistake and need to delete some characters, you can find help in Chapter One.

Inserting the Date

The date belongs on the first line, so check the Status line to see if you are at the very beginning, which is page 1, line 1, position 10. If not, move your cursor to the top left by pressing the ↑ key and/or the ← key on the numeric keypad.

At this point, you can either type the date as shown in Figure 2.1, or use a special WordPerfect Key which can do the typing for you. Appropriately named the Date Key, this keystroke combination will enter the current date at the cursor position (if you were diligent enough to type the date in when you turned on your computer). To see how the Date Key works, press Shift-F5. (Remember to hold down the Shift key while pressing F5.) You will see a prompt in the lower-left corner of your screen, as shown below:

Date 1 Insert Text; 2 Format; 3 Insert Function: 0

November 15, 1985

Mr. Raymond Vaughn
Western District Sales Manager
2134 Main St.
San Ramon, CA 90122

Dear Ray:

We sure are proud of you! Once again you've outdone everyone in
the district with phenomenal sales figures. Keep up the good
work and you'll soon be drinking Mai Tais on a beach in Maui:
the contest ends next month!

Best Regards,

Janet Jones
National Sales Manager

Figure 2.1: *Sample letter 1*

Selections 2 and 3 will be covered in detail in Chapter 7. For now, select
the first option: Insert Text. The current date will appear almost instantly at
the cursor position and the message on the Status line will disappear.

The Inside Address

Next, move the cursor down by pressing the Return key twice, then type
the following inside address. Be sure to press Return after each line.

Mr. Raymond Vaughn
Western District Sales Manager
2134 Main St.
San Ramon, CA 90122

The Salutation

Skip two more lines by pressing Return then type this salutation:

Dear Ray:

followed by two more Returns.

Now you are ready to type the body of the letter. First, though, a word of caution. Since the next four sentences belong together as one paragraph, do not press Return until you reach the last word. Remember that in word processing, instead of signaling the end of a line, pressing the Return key signals the end of a paragraph. (In case you accidentally press the Return key before the end of the paragraph, simply press the Backspace key and the cursor will move back up to the preceding line so you can continue typing the rest of the paragraph.)

Now go ahead and enter the following paragraph as shown in Figure 2.1. (Note that the line breaks on the screen may not correspond to those below.)

We sure are proud of you! Once again you've outdone everyone in the district with phenomenal sales figures. Keep up the good work and you'll soon be drinking Mai Tais on a beach in Maui: the contest ends next month!

Using Word Wrap

As you have seen, when the cursor reaches the right margin, it automatically moves down a line and may push the word you were typing down with it. This is called word wrap since words are literally being wrapped around to a new line. It is among the most useful features of any word processing program. Word wrap is the reason you can perform unlimited additions, deletions, and alterations in the middle of a paragraph and never have to retype your work.

Inserting a New Sentence

A demonstration is worth a thousand words, so let's go back and make some changes in the letter to see how word wrap works. Using the ↑ and ← keys on the numeric keypad, position the cursor at the first letter of the third sentence, which starts with *Keep up the good work.*

Now type the following sentence and watch carefully:

In fact, if you close the deal with Johnson next week, you'll probably set a new national sales record, unprecedented for the month of January.

As you type, you will see some of the text disappear off the right side of the screen. However, if you keep on typing, the lost words will eventually reappear on the line below, pushing the rest of the paragraph forward and/or down to the next line to make room.

Immediately after you have typed the last word, *January,* stop and look at the screen. As illustrated in Figure 2.2, it will be obvious that several words are missing, since the last sentence now appears to say

Keep up the good on a beach in Maui: the contest ends next month!

To bring back the missing words, just press the ↓ key, which will move your cursor down one line, and watch the paragraph realign itself.

Now you're beginning to understand the power of word wrap. If you had pressed Return after typing each line in the paragraph, you would not have been able to perform this feat!

```
November 15, 1985

Mr. Raymond Vaughn
Western District Sales Manager
2134 Main St.
San Ramon, CA 90122


Dear Ray:

We sure are proud of you! Once again you've outdone everyone in
the district with phenomenal sales figures. In fact, if you close
the deal with Johnson next week, you'll probably set a new
national sales record, unprecedented for the month of January. Keep up the good
on a beach in Maui: the contest ends next month!



Best Regards,


Janet Jones
                                  Doc 1  Pg 1  Ln 15    Pos 73
```

Figure 2.2: *Before rewriting the screen*

Now let's go back and see how word wrap works when we delete the same sentence.

Deleting a Sentence

Using the arrow keys, move the cursor to the word *In* (*In fact, . . .*) and press the Del key. Keep pressing it until the first two words, *In fact,* disappear. As you can see, this method erases text character by character.

As you learned in Chapter One, a quicker way to get rid of the unwanted sentence is to delete word by word by pressing Ctrl-Backspace. Erase the words one by one until you get to the word *deal.* As you see, the words move up from below to fill in the empty space. Word wrap is again helping you realign your paragraph. Now, continue deleting until the entire sentence is gone. If any misalignment remains when you are done deleting, press ↓ to make the realignment complete.

The Complimentary Close

The final step is to type the complimentary close and name. By now you are an old pro at moving the cursor, so go ahead and move it down two lines (press Return twice) and type this close:

Best Regards,

Press Return two more times to insert blank lines. Finish by typing the name and title with a Return in between.

Janet Jones
National Sales Manager

See how easy that was! Now that you have perfected your sample letter, it is time to save it on the data disk.

Saving the Letter to Disk

When you are using WordPerfect to create a new document, the document exists only in your computer's on-line memory, until you *save* it to disk. Since memory disappears as soon as the computer is turned off (whether it is done on purpose by you or by some unintentional cause such as a power failure), it is imperative that you save your file to disk if you will be using it again. Likewise, when you retrieve a saved file from the disk to make changes in it, you are only changing the copy of that file in memory and must save it once again if you wish to retain the modified version.

There are two methods of saving your work and both are simple.

The Save Key

This first method allows you to save the document in its current form and then continue working on it. After the command is executed, your file remains on the screen and in the computer's memory, available for further work.

Pressing the Save Key (F10) initiates this process. Press it now and you will see the following message in the lower-left corner of your screen:

Document to be Saved:

As this prompt suggests, you must then enter a name for your file. The name can have a maximum of eight characters optionally followed by a period and another one to three characters such as **.doc** or **.ltr**, which you can add as the file name extension. For your file name, type

testfile

(it doesn't matter whether you use uppercase or lowercase), then press Return. (Incidentally, once you have used this procedure to assign a file name to a document, the next time you press F10 you will see that name already filled in on the screen following the *Document to be Saved:* prompt. Unless you want to change the name or retain the original version on disk, just press Return to use the same file name you see.)

While the file is being saved, you will see a message on the prompt line. If you are using a system with floppy disk drives, the message will appear as follows:

Saving **B:\TESTFILE**

In this example, B is the default drive where the file is being stored and TESTFILE is the name of the file.

If you are using a hard disk, the message will be like this:

Saving **C:\WP\TESTFILE**

After the file has been saved, a new message will appear on the Status line in the lower-left corner of the screen, indicating the name of the file and the drive and directory where it has been saved.

It is strongly recommended that you save your documents frequently while working (about every five minutes), especially if you live in an area where the power supply is unstable or if you are working during a storm. Losing five minutes worth of work is much less traumatic than losing a few hours worth.

Save and Exit

You have already been introduced to the second method of saving to disk. This one is useful if you have finished working on a document and want to clear the screen to start working on a different one, or if you want to leave WordPerfect altogether. To use the second method, press the Exit Key (F7). You will see the following message in the lower-left corner of the screen:

Save Document? (Y/N) Y   (Text was not modified)

If you press any key other than N (upper- or lowercase) you will be answering yes and will then see the *Document to be Saved:* prompt. Notice the *(Text was not modified)* message on the Status line. This means that no revisions have been made since you last saved the file, so the file on disk is identical to the screen version. If this is the case, it is not necessary to save it again before exiting.

Go ahead and press Return or Y to indicate that you want the letter saved. If you already saved this letter in the previous exercise under the name TESTFILE, the name of the document will be filled in by the program and the prompt line will appear as follows for those using floppy disks:

Document to be Saved: **B:\TESTFILE**

If you have a hard disk, the message will read

Document to be Saved: **C:\WP\TESTFILE**

Press Return to use this file name again and you should see another message asking if you wish to replace the existing file named TESTFILE (which resides on the data disk) with the new version on your screen. The message for floppy disk users is

Replace **B:\TESTFILE?** (Y/N) N

On a hard disk, the message will read

> Replace **C:\WP\TESTFILE?** (Y/N) N

Since you normally do want to replace the old file, press Y. As the file is being saved, the message in the lower-left corner will change for floppy disk users to

> Saving **B:\TESTFILE**

or, for hard disk users, to

> Saving **C:\WP\TESTFILE**

Next you will be asked if you wish to exit from WordPerfect.

> Exit WP? (Y/N) N

If you were to press Y (don't do it though!) you would find yourself back in the operating system, with one of the DOS prompts on the screen: B> or C>.

If you press N (upper- or lowercase) or any other key except F1 (don't do this now either!), you will remain in WordPerfect, but the file will be cleared from the screen as well as from the computer's memory and you will be ready to work on a new one. The file will, of course, be safely stored away on disk for easy recall.

If you press F1, the Cancel Key, you will cancel the exit feature, and your letter will remain on the screen. Since you are going to continue working with the letter, choose the last option by pressing the Cancel Key, F1.

Printing

Now you can print your letter and see the results of your hard work! Make sure your printer is on and contains at least one sheet of paper.

If you have not yet installed your printer, please turn to Appendix A and complete the installation process before continuing.

The Print Key

As you will see, the Print Key (Shift-F7) provides you with many options, all of which will be examined in detail in Chapter 8. At the moment, all you want to do is print the sample letter, so press Shift-F7. You will see the following prompt at the bottom of your screen:

1 Full Text; 2 Page; 3 Options; 4 Printer Control; 5 Type-thru; 6 Preview: 0

Select 1 Full Text from the prompt line, and your printer should start working.

If the Printer Does Not Work

If your printer does not start printing, it may be waiting for you to issue a go command from the keyboard. This would only be the case if your WordPerfect program disk had been installed to use the Hand Feed option, which causes the printer to stop after each page so that you can insert a new sheet of paper manually. This feature prevents the printer from starting until you type G for go.

You can check to see if this is the problem by looking at the Printer Control menu (press Shift-F7 again, and then choose 4 Printer Control). If the Job Status line says

Waiting for a "Go"

as illustrated in Figure 2.3, type the letter G and the printer should start.

If your printer has an automatic sheet feeder or uses continuous paper with a tractor feed, then it does not have to be hand-fed. If this is the case, you should reinstall the program with the correct option (see Appendix A) so you will not have to type G to start it.

Exiting from WordPerfect

Now that you have created, saved, and printed your first letter, you can turn off the computer and take a well deserved break! To do this, use the Exit Key (F7) which you used earlier to save your file. This time when you see the prompt

Save Document (Y/N) Y   (Text was not modified)

press N, because you have not altered your letter since it was last saved, as the *(Text was not modified)* message indicates.

When asked if you wish to exit from WordPerfect answer Y.

```
Printer Control
                                    C - Cancel Print Job(s)
1 - Select Print Options            D - Display All Print Jobs
2 - Display Printers and Fonts      G - "Go" (Resume Printing)
3 - Select Printers                 P - Print a Document
                                    R - Rush Print Job
Selection: 0                        S - Stop Printing


Current Job

Job Number: 1                   Page Number:  1
Job Status: Waiting for a "Go"  Current Copy: 1 of 1
Message:    Place next sheet in printer--Press "G" to continue

Job List

Job  Document           Destination        Forms and Print Options
 1   (Screen)           Ptr  1             HandFed



Additional jobs not shown: 0
```

Figure 2.3: *The printer control menu*

Summary

WordPerfect's Date Key (Shift-F5) can be used to insert the current date at the cursor location.

Word wrap is WordPerfect's automatic carriage return function; it eliminates the use of the Return key after each line of text except at the end of a paragraph. When the cursor reaches the right margin, word wrap automatically moves it down to the next line along with any text that would have exceeded the margin. This feature also helps realign paragraphs after any additions, deletions, or alterations are made.

The Save Key (F10) is used to save a document and then continue working on it, since the document will remain on the screen after the operation is completed. The Exit Key (F7) can be used to save a file, and then clear the screen to work on a new one.

The Print Key (Shift-F7) is used to print your entire document or just the page on which the cursor is currently located. Option 4 of the Print Key prompt, Printer Control, can be used to determine if your program is waiting for you to type a G (for go), which would be the case if your program was set up to use the Hand Feed option.

You should feel proud of yourself by now. Not only are you capable of creating, editing, saving and printing a letter, but you have also explored some of WordPerfect's most important features, including word wrap and automatic paragraph reformatting. Armed with all this, you really can get some useful work done.

At this point you may wish to pause to digest this material, and/or practice creating some letters of your own.

If not, go right ahead to Chapter 3 where you will learn some new techniques which will help improve the appearance of your documents, and permit you to change initial format settings such as margins, tabs, and line spacing.

CHAPTER 3 KEYSTROKE SUMMARY:

The Line Format Key—display format options on prompt line

The Left Margin Release Key—move cursor (and any text) one tab position left

The Flush Right Key—align text at right margin

The Center Key—center a line of text between margins

The Caps Lock key—press to uppercase text without shifting

The Underline Key

The Boldface Key

The Tab key—press to indent a single line in a paragraph

The Indent Key—press to indent every line in a paragraph

Activate Speller

The Save Key—save document and continue

The Print Key—display print options and print

The Retrieve Key—bring a previously saved document back to the screen

FORMATTING AND ENHANCING TEXT

NOW THAT YOU HAVE GOTTEN A TASTE of the WordPerfect program, it's time to introduce some new techniques. If you're an experienced typist you're already familiar with concepts such as indenting, underlining, and setting margins and tabs, but you'll see how much more powerful these features are on a computer and also learn others such as automatic hyphenation and spell-checking, which are unique to word processing.

Start your computer and load WordPerfect so that you can begin the next set of exercises. In the course of this chapter, you will be entering the letter shown in Figure 3.1.

1001 First St.
San Mateo, CA 91123
November 11, 1985

Mr. William B. Taylor, Service Manager
ABC Parts, Inc.
423 Main Street
Santa Ana, CA 90124

<u>URGENT NOTICE</u>

Dear Mr. Taylor:

As I told you on the phone this morning, there was an
apparent misunderstanding in the order we placed on Thursday,
November 7 and we recieved the wrong parts.

As you will see on the enclosed copy of our purchase
order, we requested a replacement interface and cable for a
PC 110 and were instead sent parts for a PC 110B. We were
fairly certain that they would not work but just to be sure
we went ahead and tested anyway. As we suspected, they do
<u>not</u> work in the 110.

Our customer is furious and in dire need of his
computer. If you wish to continue to do business with us,

<u>PLEASE RUSH THE FOLLOWING PARTS VIA UPS BLUE LABEL:</u>

A PC 110 interface, part# 66A and a PC 110
cable, part# 76A, as listed in your catalog
of November 1, 1985.

As soon as they are received, I'll return the others.

Thanks for your help.

Sincerely,

Sam Jones
Ace Computer Service

Figure 3.1: *Sample letter 2*

Formatting Your Text

Margins

Let's begin by taking a look at the margins. You can change these and many other settings by using the Line Format Key (Shift-F8). Pressing this key combination summons a message on the prompt line, which offers several alternative actions:

1 2 Tabs; 3 Margins; 4 Spacing; 5 Hyphenation; 6 Align Char: 0

You'll learn about the other options later in this chapter. For now, select 3 for margins. The current settings, which are 10 for the left margin and 74 for the right margin, will be displayed as follows:

[Margin Set] 10 74 to Left =

These are called the default settings because you start out with them and unless you change them, you will be using them "by default." Assuming you use 8½ inch paper and that your printer is set for ten pitch (ten characters per inch), these settings will leave a one inch margin on each side of the paper.

Now change the margin settings to 15 and 74. Type

15

followed by a Return, then type

74

followed by a Return. (Note that since you are leaving the right margin unchanged, you could have pressed Return without entering a number to retain the previous setting.) The cursor is now at position 15, the new left margin, and the position indicator on the Status line shows the new position (15).

Margin settings can vary between 0 and 250, and can be changed as often as you wish. However, a margin change will only affect text that you type at or after the cursor position when you changed the margin settings, so if you want to change the margins for the entire document be sure to move the cursor to the beginning before initiating the change. If you have already entered text there, it will all be reformatted to fit into the new margins.

WordPerfect also has a Left Margin Release Key (Shift-Tab). To release the margin, you move the cursor to the first position on the line and press Shift-Tab. The cursor (and any existing text) then moves one tab stop to the left.

Flush Right

Let's get started on the letter. The first step is to type the return address at the upper right corner of the page. A professional look is achieved when the address is aligned against the right margin, and WordPerfect has a Flush Right Key (Alt-F6) that will do this for you.

Go ahead and try it. Press Return to bring the cursor down to line 2, then press Alt-F6 and you'll see the cursor jump to the position just past the right margin, position 75. As you type the first line, watch the characters move inward from the right side. Type

    1001 First St.

and press Return.

Since the Return key signals the end of the flush right action, the cursor moves back to the left margin. You must press the Flush Right Key again before typing the next line. Press Alt-F6 and type

    San Mateo, CA 91123

and press Return.

The Flush Right Key can be used in combination with other features. To test this, press Alt-F6, and then insert the date using the Date Key (Shift-F5 and 1) followed by a Return.

One warning about the Flush Right Key: if you type any text on a line *before* you press this Key, there is a possibility that the text will disappear from the screen, hidden by the codes inserted when you pressed Flush Right. This would happen only if you tried to type more characters in total than the margin settings allow. In such a case, after you had pressed the Flush Right Key, the new words being entered from the right side would bump into the ones which had been typed before pressing Flush Right, and some or all of the original words would disappear.

You will be learning about the codes at the end of this chapter. For now, be careful not to type anything on the same line before pressing the Flush Right Key.

Move the cursor down by pressing Return three times and type this inside address:

Mr. William B. Taylor, Service Manager
ABC Parts, Inc.
423 Main Street
Santa Ana, CA 90124

Press Return four times to skip three lines.

Print Enhancements

Since the next phrase, *urgent notice,* must grab the reader's attention, it will be centered, underlined, capitalized, and printed in boldface. That sounds like a lot to learn, but it's actually just a matter of pressing a few keys.

The Center Key

Be sure that the cursor is at the left margin, then press Shift-F6. You'll see the cursor move to the middle of the page between the two margins, waiting for you to type. Don't start typing the words yet, though, because you also have to press the Caps Lock, Underline, and Bold Keys first.

Uppercase

Press the Caps Lock key to enter the phrase in capital letters and you'll see the position indicator (Pos) on the Status line change to uppercase (POS).

The Underline Key

Next press F8 for underlining and watch the number that follows the position indicator; as soon as F8 is pressed, it will appear underlined. This signal will always appear when you press F8 or move your cursor to an area of text that has been underlined.

The Bold Key

Finally, press F6 for boldfacing and the position indicator number should appear brighter, like the rest of the text on the Status line. Then type the following *without pressing Return:*

URGENT NOTICE

The Caps Lock, Bold, and Underline Keys are toggle commands that will keep operating until you press them again to turn them off. Since you are finished capitalizing, boldfacing, and underlining, deactivate them now by pressing the same keys: Caps Lock, F6, and F8. Check the position indicator and the number following it to confirm that all three are turned off. Now press Return.

If that phrase doesn't stand out in your letter, nothing will! On your screen, it should appear brighter than the rest of the text; if not, try adjusting the contrast on your monitor. When printed, the phrase will appear darker than the rest of the letter, provided your printer is capable of printing boldface.

Incidentally, text can also be centered after it has been typed by moving the cursor to the first character and pressing the Center Key (Shift-F6) followed by the ↓ key. When you center text in this fashion the line must end in a hard Return.

You can also underline, boldface, and even change text from lowercase to uppercase after it has been entered, but we'll save that for the next chapter "Performing Block Operations."

Press Return twice to skip a line and type this salutation:

Dear Mr. Taylor:

followed by two Returns.

Tabs

As you see, the first line in each paragraph of the letter is indented five spaces. This is done with the Tab key (⇆). Since tab stops are initially set for every five spaces, each time you press the Tab key the cursor will move right five positions.

To change the tab settings, press the Line Format Key (Shift-F8) and select 1 or 2 Tabs from the menu. The lower third of your screen will then be taken over by the Tab menu, illustrated in Figure 3.2, which marks each tab setting by placing a bright L above it. The L means left tab, which is the standard type used for text; when you press the Tab key and type a word, the first letter of the word is in the same position as the tab stop. You can also designate right aligned, centered, and decimal tabs, and these are explained in detail in Chapter 7. Delete the current settings by pressing

```
                                           1001 First St.
                                        San Mateo, CA 91123
                                        November 11, 1985


        Mr. William B. Taylor, Service Manager
        ABC Parts, Inc.
        423 Main Street
        Santa Ana, CA 90124



                          URGENT NOTICE


        Dear Mr. Taylor:



        L....L....L....L....L....L....L....L....L....L....L....L....L....L....L...
        5678901234567890123456789012345678901234567890123456789012345678901234567890123
           20        30        40        50        60        70        80        90
        Delete EOL (clear tabs); Enter number (set tab); Del (clear tab);
        Left; Center; Right; Decimal; .= Dot leader; Press EXIT when done.
```

Figure 3.2: *The Tab menu*

the Delete EOL (End Of Line) Key (Ctrl-End), then reset the tabs for every ten spaces by typing

    0,10

The 0 places the first tab stop at position 0, and the 10 places another one every 10 spaces. Notice that the program automatically inserted a tab stop at position 5. This enables you to use the Margin Release Key to move the cursor back to position 5. Now press Return, and then Exit (F7).

It's not necessary to delete all the tab settings to make changes. Try inserting a single tab setting by accessing the Tab menu (press Shift-F8, 1 or 2) and typing the number of the column where you want to place another tab stop. When you press Return, the cursor in the Tab menu will move to that position and place an L there. To confirm the change, press Exit (F7). If you wish to cancel the action, press Cancel (F1).

Before continuing, change the tab settings back to WordPerfect's default settings, every 5 positions. (At the Tab menu, press Ctrl-End, 0, 5, Return and Exit).

Now type the next three paragraphs of the letter, using the Tab key at the beginning of each one. Remember to press the Underline Key (F8), before and after typing the word *not* in the last sentence of the second paragraph. Also, notice that the word *recieved* is spelled incorrectly; this was done on purpose so that you can correct it later with the spelling checker.

The phrase after "If you wish to continue to do business with us," will be capitalized, underlined, and centered, so after skipping a line, press Caps Lock, Underline (F8), and Center (Shift-F6) before typing it:

PLEASE RUSH THE FOLLOWING PARTS VIA UPS BLUE LABEL:

Don't forget to turn off Underline and Caps Lock before typing the rest of the letter.

The Tab and Indent Keys

At this point you need to learn the difference between WordPerfect's Tab and Indent Keys. To indent a single line it is perfectly acceptable to use the Tab key, as you did at the beginning of each paragraph in the body of the letter. However, if you want every line in the paragraph to begin at an indented position, you must use the Indent key (F4).

If you mistakenly use the Tab key (at the beginning of each line), you will not be able to realign the paragraph properly after any additions or deletions. Instead the indentation will just word-wrap into the middle of the line, appearing as an unwanted gap in the middle of the text. You can experiment by using the Tab key to indent each line of a paragraph and then adding or deleting a few words.

To continue with the letter, press Return three times to skip two lines, then press Indent (F4) three times (to indent the paragraph by three tab stops instead of just one), then type the following sentence:

A PC 110 interface, part# 66A and a PC 110
cable, part# 76A, as listed in your catalog
of November 1, 1985.

Next, press Return three times and type the last two sentences using the Tab key at the beginning of each one and pressing Return twice after the first sentence:

As soon as they are received, I'll return the others.

Thanks for your help.

You used Tab instead of Indent in these two closing sentences because each of them is actually a one line paragraph ended by a Return. If you add text to one of them, you *would* want the new line to start at the regular left margin and this would only happen if you use Tab instead of Indent.

Now press Return four times and Tab five times, then type this closing:

> Sincerely,
>
> Sam Jones
> Ace Computer Service

The Speller

Now that the letter is finished, it would be a good idea to proof it and check for typing and spelling errors. WordPerfect has a built-in spelling checker called the Speller that can do the job very nicely.

If you have a hard disk, the Speller should already be copied onto it, so just press Ctrl-F2 to activate it.

If you are using a floppy disk system, you will have to insert your Speller disk into one of the drives before activating it. Place it in drive B, then press Ctrl-F2.

You will see a menu on the Status line that resembles the one below:

> Check: 1 Word; 2 Page; 3 Document; 4 Change Dictionary; 5 Look Up; 6 Count

Since you want to check the entire document, press 3.

The Status line will say

> * Please Wait *

as WordPerfect begins to check your letter.

Soon you will see the word *Mateo* highlighted. The Speller contains over 100,000 commonly used words, including many proper names such as Taylor and Jones, but it does not include proper names such as cities and it assumes that these words are misspelled. A message on the Status line will indicate that the word was not found in the dictionary, and above it several possible replacements will be suggested, as shown in Figure 3.3.

Since you know the word is correct and do not need to replace it, choose 2 Skip. You could have selected 1 Skip Once, but if you had, the Speller would stop to correct it each time the word reappears in your document, an unnecessary delay. Another option, if you plan on using this

```
                                              1001 First St.
                                     San Mateo, CA 91123
                                           July 23, 1986


           Mr. William B. Taylor, Service Manager
           ABC Parts, Inc.
           423 Main Street
           Santa Ana, CA 90124


           ============================================================================

           A. mate              B. mated              C. mater
           D. mates             E. matzo              F. mad
           G. made              H. maid               I. mat
           J. mate              K. math               L. matt
           M. matte             N. mayday             O. mead
           P. meadow            Q. meadowy            R. meat
           S. meaty             T. med                U. media
           V. mediae            W. medii              X. meed

           Not Found!  Select Word or Menu Option (0=Continue): 0
           1 Skip Once; 2 Skip; 3 Add Word; 4 Edit; 5 Look Up; 6 Phonetic
```

Figure 3.3: *The Speller in action*

word frequently in other documents, would be to add it to your dictionary by selecting 3 Add Word.

The next highlighted word will be *Ana,* another proper name. Press 2 again to skip this one.

The cursor will then stop at the word *recieved,* and your screen will resemble Figure 3.4. This time the word definitely is misspelled: remember the rule "i before e except after c"? Notice that the correct spelling appears twice. This happened because the Speller checked two dictionaries, a common word list and a main word list, and located the word in both dictionaries. The common word list is always checked first; it contains about 1,550 of the most frequently used words in the language. If the word is not found there, the main list (which contains over 100,000 words) is checked.

Press A to choose the correct spelling. The misspelled word will be corrected and the Speller will continue. The last "word" to be highlighted will be *110B.* The WordPerfect Speller does not recognize words containing numbers (the presence of a letter makes it a word), so choose 3 *Ignore words containing numbers*, as shown in Figure 3.5. This is preferable to selecting Skip because there are two more words in the letter that contain

```
    Dear Mr. Taylor:

         As I told you on the phone this morning, there was an
    apparent misunderstanding in the order we placed on
    Thursday, November 7, and we recieved the wrong parts.
         As you will see on the enclosed copy of our purchase
    order, we requested a replacement interface and cable for a
    PC 110 and were instead sent parts for a PC 110B. We were
    fairly certain that they would not work but just to be sure
    we went ahead and tested anyway. As we suspected, they do

    =================================================================

    A. received            B. relieved            C. received




    Not Found!  Select Word or Menu Option (0=Continue): 0
    1 Skip Once; 2 Skip; 3 Add Word; 4 Edit; 5 Look Up; 6 Phonetic
```

Figure 3.4: *A misspelled word*

numbers and the Speller would otherwise stop two more times trying to correct them.

When the Speller is finished it will display a count of the total number of words along with this message:

Word Count: 181   Press any key to continue

Now you know enough to use the Speller effectively. In Chapter 18 you will study its more advanced features including how to check words phonetically and how to add or delete words from the dictionary.

If you are using a floppy disk system, be sure to remove the Speller disk from drive B and replace it with your data disk before continuing.

Saving and Printing the Letter

You learned how to save and print in Chapter 2, but you may need a refresher. To save the letter, press F10, name the document Sample2, and

```
        As I told you on the phone this morning, there was an
   apparent misunderstanding in the order we placed on
   Thursday, November 7, and we received the wrong parts.
        As you will see on the enclosed copy of our purchase
   order, we requested a replacement interface and cable for a
   PC 110 and were instead sent parts for a PC 110E. We were
   fairly certain that they would not work but just to be sure
   we went ahead and tested anyway. As we suspected, they do
   not work in the 110.
        Our customer is furious and in dire need of his
   computer. If you wish to continue to do business with us,

   ============================================================================

   A. b                B. ba               C. bc
   D. be               E. bp               F. bs
   G. by               H. b                I. be





   Not Found!  Select Word or Menu Option (0=Continue): 0
   1 2 Skip; 3 Ignore words containing numbers; 4 Edit
```

Figure 3.5: *Words containing numbers*

press Return. When the status line clears, print the letter. Press Shift-F7 and select 1 Full Text.

Experimenting with the Margins

The letter is now safely saved on disk so it's alright to experiment with it trying to improve its appearance. First, let's change the margin settings back to the original ones, 10 and 74. To do this, move the cursor (using the arrow keys on the numeric keypad) to Line 1 Position 15, which is the very beginning of the document. Then press the Line Format Key (Shift-F8) followed by a 3 for Margins. Type 10, Return, then 74, Return.

You should see the effects immediately, as the entire letter is readjusted to fit the expanded margins. WordPerfect allows you to change margins anytime and as often as you need to throughout your document.

Spacing

Line spacing is another variable feature that can improve the appearance of your letter. Let's change the body of the letter to double spacing and see how it looks.

Move the cursor to the beginning of the first paragraph, which starts with *As I told you*. Press the Line Format Key (Shift-F8) and then 4 for Spacing. Because WordPerfect's default is single spacing, the Status line will indicate that the current spacing is 1.

[Spacing Set] 1

Change to double spacing by pressing 2 followed by Return and watch the screen. The rest of the letter from the cursor onward will be double spaced and will expand to a second page. To see this, move the cursor to the end of the letter by pressing the Home key twice followed by ↓. Incidentally, you can set line spacing in increments of half spaces (to .5, 1, 1.5, 2, 2.5, and so on.)

It is possible to use different spacing for different parts of your document, which is fortunate because the paragraph that describes the items being rushed via UPS looks best single spaced. Change to single spacing by moving the cursor to the word *LABEL* and repeating the operation: press Shift-F8, 4, 1, and Return. Now the rest of the letter is single spaced, as shown in Figure 3.6. Notice that changing the line spacing only alters text starting at the position where the cursor was located when you initiated the change.

If you prefer the single spaced version of the letter, one way to get it back is to exit from this revised version without saving it and then recall the version you saved before you changed the spacing. Try this procedure now, since you'll need the original version (with margin settings of 15 and 74) for the exercise on hyphenation that follows this one.

Press the Exit Key (F7) and enter N in response to the prompt asking if you wish to save the document. Next you'll be asked if you wish to exit from WordPerfect and you should press N once again. Then press the Retrieve Key (Shift-F10), and you will see the following prompt:

Document to be Retrieved:

Type the name Sample2 followed by Return and your original letter will reappear on the screen.

```
        fairly certain that they would not work but just to be sure

        we went ahead and tested anyway. As we suspected, they do

        not work in the 110.

            Our customer is furious and in dire need of his

        computer. If you wish to continue to do business with us,


            PLEASE RUSH THE FOLLOWING PARTS VIA UPS BLUE LABEL:


                    A PC 110 interface, part# 66A and a PC 110
                    cable, part# 76A, as listed in your catalog
                    of November 1, 1985.


            As soon as they are received, I'll return the others.

            Thanks for your help.
C:\WP2\SAMPLE2                              Doc 1  Pg 1  Ln 39     Pos 70
```

Figure 3.6: *The letter with mixed spacing*

Hyphenation

WordPerfect has a built-in hyphenation system that can be used to improve your document's appearance. It is activated whenever a word starts before or at a certain position near the end of the line and extends beyond the right margin. The feature helps you decide where to hyphenate the word and inserts a special type of hyphen, called a *soft hyphen,* which disappears when the word moves away from the right margin. Hyphenation is useful if you use a ragged right margin, because it eliminates the most noticeable gaps at the right side. If you use right justification (see Chapter 7), the right margin will always be even, but hyphenation can help reduce large blank gaps between words.

The sample letter you just created has a large blank space at the end of the second line, after the word *on,* which could be eliminated by using hyphen help. To activate this feature, move to the beginning of the letter, press the Line Format Key (Shift-F8) and select 5 for Hyphenation. You will see a prompt on the Status line, informing you that the hyphenation zone is 7 and 0 and that hyphenation is presently turned off (the "off aided" message).

[HZone Set] 7,0 Off Aided 1 On; 2 Off; 3 Set H-Zone; 4 Aided; 5 Auto: 0

There are two types of hyphenation assistance available, aided and automatic. The automatic method hyphenates words automatically, following certain rules set up in the program (except in certain cases where the rules don't apply and you are asked to decide where the hyphen belongs). The aided method stops at each word that could use a hyphen and lets you decide where to place it. Press 1 to turn aided hyphenation on, then press Return.

The hyphenation zone refers to the area between two positions that serve as flags to activate hyphenation assistance. The left boundary, called the Left H-Zone, is set to seven spaces before the right margin. The right boundary, called the Right H-Zone, is set at the right margin itself. Whenever a word begins before or at the Left H-Zone and extends past the Right H-Zone, hyphenation will occur. In Chapter 7 you will learn how and why to alter these positions; for now it is only necessary to understand how they work.

After you turn hyphenation on, press the ↓ key and the program will check your letter and stop at the first paragraph to ask you to hyphenate *Thursday,* as illustrated in Figure 3.7.

If you do not want the word hyphenated, simply press the Cancel Key (F1) and the entire word will remain on the next line. Otherwise, use the ← key to move the cursor one position to the left (in between the *s* and *d*) and press Esc. The word Thursday will be hyphenated and split into *Thurs* and *day.* As you can see, the paragraph is lined up more evenly now:

As I told you on the phone this morning, there was an apparent misunderstanding in the order we placed on Thursday, November 7 and we received the wrong parts.

Note that if you add or delete text in the sentence with the hyphenated word and that word moves away from the right margin, the hyphen will no longer be visible.

The Reveal Codes Key

Earlier in this chapter, you learned that special hidden codes are inserted in the text when you press the Flush Right Key, and you were promised an explanation of this fact. Nearly all of WordPerfect's formatting features insert codes, including several of the ones you have just studied such as underline, center, boldface, line spacing, margins, and tabs. These codes are not shown on the screen; that way the document you see on your screen resembles the printed version as closely as possible. However, it is often necessary to see where the codes are located in case there is an unwanted one which is disrupting the document's appearance.

Let's consider the Underline Key (F8) as an example. As you know, you have to press this key twice, to signal the beginning and end of the text to be underlined. When you do this, you are actually inserting codes which turn underline on and off. It is easy to forget to press Underline the second time to turn it off. When you do this you'll realize it immediately because after you've typed the text you want underlined, any new characters you enter will continue to be underlined.

To test this, clear the screen (press F7, N, N), press Return once, then press the Underline Key (F8) once and type the following phrase:

THE WORDPERFECT REVEAL CODES SCREEN

Next, press Return and type

testing

As you can see, the word *testing* is underlined, contrary to what we had intended. In fact, until you press F8 again, WordPerfect will continue to underline anything you type.

To fix the problem, let's look at the Reveal Codes screen shown in Figure 3.8. Press the Reveal Codes Key (Alt-F3) and don't panic! Although it looks confusing the first time, this screen is actually quite logical.

The screen is divided into two parts. The top part displays several lines of text around and including the one on which the cursor is currently located. In the bottom part, the same text appears along with formatting codes, each one surrounded by brackets. A thick highlighted band separates them, and the familiar Status line appears at the top of this band. Called the Tab Ruler, this band shows where each tab stop and margin setting is located. The triangles represent tab stops, and a brace or bracket is used to represent the margins. A brace indicates that the margin coincides with a tab stop, as the left margin does in our example. Otherwise a bracket is used, as with the right margin on our screen.

The cursor on the bottom of the Reveal Codes screen is located in exactly the same place as on the top, but it appears bolder.

```
                                          1001 First St.
                                     San Mateo, CA 91123
                                        July 23, 1986



        Mr. William B. Taylor, Service Manager
        ABC Parts, Inc.
        423 Main Street
        Santa Ana, CA 90124



                           URGENT NOTICE


        Dear Mr. Taylor:

             As I told you on the phone this morning, there was an

        apparent misunderstanding in the order we placed on

        Thursday, November 7, and we received the wrong parts.
        Position hyphen; Press ESC Thursd_ay,
```

Figure 3.7: *Hyphenation in action*

The first code on the screen is [HRt], symbolizing a hard return. It indicates the Return key was pressed at that position, in this case to leave a blank line. Next is the first underline symbol, [U]. A capitalized U is the code to begin underlining.

The [U] is followed by the text *THE WORDPERFECT REVEAL CODES SCREEN,* which appears underlined above the Tab Ruler but not below it in the Reveal Codes screen. It is followed by another [HRt] code. The word *testing* appears on the next line, followed by a [u]. The [u] is the code to end underlining. Text which is underlined is always surrounded by a pair of these bracketed Us, the first in uppercase and the second in lowercase.

When you press F8 to begin underlining, the pair of bracketed Us is created, with the cursor in between. As you type, the ending [u] moves on ahead; everything you type is inserted between the pair and is underlined. When you press F8 a second time to end the underlining, the cursor jumps past the ending [u], outside the underlining area.

As you've probably figured out by now, if you don't want the word *testing* underlined, the lowercase [u] code should be at the end of the first

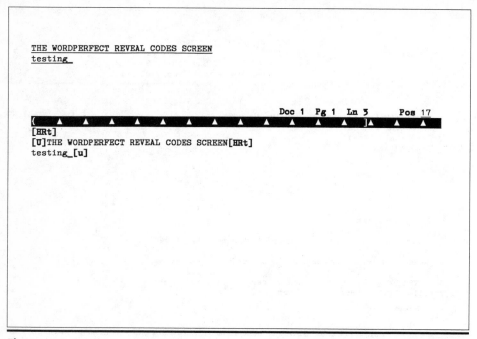

```
THE WORDPERFECT REVEAL CODES SCREEN
testing_



                                    Doc 1  Pg 1  Ln 3      Pos 17
⌐     ▲    ▲    ▲    ▲    ▲    ▲    ▲    ▲    ▲    ]▲    ▲    ▲
[HRt]
[U]THE WORDPERFECT REVEAL CODES SCREEN[HRt]
testing_[u]
```

Figure 3.8: *The Reveal Codes screen*

line, after the word *SCREEN*. To fix it, exit the Reveal Codes screen by pressing any key, move the cursor to the end of the first line after the word *SCREEN*, and press F8. Now check the Reveal Codes screen. Because you pressed F8 in the midst of already underlined text, you have created a second pair of bracketed Us, with the cursor in between the two *pairs*.

To remove underlining from the word *testing*, delete the extra pair, which begins with the second uppercase [U] code. Since the cursor is right next to it, all you have to do is press the Del key. You can do this from within the Reveal Codes screen. As soon as you delete the [U], its ending [u] will be erased as well, and the underlining will disappear from the word *testing* above the Tab Ruler. Now you can return to the normal screen by pressing any key except those on the numeric keypad (all of which are either cursor movement keys or ineffective).

The Reveal Codes screen is extremely helpful and it's important to become comfortable with it, so you will be directed to use it frequently throughout the rest of this book. Nearly all of WordPerfect's formatting features insert codes. Many are in plain English with very obvious meanings, such as [Tab], which signifies the Tab key was pressed, [Block], which signifies the beginning of a block, and [Hyph on], which means that hyphen help is being used. To help you decipher the more cryptic ones, they are summarized in Appendix B.

Let me give you one more example of how the Reveal Codes screen can help you. Suppose you have moved your cursor to the beginning of the file to change the margin to 20,70. You press the correct keys and insert the hidden code that does the job. Later on you change your mind and wish to reset the margins again. You go to the beginning of the file, press the keys to change the margins to 15,74 and . . . nothing happens! To see what went wrong, you consult the Reveal Codes screen. You find that your cursor is at the very top of the file and that there are two bracketed Margin Set codes in the document (changing a formatting code such as margin settings does not delete other margin settings that have been inserted). The code for the margin setting you just selected (15,74) is to the left of the original one (20,70):

[Margin Set:15,74][Margin Set:20,70]

WordPerfect is still following the original setting (20,70), because it reads them in order and follows the last one it sees. Now you can delete the outdated code and your new instruction will take effect.

In general, when you are puzzled by WordPerfect's behavior, use Reveal Codes to look behind the scenes at what is really going on. Then you will be able to find the problem and correct it.

Summary

The default margin settings are 10 and 74, and can vary between 0 and 250. To change them, press the Line Format Key, (Shift-F8) and choose the Margins option (3). If you want to change the settings for the entire document, it is necessary to move the cursor all the way to the beginning of the document before initiating this procedure.

The Flush Right Key (Alt-F6) is used to align text against the right margin. The Return key signals the end of a flush right operation.

The Center Key (Shift-F6) is used to center text on a line.

The Underline Key (F8) is used to underline text; it must be pressed before and after typing the text to be underlined. After text has been entered, it can only be underlined by combining this Key with the Block Key (see next chapter).

The Bold Key (F6) is used to boldface text and must be pressed before and after typing the text. After text has been entered, it can only be bold-faced by combining this Key with the Block Key (see next chapter).

The Tab key is used to indent the first line of a paragraph. Tabs are set for every five spaces, but these can easily be altered using the Tab option (1 or 2) on the Line Format Key (Shift-F8).

The Indent Key (F4) is used when you want the entire paragraph to begin at an indented position, as in an outline. If you use this key instead of repeatedly using the Tab key, you can make unlimited additions and deletions and the paragraph will be realigned automatically after each one.

The Speller (Ctrl-F2) can be used to check for spelling errors in a single word, on the current page, or in the entire document. It also pro-vides a count of the total number of words in the document. Although it has a vocabulary of over 100,000 words, you can add words of your own to customize the Speller's list.

Line spacing can be altered both in your printed document and on screen by selecting the Spacing option (4) with the Line Format Key (Shift-F8). The default setting is for single spacing, and it can be adjusted in increments of half spaces (to .5, 1, 1.5, 2, 2.5, and so on).

Hyphen help is useful if you are using a ragged right margin, for it will help eliminate blank spaces at the right margin. To use it, select the Hyphenation option (5) with the Line Format Key (Shift-F8) and indi-cate that you want the option turned on.

The Retrieve Key (Shift-F10) is used to bring a previously saved copy of a file from the disk to the screen so you can edit, print, or otherwise work with it.

The Reveal Codes screen is used to locate and (if necessary) to delete for-matting codes such as underline, center, and line spacing. These codes are inserted into your document when you select these for-matting options, but are visible only on the Reveal Codes screen.

This allows the document on the normal WordPerfect screen to look exactly like the printed version.

Once again you've covered a great deal of material and should feel very accomplished. By now you are comfortable with several formatting techniques such as margins, tabs, indentation, hyphenation, and spacing. Furthermore, you won't have to use a dictionary to check your spelling; as you've seen, WordPerfect can do it much faster!

You have also been introduced to the Reveal Codes screen and will be encountering it frequently in the remaining chapters. Chapter 6 will cover embedded codes in more depth, teaching you how to use search and replace to delete unwanted codes, how to tell which appearance of a code is controlling your document if it appears more than once, and much more.

The next chapter will introduce block operations, which allow you to mark a section of text and perform many different operations on it. You will learn how to use the Block Key with features you've already studied such as underline, delete, and print, as well as with new ones such as move and copy.

CHAPTER 4 KEYSTROKE SUMMARY:

The Block Key—press to mark off a block of text for printing, copying, saving, deleting, etc.

The Move Key—press to display Copy, Cut, and Retrieve options on Status line

The Print Key—display print options and print

The Cancel Key—press to cancel any function key command

The Switch Key—press with Block on to change text between uppercase and lowercase

BLOCK
OPERATIONS

THE BLOCK KEY IS ONE OF WORD-
PERFECT'S most useful features and you'll
undoubtedly be using it often. Simply stated,
it allows you to mark off a block of text
ranging in length from one character to the
entire document, in order to perform operations that affect only that section of text. For
instance, you can mark a block as a separate
unit to be saved to disk, sent to the printer,
copied, deleted, moved to another location,
or converted from lowercase to uppercase.

Block mode is more than an amenity though;
in many cases it is a necessity. In the last chapter you learned how to use the Underline and
Boldface Keys when entering text, and I mentioned that neither of these features can be
used by itself to underline or boldface text once
it has been entered. Instead, such text must first
be defined as a block.

Despite its power, the Block Key is not complicated. After you type the following paragraph, you'll use Block mode to copy a few sentences and find out just how easy it can be.

WordPerfect fully utilizes the PC keyboard and cursor control is outstanding. The arrow keys are used to move one space to the left or right and one line up or down. You can get to the beginning of a document by pressing the Home key twice followed by the Up Arrow key, and to the end of the document by pressing the Home key twice followed by the Down Arrow key. The Ctrl-Home combination allows you to select a page number and the cursor will quickly jump to the top of that page.

The Block Key

Start the exercise by moving the cursor to the beginning of the paragraph and pressing the Block Key (Alt-F4). Notice the flashing message that appears on the Status line:

Block on

Use the ↓ key to move the cursor down a few lines and watch as the text is highlighted, as shown in Figure 4.1. This highlighted area is the currently defined block; you can keep moving the cursor down to expand the block or else move the cursor back up to shrink it.

Some unique methods of cursor movement are available when you use Block mode. For instance, pressing Return will move the cursor and highlighting to the end of the paragraph (the next hard Return). Typing a period (.) will move the cursor and highlighting to the end of the sentence (the next period). Typing any other character will move the cursor to that character's next appearance in the text. You can repeat any of these operations and mix them as much as you like. As with most other operations, pressing Cancel (F1) will abort the Block operation altogether, so feel free to experiment a bit.

When you're finished experimenting, move the cursor and highlighting to the last word in the fourth line, *followed*. Next, you will be making a copy of the highlighted lines and inserting the copy below the first paragraph.

WordPerfect fully utilizes the PC keyboard and cursor control is
outstanding. The arrow keys are used to move one space to the
left or right and one line up or down. You can get to the
beginning of a document by pressing the Home key twice followed
by the Up Arrow key, and to the end of the document by pressing
the Home key twice followed by the Down Arrow key. The Ctrl-Home
combination allows you to select a page number and the cursor
will quickly jump to the top of that page.

Block on   Doc 1 Pg 1 Ln 5   POS 10

Figure 4.1: *The blocked text*

Copy and Cut

Press the Move Key (Ctrl-F4). The Status line will present five choices:

1 Cut Block; 2 Copy Block; 3 Append; 4 Cut/Copy Column; 5 Cut/Copy Rectangle: 0

(Besides marking a block of standard text in the ways just discussed, WordPerfect allows you to mark a rectangular block such as a line drawing or formula (option 5 on the prompt line). This will be covered in Chapter 17. You can also mark a column (option 4) that has been defined by using any of the following features: tab, tab align, indent or hard return. Marking and moving columns will be discussed in Chapter 14. However the block is marked, the operations of copying, moving, and deleting are the same as with standard blocked text.)

Press 2 to make a copy of the block. The highlighting will disappear and you may be left wondering what happened, since the paragraph seems to have returned to its original state. Appearances are deceptive in this case for the block of text you copied is actually retained in memory, waiting to be retrieved.

If you had chosen 1 Cut Block instead of Copy, the block would also have been stored in memory (waiting to be "pasted" at a location of your choice). The difference is that with Cut, the text would have disappeared from its original position; with Copy, the original text remains intact.

Move

The next step is to retrieve (paste) the copied text using the Move Key. The Move Key has two sets of functions, depending on whether it's used alone or while the Block Key is in operation. As you just saw, when used with Block, it can be used to cut or copy a user-defined section of text (options 1, 2, 4, and 5 on the prompt line above). Block and Move can also be used together to add a block of text to the end of an existing file on disk (option 3, Append).

The Move Key can be used alone (see the prompt line below) to cut or copy by the sentence, paragraph, or page. These three units do not have to be highlighted beforehand by a Block operation. The Move Key is also used by itself to retrieve (paste) text from memory after it has been cut or copied. You use the Move Key for retrieval (pasting) regardless of how the cut or copy was originally done—whether by Block plus Move (user defined) or by Move alone (sentence, paragraph, page). All these maneuvers will be made clear by the following exercises.

Move the cursor a few lines below the end of the paragraph and press the Move Key (Ctrl-F4) again. Compare the prompt line that now appears on your screen to the one that the Move Key summoned while Block was on.

Move 1 Sentence; 2 Paragraph; 3 Page; Retrieve 4 Column; 5 Text; 6 Rectangle: 0

Select the Retrieve Text option (5). A perfect copy of the lines you blocked earlier will appear with the first word located at the cursor position, as shown in Figure 4.2. These lines still remain in memory and you can keep making copies of them anywhere you like until you cut or copy a new text block. Move the cursor and repeat the operation a few times to make a few more copies.

```
WordPerfect fully utilizes the PC keyboard and cursor control is
outstanding. The arrow keys are used to move one space to the
left or right and one line up or down. You can get to the
beginning of a document by pressing the Home key twice followed
by the Up Arrow key, and to the end of the document by pressing
the Home key twice followed by the Down Arrow key. The Ctrl-Home
combination allows you to select a page number and the cursor
will quickly jump to the top of that page.

WordPerfect fully utilizes the PC keyboard and cursor control is
outstanding. The arrow keys are used to move one space to the
left or right and one line up or down. You can get to the
beginning of a document by pressing the Home key twice followed




                                    Doc 1  Pg 1  Ln 10     POS 10
```

Figure 4.2: *The copied text*

If you were retrieving a column block, you would use option 4; for a rectangle block, use option 6. Note that cutting or copying a column or rectangle block does not disturb a text block stored in memory. WordPerfect has three places in memory for the three kinds of blocks.

Delete

Now alter and then delete the duplicated lines. Change the first sentence to read

Cursor control is outstanding in WordPerfect.

Next, move the cursor to the beginning of the extra lines, then block them by pressing the Block Key (Alt-F4) and moving the cursor to the end of the last unwanted line. Then press the Move Key (Ctrl-F4). This time, select the Cut Block option (1) and the text will be deleted (cut). The whole block of extra lines is now in memory, but it is up to you whether you choose to paste it anywhere or not.

WordPerfect is very forgiving and allows you to undo the damage you may cause if you delete a block accidentally or simply change your mind after cutting it. Until you copy or cut new text, you can retrieve accidentally cut text by using the same option you just used above to paste in a text copy. Press the Move Key (Ctrl-F4) and option 5 (Retrieve Text). Try it now. Since you have not moved the cursor, you are simply pasting the cut text back where you cut it.

Another way to delete a block is to mark the sentences using the Block Key in the usual way, then with the *Block on* message still flashing, press the Backspace or Del key. The following prompt will appear on the Status line:

Delete Block? (Y/N) N

If you type a Y, the block will be deleted. When you use this method to delete text, you cannot retrieve it using the Move Key (as described above). Instead, you will have to use the Undelete feature on the Cancel Key (F1), which you learned about in Chapter 1. Press F1,1 to try it.

Using the Move Key Alone

In the exercises so far you have used the Move Key (Ctrl-F4) in conjunction with the Block Key (Alt-F4) to copy, move, and delete text. If you have the impression there were a lot of keystrokes involved, you are right! No fewer than eight steps were used to make a copy of the text:

1. You moved the cursor to the beginning of the text to be copied.
2. You pressed Alt-F4 to begin marking the block.
3. You moved the cursor to the end of the block.
4. You pressed the Move Key (Ctrl-F4).
5. You pressed 2 to copy the text.
6. You moved the cursor to the location where you wanted the copy to appear.
7. You pressed the Move Key again.
8. You pressed 5 to retrieve the copy.

As mentioned earlier, if you wish to cut or copy by the sentence, paragraph, or page, it is not necessary to use the Block Key at all. Instead you can use the Move Key alone, eliminating steps 2 and 3.

Move the cursor to any location in the original paragraph and press the Move Key (Ctrl-F4) followed by a 2 for Paragraph. As illustrated in Figure 4.3, the entire paragraph is highlighted. If the paragraph were indented, the indent would be included too. The Status line prompt now asks whether you wish to cut, copy, or delete the block. The cut and delete options both delete the highlighted sentence, paragraph, or page from the screen. The difference in the two is that the cut option deletes the text but retains it in memory so that it can be retrieved and pasted in another location using the Move Key (Ctrl-F4,5), whereas the delete option does not save the text in memory and it can never be retrieved again. Press 2 to copy, then move the cursor to a new location and press Move again, followed by a 5 to retrieve the text.

Remember, when you want to cut and paste, copy, or permanently delete a sentence, paragraph, or page, you can save a few steps by using the Move Key alone.

Before proceeding further, delete all the duplicate paragraphs.

```
WordPerfect fully utilizes the PC keyboard and cursor control is
outstanding. The arrow keys are used to move one space to the
left or right and one line up or down. You can get to the
beginning of a document by pressing the Home key twice followed
by the Up Arrow key, and to the end of the document by pressing
the Home key twice followed by the Down Arrow key. The Ctrl-Home
combination allows you to select a page number and the cursor
will quickly jump to the top of that page.




1 Cut; 2 Copy; 3 Delete: ▊
```

Figure 4.3: *Cut or copy with the Move Key*

Relocating a Sentence within a Paragraph

The Move Key is also useful for rearranging sentences within a paragraph. In the next exercise, you will be cutting the second sentence and moving it to the end of the paragraph. Remember WordPerfect's automatic rewrite feature? Observe how quickly it will realign the paragraph after the move.

Move the cursor to any character in the second sentence and press the Move Key (Ctrl-F4). Select 1 Sentence and observe that the whole sentence is highlighted on the screen. No matter where the cursor is located in the sentence, WordPerfect is able to figure out where it starts and ends by searching for periods, exclamation points or question marks which normally designate the end of the sentence you want to highlight, and the end of the previous sentence.

The next step is to press 1 to cut the sentence. It disappears and leaves a gap between the words *the* and *beginning,* as illustrated below:

WordPerfect fully utilizes the PC keyboard and cursor control is
outstanding. You can get to the
beginning of a document by pressing the Home key twice followed
by the Up Arrow key, and to the end of the document by pressing
the Home key twice followed by the Down Arrow key. The Ctrl-Home
combination allows you to select a page number and the cursor
will quickly jump to the top of that page.

You know from Chapter 2 that as soon as you move the cursor down a line, the paragraph will be realigned. Now move the cursor to the end of the last line (after the word *page*) and insert the cut sentence by pressing Ctrl-F4 again and 5 for Retrieve Text.

Printing a Block

The Print Key (Shift-F7) allows you to print an individual page or an entire document, but nothing smaller than a page and nothing in between a page and a document. It is often desirable to print a section of your work that does not fit these categories: the Block Key makes this possible.

Printing by blocks is especially useful when you are working with long documents. If you're in the habit of printing and proofreading each section after it's been typed, this will save you a lot of paper. Rather than printing the entire document after finishing each section, you can block, print, and proofread the sections individually.

Try printing the first two sentences of the sample paragraph. Move the cursor to the first word, *WordPerfect,* and press Block (Alt-F4), then press the period key twice to move the cursor to the end of the second sentence. (You will see that the first two sentences are highlighted.) Next, press the Print Key, (Shift-F7). A message will appear on the Status line asking if you wish to print the block, as illustrated below:

Print Block? (Y/N) N

Press Y. A message will appear briefly on the Status line that says

* Please wait *

and then the block will be printed.

After printing, the *Block on* message will still be flashing, so press Alt-F4 again or F1 to turn it off.

Saving a Block

Saving a block of text is equally simple and can serve many purposes. You may decide to delete a section because it doesn't really fit or doesn't sound right, but still wish to retain it in a separate file just in case you change your mind. Or you may have a paragraph that is used frequently without any changes. Rather than retyping it each time you use it, you can save it to its own disk file and insert copies of it as often as you wish.

Save the same two sentences you just printed. First, block them by pressing Alt-F4, and the period twice. Then press the Save Key (F10). As shown in Figure 4.4, the Status line now asks you to assign a file name to the block, which will then be saved in a separate file under that name. As with any file, try to assign a logical name that you will remember easily.

You'll know that the file has been saved when the light goes out on the drive. As with the block print command, the *Block on* message will still be flashing and you will have to press Block (Alt-F4) or Cancel (F1) to turn it off.

Now try retrieving the block from the disk file. Move the cursor to the end of the document, press the Retrieve Key (Shift-F10) and enter the name of the file you just saved. The block will appear at the cursor location with the cursor on the first word. In some ways this is just like retrieving a block that you have cut or copied to memory. But once the block has been saved to disk, you can still retrieve it even after another block has become the block in memory, or after the computer has been turned off and the memory cleared entirely. Delete the block before continuing.

Converting between Uppercase and Lowercase

How many times have you been typing along with your eyes glued to the paper, when you suddenly looked up at the screen to discover that all of your characters had been entered in uppercase because the Caps Lock key was on? WordPerfect has a wonderful feature that will switch the text to lowercase, saving you the effort of deleting and retyping all your work. As you've probably guessed, it works with the Block Key.

Now you are going to convert the sample paragraph to uppercase. Move the cursor to the first character and press Block (Alt-F4). Press Return to highlight the whole paragraph. Next press the Switch Key (Shift-F3) and this

```
WordPerfect fully utilizes the PC keyboard and cursor control is
outstanding. You can get to the beginning of a document by
pressing the Home key twice followed by the Up Arrow key, and to
the end of the document by pressing the Home key twice followed
by the Down Arrow key. The Ctrl-Home combination allows you to
select a page number and the cursor will quickly jump to the top
of that page. The arrow keys are used to move one space to the
left or right and one line up or down.




Block Name: _
```

Figure 4.4: *Saving a block to disk*

message will appear on the Status line asking if you wish to use lowercase or uppercase:

Block 1 Uppercase; 2 Lowercase: 0

Select 1 Uppercase, then press Alt-F4 to turn off Block mode.

The entire paragraph will now be capitalized. However, when you switch it back to lowercase, you are going to have a problem. Try it now and see if you can discover what the problem is. The results appear in Figure 4.5.

The paragraph contains several words that were originally capitalized, such as *PC* and *Ctrl*. With the text converted back to lowercase, the only words that remain capitalized are those that follow a period, with one notable exception, the first word in the paragraph. WordPerfect recognizes that words immediately following a period, question mark, or exclamation point are supposed to remain capitalized, but it is unable to capitalize the other words correctly. In fact, the *w* in the paragraph's first word, *WordPerfect,* is no longer capitalized because it does not follow a period (within the marked block).

```
    wordperfect fully utilizes the pc keyboard and cursor control is
    outstanding. You can get to the beginning of a document by
    pressing the home key twice followed by the up arrow key, and to
    the end of the document by pressing the home key twice followed
    by the down arrow key. The ctrl-home combination allows you to
    select a page number and the cursor will quickly jump to the top
    of that page. The arrow keys are used to move one space to the
    left or right and one line up or down.

    ▬

                                        Doc 1  Pg 1  Ln 10    POS 10
```

Figure 4.5: *After converting the sample paragraph back to lowercase*

As long as you recognize this limitation, the Switch feature can be very useful. In most cases, it will still be quicker than deleting and retyping the entire text.

Block Underlining and Boldfacing

As mentioned earlier, the Block Key must be used to underline or boldface text that has already been entered. The next exercise will teach you how.

Move the cursor to the beginning of the page, press Return twice, turn Caps Lock on, then move the cursor back to the first line and type the following title for your paragraph:

INTRODUCTION TO WORDPERFECT'S CURSOR CONTROL FEATURES

Next move the cursor to the first character, the *I* in *INTRODUCTION,* and press the Block Key (Alt-F4). Press the Home and → keys and watch the cursor jump to the end of the line, highlighting the whole title. Now press the Underline Key (F8) and the title will be underlined.

Notice that the highlighting disappears. This happens because the Block mode is turned off when you press the Underline Key. In addition, pressing Underline with Block on both begins and ends the underlining, so you do *not* have to press F8 again to turn underline off, as you did when underlining text as you entered it.

Repeat the steps again, except this time press Bold (F6) instead of Underline (F8). Your title should now resemble Figure 4.6.

Summary

The Block Key (Alt-F4) is used to define a block of text in order to perform operations on it as a unit.

The Block and Move Keys can be used together to cut or copy a section of text into a special area of the computer's memory so that the text can be inserted later in another section of your document. To do this, press Block (Alt-F4) and highlight the text by moving the cursor. Then press Move (Ctrl-F4) and select 1 Cut Block or 2 Copy Block. The highlighting disappears.

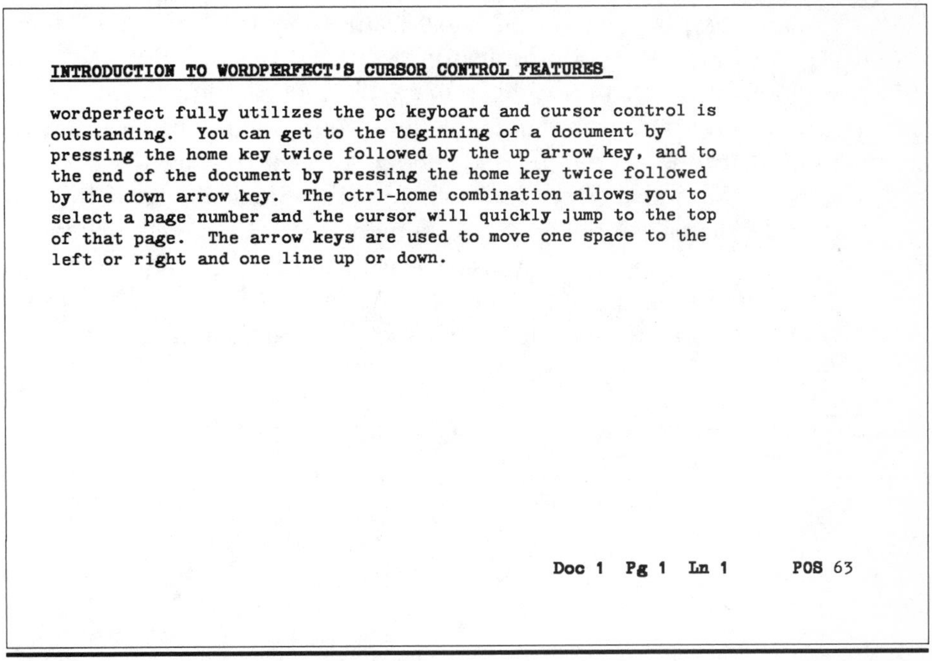

INTRODUCTION TO WORDPERFECT'S CURSOR CONTROL FEATURES

wordperfect fully utilizes the pc keyboard and cursor control is
outstanding. You can get to the beginning of a document by
pressing the home key twice followed by the up arrow key, and to
the end of the document by pressing the home key twice followed
by the down arrow key. The ctrl-home combination allows you to
select a page number and the cursor will quickly jump to the top
of that page. The arrow keys are used to move one space to the
left or right and one line up or down.

Doc 1 Pg 1 Ln 1   POS 63

Figure 4.6: *The transformed title*

The Move Key can be used without the Block Key on to cut and paste, copy, or delete by the sentence, paragraph, or page. It is also used to retrieve (paste) text once it has been cut or copied.

Any text that has been cut or copied using 1 Cut or 2 Copy (except if the Delete option on the Move Key was used) remains in memory and can be retrieved until a different block of text is cut or copied. To retrieve text, press Move and select 5 Retrieve Text.

A section of text can be printed by blocking it, then pressing the Print Key (Shift-F7).

A section of text can be saved to disk by blocking it, then pressing the Save Key (F10).

You can convert a section of text from lowercase to uppercase or vice versa by blocking it, then pressing the Switch Key (Shift-F3).

Text that has already been entered can be underlined or boldfaced by blocking it, then pressing Underline (F8) or Bold (F6).

Block mode is a powerful and valuable feature for which there are innumerable applications. Instead of disfiguring your work with the physical cut and paste method, you can use this remarkable tool to copy, move, delete, and rearrange to your heart's content, and your documents will always look terrific. Before long, you'll wonder how you ever managed without it.

You have performed many operations with the Block Key and by now you should feel familiar enough to experiment by using it with other features. For instance, you might try using it with the Speller, the Flush Right Key (Alt-F6), or the Center Key (Shift-F6). In later chapters you will learn how to use it with some new functions such as search and replace, sort, and index.

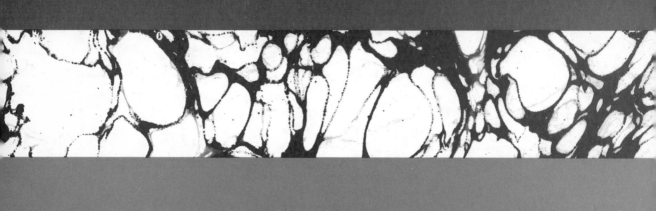

PART II

ADVANCED
WORD PROCESSING
FEATURES

CHAPTER 5 KEYSTROKE SUMMARY:

The Page Format Key—press to display Page Format Menu

The Reveal Codes Key—press to view hidden formatting codes

PAGE FORMATTING

WORDPERFECT HAS THREE MAJOR FORmatting keys: the Line Format Key, the Page Format Key, and the Print Format Key. Up to this point, you've only been introduced to one, the Line Format Key (Shift-F8). This chapter will acquaint you with the second one, the Page Format Key (Alt-F8), which controls features that affect the number of text lines on the printed page: the margins, page length, page numbering, headers and footers, and "widows and orphans." Don't worry if some of these terms sound strange to you; you'll know them all quite well by the time you finish this chapter!

The Page Format Key

Unlike most of the other Keys you've studied, the Page Format Key completely replaces your editing screen with a full-screen menu. The ten-item Page Format menu is summoned by pressing Alt-F8. The menu is shown in Figure 5.1.

Page Number Position

Unlike many other word processors, WordPerfect does not print page numbers on your documents unless you tell it to. You do this by using the Page Number Position option (1) to select a location on the page where you want the numbers printed.

```
Page Format

        1 - Page Number Position

        2 - New Page Number

        3 - Center Page Top to Bottom

        4 - Page Length

        5 - Top Margin

        6 - Headers or Footers

        7 - Page Number Column Positions

        8 - Suppress for Current page only

        9 - Conditional End of Page

        A - Widow/Orphan

Selection: 0
```

Figure 5.1: *The Page Format menu*

To view the Page Number Position menu, select option 1 on the Page Format menu. As shown in Figure 5.2, this submenu offers you eight possible locations for the page number: on each page at the top left, the top center, the top right, the bottom left, the bottom center, or the bottom right, or at the top alternating left and right, or the bottom alternating left and right.

Most of these alternatives are self-explanatory. For instance, selection 1 causes page numbers to be printed at the upper left corner of each page. The number will start at position 10 of line 1; if your printer is set for 10 pitch (10 characters per inch) and the paper size is $8\frac{1}{2}$ by 11 inches, the number will appear exactly one inch from the left side of the paper. As you will soon see, this default column position (10) can be changed using the Page Number Column Positions option (7) on the Page Format menu.

Selection 2 inserts a code that causes a page number to be printed at the top center, starting at position 42. Selection 3 inserts a code that causes a page number to be printed at the top right, starting at position 74. Selections 5, 6, and 7 will place the numbers at the bottom of each page, in the

```
Position of Page Number on Page

    0 - No page numbers

    1 - Top left of every page

    2 - Top center of every page

    3 - Top right of every page

    4 - Top alternating left & right

    5 - Bottom left of every page

    6 - Bottom center of every page

    7 - Bottom right of every page

    8 - Bottom alternating left & right


Selection: 0
```

Figure 5.2: *Selecting a page number position*

same column positions as at the top (10, 42, and 74). (If your printer is set for 12 pitch, the left, center, and right page numbers will appear in positions 12, 50, and 89, respectively.)

If you select 4 from the Page Number Position menu, the first page number will be printed on the top left side of the first page (in position 10), the second page number will be printed on the top right side of the second page (in position 74), and the third page number will be printed on the top left side of the third page. It will continue alternating like this throughout the document. Selection 8 will do the same, except that the page numbers will be placed alternatively at the *bottom* left and *bottom* right of the pages.

This alternating format is often used in books, manuals, and similar publications to allow page numbers to appear at the outer edge of the left and right hand facing pages. To present your document like this you must have text on both sides of the page, which you can accomplish by making two-sided copies on a copy machine.

The No page numbers option (0) on the Page Number Position menu is the default. It is included on the menu so that you can change back to it if necessary after choosing another option. For example, if you wanted to limit page numbering to the first five pages of your document, you would insert a page number position code on the first page, as usual. However, with your cursor on the first line of the sixth page, which you do *not* want numbered, you would select option 0 to turn the pagination feature off. This procedure would ensure that the sixth and subsequent pages would be printed without page numbers (unless you inserted another page number position code later in the document).

To add a page number, press option 1 Top left of every page. This action will restore the main Page Format menu, and you can then press any key except a selection number to exit from it back to your document. Page numbers appear only on the printed document, so don't be alarmed because a number does not appear at the top of your screen. To verify that the change was actually made, check the Reveal Codes screen by pressing the Reveal Codes Key (Alt-F3). You should see the following code at the top left of the page confirming that you selected option 1 for the page number position:

[Pos Pg#:1]

Printing a page number eliminates two lines of text from each page of single-spaced text, one for the page number and one for a blank line that is skipped to separate the number from the main text. Although the page numbers themselves are not shown until printed, each page on the screen will now end at line 52 instead of the normal 54. To verify this, press Return repeatedly to move the cursor down to the bottom of the page and watch the Status line. When a line of dashes appears on the screen with the cursor beneath it, it means you have reached the second page, and the page number indicator will read Pg 2. Now use ↑ to move the cursor up one line (to the end of the first page), and notice that the line number indicator says 52 rather than 54.

Page Number Column Positions

You have learned how to select a general location for the page number, such as top right or bottom center. You can also alter the specific position on the line for each of these settings by using the Page Number Column Positions option (7) on the Page Format menu. This is especially useful if you are using wide paper, because the page number column can be any column up to 250.

To see how this works, press Alt-F8 and select option 7. As shown in Figure 5.3, a new screen appears displaying the current settings. Since these have not been altered, they are defaults: 10, 42, and 74. You are provided two choices: *Set to Initial Settings* and *Set to Specified Settings.*

You would need to use the first choice only if you had already changed the settings earlier in your document and now wanted to set them back to the initial ones (10, 42, 74) for the remaining pages.

The second choice on the Page Number Column Positions screen allows you to name your own settings. Press 2. The message on the Status line indicates your selection, 2. As you can see in Figure 5.4, the letter L (for left) appears below the line that displays the current settings. To change L, type the new number, then press Return. To retain the existing setting, just press Return. Now you are asked to provide a setting for C (center) and R (for right). After you have changed or retained all three settings, the screen disappears and you return to the Page Format menu. Now press Return to exit from the Page Format menu and call up the Reveal Codes screen (Alt-F3). In the upper left you will see your new settings displayed.

```
Reset Column Position for Page Numbers

   (L = Left Corner, C = Center, R = Right Corner)

      1 - Set to Initial Settings (In tenths of an inch)
                L=1  C=42 R=74

      2 - Set to Specified Settings

Current Settings

      L=1  C=42 R=74




Selection: 
```

Figure 5.3: *The Page Number Column Positions screen*

New Page Number

The third and final option on the Page Format menu that relates to page numbering is 2, New Page Number. You use this option if you want page numbering to begin with a number other than 1. For example, if you were writing an exceptionally long document such as a book, you would probably save each chapter as a separate file so that the document wouldn't become too cumbersome. However, you would not want the first page of your tenth chapter to be numbered as page 1 when printed. Option 2 allows you to place the desired page number on the first page of each chapter, and all of the following pages in the chapter would be renumbered in the correct sequence.

To try this, press the Page Format Key (Alt-F8) and select option 2. This time you will not see a new screen or menu. Instead, a message appears

```
Reset Column Position for Page Numbers

   (L = Left Corner, C = Center, R = Right Corner)

      1 - Set to Initial Settings (In tenths of an inch)
              L=10 C=42 R=74

      2 - Set to Specified Settings

Current Settings

      L=10 C=42 R=74

      L=_




Selection: 2
```

Figure 5.4: *Resetting the page number column position*

at the bottom of the Page Format menu asking you to enter the number you want printed on the current page:

New Page #:

If you want the entire document renumbered, remember to move the cursor to the top of the document's first page before starting this procedure.

For practice, enter 5 as your starting page number. After you press Return, the prompt New Page #: will disappear and you will see another message in its place asking which style you wish to use, as shown below:

Numbering Style   1 Arabic; 2 Roman: 0

Numbering Style

Arabic describes the type of numerals normally used: 1, 2, 3, 4, 5, 6, 7, 8, 9, and 0; this style is WordPerfect's default. Roman numerals such as i, ii, iii, iv, v, vi, and vii are probably familiar to you, since they are frequently used in the prefaces, forewords, and tables of contents of books. When you choose this style, the numbers appear in lowercase. You can use option 2 on the Page Format menu to obtain Roman numerals even when you don't change the number of your starting page (but you have to enter the current page number to get the Numbering Style prompt).

Select 1 for Arabic and when the Page Format menu appears again, press Return. Next, check the page number indicator (Pg) on the Status line; although you haven't even entered any text and know this is the first page of your file, it should read Pg 5. (If you just press Return without selecting a style, the page number change will not be made, and you will not see the page number code on the Reveal Codes screen.)

Now enter the Reveal Codes screen (press Alt-F3) and delete the page number code, which looks like this:

[Pg#:5]

Had you selected the Roman style, your code would be

[Pg#:v]

Center Page Top to Bottom

The purpose of this option is to center the text on a page vertically between the top and bottom margins, which is useful for title pages, tables of contents, very short letters and other such documents. It only affects the printed version of the document, so don't expect to see a centered page on your screen. It is pointless to use this feature when the page is full because if it is, the text will automatically be centered between the normal top and bottom margins.

Type the text of the title page illustrated in Figure 5.5 to see how page centering works. A word of advice about horizontal centering: instead of centering each individual line as you type, it is easier to use the Block (Alt-F4) and Center (Shift-F6) Keys to center the entire text in one operation *after* you have typed it.

To use the page centering option, move the cursor to the beginning of the document, because the centering code must come before any other codes. To be certain that there are no invisible codes placed before the

```
                    THE UNIVERSITY OF CALIFORNIA


              WORD PROCESSING AND CORPORATE POLITICS



                    A DISSERTATION SUBMITTED TO
                 THE FACULTY OF THE BUSINESS SCHOOL
                  IN CANDIDACY FOR THE DEGREE OF
                        MASTER OF BUSINESS



                              BY

                        JANET R. SMITH



                      SAN FRANCISCO, CA
                         MAY 1986
```

Figure 5.5: *The sample title page*

cursor, you can do one of two things. The first is to check the Reveal Codes screen (Alt-F3) and, if necessary, move the cursor to the left of any codes you find. The second is to use the following keystroke combination, which moves the cursor to the extreme left position on the line before any codes: Home, Home, Home, ←.

Now, with your cursor in position, press the Page Format Key (Alt-F8) and select option 3, Center Page Top to Bottom. After you do this, it will appear as though nothing has happened and you will still see the familiar Page Format menu. Press Return to exit to the editing screen.

You have a problem here. Not only are you unsure that your entry was accepted, but you also can't confirm by looking at the screen that the page has really been centered, since page centering only appears on the printed version. To alleviate your fears, check the Reveal Codes screen to verify that the proper code has been included. Press Alt-F3 and look for the following code:

[Center Pg]

Continue by printing the title page to see how professional it looks centered on the page. After the page is printed, save the practice file and clear the screen using the Exit Key (F7), but don't exit from WordPerfect.

Page Length

As you have seen, there are 54 lines of single spaced text on a standard page but the actual page length is 66 lines, which corresponds to the physical page length of 11 inches. The page length is always set in terms of six lines per inch (even when you are using eight lines per inch for text). Twelve blank lines have been set aside for the top and bottom margins. (Any headers, footers, or page numbers that have been added are printed within the 54 text lines.) These default settings assume the use of letter size paper, which is 8½ by 11 inches, and text printed at 6 lines per inch. Like most other settings, the page length (or *form* length) and number of text lines per page can be changed as often as necessary throughout the document. Such changes are usually made to adjust page length for mailing labels or other variably sized print jobs.

To vary these settings, select the Page Length option (4) from the Page Format menu. As illustrated in Figure 5.6, this screen displays the current

```
Page Length

    1 - Letter Size Paper: Form Length = 66 lines (11 inches)
        Single Spaced Text lines = 54 (This includes lines
        used for Headers, Footers and/or page numbers.)

    2 - Legal Size Paper: Form Length = 84 lines (14 inches)
        Single Spaced Text Lines = 72 (This includes lines
        used for Headers, Footers and/or page numbers.)

    3 - Other (Maximum page length = 108 lines.)

Current Settings

    Form Length in Lines (6 per inch):  66

    Number of Single Spaced Text Lines: 54




Selection: 0
```

Figure 5.6: *The Page Length screen*

settings and allows you to choose from among three options: the displayed standard settings for letter size paper, the displayed standard settings for legal size paper, or your own customized settings.

Calculating Customized Settings Using Option 3—Other

An important consideration when choosing your own settings is leaving enough room for the top and bottom margins. The default settings for both letter size and legal size paper leave six lines (1 inch) for each margin by setting the total number of text lines to be 12 lines less than the form length. Assuming you are using six lines per inch, if you subtract the number of text lines from the total page length, you will have the number of lines left over for the two margins:

      66 total page (form) length
    −54 text lines
    ─────
      12 lines

The top margin setting can be altered using another option on this menu, but the bottom margin can only be altered by decreasing or increasing the number of text lines.

When customizing your form and text length settings, it is up to you to make sure that the text plus the margins equals the total length of the page, which is called the form length. However, the top margin setting will also affect the page length settings so these two features must be changed simultaneously.

Top Margin

As you know, the default for the top margin is one inch (6 lines). If you customize the page length settings, (with option 3) you may need to recalculate the top margin. This option also permits you to leave adequate room for letterhead, which usually requires a two-inch margin at the top. Finally, if you want the printer to begin printing at the very top of a form, set the top margin to 0. When you select the Top Margin option (5) on the Page Format menu, the following prompt appears at the bottom of the screen:

Set half-lines (12/inch) from 12 to

This indicates that the current setting is 12 half lines—the equivalent of 6 whole lines, and prompts you to enter a new figure. Enter the number of half lines you want to have in the top margin.

To create a two-inch margin, change this figure from 12 half lines to 24. Since you are adding one inch to the top margin, you must take one inch away from the total number of text lines on the page. If you don't, there won't be enough room for both the top and bottom margins on the page, and an extra sheet of paper will be used for the bottom margin. Use the Page Length option (Alt-F8, 4, 3) to alter the current settings. Press Return or ↓ to bypass the Form Length setting (this should still be 66) and decrease the number of text lines by six (from 54 to 48). If you were using letterhead only for the first page, you would restore the default settings for page length and top margin at the top of page 2.

Press the Reveal Codes Key (Alt-F3) to see the codes for these settings. They should appear as follows:

[Top Mar:24][PgLnth:66,48]

After you have successfully completed the exercise, delete the codes so they won't affect the exercises in the following sections.

Headers and Footers

A header is one or more lines of standard text that appears at the top of each page and a footer is a line that appears at the bottom. They are often used in books, reports, and reference works to insert titles, labels, and even page numbers. The "running heads" at the top of the pages of this book are an example. WordPerfect has the ability to place headers and footers at the top or bottom of every page, every odd-numbered page, or every even-numbered page.

There is no practical limit to the number of lines that headers and footers can contain except common sense. A header of 25 lines is possible but certainly not practical, because it would leave only 29 out of the 54 text lines on each page for the rest of the text. You can create two different headers and two footers per page, or you can create a header and footer for the even-numbered pages and a different header and footer for the odd-numbered pages. You can enter two headers (or footers) on the same line if they are short enough, but you should use the Flush Right Key (Alt-F6) before entering the second one, so that the first is placed at the extreme left and the second at the extreme right of the page.

Each header or footer uses a minimum of two lines, at least one for the text itself and another one to separate it from the main text on the page. (Remember that WordPerfect subtracts these lines from the text lines on the page.)

The Header/Footer Screen

Creating headers and footers is quite easy. To enter a header, select option 6 from the Page Format menu, and the screen illustrated in Figure 5.7 will appear.

Notice the two lists, headed **Type** and **Occurrence.** The Type list asks whether you want to create Header A (your first header), Header B (your second header), Footer A (your first footer), or Footer B, (your second footer). Since you have not created another header, press 1 to select Header A.

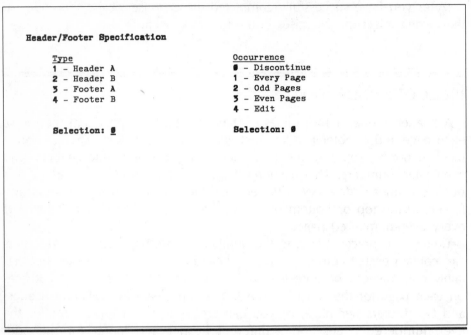

Figure 5.7: *The Header/Footer Specification screen*

The second list, Occurrence, allows you to choose a location for the header or footer you just specified. Option 1 causes the header or footer to be printed on every page in the document; with option 2, they will be printed only on odd-numbered pages; with option 3, they will be printed only on even-numbered pages. You use option 0 when you want to permanently discontinue a header or footer that you had previously entered. It will be discontinued on all remaining pages (starting from the page on which the cursor is located). You use option 4 when you want to edit a header or footer after it has been entered.

To experiment with these features, enter the following paragraph and then place a header on the page to describe it:

> The word ambition has an interesting history. The Latin noun ambitio was used by the Romans to describe a political candidate; it meant the act of going around or going about to get votes. It came from the verb ambire, which literally means "to go about." Like their modern counterparts, Roman politicians were probably as interested in the power and wealth that came with the office as they were with the honors, but the word ambition came to describe their craving for fame and honors.

Next, move the cursor back to the top of the page and add a header by following these steps:

1. Select option 6 from the Page Format menu (Alt-F8).
2. Select option 1 for Header A.
3. Select option 1 for Every Page.

You will then see a blank screen with the following message on the Status line:

Press EXIT when done   Ln 1 Pos 10

Next, type

CHAPTER FIVE
THE HISTORY AND MEANING OF WORDS

When you're done, press Exit (F7) and you will return to the Page Format menu. To exit from that, press any key except one of the numbered selections.

Viewing Headers in the Reveal Codes Screen

Like page numbers, headers and footers are invisible on the editing screen. They only appear when printed, so on screen you have to use the Reveal Codes Key to verify that they have been correctly added to your document. Press Alt-F3 now and your screen will resemble Figure 5.8.

The 1,1 inside the brackets confirms the choices you just made from the two lists on the Header/Footer Specification screen: the first 1 stands for Header A and the second 1 stands for every page. You will also see the text of your header, and the two lines will be separated by the hard return code, [HRt], signifying that you pressed Return after the first line.

Since you can only see how your header actually looks in the printed version of your document, go ahead and print the page now. It should resemble Figure 5.9. Save this paragraph for a later exercise.

Note that you could have used boldface or underline when creating the header to distinguish it further from the text which follows it on the page. If you wish, you can still add one or both of them by using the edit option (4) on the Header/Footer Specification screen. To do this, press Alt-F8 and 6, then select 1–Header A from the Type list and 4–Edit from the Occurrence list. Block the text you want underlined or boldfaced, then press either F6

```
    _      The word ambition has an interesting history. The Latin noun
     ambitio was used by the Romans to describe a political candidate;
     it meant the act of going around or going about to get votes. It
     came from the verb ambire, which literally means "to go about."
     Like their modern counterparts, Roman politicians were probably
     as interested in the power and wealth that came with the office
     as they were with the honors, but the word ambition came to
                                          Doc 1  Pg 1  Ln 1      Pos 10
{ ▲    ▲    ▲    ▲    ▲    ▲    ▲    ▲    ▲    ▲    ▲   ]▲   ▲    ▲
 _[Hdr/Ftr:1,1;CHAPTER FIVE[HRt]
THE HISTORY AND MEANING OF WORDS[HRt]
][TAB]The word ambition has an interesting history. The Latin noun[SRt]
[U]ambitio[u] was used by the Romans to describe a political candidate;[SRt]
it meant the act of going around or going about to get votes. It[SRt]
came from the verb [U]ambire[u], which literally means "to go about."[SRt]
```

Figure 5.8: *The Header/Footer Definition code*

```
CHAPTER FIVE
THE HISTORY AND MEANING OF WORDS

     The word ambition has an interesting history. The Latin noun
ambitio was used by the Romans to describe a political candidate;
it meant the act of going around or going about to get votes. It
came from the verb ambire, which literally means "to go about."
Like their modern counterparts, Roman politicians were probably
as interested in the power and wealth that came with the office
as they were with the honors, but the word ambition came to
describe their craving for fame and honors.
```

Figure 5.9: *Sample printed paragraph with Header A*

(Bold) or F8 (Underline). Press Exit (F7) when you are finished. The Reveal Codes screen will show bold or underline codes.

A problem arises when you change the margins in a document, since existing headers or footers will not be updated automatically. Instead, you have to do it manually. The steps are as follows:

1. Select option 6 on the Page Format menu.
2. Select the first header or footer from the Type list.
3. Select 4 from the Occurrence list to edit it.
4. Press F7 (Exit).
5. Repeat this operation for each header or footer in your document.

In this procedure, all you actually do is enter and exit from the edit screen, and you don't receive any messages or other evidence to confirm the update.

Placing a Page Number in a Header or Footer

If you are using headers and/or footers in your document and also including page numbers, you can avoid using two lines specifically for the page numbers by placing the number within the header or footer itself. (Remember that page numbers utilize two lines, one for the page number and one that separates it from the rest of the text.)

To do this, use the method already described to create a standard header or footer and insert a special code for the page number

    ^B

or

    ^N

This is done by pressing the Ctrl key with the B or N key, and it can be placed anywhere you choose. To create a footer with a page number, you would follow these steps:

1. Press the Page Format key (Alt-F8).
2. Select option 6 (Headers or Footers).
3. Select option 3 (Footer A).
4. Select option 1 (Every Page).

5. Type Ctrl-B or Ctrl-N, skip a few spaces, then type the text of your footer.

6. Press Exit (F7), then press any key to return to the editing screen.

Incidentally, you can add the page number code anywhere in your document; its use is not limited to footers and headers. It is no substitute, though, for standard page numbering or page numbering in a header or footer because as you add or delete text, the page number code will move with the text rather than retaining its position at the page break. You may end up with printed pages that have page numbers everywhere except where they're supposed to be!

Suppress for Current Page Only

You may want headers, footers, and/or page numbers to be omitted from a specific page in your document, such as one that contains a chart or illustration. Option 8 (Suppress for Current page only) on the Page Format menu prevents any or all of these from appearing on an individual page. Press Alt-F8 and 8, and you will see, as illustrated in Figure 5.10, that there are eight selections on this screen. Most of them are self-explanatory except for option 3, which is used to print the page number at the bottom center of the current page and overrides any other page number position code in the document. You must use these options to insert a suppress code at the top of each page you want altered since these codes affect only the current page.

If you wish to prevent headers, footers, or page numbers from appearing on all of the remaining pages in your document, do not use this option. Instead, to discontinue headers or footers, press option 0 (Discontinue) on the Header/Footer Specification screen. To discontinue page numbers use the Page Number Position option on the Page Format Key and select 0—No page numbers.

As the Suppress Page Format screen indicates, if you wish to include more than one of the selections you can type the corresponding numbers with a plus sign (+) in between. For instance, to turn off both page numbering and Header B, you would enter 2+6, as shown below:

Selection(s): 2+6

```
Suppress Page Format for Current Page Only

   To temporarily turn off multiple items, include a "+" between menu entries.
   For example 5+6+2 will turn off Header A, Header B, and Page Numbering
   for the current page.

      1 - Turn off all page numbering, headers and footers

      2 - Turn page numbering off

      3 - Print page number at bottom center (this page only)

      4 - Turn off all headers and footers

      5 - Turn off Header A

      6 - Turn off Header B

      7 - Turn off Footer A

      8 - Turn off Footer B

   Selection(s): ▮
```

Figure 5.10: *The Suppress Page Format screen*

In case you try this procedure and find yourself unexpectedly back in the Page Format menu, it is probably because you used the Plus key on the numeric keypad without turning Num Lock on or pressing Shift first. Unless you have Num Lock on, the Plus key works just like any other key, returning you to the Page Format menu. To avoid this problem, you can use the Plus key on the top row of the keyboard instead.

Soft Page

As you may have noticed, you never need to specify page breaks when using WordPerfect. Like most word processors, the program has a feature known as *soft page,* which works at the end of each page as word wrap does at the end of each line. When you have typed enough lines to fill a page (as dictated by the page length and top margin settings), a soft page code is inserted and the program automatically creates a new page while you are typing. You will see a dashed line appear across the entire screen, and your cursor will then move down to the new page as you continue typing. You can easily recognize the soft page code on the Reveal Codes screen:

[SPg]

This feature is not always desirable, though, because after editing changes it can break up lines and paragraphs you want kept together on the same page. For instance, the very last line of a paragraph may start a new page or numeric expressions such as formulas may be split between two pages. WordPerfect provides three methods to alleviate these types of problems: conditional end of page, widow and orphan protection, and block protection.

Conditional End of Page

Selection 9 (Conditional End of Page) on the Page Format menu (Alt-F8) does just what the name implies: it forces a page break when a certain condition is met. You define the condition as a certain number of lines you want kept together on the same page. If these lines are moved near the end of a page, the entire block will be pushed down onto the next page, rather than divided between two pages.

To use this feature, move the cursor to the line before the first one of the block you wish to keep together. Press Alt-F8, 9, then, in response to the prompt, enter the total number of lines in the block:

Number of lines to keep together =

Blank lines (that is, those in multiple spacing) are considered to be the same as text lines and must be counted in your calculation of the number of lines that are to be kept together. Thus, if you use double spacing and want to keep four lines of text together, press 8 in response to the prompt.

Block Protect

Fortunately, there is an easier way to protect a group of lines from being separated other than struggling to calculate the exact number of lines you want to keep together. You simply block your lines and, with Block still on, press the Page Format key.

Let's see how it works. If you still have the paragraph that you created in the section about headers and footers, you'll be using it in this example. If not, type that paragraph now. In either case, make sure it ends with a Return (check Reveal Codes, Alt-F3). Next, follow these steps to fill the page with text:

1. Press Alt-F3 to enter the Reveal Codes screen, delete the code for headers, and return to the editing screen.
2. Press Ctrl-F4 (Move), 2, 2 to copy the paragraph.
3. Move the cursor to the first line below the original paragraph and press Ctrl-F4 and 5 three times to produce three copies.
4. Move the cursor back to the top of the page and press Shift-F8, 4, 2, using the Line Format Key to change to double spacing.

If you move your cursor to the end of the document, you will see that the last paragraph has been split between pages 1 and 2.

To prevent this, you can protect the entire fourth paragraph using the Block Protect feature. To do this, use the following steps:

1. Move the cursor to the first character in the last paragraph (the *T* in *the*).
2. Press the Block Key (Alt-F4).
3. Press Return to move the cursor to the end of the paragraph, which is then highlighted.
4. Press the Page Format Key (Alt-F8). You will see the following message:

Protect Block? (Y/N) N

5. Reply with a Y and the block will be protected.

The block highlighting will immediately disappear and you will see that the protection feature has already been implemented, for it has moved the entire paragraph to the second page. If you move the cursor up to the last text line in the third paragraph, which is the last sentence on page 1, you'll see that it is actually not at the normal end of page (line 54).

Block protect is also useful for preserving the integrity of charts, tables, and similar groupings that you want to keep together on a page, particularly when the groupings contain numeric data. For instance, look at Figure 5.11, which is part of a marketing survey. The entire last rating question, number 8, should have been printed on one page, which would have been the case if block protection had been used. As it is, it is hard for respondents to grade the brands on page two since they have to keep turning back to the previous page to see the original question and explanation of the scale. Market researchers have enough trouble just finding willing participants for these surveys, so why make their task more difficult?

Widows and Orphans

Widows and orphans are the most demonstrative terms used in word processing so their meanings are not as cryptic as you might think. A widow is the first line of a paragraph that is left alone (widowed) at the bottom of a page when the soft page feature pushes the rest of the paragraph to the next page. Orphans are also created by the soft page feature. When the last line of a paragraph is pushed to a new page, that line becomes an orphan, stranded alone at the top of the page without the rest of its paragraph. (I am following WordPerfect's terminology here, though it departs somewhat from the standard definitions used in typesetting.)

The widow and orphan feature is a toggle key, meaning it is either on or off. To see how it works, press selection A (Widow/Orphan) from the Page Format menu (Alt-F8) and you'll see the following prompt:

Widow/Orphan Protect (Y/N) N

The default setting is off (that is, no widow/orphan protection) so you'll always see the N unless it has been changed earlier in the document. If you enter a Y, WordPerfect will protect widows and orphans from that point forward in your document. Protection means that widow lines will always be moved to the next page, and orphan lines will never appear alone at the top of a page because the line that comes before them in the paragraph will also be moved to the new page. You can turn this feature on and off whenever you wish, but if you want widow/orphan protection for the entire document, you should move the cursor to the beginning before turning it on.

6. Please rate the overall quality of products that are
    produced by the following corporations. Circle the number
    corresponding to your answer, 1 being the lowest quality and
    10 being the highest.

<u>Product Quality</u>

Company #1	1	2	3	4	5	6	7	8	9	10
Company #2	1	2	3	4	5	6	7	8	9	10
Company #3	1	2	3	4	5	6	7	8	9	10
Company #4	1	2	3	4	5	6	7	8	9	10
Company #5	1	2	3	4	5	6	7	8	9	10

7. Please rate these brands according to how good a value they
    are for the money. Again, the scale of values if from 1 to
    10 with #10 being the highest value and #1 the lowest.

<u>Value for the Money</u>

Brand #1	1	2	3	4	5	6	7	8	9	10
Brand #2	1	2	3	4	5	6	7	8	9	10
Brand #3	1	2	3	4	5	6	7	8	9	10
Brand #4	1	2	3	4	5	6	7	8	9	10
Brand #5	1	2	3	4	5	6	7	8	9	10

8. Please rate these brands according to whether you think they
    are important items to own. Rate them on a scale of 1 to 10,
    with 1 being the least important and 10 being the most
    important.

<u>Importance</u>

Brand #1	1	2	3	4	5	6	7	8	9	10

Figure 5.11: *The marketing survey with list split over two pages*

Brand #2	1	2	3	4	5	6	7	8	9	10
Brand #3	1	2	3	4	5	6	7	8	9	10
Brand #4	1	2	3	4	5	6	7	8	9	10
Brand #5	1	2	3	4	5	6	7	8	9	10

Figure 5.11: *The marketing survey with list split over two pages (continued)*

Obviously, using widow/orphan protection will decrease the number of lines on any page that is affected by the feature, so don't worry if you have several pages with only 52 or 53 lines of text. These pages will be reformatted if you add or delete text, and the protected lines will readjust in the normal manner.

Summary

The Page Format Key (Alt-F8) controls features that affect the length of the text on the printed page: page length, top and bottom margins, page numbering, headers and footers, and widows and orphans.

Page Number Position, option 1 on the Page Format Key, inserts a page number in one of eight different locations on each page in your document: top center, bottom center, top left, top right, bottom left, bottom right, bottom alternating left and right, or top alternating left and right. Inserting a page number reduces the number of lines available for text by two, one for the page number itself and one that separates it from the text. Page numbers appear only on the printed document.

Page Number Column Positions, option 7 on the Page Format Key, alters the column positions of the page numbers. The default settings are 10 for the left position, 42 for the center position, and 74 for the right position.

New Page Number, option 2 on the Page Format Key, is used to select a number other than 1 as the first page number for the current document. This is useful when a lengthy document such as a book is stored in several separate files. In such a case, this option is used to set new page numbers on the first page of each chapter, so that each chapter can start with the page number following the last one in the preceding chapter.

Center Page Top to Bottom, option 3 on the Page Format Key, centers a printed page between the top and bottom margins and is useful for centering title pages, tables of contents and other short documents. It does not affect the appearance of the document on screen.

Page Length, option 4 on the Page Format Key, alters the number of text lines and total blank lines left for the top and bottom margins on a page. The default page length settings are for letter size paper and they can be changed to standard settings for legal size paper or customized to your own settings.

Top Margin, option 5 on the Page Format Key, is used to change the number of blank lines left for the top margin. The default setting is for 1 inch (12 half lines), and it can be altered in increments of half lines. When the top margin setting is changed, it is also necessary to use the Page Length option (4) to change the number of text lines on the page. This guarantees that there will be enough blank lines for the bottom margin.

Headers or Footers, option 6 on the Page Format Key, is used to insert one or more lines of repeated text such as titles, labels, and other designations at the top or bottom of each page, every odd-numbered page, or every even-numbered page. Inserting a header or footer reduces the number of lines available for text by the number of lines in the header or footer plus one additional line to separate it from the rest of the text.

Suppress for Current Page Only, option 8 on the Page Format Key, is used to prevent page numbers, headers, and/or footers from appearing on the current page. In addition, it can be used to print the page number at the bottom center of the current page, overriding any other page number position code in the document.

Conditional End of Page, option 9 on the Page Format Key, is used to protect a specified number of lines so that they will not be split between separate pages by WordPerfect's soft page feature. Soft page automatically creates a new page when the page is full, and it often breaks up lines that should remain together on a single page.

Block protection is an alternative to the Conditional End of Page feature, and it is much easier to use. You simply block (Alt-F4) the text you want kept together on a page, then press Page Format (Alt-F8) and reply with a Y to the prompt "Protect Block? (Y/N)". This feature is also useful for marking and protecting charts, tables, and similar blocks that must remain together on a page.

Widow/Orphan, option A on the Page Format Key, is used to prevent widows and orphans. A widow is created by the soft page feature when the first line of a paragraph is left alone as the last line of a page. An orphan is the last line of a paragraph that is pushed by itself to the top of a new page by the soft page feature. When widow/orphan protection is on, widows will be moved to the top of the new page containing the rest of their paragraph, and an orphan will always be joined on the new page by the line that comes before it in the paragraph.

Congratulations again! You just endured an extensive study of WordPerfect's many page formatting features, and have progressed beyond the rank of novice. In fact, many of these features are quite complex and difficult to use, so unless you have unusual needs, you may never have to alter the settings established by the program. The default page length and top margin, for instance, were designed to conform to standard business usage, so they are acceptable for nearly all applications.

Other settings, such as page number position, are used frequently but not in one standard manner, so WordPerfect assumes nothing and provides several different methods for you to choose from.

All of the selections on the Page Format menu share a common characteristic: they affect the total length of the printed page. Consequently, it is important that you understand them and learn how to use them properly so that your work appears as attractive and cohesive as possible.

CHAPTER 6 KEYSTROKE SUMMARY:

F5 The List Files Key—retrieve, delete, rename, print, or copy any number of files

F2 The Forward Search Key—search all text following cursor

Ctrl **7 Home** The Go To Key—press twice after search to return cursor to previous position

⇧ **F2** The Reverse Search Key—search all text that comes before cursor

Ctrl **X** The Wildcard Character—use in a search string to stand for any character(s)

Alt **F2** The Replace Key—specify text (or nothing) to substitute for the search string

SEARCH
AND REPLACE

THIS CHAPTER WILL INTRODUCE SEARCH as well as Search and Replace, two closely related operations that are among Word-Perfect's most useful features. Search gives you the ability to locate any word, any combination of words of up to 59 characters, or any hidden function code(s) wherever they may appear in your document. Search and Replace can find the text or code and either erase it or replace it with something else. Since the Search feature automatically moves the cursor to the located text, it is often the fastest method for cursor movement, particularly in larger documents. WordPerfect can search either forward or backward through your document, ignore uppercase and lowercase when performing the operation (if the search is conducted using lowercase), and use a wildcard character to substitute for any other character, so that you can search for similar but not identical text (for example, when you're unsure of the exact spelling that was used).

Type in the following paragraphs so you can experiment with these commands:

Unlike other word processors, with WordPerfect it
is difficult, if not impossible, to lose files when you
run out of disk space. If you try to save a file and
receive a message indicating there is not enough room
on the default disk, don't worry. By pressing the List
Files Key (F6), you can search the directory for files
you don't need anymore and delete them to make
more space available. However, it is usually easier and
always safer to insert another formatted disk that
has some room left on it into the drive and then
save the file.

The List Files Key (F6) has many other functions. It
can be used to retrieve, delete, rename, print, or copy
a file or perform these operations on any number of
files that you have marked. If you forget the name of a
file you wish to retrieve you can use the List Files
Key (F6) to perform a word search, and the program will
then find and list all files containing a certain word
or combination of words. You can also use the List
Files Key (F6) to import a DOS text file into
WordPerfect, to change the default directory, or to
look at a file without retrieving it for editing.

Search

You may have noticed that these paragraphs contain a significant error: the List Files Key is incorrectly identified as F6, whereas it is actually F5. Let's locate and fix the problem with WordPerfect's Search feature.

Make sure that the cursor is located before the first word of the first paragraph and then press F2, the Forward Search Key. You will see the following prompt:

→ Srch:

The cursor will appear to the right of this prompt, indicating that you can now type the word or words you want to find. The word or combination that you enter is called the *search string;* in this case it will be F6. Note that you do not have to capitalize the F, because whenever you enter lowercase letters, the program searches for both lowercase and uppercase matches. However, the reverse is not true; uppercase letters in a search string will only locate uppercase letters. If you're searching for a word that is not capitalized, you must type only lowercase characters in the search string.

Now type

    F6

then press either F2 or Esc to signal WordPerfect that you want it to begin searching. (Do not press Return; if you do, you will actually enter the code for a hard return, [HRt], which will appear next to the F6 on your prompt line. This code will then become part of what the program searches for.)

The cursor should now be in the position just after the first F6 in your text, which is a close parenthesis. Erase the 6 by pressing Backspace, then type a 5 in its place.

Repeating the Search

As you can see, F6 appears three more times in the second paragraph. To repeat the search action, press the Forward Search Key (F2) again and you will see that the last search string you entered, F6, will already be in place next to the prompt. The program always remembers the last string you searched for and assumes you want to continue using it unless you type something else. If you type any other character at this point, the old string will immediately be replaced by the new character(s). However, since you want to continue searching for F6, accept it by pressing F2 or Esc. Note that you can use the regular cursor-movement and edit keys to alter the search string.

The cursor will move to the next appearance of F6. This time, do not delete it. Instead, keep pressing Forward Search until you reach the last F6. (You will press F2 four more times.) Now press Forward Search twice and the following message will appear very briefly:

    ∗ Not Found ∗

The cursor will reappear at the last occurrence of the string.

This prompt indicates that there are no more occurrences of the search string in the document; you can confirm this by looking at the paragraph. If you wish, you can set up your WordPerfect program so that the computer beeps each time this message appears. To find out how to do this, turn to the section in Appendix A that describes the WordPerfect Set-up menu.

In the event that you find what you are looking for in the first search attempt, you can return to the original cursor position by pressing the Go To Key (Ctrl-Home) two times. This only works after the initial search; once you have repeated the search, the double Go To only takes you back as far as the last location of the search string, not to your original starting point. You can't keep backing up step by step; instead you will just find yourself jumping back and forth between the two later occurrences of the string.

Search is particularly helpful for cursor movement in longer documents. Although you can move the cursor page by page and screen by screen, these are relatively slow methods in long documents. You can also move the cursor to a specified page, but this method is worthless if you don't know which page contains the text you wish to move to. On the other hand, if you are looking for a section that has a particular subheading or contains a unique word or phrase, you can use Search to find it almost immediately. Also, Search takes you directly to the word you want to work with, not just to the general area.

In my own case, after printing each of the chapters in this book for the first time and making editing changes on the hard copy, I used Search to locate the specific words and sections I had marked for revision. Positioning the cursor using Search saved me a lot of time as well as the eyestrain caused by searching the text visually as it scrolls by.

Another application for Search is to check for overused words. If you suspect that you are using a word too frequently, just use Search to find out. If your suspicions are confirmed, you can then use WordPerfect's Thesaurus, which you will learn about in Chapter 18, to find substitutes.

Reverse Search

WordPerfect can search backward as well as forward through a document. Try this by moving the cursor to the end of the file (Home, Home, ↓) and pressing the Reverse Search Key (Shift-F2). This time the search prompt will appear with an arrow pointing backwards, as follows:

← Srch: F6

If you performed the exercise in the preceding section, the prompt will still have the F6 search string next to it, since that was the last one you used. If not, type F6. Then press F2 or Esc and watch as the cursor moves up to the last F6. To repeat the operation, press Shift-F2 again followed by F2 or Esc.

Restricting the Search

Searching for a string such as F6 is uncomplicated because it is unlikely that it will ever be contained within another word. However, many commonly used words such as *to* are frequently found within other words such as in*to* and s*to*p. To see how WordPerfect handles these situations, try searching for *the* and see what happens. Move your cursor to the beginning of the document (Home, Home, ↑) and press Forward Search (F2). Next enter the word *the* (in lowercase) and press F2 again.

The cursor will stop at the *r* in the word o*the*r, which follows the first occurrence of the string *the*. Press F2 twice more and the cursor will stop at the *r* in the word *the*re. As you can see, you have yet to find the word you were looking for! If you press F2 two more times, you will finally come to the word *the*.

To prevent this confusion, you have to place a space before and after the search string, which signals that this is a separate word, not connected to or included within any other. Move the cursor back to the beginning of the file and press Forward Search (F2) again. This time, use the Spacebar to enter a blank space before and after the word *the*. Press F2 again and the cursor will stop at the *d* in *default,* which follows the word *the* (with the blank space). If you continue searching, you will see that this method only locates *the*.

When using a blank space in a search string, you must be certain that there is no punctuation mark such as a period or comma immediately following the word or phrase, because if there is one, it must be included in the search string before pressing the Spacebar. For example, to search for the word *file* where it appears at the end of a sentence, the search string would have to be as follows:

[blank space]file.

Searching with Ctrl-X, the Wildcard Character

Ctrl-X functions as a *wildcard* and can be used as a substitute for any character on the keyboard (not including a blank space). It is entered by pressing the Ctrl key, and holding it down while pressing V, then X. If you are unsure of the exact wording that was used in a phrase, the Ctrl-X combination can help locate it. It can also help you find words if you suspect they were misspelled. The only significant limitations are that a wildcard character cannot be the first one in the string, and that it cannot be used to locate a function code.

Now your short document identifies the List Files Key as F5 one time and F6 three others. The only way you can locate all occurrences with a single search string is to use the wildcard in place of the 5 or 6. To do this, move the cursor to the top of the file and press F2. When you see the Search prompt, type an F (remember that the case doesn't matter), press Ctrl-V (the n= prompt will appear), and then press Ctrl-X followed by a close parenthesis. Your prompt will appear as follows:

→ Srch:F^X)

Press F2 to begin the search. The cursor will stop first at F5. When you press F2 two more times, the cursor will move to the first occurrence of F6. If you continue to press F2, the program will find the other two F6s in the paragraph.

Now try using the wildcard to locate a misspelled word. First you'll have to change a word so that it is spelled incorrectly. Move the cursor to the word *retrieve* in the second sentence of the second paragraph, and change the spelling to *retreive*. Next, move the cursor back to the top of the page and press Forward Search (F2). In response to the Search prompt, enter the following string:

retrieve

Press F2 again, and watch how the misspelled version is skipped. To locate it, move the cursor back to the top of the page, press F2 and enter the following string:

retr^X

When you press F2 again, the cursor will find the misspelled version of the word (retreive), and if you continue to search it will find *retrieve* in the third sentence of the paragraph and *retrieving* in the last sentence. Note that the same search string would locate such words as *retry* and *retribution,* if they occurred in the text. The wildcard can also be used with the Search and Replace feature, which you will study next, to locate and change the incorrect spelling.

Search and Replace

Move the cursor back to the beginning of the first paragraph so that you can practice using Search and Replace to change the remaining F6s to F5s. As you will see, this method is much more efficient than searching for each F6, then deleting and retyping each one individually. Since Search and Replace works only in the forward direction, you must start at the beginning of the document.

There are two different methods of using Search and Replace. The program can pause each time it locates the search string and ask you to confirm that you want it replaced, or it can zip through the document and make all of the changes automatically with no further confirmation from you. The latter method should only be used when you are absolutely certain that you want the string replaced every time it occurs. In the exercise following this one you will see how risky this procedure can be.

Press the Replace Key (Alt-F2) and you will see the following prompt:

w/Confirm? (Y/N) N

If you respond with Y, each time F6 is located the program will stop to ask if you wish to replace it. If you press N (or any other key), all of the changes will be made without your confirmation. In fact, you might not even see all of them because the Search and Replace happens so fast. To be on the safe side, press Y this time.

The next message you will see is the familiar Search prompt. Once again, type F6 as the search string and press F2. You will then see the following prompt:

Replace with:

Since you want to change each F6 to F5, type

F5

Then press F2 (or Esc) to start Search and Replace. For an instant, you will see the message

* Please Wait *

and the cursor will move quickly to the first F6. Next, you will see the following prompt:

Confirm? (Y/N) N

If you press any key other than Y the replacement will not be made, and the cursor will move to the next occurrence of the F6 string. However, since you do wish to make the change, press Y and continue to do this each time you are asked. When the replace operation is completed, the cursor will be located on the 5 in the last F5.

Note that if you type lowercase f6 instead of the capitalized F6, the program still replaces each F5 with a capitalized F6. This happens because the case of the replacement string always matches the case of the word it is replacing in the text. This allows you to make a replacement throughout a document and have it come out capitalized appropriately when it replaces the first word in a sentence, while appearing in lowercase when it replaces a lowercase occurrence.

Now repeat the operation without using the confirm option. Move the cursor back to the first word in the first paragraph, press Replace (Alt-F2), and this time press N when asked "w/Confirm?" Instruct WordPerfect to search for F5s and replace them with F6s.

Happily, this was a straightforward procedure and the program replaced only the words you specified. However, using Search and Replace without confirm can be dangerous, because it will often replace words you had not intended to change. The next example will illustrate this problem.

In this exercise, you are going to reword a phrase that appears in the third sentence of the first paragraph. The phrase *search the directory for files* will be replaced by *search the directory to find files,* so you are going to replace the *for* with *to find.* To do this, follow these steps:

1. Move the cursor to the beginning of the first paragraph.
2. Press Alt-F2 (Replace).
3. Press N when asked "w/Confirm?"
4. Type the following search string:

   for

5. Type this replacement string:

   to find

6. Press F2.

After the operation is completed, your screen will resemble Figure 6.1.

As you can see, you've really made a mess! The word *formatted* (in the second to last sentence of the first paragraph) has been changed to *to*

```
        Unlike other word processors, with WordPerfect it is
difficult, if not impossible, to lose files when you run out of
disk space. If you try to save a file and receive a message
indicating that there is not enough room on the default disk,
don't worry. By pressing the List Files key (F6), you can search
the directory to find files you don't need anymore and delete
them to make more space available. However, it is usually easier
and always safer to insert another to findmatted disk that has
some room left on it into the drive and then save the file.
        The List Files key (F6) has many other functions. It can be
used to retreive, delete, rename, print, or copy a file or perto
findm these operations on any number of files that you have
marked. If you to findget the name of a file you wish to
retrieve, you can use the List Files key (F6) to perto findm a
word search, and the program will then find and list all files
containing a certain word or combination of words. You can also
use the List Files key (F6) to import a DOS text file into
WordPerfect, to change the default directory, or to look at a
file without retrieving it to find editing.
```

Figure 6.1: *The paragraphs after replacing the word* for *with* to find

findmatted, the word *perform* has been changed to *perto findm* (in two separate places), the word *forget* has been changed to *to findget,* and the phrase *for editing* has been changed to *to find editing.* Fortunately, the original paragraphs did not contain the words *to find,* so you can use Search and Replace to reverse the operation replacing each *to find* with a *for.* Reversing the damage will not always be this easy, though, so you can see why Search and Replace should be used with great care, preferably with the confirm option. Although using confirm is slower, you can clearly see that it has the potential of saving you an enormous amount of clean-up work.

Search and replace has many other interesting applications. For instance, it can be used when a proper name needs to be retyped throughout a lengthy document, as in a report that frequently mentions an employee whose name has been changed or misspelled. If you find yourself frequently typing a long phrase in a document, you can save some time and aggravation by using Search and Replace to let the computer do the typing. Simply enter a few unique characters such as X1 to represent the phrase and, when you are finished typing the document, replace X1 with the correct phrase. (WordPerfect's macro feature, which you will study in Chapter 16, can also be used to perform this task, and it has some additional benefits.)

Finding and Deleting Codes
with Search and Search and Replace

One of the most useful applications of Search and Replace is to locate and erase hidden codes that are disrupting your document's appearance. It's easy to accidentally insert extra codes such as underline, bold, and indent, since the same function keys used to implement them are used constantly for other operations too.

Extra codes can also be left behind when you delete or move the text associated with them. You normally initiate these move or delete operations by placing the cursor on the first character in the word, sentence, paragraph, or block you are working with, but this sometimes fails to include the invisible formatting codes that are located immediately before the first character. On the normal text screen, there is no way to tell if you've excluded a code. You may see the cursor on the first character of a bold-faced word, but that doesn't tell you whether the cursor is to the right or the left of the hidden code—it looks the same in both cases. It helps to check the Reveal Codes screen before any block or move operations, but even with this procedure you'll probably only remember to look for such codes as bold and underline whose effects on the text being deleted are quite obvious. Those with more universal or subtle effects such as line spacing, margin settings, and page length will not always be as conspicuous, and can easily be overlooked. If you leave an extra code and later suspect that something is wrong, the Search feature can be invaluable.

To try it out you'll need some codes to search for, so use Line Format to insert three different margin settings in your document, one at the beginning, one after the first paragraph, and one in the middle of the second. In each case move your cursor into position and press the Line Format Key (Shift-F8), select option 3 (Margins), and fill in whatever settings may occur to you. Your document will be reformatted to fit into these margins. It may look ridiculous, but that doesn't matter since you're going to be deleting the margin settings right away.

Next move the cursor to the beginning of the file and press Search (F2). When you see the Search prompt (→ Srch:), press Line Format (Shift-F8) again. Note that the menu of choices on the Line Format Key has changed slightly, as illustrated below, and now shows a menu of options that insert formatting codes.

1 2 Tab; 3 Margin; 4 Spacing; 5 HZone; 6 /; 7 AlChar; 8 HyOff; 9 HyOn: 0

Press 3 for Margins, and you will see the bracketed code for margin settings appear next to the prompt, as illustrated below:

→ Srch: [Margin Set]

This asks WordPerfect to search for all margin settings regardless of the different position numbers they may contain. Search works like this for any kind of code that contains a varying number. If you had pressed 4 for Spacing, it would have searched for all line spacing codes, even though they might differ in their specific settings.

Press F2 and the cursor will move to the first margin setting. To verify this, press the Reveal Codes Key (Alt-F3) and you will see the code with the margin setting you entered (it will appear to the left of the cursor). As you know, you can delete it by pressing Backspace, but don't do that now.

You can continue searching for and deleting the codes this way, but it's much easier to use Search and Replace, so try that method now. Exit the Reveal Codes screen and move the cursor to the top of the page again and press Replace (Alt-F2). Press N in response to the Confirm prompt, then press F2 to accept your search string, the margin setting code (it will appear if you have completed the previous exercise correctly). The next prompt will ask for the string you want to replace it with. If you leave this blank by pressing F2 again, all the margin codes will be erased (since they will be replaced, literally, by nothing).

You will see the immediate effects of this procedure because the document will be reformatted to fit into the default margin settings, 10 and 74. Move the cursor back to the top to confirm this.

Search and Replace can be used to replace certain formatting codes, including hard spaces, subscripts and superscripts, advance up or down, overstrike, and hyphenation codes (these features will be studied in the next chapter). However, the only other codes that can be included in the replacement string have more universal applications and are not normally added to a specific word or phrase: center page, columns on/off, justification on/off, math on/off, math operators, merge codes, and widow/orphan protection. (You will be studying these features in other chapters also.)

You can also use Search and Replace to add features such as bold and underline to specific text in your document. For example, try using Search and Replace to underline all occurrences of the phrase *List Files Key* in your document. To do this, press Alt-F2, N, and type *List Files Key* as the search string. Press F2 again, press F8 to insert the underline code, [Undrline], then type *List Files Key* and press F8 again to insert the second underline code (which ends underlining). Press F2 to begin the search. Now try boldfacing the phrase (List Files key), following the above instructions but pressing F6 instead of F8.

One limitation to using Search and Replace with codes is that codes for features such as tab settings and line spacing can be located and erased, but you cannot change their specific settings. To understand why, look at the prompt that appears after you press the Search key (F2) followed by the Line Format Key (Shift-F8). As you can see, Tab is option 1 and Spacing is option 4; there is no way to signify that you want to search for double spacing or triple spacing, or for a particular tab setting.

Extended Search

You can extend Search or Search/Replace so that headers, footers, footnotes, and endnotes are also checked for the word or phrase in the search string. To do this, you press the Home key before pressing the Forward or Reverse Search Keys (F2 or Shift-F2). The following prompt appears:

Extended Srch:

If you are using Search/Replace (Alt-F2), the above prompt appears after you choose N or Y to confirm. You then type your search string and proceed as usual. If you are using Search, when the word is found inside a header, footer, footnote, or endnote the cursor stops inside the appropriate screen (Header/Footer screen or Footnote/Endnote screen), and you can then edit it. When you are ready to continue, press Home F2, F2 for a forward search or Home Shift-F2, F2 for a reverse search. If you are using Search/Replace with confirm, the cursor stops in the appropriate screen and waits for you to type Y or N, then moves to the next occurrence of the search string (which can be in one of the special screens or in the regular text). If you are using Search/Replace without confirm, the cursor changes the text in the Header/Footer and Footnote/Endnote screens, but you don't see it stop inside the screens.

Summary

Search can be used to locate any word, phrase, or hidden formatting code in a document as well as for rapid cursor movement. WordPerfect has a Forward Search Key (F2) and a Reverse Search Key (Shift-F2) so it can search in any direction from the cursor position.

The word, combination of words, or formatting code you ask WordPerfect to locate is called the *search string.* If you want the program to ignore case when searching, type the search string in lowercase letters. To restrict the search to whole words, type a space before and after the word or words in the search string.

Ctrl-X is used as a wildcard in search operations and can be used to substitute for any character except the first one in a search string. It is a useful method of locating words or phrases when their exact wording or spelling is unknown.

The Replace Key (Alt-F2) is used to locate a search string and either erase or change it. You can ask WordPerfect to replace the string automatically each time it finds a match, or you can have the program pause for your confirmation (Y/N) at each occurrence. Replace is also used to locate and erase formatting codes that were accidentally or erroneously placed in a document.

Search and Replace can be used to locate and eliminate hard return codes, to delete line spacing codes in a document, to locate extra spaces accidentally inserted by pressing the Spacebar (this can be helpful when using Sort and Select), in combination with a macro (see Chapter 16) to locate the periods that mark the end of sentences and capitalize each word that follows, and in combination with a macro to strip all formatting codes so you can export the document to another program more easily.

As you have seen, Search and Search and Replace are valuable features that can improve your productivity enormously. Their applications are limited only by your imagination. Some other possible uses for Search are to locate headings and subheadings in order to mark them for your table of contents (see Chapter 9), to locate words or phrases to mark for an index (see Chapter 9), and to find a special word you have entered as a marker in your text (I use my first name) so you can jump around in the document and always find the last area you worked on.

CHAPTER 7 KEYSTROKE SUMMARY:

Insert a soft hyphen

Insert a hard hyphen or a minus sign

Insert a dash

The Tab Align Key—create and align columns against a decimal point, asterisk, dollar sign, or other symbol

Insert a hard space

The Date Key—display the Date Format screen

The Super/Subscript Key—display the options menu for super/subscript, overstrike, and text-advancing features

The Mark Text Key—display options menu for Redline and other text marking features

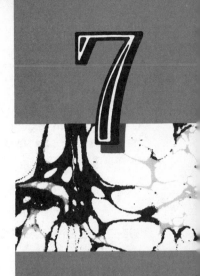

ADVANCED FORMATTING FEATURES

THIS CHAPTER WILL INTRODUCE SEVERAL new formatting features such as subscripts and superscripts, hard spaces, hanging paragraphs, overstrike, hard and soft hyphens, the alignment character, left, right, center, and decimal tabs, redline, strikeout, and line numbering. It will also further explore some other features that have been mentioned only briefly in earlier chapters. Among these are the hyphenation zone and the Date Key.

Many who use word processors do not bother to learn the more advanced formatting features unless required to, because none of them is absolutely essential, and many of them seem to be esoteric and difficult to learn. If you think of yourself as this type of user, you are still encouraged to skim this chapter and familiarize yourself with the advanced features so that if you are ever in a situation where one of them could help, you'll at least be able to recognize it and go back to find out how to use it. It is not an exaggeration to say that features such as hard space and hard hyphen can save you a lot of frustration and an enormous amount of time and energy.

Hyphenation

You have already worked with WordPerfect's Hyphenation feature and have been briefly introduced to the hyphenation zone. To refresh your memory, it is the area on each line between two positions called the Left H-Zone and the Right H-Zone. By default, the Right H-Zone is located at the right margin, and the left one is located seven positions before the right margin.

If the Hyphenation feature is on, whenever a word begins before or at the Left H-Zone and extends past the Right H-Zone, the following prompt will appear asking you where to split the word:

Position hyphen; Press ESC

By contrast, word wrap takes over if a word begins *after* the Left H-Zone and extends past the Right H-Zone, automatically pushing the whole word to the next line.

Like most other settings in WordPerfect, the hyphenation zone can easily be changed. If you make it smaller, you will be asked to hyphenate more frequently; if it is larger, less hyphenation will be called for and more words will be word wrapped to the next line in their entirety. You will learn how to alter the hyphenation zone later in this section.

To see how hyphenation works, look at Figure 7.1. The asterisks represent single positions on a line and the word PRODUCTIVE is preceded by a full line of text that you don't see here. (Note that the Right H-Zone is at the default setting for the right margin, 74.) In the top diagram, the word starts before the Left H-Zone and extends past the right margin, so you will be requested to hyphenate it. In the second diagram, the word starts after the Left H-Zone and extends past the right margin; therefore, it will be automatically wrapped to the next line. (If the word doesn't extend beyond the right margin at all, it remains intact where it is, regardless of where the word begins.)

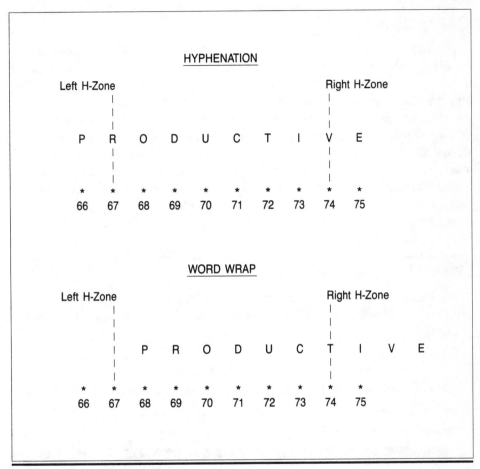

Figure 7.1: *The hyphenation zones*

When you see the hyphenation prompt and you prefer not to hyphenate the word, you can press Cancel (F1) and the entire word will be wrapped to the following line. If you do this, the Reveal Codes screen will display a bold slash line (/) in front of the word. This is called the Cancel Hyphenation code; it will always be found in front of a word that you declined to hyphenate (after the hyphenation message asked you to). If you later change your mind and decide you do want to hyphenate it, you can delete the slash. Search or Replace can be used to locate Cancel Hyphenation codes. Just press one of the Search Keys (F2 or Shift-F2), or Search/Replace (Alt-F2), followed by the Line Format Key (Shift-F8), then select option 6, and press F2 or Esc.

Soft Hyphens

The hyphen that is inserted when you are using the Hyphenation feature is called a *soft hyphen.* It is important that you understand the meaning of this term. If you add or delete text near a word that contains a soft hyphen and the document is then reformatted so that the word is moved away from the right margin, WordPerfect will remove the hyphen that is visible on your editing screen (and in the printed version). However, if you look at the Reveal Codes screen (Alt-F3) you will still see a bold hyphen where you had inserted the soft hyphen. In Figure 7.2, for example, you can see a soft hyphen in the word *WordPerfect,* since it was originally hyphenated until the word *then* was inserted to the left of it, which caused *WordPerfect* to be wrapped to the following line.

Other Hyphens

You can insert a Soft Hyphen code yourself, without prompting from the program, by pressing the Ctrl key followed by the hyphen key. This hyphen

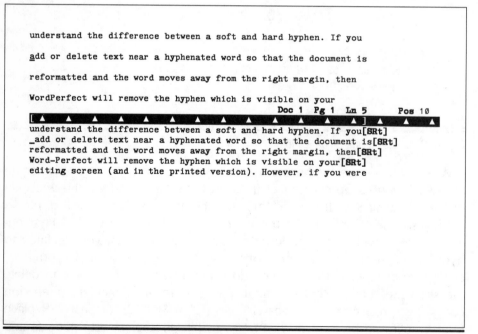

Figure 7.2: *The soft hyphen in the Reveal Codes screen*

will only appear on the screen if the word is moved to a position at the right margin where hyphenation or word wrap would be required.

A plain hyphen that you insert using the hyphen key alone, without any prompting from WordPerfect, will appear on screen and in print wherever the word appears on a line. If the word has to be split between two lines, WordPerfect will use your hyphen for the break.

If you wish to prevent a hyphenated word from being split between two lines under any circumstances, press the Home key before pressing the hyphen key. This type of hyphen should also be used to represent a minus sign in a numeric equation such as $15-5=10$. If it is not, WordPerfect considers the sign to be a hyphen, and may split the equation into two lines against your intentions. Finally, to create a dash between two words, you must use the double hyphen (press Home, hyphen, hyphen).

In the Reveal Codes screen, the hyphen created by pressing the hyphen key alone appears as follows:

[-]

The soft hyphen, created by WordPerfect's hyphenation feature or by pressing Ctrl hyphen, appears as a bold hyphen. The dash (double hyphen) appears like this:

-[-]

Finally, the hyphen created with Home and the minus sign, used to keep text from being split at the hyphen, appears as follows:

-

Changing the Hyphenation Zone

To change the settings for the hyphenation zone, press Line Format (Shift-F8) followed by 5 (Hyphenation). You will then see the following prompt line:

[HZone Set] 7,0 Off Aided 1 On; 2 Off; 3 Set H-Zone; 4 Aided; 5 Auto: 0

Next, select option 3 and enter the new settings for the left and right zones, following each entry with a Return. Normally, you should not alter the right one or you may end up with lines printed beyond the right margin.

If you reduce the size of the hyphenation zone, you will encounter the hyphenation prompt more frequently. To understand why, look at Figure 7.3 in which the Left H-Zone setting has been decreased from 7 to 4.

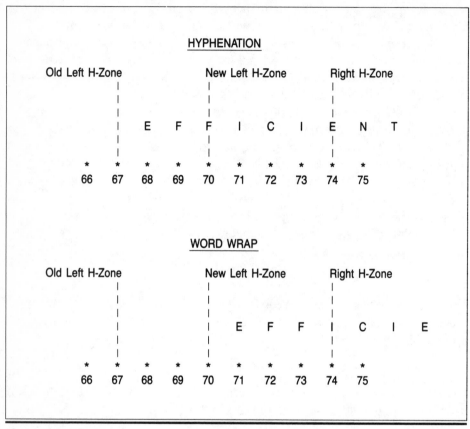

Figure 7.3: *Effects of a smaller hyphenation zone*

Using the old settings, the word EFFICIENT would have automatically been wrapped to the next line because the first character in the word appears after the Left H-Zone setting (7 positions to the left of the right margin). With the new settings, the word begins before the Left H-Zone setting, (4 positions to the left of the right margin), so the hyphenation prompt will appear.

If you increase the size of the hyphenation zone, you will be asked to hyphenate less frequently, and more words will be wrapped to the following line. To visualize this, look again at Figure 7.1. If the Left H-Zone were changed to 9, it would be located at position 65. Since the P would then appear after the Left H-Zone, instead of hyphenating the word PRODUC-TIVE, WordPerfect would automatically wrap it to the next line.

Left, Center, Right, and Decimal Tabs

In Chapter 3 you were introduced to the subject of left justified tabs and promised further explanation of the other types of tabs: center, right, and decimal. As you may recall, left tabs are the standard type of tab used for aligning text. When you press the Tab key and type a word, the first letter of the word is actually in the same position as the tab stop and the remaining characters in the word are entered to the right of the tab stop, as shown below:

```
15     20     25     30     35     40     45     50     55     60     65
Dear
```

In the above case, left tabs are set every 5 positions (WordPerfect's default) and the word *Dear* was typed after pressing the Tab key once. Left tabs are set for every 5 spaces up to column 160, then every 10 spaces up to column 250 unless you change them using the Line Format Key (Shift F8, 1 or 2). You cannot set right, center, or decimal tabs after the first 40 tab stops have been set.

Center tabs are used primarily to center a heading over a column of text or numbers. The previous example looks like this when a center tab is used:

```
15     20     25     30     35     40     45     50     55     60     65
Dear
```

Decimal tabs are most often used to align a column of numbers around the decimal point, as shown below. Note that the decimal points are all directly under the tab stop at position 15; this happens automatically when you press the Tab key after setting a decimal tab.

```
   15      20     25     30     35     40     45     50     55     60     65
  199.99
   99.99
 1999.99
```

Right aligned tabs are also used for numbers when they do not include decimal points. As shown below, the blank space following the last digit (0) in each number is aligned under the tab stop. For instance, when you round off the numbers shown above (let's hear it for truth in advertising!)

and use a right tab instead of a center tab, they look like this:

	15	20	25	30	35	40	45	50	55	60	65
200											
100											
2000											

Incidentally, there are other methods for aligning decimal points under the Tab position, including the Tab Align Key (Ctrl-F6) and WordPerfect's Math feature (Alt-F7, 1). You will study Tab Align in the next section, and Math in Chapter 14.

In Chapter 3 you learned how to change tab stops. To refresh your memory, press the Line Format Key (Shift-F8, 1 or 2) and delete all the default tab stops by pressing Ctrl-End (the Delete EOL Key). Next, either type the number of the new tab stop and press Return or set evenly spaced tab stops every N positions by typing N,N. For example, to set them every 10 positions starting at position 10 type

      10,10

Both of these methods insert left tab stops. To change the type to right, center, or decimal (and insert tabs every 10 positions) the procedure is slightly different. After using Ctrl-End to delete all tab stops, type the letter corresponding to the type of tab you wish to set (R, C, or D). Next, type

      10,10

and press Return.

To change individual tab settings, use the ← or → keys or the Spacebar to position the cursor over the tab stop, then press either L, R, C, or D. To delete individual tab settings, position the cursor over the tab stop and then press the Del key.

A word of warning: whenever you change tab stops, you must use the Exit Key (F7) to leave the Tab menu and register the changes you just made. Do not try to exit by pressing Cancel (F1) or you will, in effect, cancel the new tab stops. Observe the *Press EXIT when done* message in the lower right corner of the screen illustrated in Figure 7.4; this notice refers to the F7 key.

```
C.........R.........D.........L...................C.........C.........C.......
0123456789012345678901234567890123456789012345678901234567890123456789012345678
        20        30        40        50        60        70        80
Delete EOL (clear tabs); Enter number (set tab); Del (clear tab);
Left; Center; Right; Decimal; .= Dot leader; Press EXIT when done. 10,10
```

Figure 7.4: *The Tab menu with left, center, right, and decimal tabs*

Leader Characters

Selecting a leader character fills the space between the tabs with a row of dots, as shown below:

```
RENT...............................................1000.00
UTILITIES ...........................................45.66
SUPPLIES ...........................................39.75
```

In this example, a decimal tab was used to align the numbers. To set the leader character, you simply type a period over the L, R, or D when setting tab positions in the Tab menu (you cannot use dot leaders with center tabs). A bright box appears over the character, indicating the text at that tab position will be preceded by a dot leader.

In the example shown above, I set a decimal tab with a dot leader at position 50. After typing each heading (RENT, UTILITIES, SUPPLIES), I pressed the Tab key to move the cursor to position 50 and typed the numbers, as shown in Figure 7.5. As I typed, the cursor remained stationary at the tab stop and the numbers were pushed to the left until the decimal point (period) was pressed. Notice (in Figure 7.5) the message *Alignment Char = .* and the dot leaders that were automatically inserted when I pressed Tab. The Alignment Character message means that the decimal point will be directly under the tab stop, ensuring that all the numbers are correctly aligned. In the next section, you will learn how to change the Alignment Character to a different one such as a blank space, dollar sign, or anything you wish.

The Alignment Character

The only other option on the Line Format menu that has not yet been explained is the Alignment Character. This feature works in conjunction with the Tab Align Key (Ctrl-F6), to create and align columns against or

```
        RENT . . . . . . . . . .1000.00
        UTILITIES. . . . . . . . .45.66
        SUPPLIES . . . . . . . . .39_




        Align Char = .                        Doc 2  Pg 1  Ln 6      POS 50
```

Figure 7.5: *Using a decimal tab with dot leaders*

around a character such as a decimal point, asterisk, or a blank space that is inserted using the Spacebar. Although more commonly used with Word-Perfect's math feature, the Alignment Character can also be used to establish columns of text. You will learn about math columns in Chapter 14, so this section will be limited to exploring text columns.

Using Tab Align with text columns is similar to using the Flush Right Key to align text against the right margin, except that the Alignment Character replaces the right margin as the position against which the text will be aligned. Characters that are typed after pressing Tab Align are inserted to the left of the cursor, and the cursor remains stationary at the tab stop until the Alignment Character is entered. For example, in Figure 7.6, an excerpt from a legal document, the text in the last three lines is aligned against the dollar sign ($).

The procedure that was used to align these sentences is simple, and certainly easier than trying to align them visually. The first step is to designate the Alignment Character, in this case the dollar sign. Since it is used most often for mathematical and financial typing, the default value for the Alignment Character is a period, which serves as a decimal point. To change it, press Line Format (Shift-F8) and choose option 6, Align Char. You will then see the following prompt, which shows that the Alignment Character is currently a period:

Align Char = .

Replace it with a dollar sign and the entire message will disappear. As you can see, this is one of those prompts that does not wait for you to press Return, so you do not see if it has accepted your entry. To verify that the

```
        The undersigned Applicant and representative hereby certify
    that no other fees have been charged or will be charged by the
    representative in connection with this loan, unless provided for
    in loan authorization specifically approved by the agency.


        Amount Heretofore Paid  $  _____

    Additional Amount to be Paid  $  _____

          Total Compensation  $  _____
```

Figure 7.6: *Text aligned against the dollar sign*

Alignment Character has been changed to a dollar sign, you'll have to turn to the Reveal Codes screen (Alt-F3) where you'll see the following code:

[Align Char:$]

Now press the Tab key five times, then press the Tab Align Key (Ctrl-F6). You will see this prompt on the Status line, which stays on the screen until you enter the $:

Align Char = $

Next, type the first sentence:

Amount Heretofore Paid $

As soon as you typed the dollar sign, the prompt disappeared. This indicates that the alignment feature has been turned off, and whatever you type next will be entered in the usual manner.

When using tab alignment, you must be sure to leave enough space for all the characters in your sentence, which is why you were instructed to press the Tab key five times before pressing Tab Align. It is apparent that there are more than five characters in each of the sentences in this example, and if you had pressed the Tab Alignment Key once without inserting extra tabs, the words would have been pushed all the way to the left margin. Once you had typed more than 15 characters, the Align prompt would have disappeared and you would no longer have been in Alignment mode.

The reason for this is not complicated. As you type the first 5 characters, they move to the left of the cursor (which remains at the tab stop at position 15) until the first one is at position 10, the left margin. The next 9 characters you type release the margin and continue to move to the left until the first character appears at position 1. If you enter one more character, they can go no further; with no more room at the left edge, tab alignment ends and any other characters you type from that point on are entered in the standard method, with the cursor moving to the right of each character after it is typed.

Now add the line to the right by typing 27 underlines (using Shift with the key on the right of the top row), or by using the Esc key in the convenient method described below.

The Esc key can be used to repeat a function or character any number of times. To try it, press Esc and you will see the following prompt:

n = 8

N represents the number of times your action will be repeated. Eight is the default so replace the 8 with 27. Next, type an underline and voilà, your line appears instantly! Esc can also be used in the same manner to move the cursor up, down, right, or left a specified number of lines or positions, to delete several lines or characters following the cursor, and much more. To learn more about these applications, you can use Help (press F3, then Esc) or turn to Appendix B of this book, which describes all of them.

Editing Text that Has Been Aligned

There is one hazard to watch out for when you use the Tab Align feature: if you try to edit the words that were aligned, the cursor will behave in a bizarre and unpredictable manner unless it is correctly positioned. Even worse, new text that you enter may not appear on the screen at all. This is not a flaw in WordPerfect (which appears to be nearly free of such problems). Instead, it stems from a misunderstanding you can only correct by looking at the Reveal Codes screen to understand how the alignment codes have been placed.

Do this now by pressing Alt-F3 (Reveal Codes). You will see a pair of alignment codes, [A] and [a], and the screen will resemble Figure 7.7.

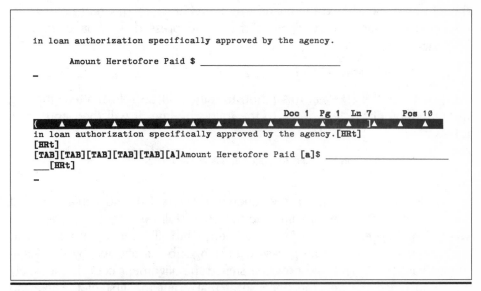

Figure 7.7: *The Reveal Codes screen with tab alignment codes*

Like the boldface codes, alignment codes always appear in pairs with the first one, [A], signalling the beginning of the text being aligned, and the second, [a], signalling the end. The problem arises when you try to edit the text without checking the cursor location. Since the codes are invisible on the editing screen, it's easy to accidentally place the cursor in the wrong position when you are trying to edit the aligned text. Also, unless you use the Reveal Codes screen, it will seem as though the cursor refuses to stop at the first character of aligned text.

Use the Reveal Codes screen to help you move the cursor to the position following the uppercase alignment code, [A]. Next, press the Spacebar to exit to the editing screen. Notice that it appears as though your cursor is positioned on the first character of the sentence (the A in Amount). Now type the following:

This represents the

Press the Spacebar after you've finished typing the word *the* but don't press any other keys yet.

Did you see how the words were entered as you typed them? As you typed *This represents,* these two words were pushed to the left by the alignment character, but when you typed the *t* in *the,* the first tab code in your sentence bumped into position 0 and could be pushed no further to the left. Next, you typed the *h* and saw the characters *This represents t* disappear altogether. After you typed the *e* and pressed the Spacebar, your line appeared like this:

he Amount Heretofore Paid $ _____

If you press the ↓ key at this point, the line will be reformatted, moving the underline characters down to the following line. It will then appear as follows:

This represents the Amount Heretofore Paid $

_____

Look at the Reveal Codes screen shown in Figure 7.8, and you'll see what has happened. The line contains five tab codes followed by the [A] and the words *This represents.* The [a], which ends tab alignment, appears next, meaning that the rest of the phrase is no longer being affected by the Alignment Character. In fact, the program shifted the alignment code immediately after you typed the *t* in *the* because at that point the first of the five tab codes hit position 0, and alignment ended. If you had inserted a few more

```
     representative in connection with this loan, unless provided for
     in loan authorization specifically approved by the agency.

              This represents the Amount Heretofore Paid $
     _____



     C:\WP2\REVISED\FIG74                     Doc 1  Pg 1  Ln 6      Pos 44
     [  ▲    ▲    ▲    ▲    ▲    ▲    ▲    ▲    ▲    ▲    ▲    ]▲    ▲    ▲
     representative in connection with this loan, unless provided for[SRt]
     in loan authorization specifically approved by the agency.[HRt]
     [HRt]
     [TAB][TAB][TAB][TAB][TAB][A]This represents [a]the _Amount Heretofore Paid $[SRt
     ]
     _____[HRt]
```

Figure 7.8: *The Reveal Codes screen with* This represents *added*

tabs in front of the original sentence and shortened the line of underline characters, this problem would have been avoided.

Now you understand why you have to be so careful when using the tab alignment feature! It can be extremely confusing, especially when words disappear from your editing screen, or the cursor jumps around unpredictably when you try to edit. If this ever happens, it is likely that the new text has disappeared between a set of alignment codes ([A] and [a]), or that the cursor was accidentally placed in the wrong position before editing. To correct the problem, you must check the Reveal Codes screen and position the cursor properly.

Hard Spaces

You have already been introduced to the concepts of hard and soft hyphens, so you should have little trouble understanding hard spaces.

Hard spaces are used to prevent the program from splitting words between two lines. This is often necessary with a mathematical formula, a date, or a name such as Henry VIII. To see why, look at the paragraph in Figure 7.9.

The date, November 23, and the address, 54 Main Street, would be much easier to read if they had remained unbroken; your eyes tend to read each of them as a unit and slow down considerably when the words are separated. To prove this, read the revised version in Figure 7.10, in which hard spaces were used to keep the name and date on the same lines.

To insert a hard space, you press the Home key first, then press the Spacebar, rather than the Spacebar alone. As you would expect, this action inserts a formatting code that is visible on your Reveal Codes screen. It is a space surrounded by brackets, [ ], and appears between the words instead of a normal space.

If you use hard spaces, you will occasionally end up with excessive blank space at the end of a line when you add or delete text, just as with any long, unbroken word that word wraps. If this happens, delete the hard spaces using the Reveal Codes screen. Another problem with hard spaces occurs when you are using WordPerfect's hyphenation feature. Since WordPerfect considers words separated by hard spaces to be one word, it may ask you to place an inappropriate hyphen in between them if they

```
        The bone-chilling event occurred on the night of November
23, long after Halloween's raucousness had faded into memory and
the town had taken on a prim demeanor for the new holiday. The
slovenly old house whose remains barely covered the site at 54
Main Street had been empty for years ...
```

Figure 7.9: *A paragraph that needs hard spaces*

```
        The bone-chilling event occurred on the night of
November 23, long after Halloween's raucousness had faded into
memory and the town had taken on a prim demeanor for the new
holiday. The slovenly old house whose remains barely covered the
site at 54 Main Street had been empty for years ...
```

Figure 7.10: *The paragraph with hard spaces added*

appear at or near the right margin. To prevent hyphenation in these cases, simply press the Cancel Key (F1).

The Date Key

You have already learned that pressing the Date Key (Shift-F5) and selecting option 1 (Insert Text), places the current date (based on the computer's clock or the entries you make at start-up time) at the cursor location. In this section, you will learn about the remaining two options on the Date Key: Format and Insert Function. Format allows you to customize the appearance of the date and can also be used to include the time of day. Insert Function allows you to insert the date as a function code (although it will appear in your document as text, as in option 1), so that in the future it will always show the current date and/or time when you print the document or bring it from the disk to the screen for editing.

Date Format

Let's experiment with the formats. Press the Date Key (Shift-F5). Select option 2, Format, and you will see the screen shown in Figure 7.11.

Notice the boldfaced prompt line that displays the default format in the lower part of the screen:

Date Format: 3 1, 4.

Two columns are visible on the Date Format screen, one with numbers and one that explains their meanings. To change the date format, you must enter one or more of these numbers in the prompt line, then press Return. For instance, if you want the date to appear as all numbers with hyphens but no spaces between the numbers, you type the numeric codes for the parts of the date. The code for each part is entered in the order you want in the date itself, and you type codes with hyphens but no spaces, as follows:

2-1-5

After pressing Return, you will see the Date Key prompt again, and if you select option 1 or 3 the date will be placed at the current cursor position in your new format. For example, if the date in your computer is

```
Date Format

    Character    Meaning
       1         Day of the month
       2         Month (number)
       3         Month (word)
       4         Year (all four digits)
       5         Year (last two digits)
       6         Day of the week (word)
       7         Hour (24-hour clock)
       8         Hour (12-hour clock)
       9         Minute
       0         am / pm
       %         Include leading zero for numbers less than 10
                    (must directly precede number)

    Examples:  3 1, 4      = December 25, 1984
               %2/%1/5 (6) = 01/01/85 (Tuesday)
Date Format: 3 1, 4
```

Figure 7.11: *The Date Format screen*

January 9, 1986, it will appear as follows:

　　1-9-86

The table below shows what each of the numbers would insert in your document on January 9, 1986 at 8:45 p.m.

Number	Meaning	Example
1	Day of the month	9
2	Month (numbers)	1
3	Month (text)	January
4	Year (4 digits)	1986
5	Year (last 2 digits)	86
6	Day of the week (text)	Thursday
7	Hour (military time)	20
8	Hour (12 hour clock)	8
9	Minute	45
0	am / pm	pm
%	Include leading zeros	01-09-86

When you use these numbers to change the date format, you can also include any other symbols or characters such as slashes, hyphens, spaces, or commas. You have already used hyphens in the first exercise, and can probably think of applications for the others. For example, it is standard practice to insert a colon between the hour and minute, so typing

    8:9 0

will return the current time in the correct format, as follows:

    8:45 pm

The only restriction in your date format pattern is that the total number of characters cannot exceed 29.

Each time you start WordPerfect, the default format, 3 1, 4, will automatically appear when you select option 2 from the Date Format Key. However, once you change it, the new format will continue to appear each time you press Shift-F5, 2 and will be the same until you exit from the program or change it once again. Unlike most other features in WordPerfect, changing the date format does not insert a special code into your document (you won't see any indication on your Reveal Codes screen that this has been done). When you insert the date into your text as a function (using Shift-F5, 3), the date code in your Reveal Codes screen will show the new format you have selected.

Insert Function

The Insert Function option inserts a date that appears to be just like any other text in your document, but it is actually a code. This date will change to match the one that is in your computer at the time you print the document or retrieve it from disk to be edited.

To use this feature, simply select option 3 after pressing the Date Key (Shift-F5). The date in your computer's memory when you make this selection will be inserted into your text, using the default format. If you have changed the format (since you started this session with WordPerfect), the date will conform to the most recent format used. I find this feature to be of great value and use it often. For instance, while writing this book I have been saving each chapter as a separate file, inserting a function code at the end that tells me the date and time. By doing this, I can always tell how long I have been working in each session (that is, since I last retrieved the file from the disk) by comparing it to the time on my watch. (It helps me maintain self-discipline!) I also use it on printed drafts of the chapters so I'll know which of several printouts is the most recent revision. I use this format:

> 6, 3 1, 4 8:90

It shows up as follows:

> Thursday, January 30, 1986 9:00pm

This date function appears on the Reveal Codes screen as follows:

> [Date:6, 3 1, 4 8:90]

Hanging Paragraphs

A hanging paragraph is one in which the entire paragraph is indented one or more tab stops to the right, except for the first line, which hangs out from the rest of the text at the left side because the indented margin has been released. This is especially useful in numbered outlines, so that the numbers or letters that are used to label each paragraph or section are set off from the body of text that follows. Note that the chapter summaries in this book use hanging paragraphs for emphasis.

Figure 7.12 shows three journal entries that are to be recorded in a general ledger with the date listed to the left of the transaction for emphasis. Each of the transactions is a hanging paragraph.

You create a hanging paragraph by using the following steps:

1. Press the Indent Key (F4) (one or more times).

```
August 3: Spent $20,000 in cash to purchase computer equipment.

August 6: Paid by check the amount of $633.45, for invoice #4020
          from the phone company for the July bill.

August 9: Received a check for $5,455 from clients Smith, Jones,
          and Brown for work performed from July 1 through July
          9, billed on invoice #1355.
```

Figure 7.12: *Hanging paragraphs*

2. Use the Margin Release Key (Shift-Tab) to release the temporary margin (just created by using the Indent Key) and move the first line one or more tab stops to the left.

3. Type your paragraph. Pressing Return at the end of the paragraph terminates automatic indentation and ends the paragraph. Note that in the example shown in Figure 7.12, the Indent Key was pressed twice so that the sentences begin at position 20, and the Margin Release Key was pressed twice so that the date begins in the left margin, in position 10.

Superscript and Subscript

Superscripted characters are ones that are printed in a position slightly above the standard line, as in the number:

1.05^2

Subscripted characters appear in a position slightly below the standard line, as in the chemical formula for copper sulfate:

Cu_2SO_4

According to the WordPerfect manual, superscripted and subscripted characters are supposed to print one-third of a line above or below the rest of the text on the line on which they are placed, but this placement can vary with the printer. In addition, not all printers can produce subscripts and superscripts, so you may want to test your printer before trying to use this feature. For details about printer installation and testing, please refer to Appendix A.

You can place a superscript or subscript code in front of a single character before typing it or you can designate a block of characters that have been marked with the Block Key (Alt-F4). To insert the code, press Shift-F1 (the Super/Subscript Key). The following menu appears:

1 Superscript; 2 Subscript; 3 Overstrike; 4 Adv Up; 5 Adv Dn; 6 Adv Ln: 0

If you press 1 for Superscript, you will see a boldfaced uppercase S at the lower left corner of the screen, and if you press 2 for Subscript, you will see a boldfaced lowercase s. At this point, type the character to be subscripted or superscripted. The S or s will disappear as soon as you do. Your subscripted or superscripted character does not appear to be different on screen, since these features only alter the printed version of your work. To verify that you have inserted the code correctly, you can check the Reveal Codes screen (Alt-F3). The code for superscript is

[SuprScrpt]

and the one for subscript is

[SubScrpt]

Note that this method can only be used to type a single subscripted or superscripted character at a time, so if you intend to alter an entire word or phrase, it is much easier to type it first and then mark it with the Block Key (Alt-F4). When you press the Super/Subscript Key with the Block Key on, you will see this prompt:

Block 1 Superscript; 2 Subscript: 0

You can press 1 or 2 to alter the entire block.

Advance

If Subscript and Superscript don't work correctly with your printer, or if you want to move a character or phrase up or down the page in different increments, you can use WordPerfect's Advance feature. It is accessible from the Super/Subscript Key and causes text to be printed up or down one-half a line from the rest of the text on the line.

Advance is used differently from the Subscript and Superscript features, primarily because it is a toggle key. Like the Underline and Bold Keys, this one must be turned on in front of the text you want altered and turned off immediately afterward. As with the Subscript and Superscript features, not all printers can take advantage of this feature, so it's helpful to test your printer before using it.

To use Advance, follow these steps:

1. Press Shift-F1, (Super/Subscript).
2. Select either option 4 to advance the characters you are going to type one-half line up, or option 5 to advance them one-half line

down. You will see a solid arrow head in the lower left hand corner of the screen, pointing either upward or downward to show which direction you have selected. As soon as you type a character, the arrowhead will disappear.

3. Type the text you want to have advanced.

4. To turn the feature off, press Shift-F1 again. If you selected option 4, your next step is to select option 5 to move the cursor back down to the original line. If you selected option 5, your next step is to select option 4 to move back up to the original line.

Figure 7.13 shows the Reveal Codes screen for a line of text that has been advanced. The bracketed code representing Advance Up appears at the beginning of the line, indicating that the words *IT'S FUN UP HERE* have been advanced up by half a line. The Advance Down code follows this phrase, and turns the feature off. The code representing Advance Down appears again after the word *BUT*, indicating that the words that follow, *IT'S NO FUN AT ALL DOWN HERE*, have been advanced down half a line. At the end of the sentence, another code for Advance Up appears, which serves to turn the feature off once again.

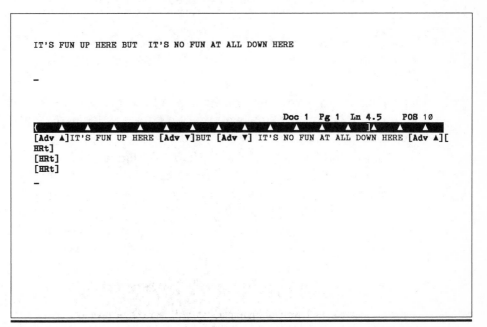

Figure 7.13: *The Reveal Codes screen with advance up and advance down codes*

Although this sentence was started on line 3, the only word that will appear on line 3 of the printed text is the word *BUT,* which was unaffected by the codes. If you type this sentence (including the advance codes) and then move your cursor to the word *UP,* the line indicator on the Status line shows that the cursor is on line 2.5. If you move your cursor to the word *DOWN,* the line indicator reveals that the cursor is on line 3.5.

Advance by Lines

Option 6 on the Super/Subscript Key permits you to advance the printed text up or down one or more whole lines. It can be used to insert blank space on a printed page, without the blank lines appearing on the monitor. If you use this feature, you have to rely on the line indicator to tell you which line you are currently typing on.

Since this option is slightly harder to understand unless you try it, do so now by following these steps:

1. Start at the first line in the page and type the following sentence without pressing Return. (Your line breaks will differ from those below):

   The Line Advance option can be used instead of the Return key if you want to eliminate all the blank spaces on the monitor that are inserted by pressing the Return key.

2. After typing the last word in the sentence, check the Status line and note the number of the line where your cursor is located. If you started typing at line 1, the cursor should now be on line 3.

3. Press Return and make sure the cursor is positioned on line 4 by checking the line indicator. Next, press Shift-F1 (Super/Subscript). From the menu, select option 6, Adv Ln. You will see the prompt Adv. in the lower left corner of the screen.

4. Press 8 to move to line 8, then press Return. The line indicator will show that you are now on line 8, even though you do not see any blank space on the screen between lines 3 and 8.

5. Type the following sentence (without pressing Return):

   However, just remember when using Line Advance that what you see on screen will not be the same as what you get on paper.

When you're finished, the line indicator will show that the cursor is on line 9, though only five lines will be visible on the screen.

The printed version of this page will resemble Figure 7.14, with four blank lines appearing between lines 3 and 8.

Overstrike

Overstrike, option 3 on the Super/Subscript Key, allows you to print two characters in the same position, if your printer is capable of this. This feature can be used to print certain foreign characters such as the accents and circumflexes that are often placed over vowels to clarify pronunciation. For example, many French words include an accent over the e, as in that most famous street, the Champs Elysée, and in the original version of the word *résumé*.

```
The Line Advance option can be used instead of the Return key if
you want to avoid all the blank spaces on the monitor that are
inserted be pressing the Return key.



However, just remember when using Line Advance that what you see
on screen will not be the same as what you get on paper.
```

Figure 7.14: *The printed version of two paragraphs that have been separated by line advance*

To use Overstrike, you type the character to be affected, such as the first *e* in *résumé*, then press the Super/Subscript Key (Shift-F1) and select option 3 for Overstrike. This moves the cursor back one position and places it on the original character. Next, you type the second character, such as the acute accent mark (´), which will appear to replace the original character (e) on the screen, as shown in the top half of the Reveal Codes screen illustrated in Figure 7.15. However, the lower half of the screen confirms that both characters are still in your document, separated by the formatting code, [Ovrstk]. If your printer is capable, when you print this word both the e and the ´ will appear.

Redline and Strikeout

Redline and Strikeout are two special purpose formatting features used to designate editing changes. Strikeout is often used in legal documents to mark text that is to be deleted, by placing a line of dashes through the

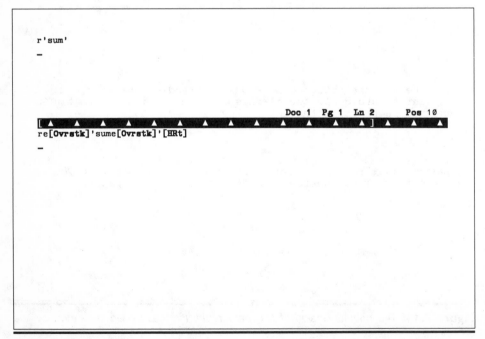

Figure 7.15: *Overstrike*

characters that will be removed. Redline has the opposite function; it is used to mark text that is being added to the document, by placing a vertical bar or a plus sign (depending on your printer) in the left margin next to each line that will be added. Figure 7.16 shows the printed version of a line of text marked with redline, and one marked by strikeout. The redline bar or plus sign appears next to a line when any part of the line has been redlined.

To use Redline, press the Mark Text Key (Alt-F5). The prompt line will appear as follows:

1 Outline; 2 Para #; 3 Redline; 4 Short form; 5 Index; 6 Other Options: 0

Then select option 3, Redline. You will see a plus sign appear next to the position number on the Status line. Anything you type after this will be printed with a vertical bar or a plus sign in the left margin. This is a toggle key, so when you are through, you must again press Alt-F5 and 3 to turn the feature off.

If you want to redline text that has already been typed, you mark it using the Block Key (Alt-F4), then press Alt-F5. The prompt line will be different since Block has been pressed first:

Mark for 1 ToC; 2 List; 3 Redline; 4 Strikeout; 5 Index; 6 ToA: 0

Whichever way you do the redlining, you cannot see the bar or plus sign on screen that will mark the printed version of your redlined text, but when you move the cursor back through the text, the plus sign appears next to the Position Indicator on the Status line. You can check it by looking at the Reveal Codes screen (Alt-F3). When you do, your text will be surrounded with two formatting codes, [RedLn] just before the first character that was redlined, and [r] after the last one.

```
| This sentence is marked with redline
  This sentence is marked with strikeout
```

Figure 7.16: *Redline and Strikeout*

Strikeout works just like Redline when it (Redline) is used with block on; in fact, you must always block your text before using strikeout. Look again at the two prompt lines above and you will see that the Strikeout option can only be selected from the Mark Text Key after the Block Key has been pressed.

To use Strikeout, mark your text using Block (Alt-F4), then press the Mark Text Key (Alt-F5) and select option 4, Strikeout. The highlighting disappears and you can continue typing. If you move the cursor back through the text marked for strikeout, you will see a minus sign next to the position number on the Status line. The strikeout codes that appear in the Reveal Codes screen are [StrkOut] and [s].

After marking the text with one of these features, you can use the Mark Text Key (Alt-F5) at any time to delete the redline markings and add the text to your document or delete the strikeout text. To do this, press option 6, Other Options, then select option 6, Remove all Redline Markings and all Strikeout text from document. The following prompt appears:

Delete Redline markings and Strikeout text? (Y/N) N

When you press Y, WordPerfect searches the entire document, deleting all text marked by Strikeout and erasing all the vertical bars or plus signs next to redlined text.

Line Numbering

WordPerfect 4.2 includes a Line Numbering feature that can be used to print line numbers in the left margin, as used in documents such as legal briefs. Line numbers are printed for the body of the document, as well as for all footnotes and endnotes. Although the numbers only appear when the document is printed, they can be viewed using the Print Preview feature (see Chapter 8).

Several options are available when you use this feature: you can print numbers on every line or eliminate numbering from blank lines (except the blank lines generated by changing line spacing); use continuous numbering or restart numbering on each page; print numbers every *n* lines starting with the number *n;* and change the position where the numbers will be printed. You can turn numbering on and off as often as you wish in a document. When you do, numbering restarts with the number 1.

To use Line Numbering, move the cursor to the top of the document (or wherever you want the numbers to begin) and press the Print Format Key (Ctrl-F8). Select option B, Line Numbering, and the screen illustrated in Figure 7.17 will appear.

Press 2 to turn Line Numbering on, select any other options you wish to use, then press Return twice.

The Line Numbering Options

Option 3, *Count blank lines,* is set to Yes. If you leave it this way, the program will number every line in your document as long as it ends in a hard or soft return. Note that the blank lines generated when you use double spacing (or any other spacing other than single) do not end in a soft or hard return, so they are not counted regardless of your answer to the *Count blank lines?* question. For example, Figure 7.18 shows a page from a legal brief which was formatted with double spacing, and for which the *Count blank lines* option was set to *N.* If you set the *Count blank lines* option to *Y,* the results are identical.

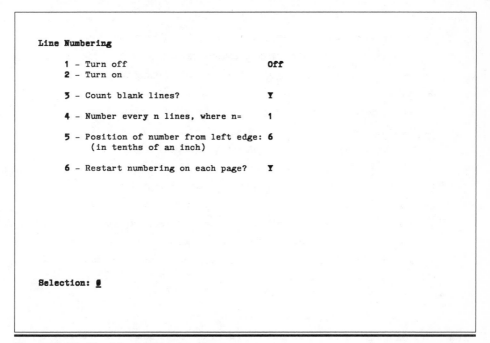

```
Line Numbering

     1 - Turn off                          Off
     2 - Turn on

     3 - Count blank lines?                Y

     4 - Number every n lines, where n=    1

     5 - Position of number from left edge: 6
           (in tenths of an inch)

     6 - Restart numbering on each page?   Y




     Selection: █
```

Figure 7.17: *The Line Numbering screen*

Selecting Y to count blank lines guarantees evenly placed numbering as long as line spacing is not mixed on a page. If a page includes varied spacing such as single spacing for the first 10 lines and double spacing for the rest, the numbers cannot be evenly placed.

```
 1  the ambiguity or uncertainty must be resolved in favor of
 2  apportionment, Smithfield, supra. at page 803.
 3      These rules of construction apply equally to determine
 4  whether the burden of California inheritance tax should be
 5  shifted from one transferee to others, Estate of Brown, 90 C.A.
 6  3d 582, 589 (1979).
 7      Finally, it is a judicial function to interpret written
 8  instruments unless the interpretations depends on the credibility
 9  of extrinsic evidence, Estate of Callahan, 6 C 3d 311,318 (1971).
10  In this case, there was no testimony as to the decedent's inten-
11  tions, and the only extrinsic evidence presented was the
12  decedent's 1975 will, various uncontested affidavits, and a
13  stipulation that the decedent's attorney had been in practice
14  since 1923. Under these circumstances, the interpretation of the
15  relevant documents is a question of law, Estate of Johnson,
16  supra., at p 801, and it is the task of this Court to arrive at
17  an independent interpretation of the decedent's trust, Estate of
18  Callahan, supra., at p. 602, Estate of Jones, supra, at p. 534.
19      In the next section, Appellant will show that the decedent's
20  expressed intention regarding payment of the death taxes
21  equitably attributable to Respondent's accumulated income is not
22  clear and unambiguous, and the extrinsic evidence which is
23  available does not provide the necessary clear and unambiguous
24  intention. As a result, the death taxes equitably attributable to
25  Respondent's accumulated income must be paid by the Respondent.

                                16
```

Figure 7.18: *A double spaced page with line numbering*

Option 4, *Number every n lines where n =* can be used to change the interval at which numbers are printed in the margin. For example, if you change *n* to 2, numbering will start with line 2 and only lines 2, 4, 6, 8, 10, 12, etc. will have a number next to them, as shown in the Print Preview screen illustrated in Figure 7.19. Note that although the odd numbered lines are counted, the numbers themselves are not printed.

Option 5, *Position of number from left edge,* allows you to change the column position where the number will be printed. It is measured in tenths of an inch from the left edge of the paper and the default is 6/10 inch. To change it, use the following guidelines:

Desired position	Number to enter
¹/₂ inch	5
1 inch	10
1¹/₂ inches	15
2 inches	20
2¹/₂ inches	25

```
        the_ ambiguity  or  uncertainty  must  be  resolved  in  favor of

    2   apportionment, Smithfield, supra. at page 803.

            These  rules  of  construction  apply  equally  to determine

    4   whether  the  burden  of  California  inheritance  tax  should be

        shifted from one transferee to others,  Estate of  Brown, 90 C.A.

    6   3d 582, 589 (1979).

            Finally,  it  is  a  judicial  function to interpret written

    8   instruments unless the interpretations depends on the credibility

        of extrinsic evidence, Estate of Callahan, 6 C 3d 311,318 (1971).

   10   In this case, there was no testimony as to the  decedent's inten-

        tions,  and   the  only  extrinsic  evidence  presented  was  the

   12   decedent's 1975 will,  various  uncontested  affidavits,  and a

  PREVIEW                                    Doc 3  Pg 1  Ln 7      Pos 13
```

Figure 7.19: *Line numbering every two lines*

Option 6, *Restart numbering on each page,* is set to Yes, meaning that the printed numbers on each page will always begin with the number 1. If you change it to *N,* numbering will start with 1 and be continuous on consecutive pages until the end of the document or until you turn Line Numbering off. To turn Line Numbering off before the end of the document, select option 1. Turning the feature on and off inserts the following codes in your document, visible in the Reveal Codes screen:

[LnNum:On]   [LnNum:Off]

Summary

This chapter has given you some new tools, and provided you with a more advanced understanding of a few of the old ones.

The (default) hyphenation zone is the area between the right margin and the position seven spaces to the left of it. If Hyphenation is turned on by selecting option 5 from the Line Format Key (Shift-F8), then whenever a word begins before or at the left hyphenation zone and extends past the right one, you will be asked to hyphenate it. By contrast, if a word begins after the left hyphenation zone and extends past the margin, WordPerfect's automatic word wrap feature will move the word to the next line. The hyphenation zone can be enlarged or reduced: enlarging it will cause the program to ask you to hyphenate less frequently.

The hyphen inserted using WordPerfect's Hyphenation feature or by pressing Ctrl and hyphen is called a soft hyphen. If a word with a soft hyphen is later moved away from the margin due to editing changes, the hyphen becomes unnecessary and will disappear from the editing screen and printed document. If you want a hyphen to remain permanently in a word such as one-half, press the Home key before pressing the hyphen key. This combination should also be used to type a minus sign. Finally, a double hyphen—Home, hyphen, hyphen, should be used when a dash is required in your text.

The Tabs option, 1 or 2 on the Line Format Key (Shift-F8), is used to set left, right, center, and decimal tabs. You can also use the Tabs option to fill the spaces between tabs with dots, called leader characters.

The Tab Align Key (Ctrl-F6) is used to align columns of text (characters or numbers) against or around an Alignment Character such as a decimal point or a dollar sign. When you press the Tab Align Key, any characters that are typed will be inserted to the left of the cursor until you enter the chosen Alignment Character. Editing text that has been entered by this method can be problematic, unless the cursor is properly positioned by using the Reveal Codes screen.

Hard spaces are formatting codes that you insert between two words or characters; they are used instead of normal spaces to prevent WordPerfect from splitting up words (or numbers) that should remain together on one line. They have many applications, and are especially useful in mathematical formulas, dates, proper names, and titles. To add a hard space, you press the Home key followed by the Spacebar instead of just the Spacebar alone. Although words or characters separated by a hard space appear to be two distinct words, WordPerfect treats them as though they were one word.

The Date Key (Shift-F5) has three options: one to insert the date in your computer's memory into the document, one to customize the appearance of the date and/or to insert the time of day, and one to insert the date and/or time as a formatting code, so that the date in your document will always match the one in your computer's clock at the time when the document was retrieved for editing or sent to the printer.

A hanging paragraph is one that is indented one or more tab stops to the right, but the margin is released before typing the first line so that it starts to the left of the indent position where the remaining lines begin. This is especially useful in numbered outlines, so the numbers or letters used to label each paragraph or section are set off from the body of text that follows.

Superscripted characters are printed in a position one-third of a line above the standard line, while subscripted characters appear in a position one-third of a line below it. You can place a superscript or subscript code in front of a single character by pressing the Super/Subscript Key (Shift-F1) before typing the character. You can also designate a block of characters that has been marked with the Block Key (Alt-F4). Subscript and superscript appear only in printed work, not on screen, but since some printers cannot produce subscripts and superscripts, the printer should be tested before using them.

Advance Up and Advance Down, options 4 and 5 on the Super/Subscript Key, are similar to Superscript and Subscript. They move text up or down one-half line, and work as toggle keys that must be turned on in front of the text to be altered and turned off immediately afterward. Like Subscript and Superscript, advanced text does not appear to be advanced on the editing screen, but will be when printed, if the printer is capable.

WordPerfect's Advance by Line feature, option 6 on the Super/Subscript Key, moves the cursor to a line you specify by its line number. It can be used to insert blank space on a printed page without the blank lines appearing on the monitor.

Overstrike, option 3 on the Super/Subscript Key, is used to print two characters in the same position, as in foreign words that use accents and other marks to clarify pronunciation. Overstrike does not appear on the editing screen, only on the printed page.

Redline and Strikeout are two special formatting features used to designate editing changes. Strikeout is used to mark text that is to be deleted, by placing a dashed line through the characters. Redline is used to mark text being added to the document, by placing a vertical bar or plus sign in the left margin next to each line affected. These features only appear on the printed version of your documents; you must use the Reveal Codes screen to see them on your monitor.

Line Numbering, option B on the Print Format key (Ctrl-F8), can be used to print line numbers in the left margin, as in legal briefs. The numbers appear only in the printed version, but can be seen using WordPerfect's Print Preview feature.

Now that you've read this far, you have literally mastered all of WordPerfect's formatting features. The remaining chapters cover the WordPerfect extras, those techniques that really set this program apart from the profusion of word processors on the market.

CHAPTER 8 KEYSTROKE SUMMARY:

The Print Key—display print options and print

The Print Format Key—display options for print style (including: pitch, font, underline style, justification, proportional spacing)

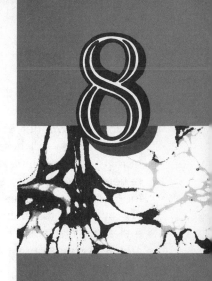

PRINTER CONTROL AND OPTIONS

WORDPERFECT'S PRINTING OPERATIONS are comprehensive, flexible, and varied, but they can be confusing to the uninitiated. Two major key combinations with over ten menus and prompts are used to direct the operations and select various options, and no less than seven different methods of printing are available using these and a few other keys, including the Block Key and the List Files Key. The Print Key can print an entire document or a single page; select one or more documents from the disk and place them in a queue (waiting list) to be printed in turn; or emulate a typewriter, typing text immediately onto a sheet of paper in the printer as you enter it. In addition, you can use the Block Key to print a marked section of a document, the List Files Key to print a document from a directory listing without retrieving it for editing, and the Print Screen

Key to make a quick copy of the text on your screen. With all these choices, no wonder it's so bewildering!

This chapter will describe the various printing methods, explain the terminology, and examine WordPerfect's print formatting and printer control options. It will also cover the Print Preview option, which allows you to view the document on screen much as it will appear on paper, displaying features not shown on the editing screen. By the end of the chapter, you should have a clear understanding of WordPerfect's printing operations, which are, after all, among the most important functions of a word processor.

The Printing Methods

The first thing you should learn is how to print your documents; WordPerfect provides you with many different methods. The two you will probably use most often are found on the Print Key (Shift-F7). When you press it you will see the following menu:

1 Full Text; 2 Page; 3 Options; 4 Printer Control; 5 Type-thru; 6 Preview: 0

Note that in earlier versions of WordPerfect, the Print Key was Ctrl-PrtSc; this combination can still be used to summon the prompt shown above.

The Full Text and Page Printing Options on the Print Key

By selecting option 1, Full Text, you can print the entire document that is currently on your editing screen. When you select Option 2, Page, only the page on which the cursor is located is printed. The page method prints the entire page, not just the part visible on your screen, and will do this regardless of where the cursor is placed on the page.

Both of these methods will create a temporary copy of the file in RAM or, if there is not enough room in your computer's memory, on the default disk. If you are printing a lengthy document and the disk does not have enough room for another copy, you will see a *disk full* error message on your screen. To avoid this problem, use one of the two methods of printing from the existing disk file, as described in the next section.

Bear in mind that when you print directly from disk, you are printing the document as you last saved it, without any of the changes you have made since then. Thus, if you have made changes since retrieving it and want to print the most current version using the methods below, first save your document to disk and then print the file.

Two Methods of Printing a Document from Disk

Pressing option 4, Printer Control, will bring up the Printer Control screen shown in Figure 8.1. As you can see, this screen serves many purposes, and you will study them individually later in this chapter. For now, the only one to be concerned with is option P, Print a Document, since this allows you to print files directly from the disk (as opposed to the other methods you have learned thus far, which only print files from the editing screen).

Take another look at Figure 8.1. The cursor appears next to the Selection prompt and when you select P, a message appears under the Selection line asking you to enter the name of the document to be printed. You then enter the name of any file on your data disk and either press Return to accept (All) and print the entire document or enter the page numbers you

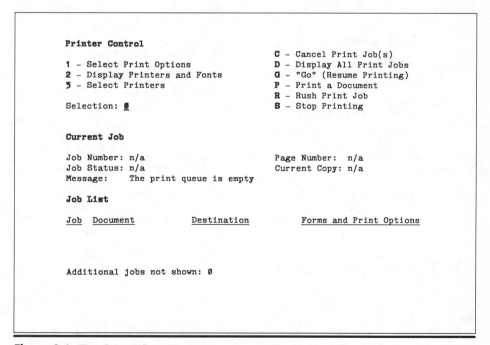

```
Printer Control
                                   C - Cancel Print Job(s)
1 - Select Print Options           D - Display All Print Jobs
2 - Display Printers and Fonts     G - "Go" (Resume Printing)
3 - Select Printers                P - Print a Document
                                   R - Rush Print Job
Selection: 0                       S - Stop Printing


Current Job

Job Number: n/a                    Page Number:  n/a
Job Status: n/a                    Current Copy: n/a
Message:     The print queue is empty

Job List

Job  Document          Destination           Forms and Print Options



Additional jobs not shown: 0
```

Figure 8.1: *The Printer Control screen*

want printed as shown in Figure 8.2. You can enter individual page numbers such as 5,7,9 or a range such as 2-12, or mix both a range and individual numbers, such as 1-5,12,15. Typing a page number followed by a
dash (such as 6-) prints everything from that page through the last one in
the document, and typing a page number preceded by a dash (-6) prints
everything from the first page through that page.

If you want to print more than one document (and are using continuous
paper or a cut-sheet feeder), you can continue selecting documents using
this method, and they will be printed in the order you select them (the
print queue). If you forget the sequence, the *Job List* section of the Printer
Control screen displays the name of each document and a job number
corresponding to it. The information provided on this list will be explored
in depth later in this chapter, in the section that examines printer control.

If you forget the exact name of a file you want to print, you can use the
second method of printing from disk, the List Files Key (F5). When you
press it you will see the DOS directory command, DIR, followed by the
letter corresponding to your default drive (and directory if you have a hard

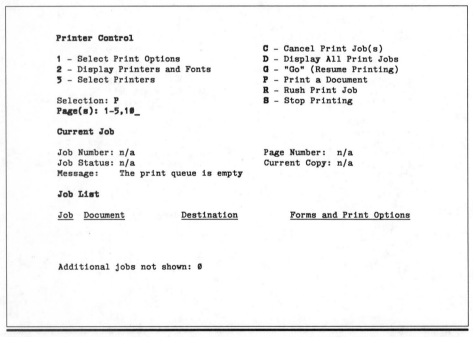

```
Printer Control
                            C - Cancel Print Job(s)
1 - Select Print Options    D - Display All Print Jobs
2 - Display Printers and Fonts  G - "Go" (Resume Printing)
3 - Select Printers         P - Print a Document
                            R - Rush Print Job
Selection: P                S - Stop Printing
Page(s): 1-5,10_

Current Job

Job Number: n/a             Page Number:  n/a
Job Status: n/a             Current Copy: n/a
Message:    The print queue is empty

Job List

Job  Document         Destination        Forms and Print Options




Additional jobs not shown: 0
```

Figure 8.2: *Using the Printer Control screen to print a document directly from the disk*

disk), and the wildcard characters **.**. These characters will produce a list of all files on the drive. You can narrow the search to all files with a certain extension, to files that start with a certain character, or use many other criteria if you are familiar with the DIR command and the wildcard characters. For those of you who are unfamiliar with this command, Chapter 12, "File Management and Security," thoroughly explores the List Files Key.

If you accept the default DIR command by pressing Return, the screen will be replaced by a list of all files on the data disk. (If you are using a hard disk, the default drive is usually C, and if you are using floppy disks, it is usually B.) To print from the listing, you move the selection bar using the arrow keys until the file you want to print is highlighted, then select option 4, Print, as shown in Figure 8.3. If you want to print more than one file, move the bar to each one and mark it by pressing the asterisk key (it has the ***** symbol and PrtSc on it), then select option 4. The marked documents will then be printed in the order in which they were selected. To exit from List Files, press the Spacebar. If you turn to the Print Control screen by pressing Shift-F7, and then 4, your job list will display this order.

```
03/01/87  10:46              Directory C:\WP2\*.*
Document Size:          0                    Free Disk Space:   1826816

   . <CURRENT>    <DIR>              .. <PARENT>    <DIR>
   REVISED .      <DIR>  02/22/87 10:07    ALTB   .MAC       6  10/17/86 15:55
   ALTC   .MAC        5  02/16/87 22:23    ALTF   .MAC       7  02/16/87 22:28
   ALTP   .MAC        2  09/29/86 11:15    ALTQ   .MAC       5  02/16/87 22:27
   ALTR   .MAC        7  02/16/87 22:33    ALTU   .MAC       4  02/14/87 16:15
   ALTW   .MAC       12  09/26/86 15:29    ALTX   .MAC       4  09/26/86 15:30
   ALTZ   .MAC        4  09/26/86 15:30    BACKUP .DOC    1578  02/23/87 13:21
   CHANGES .       5198  02/23/87 15:49    COL    .       2498  02/23/87 11:51
   CONVERT .EXE   45056  10/28/86 14:47    CURSOR .COM    1451  10/28/86 14:47
   DOSINFO .       2807  02/23/87 14:19    FIG114 .       1329  02/15/87 11:08
   FIG72  .         267  02/14/87 13:29    FIGURE4 .       483  02/23/87 12:17
   FNTTEST1.MAC     169  10/28/86 14:47    FONTTEST.MAC   3811  10/28/86 14:47
   IMCAP  .COM     5640  02/06/85 22:35    IMMGR  .EXE   38994  11/25/84 20:52
   LEX    .WP    290310  02/19/87 09:30    LOTUS  .WBK   60508  02/25/87 17:07
   MAC    .MEX     6419  10/28/86 14:47    MSWORD .WBK  153540  02/20/87 19:41
   SAMPLE2 .       1151  02/24/87 16:27    SPECIAL .      2783  02/23/87 09:06
   SPELL  .EXE   52592  10/20/86 15:50    TESTFILE.       2807  02/23/87 14:19
   TH     .WP   362303  10/20/86 15:58    UB     .MAC      10  02/14/87 15:45
   WORDCONC.       2719  02/20/87 18:54    WP     .EXE  265098  02/14/87 20:15

   1 Retrieve; 2 Delete; 3 Rename; 4 Print; 5 Text In;
   6 Look; 7 Change Directory; 8 Copy; 9 Word Search; 0 Exit: 6
```

Figure 8.3: *The List Files screen*

Printing by Block

As you learned above, the Print Key (Shift-F7) allows you to print an individual page or an entire document, but nothing in between. The two methods of printing from disk can print the whole document or a range of pages that you specify. When you want to print a portion of a document that does not fit into page units, you can mark the section with the Block Key, then print it. Since we've already covered this subject in Chapter 4, "Performing Block Operations," we'll limit this discussion to a brief review. To print a block, follow these steps:

1. Move the cursor to the beginning of the section you want printed and press Block (Alt-F4). You will see a flashing *Block on* message in the lower left corner of the screen.

2. Move the cursor to the end of the section you wish to print. The entire block will appear highlighted on the screen (the Block on message will still be visible).

3. The next step is to press the Print Key (Shift-F7). A prompt will appear on the Status line asking if you wish to print the block, so press Y. A message will briefly appear on the Status line, * *Please wait* *, then the block will be printed.

4. Once the printer starts working, you can press F1 to cancel Block mode and continue editing without stopping the print operation.

The Print Screen Key

If you want a "quick and dirty" printout, use the Print Screen Key (Shift-PrtSc). This method will print the text that is currently visible on your screen as though it were taking a picture of it and sending it to your printer. Note that the Status line and any prompt lines that may be on your screen when you press these keys will also be printed, which may be acceptable for rough drafts but never for your final work.

Typewriter Mode

Even though the typical business office is well stocked with word processors, that old white elephant known as the typewriter can still be found on many desks, where it is occasionally used for odd jobs such as envelopes, loan applications and other printed forms that do not lend themselves well to a standard word processor. However, WordPerfect's Type-thru feature may convince you to abandon this quaint mechanism once and for all, because Type-thru effectively converts your computer and printer into a typewriter and prints text immediately onto a sheet of paper while you are typing it. Type-thru can be used to type character by character or line by line. Either way, it's a convenient and readily accessible feature.

There are several printers, however, that cannot use Type-thru, including the Cannon Laser printer and the Hewlett Packard LaserJet. Others can use it but are limited to the line-by-line typing method, including the Brother HR1, the Epson LQ-1500, the Epson RX-80, the Texas Instruments 855, the Okidata 84 Microline, and the MPI Printmate.

You can use Type-thru to type an envelope or form even if you are already working on both document editing screens (Doc 1 and Doc 2). Whatever you do in typewriter mode will only affect the sheet of paper in your printer and, as with a typewriter, once you have finished typing, it is forgotten. In other words, the text that has been typed is not retained in memory or in a disk file.

Line Type-thru

To use Type-thru, press Print (Shift-F7) and select option 5. This prompt then appears, asking you to select one of the two methods:

Type-thru printing: 1 by line; 2 by character: 0

If you select option 1, by line, you will see the screen shown in Figure 8.4.

The next step is to position your paper in the printer so the printhead is placed on the first line to be printed, just as you would in a typewriter, then type the first line of text. If you want the text printed to the right, as in addressing an envelope, press the Spacebar to move the cursor over before typing the text. As soon as you press Return (or "Enter," as it is called on this screen), the line will be printed and a carriage return signal will be sent to the printer, moving the printhead to the next line.

If you make a mistake before you press Return, you can move the cursor back and fix it, but cursor movement methods are limited compared to those in normal Edit mode. The arrow keys on the numeric keypad can be used to move the cursor right or left one position at a time, and Home with the → or ← keys can be used to move to the beginning or end of a

—

Line Type-thru Printing

Function Key	Action
Move	Retrieve the previous line for editing
Print Format	Do a printer command
Enter	Print the line
Exit/Cancel	Exit without printing

Figure 8.4: *The Line Type-thru screen*

line. Press Return when you are done editing; the cursor does not have to be at the end of the line. According to the manual, if you press the ↑ or ↓, the printhead will move up or down a line on your sheet of paper (don't press Return), but on some printers, ↑ does not work. Pressing Return by itself will also move the paper down by a line.

As the screen indicates, the Move Key (Ctrl-F4) can be used to place a copy of the previous line on the current line, so that you can use it over again, either without change or in an edited form.

When using Type-thru, the Print Format feature permits you to send a special command to your printer in order to change the print style. For instance, you may want to switch your dot matrix printer to condensed mode, in order to fit more characters on the line. To do this, find the appropriate code in your printer manual, press the Print Format Key (Ctrl-F8) and type the appropriate printer code in response to this prompt that appears on the screen:

Cmnd:

Using Type-thru, you can type up to 250 characters on a single line. The text will not word wrap; the screen just "pans" to the right on the same line to keep the cursor in view. However, when you press Return the printer will print only as much as it can fit on a line (on a wide printer this can be a large number). If it runs out of space you see this error message:

Printer is not accepting characters. Press EXIT or
Cancel to quit or fix the printer and then press any
other key to continue.

When this happens, press Exit (F7) or Cancel (F1) and start over. When the screen starts to "pan," you have typed 80 characters. If you are unsure how many characters will fit on a line on your form, just try it out if you have a spare. If you don't, measure the line with a ruler and draw a line of the same width on a piece of scratch paper, then practice by typing on the scratch paper and counting the characters.

Character Type-thru

As you have learned, Line Type-thru has one important advantage over the character-by-character method: you have a chance to correct any typing errors on screen before you press the Return key and send the line to the printer. By contrast, the Character Type-thru method sends each character to the printer as soon as it is typed, so if you make a mistake it can ruin your form. On the other hand, you do get immediate feedback on paper and more of a typewriter feel.

To use Character Type-thru, follow the same steps outlined above, except that you press selection 2, by character, after pressing Shift-F7 and 5. The screen illustrated in Figure 8.5 will then appear.

Note that although the titles are different, the Line Type-thru screen (Figure 8.4) and the Character Type-thru screen (Figure 8.5) are otherwise identical.

As soon as you type a character, it will be printed on the paper at the printhead position (assuming your printer is capable of using this feature). Remember that you will not be able to change it after typing it. After printing one or more characters, you can clear them from the screen by using the Delete EOP Key, (Ctrl-PgDn). If you are finished typing, press either Cancel (F1) or Exit (F7).

Printer Control

If you have read the preceding sections, you are already familiar with three of the six options on the Print Key (Shift-F7): printing full text (1), printing by page (2), and Type-thru printing (5). Most of the remaining options control the printer itself, allowing you to specify the number of copies to be printed, the order in which documents will be printed, the specific printer to be used for each print job, and so on.

As mentioned earlier in this chapter, when you press option 4, Printer Control, you see the Printer Control screen illustrated in Figure 8.1. This screen is among WordPerfect's most important and useful ones, and it is likely that you will be using it frequently. It is divided into three major sections, one that controls printing and two that provide information about the current status of the printer and the documents waiting in line to be printed.

```
 -




Character Type-thru Printing

Function Key      Action

Move              Retrieve the previous line for editing
Print Format      Do a printer command
Enter             Print the line
Exit/Cancel       Exit without printing
```

Figure 8.5: *The Character Type-thru screen*

Let's begin by examining the first section, the three numbered selections on the top left side of the screen:

1 - Select Print Options
2 - Display Printers and Fonts
3 - Select Printers

We'll start at the bottom of the list and work our way up to the top.

Select Printers

Option 3, Select printers, is used to install your printer(s) for use with WordPerfect. As of this writing, the program is able to fully support 179 models of printers, and partially support 69 others. If you have not already set up your printer, turn to Appendix A, which covers printer installation in detail.

Display Printers and Fonts

You can verify that your printers have been set up correctly by selecting option 2, Display Printers and Fonts. When you do, you will see a list of available fonts for each printer you have installed, as shown in Figure 8.6.

As you can see, WordPerfect permits the use of up to eight different fonts per printer. If you are using a dot matrix printer and a variety of fonts is listed on this display, one way to find out what each font will look like is to type and print a line of text for each of the different fonts, changing the fonts before typing each line. You can do this all in one document, and save it for future reference. The Print Format Key is used to change the fonts, so you will learn more about fonts in the section of this chapter that covers option 1 on the Print Format Key: pitch and font.

Select Print Options

The first option (Select Print Options) on the Printer Control screen calls up the screen illustrated in Figure 8.7.

```
1:  HP LaserJet Series II       Continuous

       1 IBM Graphics           2 IBM Graphics
       3 IBM Graphics           4 IBM Graphics
       5 IBM Graphics           6 IBM Graphics
       7 IBM Graphics           8 IBM Graphics

2:  LaserJt Reg,+,500+ A: CourierContinuous

       1 LaserJet Rmn 8         2 LaserJet Rmn 8
       3 LaserJet Rmn 8         4 LaserJet Rmn 8
       5 LaserJet Rmn 8         6 LaserJet+ Graph
       7 LaserJet+ Box          8 LaserJet- Box

3:  LaserJt+,500+ Soft AC: Tms P Continuous

       1 HP AD TmsRmn10R        2 HP AD TmsRmn10I
       3 HP AD TmsRmn6R         4 HP AD TmsRmn8R
       5 HP AD TmsRmn8I         6 HP AD TmsRmn12R
       7 HP AD TmsRmn18B        8 HP AD TmsRmn30B




Press any key to continue_
```

Figure 8.6: *Displaying printers and fonts*

```
Select Print Options

      1 - Printer Number            1

      2 - Number of Copies          1

      3 - Binding Width (1/10 in.)  0










Selection: 0
```

Figure 8.7: *The Select Print Options screen*

Printer Number

If you are using more than one printer, this section will teach you how to change printers for one or more print jobs. Unless you tell it otherwise, the program will assume that you want to use printer 1, the first one on your list. (If you need help with printer installation, consult Appendix A.)

To change printers, select option 1, Printer Number, and enter the number of the printer you wish to use, then press Return. When you do this, the program will continue to use this printer until you change it again or exit from WordPerfect. The next time you start the program it will use the default printer, printer number 1.

Do not use this option if you are using the Full Text or Page option on the Print Key (Shift-F7) to print a document, and want to switch printers on a one-time basis. Instead, select option 3 (Options) from the Print Key menu (Shift-F7) and you will see a screen exactly like the one in Figure 8.7, except for a line at the top describing it as a temporary change. This screen is shown in Figure 8.8.

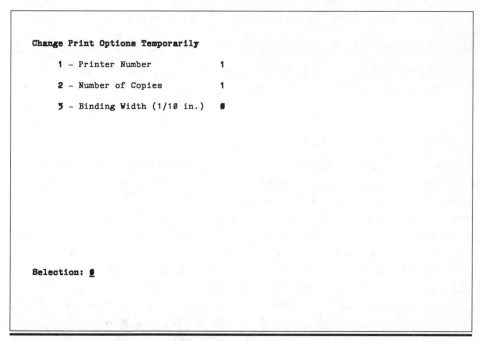

Figure 8.8: *The screen used to change print options temporarily*

Remember that as soon as the current document is printed, WordPerfect will revert to using the default printer.

Number of Copies

Option 2 (Number of Copies) on the Select Print Options screen is used to produce multiple copies of a document. To use it, just press 2, enter the number of copies you want the program to print, then press Return. The new number of copies will remain in effect for the rest of the session unless you change it again. As with the printer number option, you can use option 3 on the Print Key (Shift-F7) to change the number of copies just for one print job.

Binding Width

Option 3 on both the Select Print Options and the Change Print Options Temporarily screens is useful for printing two-sided documents that are to be bound, for it shifts the text to the left on even-numbered pages and to the right on odd-numbered pages. As you can see on the screen, you specify the binding width in tenths of an inch, so if you want the program to leave one extra inch for binding, enter 10 in response to this prompt:

Binding Width (1/10 in.)   0

If the document is to be printed on one side only, you can do the same thing by simply adding an inch to the left margin instead.

Controlling Print Jobs

When you ask WordPerfect to print a document using any of the methods described above, the program assigns a job number to the task and places a description of it in the Job List at the bottom of the Printer Control screen (see Figure 8.1). The description will remain there and in a special printer queue file on the disk until the document has been printed, so you will always know what your printer is doing.

If you ask the program to print more than one document at a time, it will assign sequential numbers to them, and line them up in a print queue to await their turn at the printer. Once a document has been placed on the list, you can continue to edit it or another document while the printer is working. However, your printer may slow down or stop while you are performing operations that access the disk, such as moving the cursor to the top of a long document or saving a document.

Figure 8.9 shows a Printer Control screen with three jobs on the list. This screen shows that Job 1, the file named CH6, is currently printing. As you can see, it appears both on the Job List at the bottom of the screen and under the Current Job heading, next to the Job Number prompt. The Job Status message confirms that Job 1 is now printing.

After Job 1 is finished, Job 2 will begin and the file named CH5 will be printed. When this is done, Job 3 will be printed. Notice that it is described as "screen," meaning it is the document now appearing on the editing screen. It was sent to the printer by pressing the Print Key and selecting option 1, Full Text. The Job List also provides details about the printer number and paper handling method (continuous, hand fed, or sheet feeder) to be used in each job number. WordPerfect will continue to assign job numbers in sequential numeric order until you exit from the program.

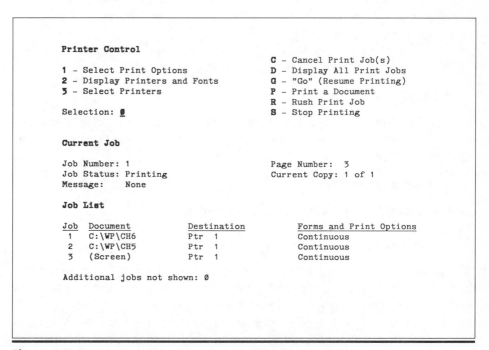

```
Printer Control
                                   C - Cancel Print Job(s)
1 - Select Print Options           D - Display All Print Jobs
2 - Display Printers and Fonts     G - "Go" (Resume Printing)
3 - Select Printers                P - Print a Document
                                   R - Rush Print Job
Selection: 0                       S - Stop Printing



Current Job

Job Number: 1                      Page Number:  3
Job Status: Printing               Current Copy: 1 of 1
Message:    None

Job List

Job   Document           Destination      Forms and Print Options
 1    C:\WP\CH6          Ptr  1           Continuous
 2    C:\WP\CH5          Ptr  1           Continuous
 3    (Screen)           Ptr  1           Continuous

Additional jobs not shown: 0
```

Figure 8.9: *A job list with three documents waiting to be printed*

Look again at the Current Job section. The right side informs you that the printer is now printing page 3 of the document, and that only one copy will be printed.

The message line, which says "None" on the screen in Figure 8.9, is reserved for error messages. We will see an example in the next section.

Stopping and/or Cancelling Print Jobs

If you need to interrupt the printer temporarily, press S—the last of the six options offered at the top right of the screen for controlling print jobs. S will immediately stop the printer, and cause it to pause until you press G.

The Job Status line indicates that the printer is

> Waiting for a "Go"

and the message explains what to do:

> Fix Printer – – Reset top of form – – Press "G" to continue

If you press G, the printer will start printing the document from the beginning, but it will not advance the paper to start on a new page. This is why the message "reset top of form" appears, to remind you to advance the paper to the appropriate position.

If you wish to cancel the print job altogether, press C. You will then see this message under the Selection prompt:

> Cancel which job? (∗ = All Jobs)

and you can enter either a single job number or an asterisk to cancel all of them. If you enter an asterisk, you will see the message shown in Figure 8.10:

> Cancel all print jobs? (Y/N) N

Press Y to cancel all printing, then G to continue.

The Rush Print Job Option

Command R, Rush Print Job, can be used to send a job to the beginning of the list and print it immediately. This is helpful when you are printing a long list of documents and suddenly discover that one is urgently needed. Rather than cancel all the print jobs and start over, you can use the Rush Print Job feature to print it either immediately or right after the current document is finished printing.

When you press R, a prompt will appear asking which job to rush. After you enter the number from the job list, another prompt will appear asking if you wish to interrupt the current job. If you type Y and press Return in response to the prompt:

Completing page, press ENTER to interrupt job immediately

then insert new paper in your printer and type G for go, the printer will stop printing the current document and start printing the rush job, resuming the current one after that. It starts the current job over at the top of the page it was printing when stopped, so it will be correctly realigned. If you type N, the printer will not print the rush job until the current document is finished.

Display All Print Jobs

Since the Job List at the bottom of the screen can only display three print jobs, command D, Display all Print Jobs, allows you to view any others. Notice the message at the bottom of the Printer Control screen:

Additional jobs not shown: 0

```
Printer Control
                                C - Cancel Print Job(s)
                                D - Display All Print Jobs
1 - Select Print Options        G - "Go" (Resume Printing)
2 - Display Printers and Fonts  P - Print a Document
3 - Select Printers             R - Rush Print Job
                                S - Stop Printing
Selection: C
Cancel all print jobs? (Y/N) N

Current Job

Job Number: 1                   Page Number:  4
Job Status: Waiting for a "Go"    Current Copy: 1 of 1
Message:    Fix printer--Reset top of form--Press "G" to continue

Job List

Job  Document          Destination      Forms and Print Options
 1   C:\WP\CH6         Ptr  1           Continuous
 2   C:\WP\CH5         Ptr  1           Continuous
 3   (Screen)          Ptr  1           Continuous

Additional jobs not shown: 0
```

Figure 8.10: *The current job listing after interrupting the printer*

If a number other than 0 appears here, use the D command to inquire about the remaining jobs. You will see a screen resembling Figure 8.11.

The Print Format Key

The Print Format Key (Ctrl-F8) is used primarily for stylistic changes such as pitch, font, underline style, justification and proportional spacing. These commands affect only the printed version of your documents, but they all insert formatting codes that are visible on the Reveal Codes screen. When you press Ctrl-F8, you will see the screen illustrated in Figure 8.12.

Pitch and Font

Option 1 on the Print Format Key is used to change the pitch and font at the printer. Pitch is the type size measured in the number of characters per

```
                              Job List

        Job   Document           Destination       Forms and Print Options
         7    C:\WP\CH1          Ptr  1            Continuous
         8    C:\WP\CH3          Ptr  1            Continuous
         9    C:\WP\CH4          Ptr  1            Continuous
        10    C:\WP\CH5          Ptr  1            Continuous

















        Press any key to continue_
```

Figure 8.11: *The additional job list screen*

inch; the one most commonly used is 10 characters per inch. Font is the type style, such as Courier, Letter Gothic, and Orator. The prompt lines shown in this book are printed in a different font from the main text. To change fonts on a letter quality printer, you also have to switch the print wheel or thimble. WordPerfect controls all pitch settings from this screen. Most dot matrix printers carry internal programs for a variety of fonts, while most laser printers supply fonts on special cartridges or disks.

Several different files are supplied on the WordPerfect Learning diskette, PRINTER.TST, PRINTER2.TST, PS.TST, and FONT.TST, to help you determine the fonts, pitches, and special features your printer can produce with WordPerfect. PRINTER.TST can be used to print features such as superscripts and subscripts, overstrike, line numbering, underlining, strikeout, tab aligning and column centering, as well as several different fonts and pitches. PRINTER2.TST prints 4 lines for each of the 8 possible fonts showing how the font looks in each of the following pitches: 10, 12, 15, and 13* (the asterisk is for proportional spacing), as well as a series of line drawings in the 8 different fonts. PS.TST is a test of proportional spacing; it

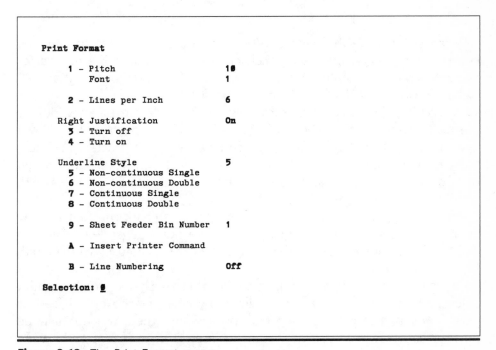

Figure 8.12: *The Print Format screen*

will help you determine the pitch you should be using to obtain proportionally spaced output. To use PRINTER.TST, PRINTER2.TST, or PS.TST, just retrieve the file to the editing screen, select the printer number of the printer you wish to test (Shift F7,3,1) and use the Print Key (Shift F7, 1) to print it. FONT.TST shows how all characters in a selected font will appear when printed, as well as their corresponding ASCII values. To use it, retrieve the file, change the font using the Print Format Key (as described below), change the print wheel if you are using a letter quality printer, then print the file.

Changing Fonts and Pitch

WordPerfect's defaults are 10 pitch and font 1. To change these, use the Print Format Key (Ctrl-F8) and select option 1. (Sometimes you have to change the pitch and font together, so consult your printer manual for specific instructions.) This procedure will insert a formatting code such as this one, which shows that the pitch and font were changed to 12 and 5 respectively:

[Font Change:12,5]

When you change the pitch and/or font, you usually have to alter the margin settings as well, because pitch changes always alter the number of characters on a line. With 12 pitch, you must set the margins to 12 and 89 to have the equivalent of the 10 pitch default (10,74).

To calculate the margins for other pitches, multiply the paper width by the pitch. Thus, a paper width of 8½ inches times a pitch of 15 yields a total of 127.5 characters per page. Since there are 15 characters per inch, the left margin must be set at 15 to equal 1 inch, and the right margin must be set at 112 (you cannot set margins in increments of .5) to leave 15 blank spaces at the right.

On many dot matrix printers, including Epsons, a change in font actually involves a change in pitch as well; the two are not independent. The new "font" is of a different size so you must be sure to adjust WordPerfect's pitch setting accordingly.

On letter-quality printers, you may be able to change fonts without adjusting WordPerfect's font setting, simply by changing the print wheel or thimble. As long as you have the right pitch setting, there will normally be no problem. However, you may want to insert a change font code when you are going to change print elements within the same document, because when the code is reached, printing will pause to allow you to change print elements.

Lines Per Inch

WordPerfect provides option 2, Lines per inch, on the Print Format Key so that you can change the number of lines per vertical inch to 8 (the default is 6). (If you select a large font that requires lines larger than 6 per inch, WordPerfect will adjust the line size automatically.)

When you change to 8 lines per inch, you must remember to change the number of text lines per page to accommodate the smaller lines. To maintain a 1 inch top and bottom margin on letter size paper, use the Page Lenth option on the Page Format key (Alt-F8). Leave the form length at 66 (it must always be set to 6 lines per inch) and change the number of text lines to 72. Since the paper is 11 inches long, 88 lines are available (11 x 8). 72 can be used for text, and 16 (2 inches) will be left for the top and bottom margins. Remember that if you change the top margin setting (using option 5 on the Page Format key), you must change the number of text lines again.

Right Justification

Right Justification produces an even right margin in the printed version of your document, and it is WordPerfect's default setting. Although text on screen appears to be uneven, it will always be justified when printed unless you use option 3 on the Print Format Key to turn justification off. When it is off, the right margins will be ragged, just like margins produced by typewriters.

WordPerfect creates even right margins by filling out short lines with blank space between words, sometimes resulting in large gaps between words (especially if you are not using hyphenation). If you find this un- attractive, turn off Right Justification by selecting option 3 from the Print Format Key. When you do this, the following code will be inserted into your document (visible only on the Reveal Codes screen):

[Rt Just Off].

If you prefer to turn off Right Justification permanently, you can change the default setting in your program. Appendix A explains this process, in the section that covers the WordPerfect Set-up menu.

Proportional Spacing

If your printer supports proportional spacing, you can use option 1, Pitch and Font, to take advantage of this professional technique. Proportional spacing produces some characters that are actually wider than others. The letter M, for example, will be wider than the letter I. To use proportional spacing, change the font and pitch settings, and type an asterisk after the pitch number. (Check your printer manual and option 2—Display Printers and Fonts on the Printer Control screen for the appropriate pitch and font for proportional spacing.)

Underline Style

When you use Underline, WordPerfect by default uses a style of underlining that creates a single (rather than double) line under the word or block of text and is *non-continuous,* meaning it does not underline the space between tabs. (If you are typing with Underline on and press either the Tab or Indent Key, underlining will stop and won't start again until you start typing text.) You can change this from the default style to either continuous single underlining (which does underline when you tab) or to double underlining, which places two lines under the text. Double underlining can also be used in either the continuous or non-continuous style. You choose an underlining style by using options 5 through 8 on the Print Format Key. The examples below show the difference between the continuous and non-continuous styles.

Non-continuous single underline style -   with tabs
Continuous single underline style -   with tabs

When you change the style, WordPerfect places the following code in your document:

[Undrl Style:*n*].

where *n* is the number of the style (5 through 8) you have chosen from the list on the Print Format Key.

Sheet Feeder Bin Number

Option 9, Sheet Feeder Bin Number, on the Print Format Key is useful if you have two sheet feeders attached to your printer, one for letter-size paper and one for legal-size paper. The default bin is 1, you can enter any number from 1 to 7. When you change it, the printer will use paper from the other bin. Like most other options on this screen, this action will insert a formatting code into your document like this one:

[Bin#:2]

You can also use the two bins to hold letterhead paper (for the first page of a letter) and plain paper (for the remaining pages).

Insert Printer Command

Option A, Insert Printer Command, allows you to send a special code to your printer to change the print style or otherwise alter the printer settings. When you select it, you will see this message on the prompt line:

Cmnd:

You then insert your printer command. This is used with dot matrix or laser printers, most of which can accept a wide variety of codes to take advantage of such features as enlarged print, condensed print, and graphics characters. For example, Esc M produces elite type on my Epson printer, so I enter this code in response to the *Cmnd:* prompt:

<27>M

(Esc is always represented by <27>). The WordPerfect formatting code that will appear on your Reveal Codes screen after you insert a special printer command will resemble this one:

[Cmnd:*n*]

where *n* is your specific printer code.

Print Preview

As you know, WordPerfect has certain features that cannot be viewed on screen and appear only when printed. Among them are right justification; proportional spacing; left, right, top and bottom margins; italics and other special print fonts; headers and footers; endnotes and footnotes; page numbers, and subscripts and superscripts. However, by using the Print Preview feature you can obtain a display that is actually much closer to the printed version and save yourself some time and paper. Not only will the left, right, top, and bottom margins be accurately portrayed in the preview document, but any headers, footers, page numbers, footnotes, and endnotes will also be included. Right justification is shown unless proportional spacing is being used.

To use the feature, make sure the file you want to preview is on the screen, then press the Print Key (Shift-F7) and select option 6 Preview. The next prompt

Preview: 1 Document; 2 Page: 0

gives you the choice of viewing the entire document (1) or limiting your preview to the page the cursor is currently on (2). If your document is quite long, be forewarned that it may take quite a while for the program to redraw the document. Until it is finished, you will be staring at the * Please wait * message for what may become an uncomfortable stretch of time (WordPerfect usually responds so fast to our commands!).

When the preview document appears, notice the *Doc 3* message on the Status line, as shown in Figure 8.13. Doc 3 is a temporary work area designed for the preview feature. You cannot edit while in this area, but you can move the cursor around, use the Search feature (F2 or Shift-F2), and use the Switch Key (Shift-F3, covered in Chapter 12) to switch back and forth between the actual document and the preview version.

When you have seen enough, you can press the Exit Key (F7) to return to edit mode. Once you do this, you can only return to Preview mode by using the Preview command all over again (press Shift-F7, 6, and 1 or 2).

Summary

As you have learned, WordPerfect's printing operations are complex and powerful. You can choose from among several different methods of printing and can vary many features. You can send a list of documents to the printer, interrupt or change their order, or cancel one or more jobs. Printing does not tie up your computer, and you can proceed to work on any document almost immediately after issuing a print command.

```
        —    Mr. William B. Taylor, Service Manager
                 ABC Parts, Inc.
                 423 Main Street
                 Santa Ana, CA 90124


                              URGENT NOTICE

                 Dear Mr. Taylor:

                     As I  told you  on the phone this morning, there was an

                 apparent  misunderstanding  in  the    order  we    placed  on

                 Thursday, November 7, and we received the wrong parts.

                     As you  will see  on the  enclosed copy of our purchase

                 order, we requested a replacement interface and cable  for a

                 PC 110  and were  instead sent  parts for a PC 110B. We were

    PREVIEW                                   Doc 3  Pg 1  Ln 14     Pos 10
```

Figure 8.13: *Print Preview*

WordPerfect supports over 248 printers, but in case yours is not one of them, a separate printer program has been included on the WordPerfect Learning diskette to help you define your printer and fonts. A booklet is also supplied with the 4.2 manual called *Defining a Printer Driver*. I do not recommend that you attempt to customize your printer unless you are technically inclined.

WordPerfect provides two print Keys, Print (Shift-F7) and Print Format (Ctrl-F8). The Print Key controls printing operations while the Print Format Key controls several formatting features such as underlining style, justification, pitch, and font.

Option 1 on the Print Key, Full Text, will print the entire document that is on the editing screen. Option 2, Page, will print the page on which the cursor is currently located.

WordPerfect provides two methods of printing a file from disk. The first is to select option P, Print a Document, from the Printer Control screen. The second is to use the List Files Key (F5) and select a file for printing from the directory listing. The List Files method is helpful if you have forgotten the exact spelling of the file name.

You can print a designated section of text from the edit screen by marking the section with the Block Key (Alt-F4), then pressing the Print Key (Shift-F7).

WordPerfect's Type-thru feature converts your printer to typewriter mode and text is printed as soon as you type it. This feature is useful for envelopes, invoices, and other forms that are not suitable for a word processor. Type-thru can be used to type on a character-by-character basis or line by line.

The Printer Control screen, option 4 on the Print Key, has three major functions: to control printing features such as installation, printer number selection, and number of copies to be printed; to provide information about the printer's current status; and to display the job list, which provides information about documents that are waiting to be printed.

To change the printer number, use option 1 on the Printer Control screen. To change the number of copies, select option 2. To change the binding width, select option 3. If you only want to change these options on a one-time basis, use option 3 Change Options, on the Print Key.

WordPerfect assigns a job number to each print job and places a description of it on a list at the bottom of the Printer Control screen. Once a document has been placed on this list, you can resume editing. To change the order of this list, use the Rush Job option, or the Cancel Print Job(s) option on the Printer Control screen.

The Current Job section of the Printer Control screen displays information about the document currently being printed, such as the number of the page being printed and the number of copies you have requested. If you detect a problem, you can use option S, Stop Printing, to temporarily stop the printer.

The Print Format Key allows you to change the pitch, font, underline style, and sheet feeder bin number; to turn Justification on or off, or switch to proportional spacing; to turn on Line Numbering; and to insert a printer command that sends formatting codes to your printer, so you can change the print style anywhere in your document.

The Print Preview option on the Print Key (Shift-F7,6) allows you to view the document on a special screen with features that otherwise appear only in the printed version, including margins, headers, footers, page numbers, footnotes, and endnotes. Right justification appears unless proportional spacing is being used.

CHAPTER 9 KEYSTROKE SUMMARY:

The Search Key—find text to be included in list, index, or table of contents

The Block Key—highlight text to be included in list, index, or table of contents

The Mark Text Key—display options for marking text, defining, and generating list, index, or table of contents

REFERENCE TOOLS

WORDPERFECT ENJOYS GREAT POPULARITY among professional writers, for it is a virtual toolbox that can simplify a variety of their projects. This chapter will cover several of its most important techniques including those used for making outlines, lists, indexes, tables of contents, and tables of authorities.

Even though you may not be a professional writer, you'll want to know about the features covered in this chapter. Although they are most commonly used in books, dissertations, and other lengthy reports, they can also serve as a wonderful method of organizing ideas and thoughts. In fact, once you find out how easy it is to use these features, they may become your favorite tools.

The procedures used to create a list, index, or table of contents, are similar and require three main steps:

A. using the Mark Text Key to designate the text from the document that is to be included

B. defining the numbering style to be used and

C. generating the structure

Text can be marked anytime, either as you create the document, or after it is written and thoroughly edited. Either way, the process is not entirely automatic and requires some careful planning.

Lists

Mastering WordPerfect includes a multiplicity of illustrations, designed to clarify step-by-step instructions and exemplify major problems and issues. The illustrations were created and incorporated into the chapters as they were being written, but once the editing process began and figures were added, changed, or deleted by my proficient editors, it was frequently necessary to reorganize and renumber the figures, so WordPerfect's list creation feature became indispensable. By providing a list of illustrations and their page locations that could be easily updated each time changes were made, it spared me hours of work.

WordPerfect permits you to keep as many as five different lists at one time, so you can have separate tables for figures, graphs, maps, charts, and whatever else you want to enumerate. However, you can include a given word or phrase in only one list, so all of the five potential lists must be mutually exclusive. (You can, however, get around this by creating separate copies of the document and using different copies to mark and generate different lists.) There is no limit on the length of the words or phrases that can be included.

The lists of figures that I kept while working on this book were created after completing the manuscript of each chapter. I used WordPerfect's Search feature to locate each illustration in the text. If you're more organized, you can mark your items for inclusion as you write. The following section provides step-by-step instructions explaining how I created my list of figures for the first chapter, and I encourage you to practice using one of your own documents.

Creating a List

A. Marking the Items to Be Included in the List

The first process is to mark the items to be included in the list. To do this, follow these steps:

1. Use the Search Key (F2) to find the text to be included in the list. In this manuscript, I was searching for occurrences of the word *Figure*. (If you are creating the list as you type the document, skip this step.)

2. At each occurrence, use the Block Key (Alt-F4) to highlight the text to be included in the list. I blocked the number and title of each illustration, as shown below:

Figure 1.2: The Function Keys

Note that this procedure may also capture formatting codes such as Bold and Underline, so if you don't want them appearing in your final list, check the Reveal Codes screen before marking the block, and position your cursor accordingly.

3. With Block still on, press Alt-F5, the Mark Text Key. The following menu will appear:

Mark for 1 ToC; 2 List; 3 Redline; 4 Strikeout; 5 Index; 6 ToA:0

4. Select 2 List and this prompt will appear:

List #:

Since this was to be my first list, I entered the number

1

5. To verify that the text was correctly marked, you should then examine the Reveal Codes screen. Each marked phrase will be surrounded by a pair of formatting codes, designating the beginning and end of the marked block, as shown below:

[Mark:List,1]Figure 1.2: The Function keys[EndMark:List,1]

Note that the 1 inside the brackets refers to List 1. Repeat these five steps until you have marked each item you want in the list.

B. Defining the Style

The second process is to define the numbering style for the list. Be sure to move the cursor to the end of the document first, to guarantee that all marked text will be included in the list. Inserting a hard page break to set the list apart from the rest of the text is also recommended.

1. With the cursor at the end of the document, define the list by pressing the Mark Text Key (Alt-F5). You will see the following menu:

   1 Outline; 2 Para #; 3 Redline; 4 Short Form; 5 Index; 6 Other Options: 0

(Note the difference between this Mark Text menu and the one that appears with Block on.)

2. Now select option 6, Other Options. You will see the Other Mark Text Options screen illustrated in Figure 9.1.

```
Other Mark Text Options

        1 - Define Paragraph/Outline Numbering

        2 - Define Table of Contents

        3 - Define List

        4 - Define Table of Authorities

        5 - Define Index

        6 - Remove all Redline Markings and all Strikeout text from document

        7 - Edit Table of Authorities Full Form

        8 - Generate Tables and Index




    Selection: ▮
```

Figure 9.1: *The Other Mark Text Options screen*

3. Select option 3, Define List and enter the list number 1.

4. After you have selected the list number, the screen illustrated in Figure 9.2 will appear; you must select one of the five numbering styles.

Each of the styles is illustrated in Figure 9.3, which displays five copies of the list of figures in Chapter 1, each one using a different numbering style. I usually use option 5, which features a page number at the right margin, preceded by a row of dots called *leaders,* because they lead the eye from the item on the left to the matching page number on the right. Without the dots, mismatches can occur. (Note that the page numbers in the word-processed manuscript are different from those in the printed book.) After completing this step, the Reveal Codes screen should include this code:

[DefMark:List,1]

This is important because it marks the position where the list will be generated.

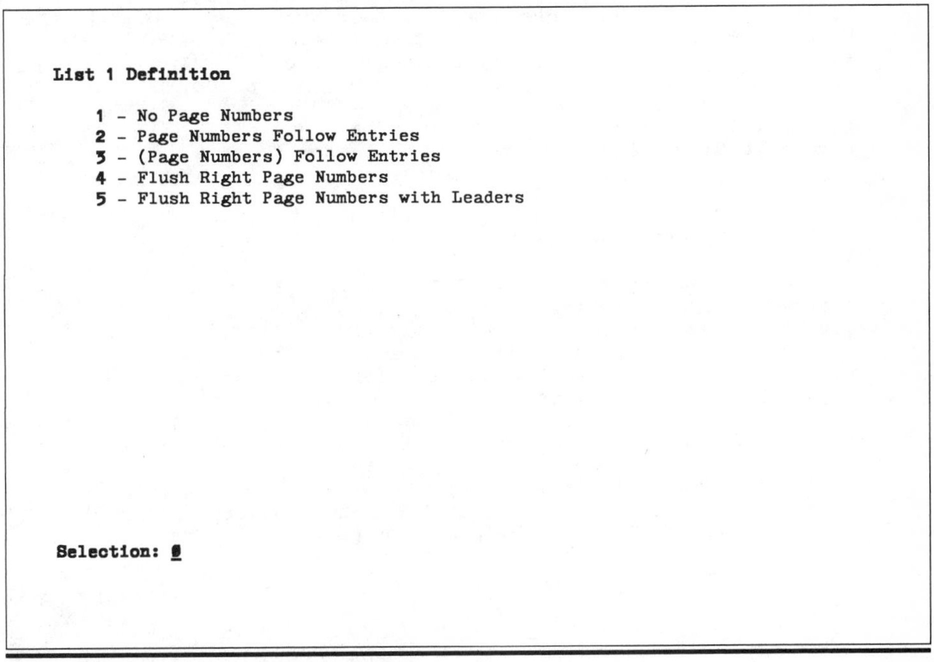

```
List 1 Definition

    1 - No Page Numbers
    2 - Page Numbers Follow Entries
    3 - (Page Numbers) Follow Entries
    4 - Flush Right Page Numbers
    5 - Flush Right Page Numbers with Leaders













    Selection: ▌
```

Figure 9.2: *The List Definition screen*

```
CHAPTER 1 ILLUSTRATIONS: STYLE 1

Figure 1.1: The Shift, Alt, and Ctrl keys
Figure 1.2: The function keys
Figure 1.3: The result of pressing Shift-F8
Figure 1.4: The Return, Caps Lock, and Num Lock keys
Figure 1.5: The Del, Backspace, and Left Arrow keys
Figure 1.6: The Ins (Insert) and Cancel Keys
Figure 1.7: The arrow keys on the numeric keypad
Figure 1.8: The Home, Page Up, Page Down, Screen Up, Screen
     Down, and End Keys
Figure 1.9: The Help screen
Figure 1.10: The Help screen for the letter S
Figure 1.11: The Exit Key Help screen


CHAPTER 1 ILLUSTRATIONS: STYLE 2

Figure 1.1: The Shift, Alt, and Ctrl keys    8
Figure 1.2: The function keys  9
Figure 1.3: The result of pressing Shift-F8   10
Figure 1.4: The Return, Caps Lock, and Num Lock keys  12
Figure 1.5: The Del, Backspace, and Left Arrow keys   16
Figure 1.6: The Ins (Insert) and Cancel Keys   17
Figure 1.7: The arrow keys on the numeric keypad   21
Figure 1.8: The Home, Page Up, Page Down, Screen Up, Screen
     Down, and End Keys         22
Figure 1.9: The Help screen  25
Figure 1.10: The Help screen for the letter S   26
Figure 1.11: The Exit Key Help screen   27


CHAPTER 1 ILLUSTRATIONS: STYLE 3

Figure 1.1: The Shift, Alt, and Ctrl keys   (8)
Figure 1.2: The function keys (9)
Figure 1.3: The result of pressing Shift-F8 (10)
Figure 1.4: The Return, Caps Lock, and Num Lock keys (12)
Figure 1.5: The Del, Backspace, and Left Arrow keys (16)
Figure 1.6: The Ins (Insert) and Cancel Keys (17)
Figure 1.7: The arrow keys on the numeric keypad (21)
Figure 1.8: The Home, Page Up, Page Down, Screen Up, Screen
     Down, and End Keys        (22)
Figure 1.9: The Help screen (25)
Figure 1.10: The Help screen for the letter S (26)
Figure 1.11: The Exit Key Help screen (27)
```

Figure 9.3: *The output: five different versions of the list of illustrations in Chapter 1*

```
CHAPTER 1 ILLUSTRATIONS: STYLE 4

Figure 1.1: The Shift, Alt, and Ctrl keys                  8
Figure 1.2: The function keys                              9
Figure 1.3: The result of pressing Shift-F8               10
Figure 1.4: The Return, Caps Lock, and Num Lock keys      12
Figure 1.5: The Del, Backspace, and Left Arrow keys       16
Figure 1.6: The Ins (Insert) and Cancel Keys              17
Figure 1.7: The arrow keys on the numeric keypad          21
Figure 1.8: The Home, Page Up, Page Down, Screen Up, Screen
    Down, and End Keys                                    22
Figure 1.9: The Help screen                               25
Figure 1.10: The Help screen for the letter S             26
Figure 1.11: The Exit Key Help screen                     27


CHAPTER 1 ILLUSTRATIONS: STYLE 5

Figure 1.1: The Shift, Alt, and Ctrl keys  . . . . . . . . . .    8
Figure 1.2: The function keys . . . . . . . . . . . . . . . .     9
Figure 1.3: The result of pressing Shift-F8 . . . . . . . . .    10
Figure 1.4: The Return, Caps Lock, and Num Lock keys . . . . .   12
Figure 1.5: The DHl, Backspace, and Left Arrow keys . . . . . .  16
Figure 1.6: The Ins (Insert) and Cancel Keys . . . . . . . . .   17
Figure 1.7: The arrow keys on the numeric keypad . . . . . . .   21
Figure 1.8: The Home, Page Up, Page Down, Screen Up, Screen
    Down, and End Keys      . . . . . . . . . . . . . . . . .    22
Figure 1.9: The Help screen . . . . . . . . . . . . . . . . .    25
Figure 1.10: The Help screen for the letter S . . . . . . . . .  26
Figure 1.11: The Exit Key Help screen . . . . . . . . . . . . .  27
```

Figure 9.3: *The output: five different versions of the list of illustrations in Chapter 1 (continued)*

C. Generating the List

The final process is actually to generate the list. To do this, press Mark Text (Alt-F5) and select option 6 (Other Options), then option 8, Generate Tables and Index. The following message will appear:

Existing tables, lists, and indexes will be replaced. Continue? (Y/N) Y

Since this is the first list you have created (and there are no old lists), the appropriate response is yes, so type:

Y or press Return

As the list is being generated, this message will appear:

Generation in progress: Counter: (*number*)

The process will take a minute or two, depending on the total number of items that have been marked for inclusion. After the list is completed, the following code will be added to the end of the list:

[EndDef]

Generating a List If Your Document Already Includes a List, Index, or Table of Contents

Your document may already include one or more lists or an index or table of contents that was previously generated. If you want to change it (or them)—either because the text in the document has been edited and differs from that in the one generated or because you want to redefine the numbering style—follow these instructions.

If you have changed the text in your document, the first step is to locate the old entries and delete or remark them if necessary with the Block and Mark Text Keys. The best way to proceed is to use the Search Key (F2) to locate each occurrence of a mark text code. Press F2 and the Mark Text Key (Alt-F5). You will see this menu:

1 List/Toc 2 Par# 3 Index 4 RedLn 5 StrkOut 6 Par#Def 7 DefMark 8 EndDef; 9 ToA: 0

Option 1 will locate the codes that mark text for a list or table of contents. When you select it, the search string will appear as follows on the Status line:

→ Srch: [Mark]

Press F2 or Esc to begin the search. When the cursor stops, press the Reveal Codes Key (Alt-F3) to see the code, which will appear to the left of the cursor. An entry for a list will be surrounded by a pair of codes:

[Mark:List,1]

and

[EndMark:List,1]

while an entry for a table of contents will be surrounded by

[Mark:ToC,1]

and

[EndMark:ToC,1]

If the edited text is correctly positioned between the codes, you will not have to remark it because, when the new list or table of contents is generated, everything that appears between the pair of codes will be included. If you need to remark the text or just want to exclude it from your new list or table of contents, delete the codes with the Backspace or Del key. You will see the prompt

Delete [Mark]? (Y/N) N

Press Y. If you are remarking it, press the Block and Mark Text Keys and select the appropriate options.

Once you have located and changed the entries (if needed) and added any new entries, move the cursor to the end of the document and select the Generate option from the Mark Text Key (Alt-F5, 6, 8). As the warning indicates, this procedure will replace any existing tables, lists, and indexes. However, the codes that define them remain intact during the procedure, so if your document includes an existing list, index, or table, it (or they) will be correctly regenerated along with the altered one whether or not any changes have been made to it (or them). Enter Y or press Return to begin generating.

Your revised list, table, or index and any existing one(s) will then be generated, completely replacing the old ones. Since the original definition codes are still in effect, they will use the same page numbering style and appear in the same location as the old ones.

Changing the Page Number Position

If you have not altered the text but just want to change the definition for page number position before regenerating, follow these instructions. As you know, the list is set off from the rest of the document by a [DefMark] code at the beginning and an [EndDef] code at the end. When you instruct WordPerfect to delete your old list, index, or table of contents by pressing Y after this prompt appears

Existing tables, lists, and indexes will be replaced. Continue? (Y/N): Y

the program regenerates the existing table, list, and/or index using the [DefMark] code you inserted when you defined a Table of Contents, List, Index, or Table of Authorities from the Other Mark Text Options Screen (options 2, 3, 4, or 5). In order to change the page-numbering style, you should delete the original [DefMark] code, or make sure that your cursor is placed in a position following the code before you select a new style. Deleting the code is the safest approach.

In either case, the easiest way to find the original code is to use WordPerfect's Search feature. To do this, press the Search Key (F2) followed by the Mark Text Key (Alt-F5). Then select option 7 [DefMark] from the menu and press F2 to start the search. When the cursor stops, you can delete it by pressing the Backspace key. When you do, you will see this prompt:

Delete [DefMark]? (Y/N) N

Type Y to delete it. Next, use the Other Mark Text Options screen to select a new page numbering style, then use the Generate option from the same screen to regenerate it using your new page numbering style.

Tables of Contents

Creating a table of contents is similar to creating a list, for it involves moving the cursor to each occurrence of the text you want included, blocking it, and inserting invisible codes with the Mark Text Key. However, you can only create one table of contents per document, so the operations differ slightly when the entries are marked. Instead of being asked which list to include the text in, you are asked to select the *level number* for each entry.

A table of contents can have up to five levels of entries, and each level will be indented one tab stop to the right of the last one. Figure 9.4 displays a table of contents with three levels. The first entry on level 1 is *Starting WordPerfect,* and the first entry on level 2 is *Starting WordPerfect on a Two Floppy Disk System.* There are several level 3 entries in the table: *The Default Drive, The Document Indicator, The Page Indicator, The Line Indicator, The Position Indicator, The WordPerfect Color Scheme,* and *The Caps Lock and Num Lock Indicators.* It's important to decide which level each entry should appear on before you begin marking them or you may end up deleting and reentering codes and regenerating the table several times. You can mark the entries as you type the document or you can wait until it is completed. Some writers feel they have a better overview after the text is complete; others prefer to specify the structure as they write. Whichever method you choose, the process is identical.

Starting WordPerfect   2
        Starting WordPerfect on a Two Floppy Disk System   2
                The Default Drive   3
        Starting WordPerfect on a Hard Disk   4

The WordPerfect Editing Screen   5
        The Status Line   5
                The Document Indicator   6
                The Page Indicator   7
                The Line Indicator   7
                The Position Indicator   7

The WordPerfect Keyboard   8
        Shift   8
        Alt and Ctrl   8
        The Function Keys   9
                The WordPerfect Template Color Scheme 11
        The Return Key 11
        Num Lock and Caps Lock 13
                The Caps Lock and Num Lock Indicators 14
        The Delete, Backspace and Left Arrow Keys 15
        Ins (Insert) 17
        Cancel and Undelete 18

Basic Cursor Movement 20
        Moving One Character at a Time 20
        Moving Word by Word 21
        Moving to the Beginning or End of a Line 22
        Page Up, Page Down, Screen Up, and Screen Down 22

Deleting Hidden Codes 23
        Unwanted Page Breaks 25

Getting Help 25

Deleting Larger Segments 27

Exiting from WordPerfect 28
        File Management and Overflow Files 28

Summary 31

Figure 9.4: *Chapter 1 table of contents*

The five numbering styles that can be used in a table of contents are the same as in a list: no page numbers, page numbers that follow the entries, page numbers in parentheses that follow the entries, flush right page numbers, and flush right page numbers with leaders. However, each level can have a different numbering style, as you will see.

Creating a Table of Contents

A. Marking the Items to Be Included in the Table of Contents

1. As in the case of making a list, find the text you want to include in the table of contents using Search (F2).

2. Using Alt-F4, block the desired text.

3. Next, with Block still on, press the Mark Text Key (Alt-F5). You will see the following menu:

> Mark for 1 ToC; 2 List; 3 Redline; 4 Strikeout; 5 Index; 6 ToA: 0

4. Select option 1, for table of contents. A prompt will then appear asking you to enter the level number for this particular entry, as shown below:

> ToC Level:

Enter the appropriate number (1–5) and press Return. Repeat these steps until all entries have been marked.

B. Defining the Style

To define the style for your table of contents,

1. Move the cursor to the end of the document and press Ctrl-Return, inserting a hard page break to separate the table from the rest of the document. You will probably want to type a heading for your table of contents at the top of the page.

2. Next, press the Mark Text Key and select option 6, Other Options, then select 2 Define Table of Contents from the Other Mark Text Options screen (shown in Figure 9.1).

3. Select option 2 Define Table of Contents and The Table of Contents Definition screen, as shown in Figure 9.5, will appear.

4. Use it to specify the total number of levels for the table, as well as the page number position (that is, the numbering style) for each level. Since I used three levels in my table, I responded to the first prompt as follows:

Numbers of levels in table of contents (1-5): 3

5. After you make the selection, this prompt will appear:

Display last level in wrapped format (Y/N) N

Wrapped format means that entries in the last (in my case, the third) level will be displayed next to each other, separated only by a semicolon, as shown in the partial table in Figure 9.6.

```
Table of Contents Definition

    Number of levels in table of contents (1-5): 0



                          Page Number Position
        Level 1
        Level 2
        Level 3
        Level 4
        Level 5


    Page Number Position
    1 - No Page Numbers
    2 - Page Number Follow Entries
    3 - (Page Numbers) follow Entries
    4 - Flush Right Page Numbers
    5 - Flush Right Page Numbers with Leaders
```

Figure 9.5: *The Table of Contents Definition screen*

```
The WordPerfect Editing Screen . . . . . . . . . . . . . . . .    5
    The Status Line . . . . . . . . . . . . . . . . . .         5
            The Document Indicator (6);  The Page Indicator (7);
            The Line Indicator (7); The Position Indicator (7)
```

Figure 9.6: *Partial table of contents with the third level in wrapped format*

In this example, the last level starts with the words *The Document Indicator* and ends with *The Position Indicator (4)*. Note that for page numbers on this level I used position option 3, (Page Numbers) Follow Entries. (When the last level is displayed in wrapped format, only options 1, 2, or 3 can be used for the page numbers position. WordPerfect won't accept 4 or 5 as an entry.) The same table was shown in Figure 9.4, where wrapped format was not used. As you are not going to use the wrapped format, type N and press Return.

6. The next step is to select the page number position for each level. Since you are not using wrapped format you may choose from among the five styles that were described and illustrated in Figure 9.3. WordPerfect's default for each level in the table of contents is option 5, the one that places page numbers at the right and connects them with dots. To accept this style, press Return for each level, otherwise select another style by typing the corresponding number. Remember that a different style *can* be used for each level. The table of contents is displayed in Figure 9.4. As you can see, a total of three levels are specified, and each level used the default page number position.

7. After you have selected the page number position, the screen disappears and you are returned to the editing screen. You can then check the Reveal Codes screen for the following code:

[DefMark:ToC,*n*]

Note that *n* corresponds to the number of levels you have selected.

C. Generating the Table of Contents

1. Now we're ready to produce the table of contents. Select option 6, then 8, Generate Tables and Indexes, from the Mark Text Key and the following message will appear:

Existing tables, lists, and indexes will be replaced. Continue? (Y/N): Y

Press Y or Return. (If there is insufficient RAM in your computer, you may also see a message asking you to clear the screen used for document 2.If this happens, use the Switch Key (Shift-F3) to move to the document 2 screen, save the document it contains, and exit from it.) The program will then begin generating your table of contents, and this message will appear:

Generation in progress: Counter: (number)

The process will take a minute or two, after which the table will appear in front of the cursor. If you used the same options, it will resemble Figure 9.4.

Indexes

As with lists and tables of contents, creating an index is not entirely an automatic process. Unless you use a concordance file, you must individually mark each occurrence of each entry you want in the index. Although this sounds like an enormous amount of work, it does not have to be if you plan carefully. For one thing, you can mark entries as you type them. For another, you won't have to use the Block Key except to mark phrases (more than one word). If you wait until after the document is completed to mark them, Word-Perfect's Macro feature can be used to expedite the task. WordPerfect macros are covered in Chapter 16.

Both headings and subheadings are permitted in an index, and each entry can include as many as 73 characters. Unlike lists and tables of contents, you do not have to use the exact words or phrases being marked in your document, but can type the entries separately, rewording them just for the index. Headings are automatically capitalized, unless you type them in lowercase (instead of using the wording in the document). Subheadings appear in lower-case, unless retyped separately in capital letters.

I strongly recommend that you spend time analyzing your document and carefully consider which words or phrases will be used as headings and subheadings before you start marking them. If a word or phrase is not spelled exactly the same way each time it is marked, it will appear as a new entry, rather than an additional page number next to the same entry. For example, Figure 9.7 shows two distinct headings, *Function key* and *Function keys,* that were obviously intended to be one heading. One way to avoid this duplication is to switch to document 2 and create a list of the correct spelling for each heading and subheading (a style sheet), and refer to it before you mark the entries.

Creating an Index

A. Marking the Text to Be Included in the Index

1. To designate a one-word entry for your index as you are typing the document, place the cursor anywhere in the word (or the blank space following it) and press the Mark Text Key (Alt-F5). The following menu will appear:

  1 Outline; 2 Para #; 3 Redline; 4 Short Form; 5 Index; 6 Other Options: 0

To index a section of text that includes more than one word, you will have to mark it first with the Block Key (Alt-F4), then press the Mark Text Key. This menu will appear:

  Mark for: 1 ToC; 2 List; 3 Redline; 4 Strikeout; 5 Index; 6 ToA: 0

2. Whichever method you are using, select option 5 Index. You will then see a prompt that asks for the index heading, followed by the word or phrase you indicated with the cursor or blocked. WordPerfect assumes this is what you wish to mark, so it is the default. For example, when I blocked the phrase *Function keys* and selected option 5 from the Mark Text Key, the prompt appeared as follows:

  Index Heading: Function Keys

```
            Carriage Return key 11
            Ctrl key   9
            Cursor  6
            Default Drive 3
            Delete
                 from cursor to end of line  28
                 to the end of a page  28
                 word  28
            Document Indicator  6
            Enter key  12
            Exit key  27, 28
            Function  10
            Function key  9, 10
            Function keys  9
            Function-key template 11
            Help key  25
            Line Indicator  7
            Num Lock key  13
                 and the position indicator  15
                 with Shift keys  14
            Overflow files  28
            Page Down key  22
            Page Indicator  7
            Page Up key  22
```

Figure 9.7: *A poorly planned index*

3. If this is the wording you want for the heading, press Return. Otherwise, type a different heading for this entry and press Return.

4. Next you will be prompted to enter a subheading:

Subheading:

If you accepted the default word or phrase as the heading (*Function keys* in step 2), nothing will appear after this prompt and you can simply type the subheading or press Return for no subheading. However, if you typed something else for the heading, the program will assume that you now want to use the default word or phrase as a subheading. You can accept this by pressing Return. To type a different subheading, press Del to erase the one now appearing after the prompt, then type a new one in its place.

5. Repeat these four steps until you have marked each item you want in the index. If you check the Reveal Codes screen, you will see that each

heading or subheading is marked with a code resembling this one:

[Index:Function keys]

where *Function keys* is the actual entry.

WordPerfect 4.2 allows you to mark entries contained in footnotes. To do this, use the edit option (2) on the Footnote Key (Ctrl-F7) and mark the text inside the footnote as described above.

B. Using a Concordance File

The Concordance feature was added to WordPerfect 4.2 to simplify the process of building an index. Rather than locating and marking each word or phrase individually throughout the document you are indexing, you can type a list of commonly used words and phrases, save it as a separate file, then instruct WordPerfect to use this concordance file when generating the index (Step D). When the index is completed, it will include entries individually marked (using the procedures described in Step A) as well as entries from the concordance file that have been matched in the document. Entries from the concordance file that are not located in the document will not appear in the index.

To create a concordance file, you simply type the list of common entries, then save the file. Although an individual entry can exceed one line, each separate entry must be followed by a [HRt] code (pressing the Return key inserts this code). It is recommended that you sort the file alphabetically using WordPerfect's Line Sort feature (see Chapter 15 for details) because this speeds up the process of index generation. Since the program ignores case when matching the entries to words in the document, you can use all uppercase (or all lowercase) when typing the list.

A word of warning: you may not be able to use this feature if your concordance file is very large and the amount of RAM memory in your system is limited. My computer is equipped with 512K of RAM, and I had no trouble using a 200-entry concordance file to generate an index for a document that is 105 pages in length (it also contained 32 entries individually marked). If your concordance file is too large for your system, when you generate the index you will be warned that there is not enough memory to use the entire file and can choose to stop the index generation process. If you do not stop it, your final index will only contain entries located up to the point where the warning was issued.

If you want the wording in your final index to differ from the wording of an entry in the concordance file, mark the entry using the Mark Text Key (Alt-F5), as described in the previous section, and assign a different expression to it. Note that when you do this WordPerfect searches for a match based on the actual entry, not the wording in the index marks. To use subheadings, you have no choice but to mark them using the Mark Text Key. For example, Figure 9.8 shows part of the concordance file for this book's index. Note that three of the entries, *Retrieve, Return key,* and *Reveal Codes Key* have subheadings.

```
Ragged right margin
RAM
Realign
Records
Rectangle
Redirecting overflow files, buffers, and temporary macros
Redline
Reformatting text
Release left margin
Relocating text
Remove redline, and strikeout text
Rename files
Renumbering pages
Repeating a macro
Repeating a command
Replace Key (Alt-F2)
Required hyphen
Required space
Required page break
Restoring deleted text
Retrieve
  blocked text
  column
  files
  rectangle
Retrieve Text Key
Return key
  block mode
  code
  outline mode
Reveal Codes Key
  in column mode
  line draw
  math
Reverse Search Key
Right justification
Run merge
Rush print job
```

Figure 9.8: *A partial concordance file*

These were marked in the concordance file by using the Block and Mark Text Keys. Figure 9.9 shows the subheading *in column mode* being marked with the heading *Reveal Codes Key.*

After typing the heading and pressing Return, the blocked subheading *in column mode* is suggested as the subheading entry, as shown in Figure 9.10. Pressing Return enters it.

Note that you can have more than one index mark for an entry, if you want the reference to appear under more than one index heading.

C. Defining the Style

The next process is to define a numbering style; it works almost exactly the same as when making a list or table of contents. Before you begin, the cursor must be at the end of the document, and you should insert a hard page break (by pressing Ctrl-Return) to isolate the index.

```
    Rename files
    Renumbering pages
    Repeating a macro
    Repeating a command
    Replace Key (Alt-F2)
    Required hyphen
    Required space
    Required page break
    Restoring deleted text
    Retrieve
       blocked text
       column
       files
       rectangle
    Retrieve Text Key
    Return key
       block mode
       code
       outline mode
    Reveal Codes Key
       in column mode
       line draw
       math
    Reverse Search Key
    Index Heading: Reveal Codes Key_
```

Figure 9.9: *Marking a subheading in a concordance file*

1. Define the index by pressing the Mark Text Key (Alt-F5) and selecting option 6, Other Options. Choose option 5, Define Index, from the screen illustrated in Figure 9.1.

2. You will then be asked to enter the name of the concordance file. If there is none, just press Return to continue. The Index Definition screen will appear, as shown in Figure 9.11. Note that this screen is nearly the same as the List Definition screen (see Figure 9.2).

3. Now select one of the five page numbering styles that are illustrated in Figure 9.3. Note that the index shown in Figure 9.7 uses option 5, Flush Right Page Numbers with Leaders.

4. After you complete step 3, the Reveal Codes screen should include this code, where N means numbering style:

[DefMark:Index,N]

Note that the index will be generated at this position.

```
Rename files
Renumbering pages
Repeating a macro
Repeating a command
Replace Key (Alt-F2)
Required hyphen
Required space
Required page break
Restoring deleted text
Retrieve
  blocked text
  column
  files
  rectangle
Retrieve Text Key
Return key
  block mode
  code
  outline mode
Reveal Codes Key
  in column mode
  line draw
  math
Reverse Search Key
Subheading: in column mode
```

Figure 9.10: *The suggested subheading*

```
Index Definition

    1 - No Page Numbers
    2 - Page Numbers Follow Entries
    3 - (Page Numbers) Follow Entries
    4 - Flush Right Page Numbers
    5 - Flush Right Page Numbers with Leaders















Selection: ▌
```

Figure 9.11: *The Index Definition screen*

D. Generating the Index

1. Select option 6, Other Options, then select 8, Generate Tables and Index, from the Mark Text Key. The following message will appear:

> Existing tables, lists, and indexes will be replaced. Continue? (Y/N): Y

Reply by typing Y. The program will then begin generating your index and this message will appear:

> Generation in progress: Counter: (*number*)

A few minutes will elapse, then the index will appear. Note that an [EndDef] code will be inserted at the end, to mark the boundary of the defined index.

Tables of Authorities

A table of authorities is a list of statutes, cases, rules of court, treaties, regulations, and other authorities that are cited in a legal brief. It is generally divided into sections such as statutes, cases, and rules of court or federal, state, and local regulations. WordPerfect permits as many as sixteen different sections, and the formatting style can vary for each section. As in an index, each citation can include references to multiple page numbers. Individual sections are sorted alphanumerically, as shown in Figure 9.12, which displays a table containing three sections: statues, cases, and rules of court.

The procedure for marking entries for a table of authorities is similar to marking index entries in that you block and mark each entry with the Mark Text Key, then edit the entry so that it appears exactly the way you want it in the table. However, you are then asked to enter a *short form*, which is an abbreviated version of the entry. If the reference appears more than once in the document, marking the others is easy because you can omit the lengthy initial step and simply enter the short form. The next step is to define the table of authorities, designating the order, location, and formatting style for each section of the table; this is followed by typing section headings. Generating the table is the last, and easiest, step.

A. Marking the Citations to Be Included in the Table of Authorities

Use the Block (Alt-F4) and Mark Text Keys (Alt-F5, 6) to mark each reference. The first time you mark a citation (or if there is only one occurrence) it must be designated as the full form. If there are multiple occurrences, be sure that you mark the *first* one in the document (in sequential order) as the full form. Before marking anything, be sure you have planned the sections so you'll know which section number to enter for each reference. Follow these steps to mark an item as the full form:

1. Highlight the citation using the Block Key (Alt-F4), then press the Mark Text Key (Alt-F5). This menu will appear:

Mark for 1 ToC; 2 List; 3 Redline; 4 Strikeout; 5 Index; 6; ToA

2. Select option 6, ToA.

3. You will be asked for the section number, as shown below.

ToA section number (Press Enter for short form only):

Be sure to type the section number, then press Return (pressing Return alone designates the entry as a short form, which is incorrect).

```
                        TABLE OF AUTHORITIES

STATUTES                                          PAGE NUMBERS


California Civil Code Section 930.03 (b) . . . . . . . . . . 16

California Civil Code Section 990.04 (d) . . . . . . . . . . 16

California Probate Code Section 1338.6 . . . . . . . . . . . 22

California Probate Code Section 1811.1 . . . . . . . . . . . 5

California Probate Code Sections 970-977 . . . . . . . . . . 10

California Revenue and Taxation Code
   Sections 12401-12443, 16101  . . . . . . . . . . . . . . . 9

United States Internal Revenue Code
   Sections 2061, 2063-2075 . . . . . . . . . . . . . . . . . 9



CASES

California First Bank v. Jones 99 CA 2D 415 . . . . . . . . . 11

Estate of Gary 94 CA 3d 582 (1965) . . . . . . . . . . . 12, 19

Estate of Kensington 491 Ca 3d 402 (1979) . . . . . . . . . 11

Estate of Lawrence  87 C 2d 976 (1958) . . . . . . . . . . . 9

Estate of Ramirez 11 Ca 3d 605 (1971) . . . . . . . . . . . 12

Estate of Randolph 196 Ca 2d 987 (1986) . . . . . . . . . . 10

Estate of Walsh 528 CA 3d 247 (1965) . . . . . . . . . . . . 22

Estate of White 210 Ca 2d 29 (1978) . . . . . . . . . . 10, 19

First National Trust Assn. v. Smith 124 CA 5D (1983). . . . . 9

Jones v. Browning  437 US 95 . . . . . . . . . . . . . . . . 9



RULES OF COURT

2(a) . . . . . . . . . . . . . . . . . . . . . . . . . . . . 7

3(b) . . . . . . . . . . . . . . . . . . . . . . . . . . . . 7
```

Figure 9.12: *A sample table of authorities*

4. The blocked entry appears on a special screen, similar to the one shown in Figure 9.13, where you can edit it to enhance the reference that will actually appear in the table of authorities (without changing it in the body of the document). For example, you can expand it to include up to 30 lines, designate formatting changes such as underline and bold, and indent the second line if it is a multiple line entry. Press F7 when you are finished. If you don't want to make any changes, simply press F7.

5. Next, you are asked to enter the short form for this citation. WordPerfect prompts you with the first 40 characters of the full form, as shown below:

Enter Short Form: Estate of Kensington 491 CA 3d 402 (1979

Use ← and → to move through the prompt, and the Del and Backspace keys to edit it, then press Return. In this example, you could change the short form to *Estate of Kensington* by pressing → until the cursor is on the *4,* then pressing the Del key or Ctrl-End until the rest of the citation is erased. If you want to use an entirely different short form, use Ctrl-End to delete the whole prompt, then type your entry. If you want the short form to match

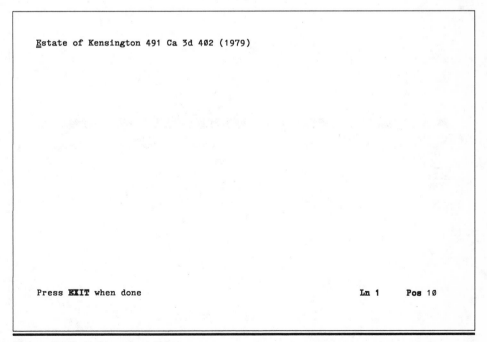

Estate of Kensington 491 Ca 3d 402 (1979)

Press **EXIT** when done   Ln 1   Pos 10

Figure 9.13: *Editing the full form entry*

the full form, just press F7. In any case, the short form must be unique, since it is used to identify this particular citation wherever it occurs in your document. If it is not unique, you will see an error message later on, when you generate the table of authorities.

6. Check the Reveal Codes screen to see the table of authorities code, as shown in Figure 9.14.

The code *ToA:2;* signifies that this is a section two entry. Next comes the short form, *Estate of Kensington,* then the code <Full Form>. Note that you do not see the text of the full form.

If you need to make editing changes to the full form or change the section number, you must place the cursor directly *after* the code, select Other Options from the Mark Text Key (Alt-F5,6) and select option 7, Edit Table of Authorities Full Form. This will place the cursor in the special screen shown in Figure 9.13 where you can edit the citation using the same keys used in normal edit mode. After you press F7 to exit, you are asked for the section number and prompted with the original one. Either press Return to accept the original section number, or type the one you want.

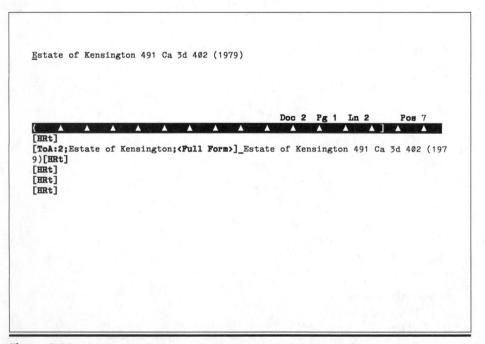

Figure 9.14: *Viewing the table of authorities code in the Reveal Codes screen*

7. If there are any other occurrences of the citation, use the short form option from the Mark Text Key to include them in your table of authorities. To do this, highlight the citation using the Block Key (Alt-F4), press the Mark Text Key (Alt-F5) and select option 6, ToA. Press Return when you see this prompt:

ToA section number (Press Enter for short form only):

The highlighted text appears in the prompt, as shown below:

Enter Short Form: Estate of Kensington

Next, you can either press Return to accept the contents of the prompt as the short form, edit it as described in step 5, or erase it and type the short form. In any case, it must match the one you entered in step 5 for this citation. In the Reveal Codes screen, the code for short form is as follows:

[ToA:;Estate of Kensington;]

where *Estate of Kensington* is the short form.

Using the Switch Key to Keep a List of Short Forms

If your document is long and contains many frequently repeated citations, you may wish to use the Doc 2 work area to keep a separate list of the short forms so that you can refer back to it if you forget the exact text of a short form. To do this, after marking each full form press the Switch Key (Shift-F3) and type the short form in the Doc 2 area. When you have finished marking all citations in the brief, save the list in case you need it for future reference.

Using Search to Mark Citations

If you are marking the entries after your document has been typed, you can simplify your task by using WordPerfect's Extended Search feature to help you locate and mark each citation. To do this, begin at the top of the document and mark the first occurrence of a citation. Next, search for the remaining occurrences using a unique word. For instance, in the above example you could search for the *Estate of Kensington* citation by entering *Kensington* as the search string (see Chapter 6, Search and Replace, if you need to refresh your memory). Next, mark the citation by selecting the Short Form option from the Mark Text Key (Alt-F5,4). WordPerfect prompts you with the short form you selected when marking the last full form, and you can simply press Return to accept it.

B. Defining the Style

To define the style for your table of authorities, you type the section headings, use the Mark Text Key to enter definition codes for each one, then (for each section) specify whether you want dot leaders, underlining, and/or blank lines separating each citation. A table of authorities usually appears at the beginning of a brief, so you should define the table at the top of the document.

1. Move the cursor to the top of page one (press Home, Home, ↑) and press Ctrl-Return to force a page break.

2. Change the page number of the first page of text, which has now become page two, back to page one. To do this, use the Page Format Key (Alt-F8, 2), enter 1 as the new page number, then select the numbering style, usually Arabic (see Chapter 5 if you need to refresh your memory). Note that if you do not change the page number in this manner, you will get an error message when the table is generated, and the page numbers listed in the table of authorities may be incorrect.

3. Press PgUp to move the cursor to the top of the document. Enter the title *TABLE OF AUTHORITIES* (optional). Next, type the heading for the first section, such as *STATUTES*. As you can see in Figure 9.12, my next step was to press the Flush Right Key (Alt-F6) and type *Page Numbers,* but this is also optional. Press Return twice to leave a few blank lines between the section heading and the entries. Although you aren't required to leave the blank lines, the entries will begin immediately after the code so it is advisable to leave at least one.

4. To enter the definition code for the first section, press the Mark Text Key (Alt-F5) and select 6 Other Options, then select option 4, Define Table of Authorities. You will see this prompt:

Selection: 4
Enter Section Number (1-16):

Since this is the first section, type 1.

5. You will then see the screen illustrated in Figure 9.15. Note the 1 at the top (Definition for Table of Authorities 1), indicating that you are defining the first section. Dot leaders appear between each entry and its corresponding page number(s) at the right margin, as shown in Figure 9.12. WordPerfect's default is to include them, so if you prefer flush right numbers without the leading dots, select option 1 and press N.

The second selection, Allow underlining, is set to N (No). If you want to include underlining in the table, press 2, then Y to change it. Note that I set it to Y in my example, since it is common practice to underline case citations.

The third selection, Blank line between authorities, is set to Y, meaning that when the table is generated, each citation will automatically be separated from the next one by a blank line. In my example, I left this setting at Y.

6. For each remaining section in your table, follow steps 3 through 5 to enter a heading and define the style.

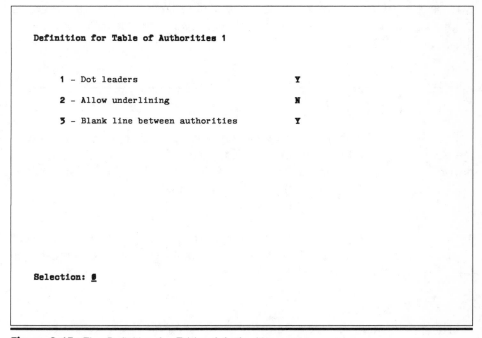

Definition for Table of Authorities 1

    1 – Dot leaders   **Y**

    2 – Allow underlining   **N**

    3 – Blank line between authorities   **Y**

    Selection: _

Figure 9.15: *The Definition for Table of Authorities screen*

C. Generating the Table of Authorities

The last step is the easiest one. After marking each citation and defining the sections, you select the Generate Tables and Index Option from the Mark Text Key (Alt-F5, 6, 8). Note that the cursor can be anywhere in the document when you do this. You will see this prompt:

Selection: 8
Existing tables, lists, and indexes will be replaced. Continue? (Y/N): Y

Press Return or Y to begin the process. After a few minutes, the table will appear with the cursor at the end of it.

Paragraph Numbering and Outlines

Very few, if any, word processors are able to create outlines and numbered paragraphs automatically. Recently, a whole new genre of software was developed to accommodate this need and several software programs in this category became best-sellers almost overnight. WordPerfect added this feature to Version 4.0.

Creating an Outline

To create an outline, you use four main keys: the Tab key, the Indent Key, the Return key, and the Mark Text Key. The Return, Tab, and Indent Keys function differently in Outline mode than in Edit mode. As you will see, when you use the Outline feature, it's almost as though you were using a different program.

1. To turn on Outline mode, press the Mark Text Key (Alt-F5) and select option 1, Outline. To verify that it is on, this message appears in the lower left corner of the screen:

Outline

2. The next step is to press Return. As you see, this inserts a number that designates the first paragraph level of your outline. Since the default value

for the style of numbering is uppercase Roman numerals, you will see this symbol: I. Press the Spacebar (or type one or more characters), then press Return again, and the numeral II will appear underneath the I. If you repeat this action five more times, your screen will appear as follows:

I.
II.
III.
IV.
V.
VI.
VII.

As you can see, pressing Return adds a paragraph number to your outline. However, if you do not press the Spacebar or type a character(s) before pressing Return, the paragraph number will be moved down a line and a blank line will be inserted above it. This happens even though your cursor is positioned after the number I.

Look at the Reveal Codes screen to see the code that WordPerfect inserted when you pressed Return:

[Par#:Auto].

The *Auto* inside the brackets indicates that WordPerfect is automatically insert-ing numbers for you and will change them as you add, delete, or move other paragraphs surrounding it. You also have the option of typing your own para-graph numbers, called *fixed numbers,* by selecting option 2, Par#. These are not renumbered if you move them over one or more tab stops, so don't use them unless you want all paragraph levels lined up against the left margin or the same tab stop. If you do use your own numbering scheme, the *Auto* inside the brackets will be replaced by the number you enter at that location. Now delete all the paragraph numbers except the first. To do this, move the cursor to the right of each one and press Backspace or place the cursor on the number and press Del.

3. Now, to continue creating the outline, position the cursor after the numeral I and type the following text:

Alternatives

Press Return and the numeral II will appear underneath, just as you would expect.

4. With the cursor positioned after the II, press Tab. The II is moved right one tab stop and converted into an A! In Outline mode, the Tab key functions to change the paragraph number, I, to the next level, which is A. Until you enter a character(s) or press the Spacebar, if you were to press Tab once more, the A would change into a 1; pressing it again would change the 1 into a lowercase a. This can continue for seven levels. For the numbers 1 through 5, this is the order:

Level 1:   I II III IV V
Level 2:   A B C D E
Level 3:   1 2 3 4 5
Level 4:   a b c d e
Level 5:   (1) (2) (3) (4) (5)
Level 6:   (a) (b) (c) (d) (e)
Level 7:   i) ii) iii) iv) v)

Figure 9.16 shows how these levels actually look in an outline. Note that if the last level is reached, and you indent yet another tab stop, WordPerfect will continue to use the seventh style.

5. In Outline mode, when you want to move the cursor one or more tab stops to the right without adding or changing a paragraph number, you can use the Indent Key or press the Spacebar once followed by Tab. The Indent Key will function just as it does in Edit mode, moving all text to the next tab stop until the Return key is pressed. Press Indent (F4) now and type this entry for level A:

Offer early retirement for senior personnel

Press Return, which inserts a II, and press Tab again to change it to a B. Next, press Indent again and type this alternative:

Performance and ability will be used as criteria to lay off and/or fire

Press Return again, inserting a II; then press Tab to convert the II to a C. Indent and type this sentence as the third alternative:

Offer all employees pay cuts so that nobody will be fired or laid off

6. Now your document is beginning to look like a useful outline! However, a few paragraphs to explain the problems these alternatives are supposed to solve might be helpful, so you should insert another level 1 entry, Problem Definition, before Alternatives.

```
I.    Introduction
II.   Background
III.  Problem definition
IV.   Principal issues
V.    Alternative solutions
      A.
      B.
      C.
      D.
      E.
            1.
            2.
            3.
            4.
            5.
                  a.
                  b.
                  c.
                  d.
                  e.
                        (1)
                        (2)
                        (3)
                        (4)
                        (5)
                              i)
                              ii)
                              iii)
                              iv)
                              v)
                                    vi)
                                    vii)
                                    viii)
                                    ix)
                                    x)
```

Figure 9.16: *Outline numbering*

Move the cursor to the beginning of the document by pressing Home, Home, and ↑. Press Return and a I will be inserted. Did you see the number in front of the entry *Alternatives* turn into a II? If you press the Spacebar and press Return once more, a II will be added and the old II will turn into a III. This happens because of WordPerfect's automatic renumbering of outline entries. Now delete the extra II and type this entry after the I:

Problem Definition

Your outline should now appear like the one in Figure 9.17.

```
I. Problem definition

II. Alternatives
    A.   Early retirement for senior personnel
    B.   Performance and ability will be used as criteria to lay
         off and/or fire
    C.   Offer all employees pay cuts so that nobody will be fired
         or laid off.
```

Figure 9.17: *The partial outline*

7. To complete the outline at level IIA, *Offer early retirement . . .,* position the cursor after the word *personnel,* press Return, and use the Tab and Return keys to add these entries:

  1. Advantages

  2. Disadvantages

  3. Issues

Remember, if you press Return too often and find you have added a number you did not want, press either the Backspace key or the Del key (depending on the cursor position) to delete it. Likewise, if you press Tab and accidentally move a paragraph number, changing it to the next level, just position the cursor on that number and press the Backspace key, then press ↓ so that WordPerfect updates the text. This will delete the extra tab code and renumber your entry correctly.

Figure 9.18 shows the completed outline; you can continue exploring WordPerfect's Outline feature by typing the rest of the entries.

Numbering and Punctuation Styles

You are now familiar with the default numbering style, as shown in Figure 9.18. If you prefer another style, you can use Option 1, Define Paragraph/ Outline Numbering from the Other Mark Text Options screen (Alt-F5,6) to change it. You can select one of two other styles supplied by WordPerfect, or you can customize the numbering style using your own symbols.

I. Problem definition

Due to poor cost control, insufficient growth, sloppy staffing practices and lax product evaluation, the company has had a $3 million loss in the last quarter. The Board of Directors has issued a mandatory order to lay off 15% of all managers, and 20% of all other workers.

Issues and guidelines are needed to formulate reduction plans.

II. Alternatives

A. Early retirement for senior personnel

1. Advantages:

a.   Less harsh feelings; optional early retirement may be welcomed by older workers

2. Disadvantages:

a.   May lose the best, most experienced employees
b.   This action alone will not meet reduction targets

3. Issues:

a.   Guidelines won't allow this option

B.   Performance and ability will be used as criteria to lay off/and or fire

1. Advantages:

a.   Potential benefits to the company to get rid of the deadwood
b.   Improve morale of better workers
c.   Fair policy

2. Disadvantages:

a.   A rating system has never been devised since the company has never fired or laid off an employee
b.   Possible union activity

3. Issues

a.   Expense of creating job review system

Figure 9.18: *Outline for the XYZ Plastics, Inc. Case*

```
    C.    Offer all employees pay cuts so that nobody will be fired
          or laid off.

          1. Advantages:

                a.    Maintains company's paternalistic image
                b.    Morale booster: everyone pitches in and works
                      hard to get wages back up, prevent their friends
                      from being laid off.

          2. Disadvantages:

                a.    Workers who disagree will be angry at having to
                      support the deadwood
                b.    Chaotic, hard to implement

          3.    Issues:

                a.    Possible legal action


    D.    Seniority

          1.    Advantages:

          2.    Disadvantages:

          3.    Issues:


III. Recommended Solution
```

Figure 9.18: *Outline for the XYZ Plastics, Inc. Case (continued)*

The two other supplied styles are paragraph style and legal style. For the numbers 1 to 5, paragraph style is as follows:

Level 1:	1. 2. 3. 4. 5.
Level 2:	a. b. c. d. e.
Level 3:	i. ii. iii. iv. v.
Level 4:	(1) (2) (3) (4) (5)
Level 5:	(a) (b) (c) (d) (e)
Level 6:	(i) (ii) (iii) (iv) (v)
Level 7:	1) 2) 3) 4) 5)

and legal style is as follows:

Level 1:	1. 2. 3. 4. 5.
Level 2:	5.1. 5.2. 5.3. 5.4. 5.5.
Level 3:	5.5.1. 5.5.2. 5.5.3. 5.5.4. 5.5.5.
Level 4:	5.5.5.1. 5.5.5.2. 5.5.5.3. 5.5.5.4. 5.5.5.5.
Level 5:	5.5.5.5.1. 5.5.5.5.2. 5.5.5.5.3. 5.5.5.5.4. 5.5.5.5.5.
Level 6:	5.5.5.5.5.1. 5.5.5.5.5.2. 5.5.5.5.5.3. 5.5.5.5.5.4. 5.5.5.5.5.5.
Level 7:	5.5.5.5.5.5.1. 5.5.5.5.5.5.2. 5.5.5.5.5.5.3. 5.5.5.5.5.5.4. 5.5.5.5.5.5.5.

You can test these styles on your practice outline by moving the cursor to the top of the file and selecting the Define Paragraph/Outline Numbering option (1) from the Other Mark Text Options screen (Alt-F5, 6, 1). You will then see the Paragraph Numbering Definition screen, as illustrated in Figure 9.19, from which you can choose a numbering style.

```
Paragraph Numbering Definition

      1 - Paragraph Numbering, e.g. 1. a. i. (1) (a) (i) 1)
      2 - Outline Numbering, e.g. I. A. 1. a. (1) (a) i)
      3 - Legal Numbering, e.g. 1. 1.1. 2.2.1 etc.
      4 - Other

Selection: 0

Levels:                1   2   3   4   5   6   7
   Number Style:       0   2   4   3   4   3   1
   Punctuation:        1   1   1   1   3   3   2

Number Style                        Punctuation
0 - Upper Case Roman                0 - #
1 - Lower Case Roman                1 - #.
2 - Upper Case Letters              2 - #)
3 - Lower Case Letters              3 - (#)
4 - Numbers
5 - Numbers with previous levels separated by a period

Starting Paragraph Number (in Legal Style): 1
```

Figure 9.19: *The Paragraph Numbering Definition screen*

Numbering Paragraphs

Paragraph numbering works almost the same way as outlining but it's easier to use because you insert the paragraph numbers one at a time by selecting an option on the Mark Text Key. The Return key behaves the same as it does in Edit mode, and the Tab key does not automatically change the number to the next level unless you position the cursor on or in front of the number. As with Outline mode, when you add or delete paragraphs (and their automatic numbers), WordPerfect automatically renumbers all paragraphs.

Instead of using Return to enter a paragraph number, you select option 2, Para #, on the Mark Text Key. Next, you have two choices: either press Return to insert the code for automatic number, [Par#:Auto], or type a number between 1 and 7, which then becomes a fixed paragraph level. (Remember that the disadvantage to using fixed levels is that they will not be renumbered automatically when you press Tab in front of them.)

To create a short outline using paragraph numbering, follow these steps:

1. Press Alt-F5, 2, and Return. This will insert a I for your first level. Next, press Tab to indent one tab stop and type

   Introduction and Overview

Press Return.

2. Repeat this procedure twice, so that you add a II and III to level one. Type these entries for them:

   II. Historical Background
   III. Principle Issues

Press Return.

3. Press Tab, then press Alt-F5, 2, Return, and Tab again. Press Return and repeat this procedure twice so that you have an A, B, and C, and type these entries for them:

   A. Fair employment practices
   B. Union activity
   C. Employee morale and impact on profits

4. Repeat step 1, and type this for the entry at IV:

   Alternatives

Your outline should look exactly like this:

```
I.    Introduction and Overview
II.   Historical Background
III.  Principle Issues
      A.  Fair employment practices
      B.  Union activity
      C.  Employee morale and impact on profits
IV.   Alternatives
```

Summary

WordPerfect can be used to create lists, an index, a table of authorities, and a table of contents for your document. The principle steps used to create each of them are similar: mark the text to be included, define the numbering style for the page numbers, and generate the structure. After editing changes, any of these structures can be easily updated by regenerating it.

Marking the text is not an automatic process, for you must move the cursor to each item in the document and mark it separately. However, WordPerfect's Search and Macro features can be used to expedite the process. There are five numbering styles to choose from: no page numbers, page numbers that follow the entries, page numbers in parentheses that follow the entries, flush right page numbers, and flush right page numbers with leaders.

WordPerfect supplies two more organizational tools for the writer, outlining and paragraph numbering. Paragraph numbering is slightly easier to work with than outlining, because Outline mode alters the functions of several common keys, including the Return and Tab keys. Other than that, the procedures used are quite similar.

WordPerfect can create up to five lists per document, so you can have separate ones for illustrations, graphs, maps, charts, and anything else you wish to keep track of, but each word or phrase in a document can only be included in one list. To mark each entry for a list, block it with the Block Key (Alt-F4), then select option 2 from the Mark Text Key (Alt-F5). After all entries have been marked, move the cursor to the end of the document, define the structure (Alt-F5, 6, 3), and generate it (Alt-F5, 6, 8).

A table of contents can contain up to five levels, and each level can have a different numbering style. Each level of entry will be indented one tab stop to the right of the last one. The procedure for creating a table of contents is similar to creating a list: you block each entry with the Block Key (Alt-F4) and mark them by selecting option 1 from the Mark Text Key (Alt-F5), move the cursor to the end of the document, then define and generate the structure.

Unlike lists and tables of contents, when you create an index, you do not have to mark each entry with the Block Key unless an entry is longer than one word. This makes it easier to mark entries as you are typing the document. Index entries can contain headings and subheadings, and each entry can have as many as 73 characters. You create an index by marking each entry, moving the cursor to the end of the document, and defining and generating the structure.

You can also use a concordance file to simplify the process of generating an index. To do this, you type a list of words and phrases that occur frequently in your document, sort it alphabetically, and save it as a separate file. Next, you create your index by selecting the generate option (Alt F5, 6, 8) from the Mark Text Key and entering the name of the concordance file. WordPerfect automatically locates and includes page numbers for all occurrences of the words and phrases in your concordance file, saving you the work of locating and marking each one individually in your document.

WordPerfect's Outline feature allows you to create outlines with as many as seven paragraph levels. Three familiar WordPerfect keys, Tab, Return, and Indent are used, but they function quite differently from the way they do in Edit mode. Return automatically inserts a number designating the first paragraph level, such as I. Tab changes the number to the next level below it, such as from I to A. Indent replaces the normal tab key, moving text to the right one tab stop. WordPerfect provides three predefined numbering styles, paragraph, outline, or legal style, and if these aren't acceptable, you can customize the settings to create your own style.

Paragraph numbering is similar to outlining, but it is easier to use because the Return and Tab keys function just as they do in Edit mode. When you want to enter a paragraph level number, select option 2 on the Mark Text Key.

WordPerfect 4.2 can be used to produce a table of authorities, which is a list of statutes, cases, rules of court, regulations, and other authorities that are cited in a legal brief. The table can include as many as sixteen different sections, with the entries in individual sections sorted alphanumerically. Page numbers can be preceded by dot leaders, as in an index, and each citation can include multiple page references. To include entries in the table, you block and mark them with the Block and Mark Text Keys, enter the text to appear in the table in *full form,* then make up a *short form,* or abbreviated version, to simplify marking the remaining entries. If you are marking entries in a document that has already been typed, WordPerfect's Search feature and the Short Form option on the Mark Text Key can be used to quickly locate and mark the entries. After marking all the entries, you type the section headings and define the style and location for each section, then use the Mark Text Key to generate the table.

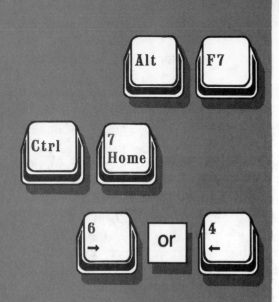

CHAPTER 10 KEYSTROKE SUMMARY:

The Math/Columns Key—use to display Text Column Definition screen and to turn columns on and off

The GoTo Key—use with → or ← to move cursor across columns to the left or right.

PARALLEL AND NEWSPAPER COLUMNS

THE ABILITY TO PRODUCE TEXT COL-
umns is among WordPerfect's most exciting
features and has many applications. There
are two types of text columns that can be
created: newspaper and parallel. Newspaper
columns are used for text that continues
from one column to another, and parallel
columns are used to keep separate blocks of
text next to each other on the same page.
WordPerfect permits as many as 24 columns
per page; the columns appear next to each
other both on the screen and in your
printed version. (Versions prior to 4.1 do not
show side-by-side columns on screen, only
in printed work.)

Creating either parallel or newspaper columns involves three basic steps:

A. defining the columns

B. turning the column feature on

C. typing the text into each column

Not all features can be used within text (newspaper or parallel) columns, (although most of the important ones are available). For example, the Tabs function cannot be used, so the decimal alignment feature, which is used to create columns of numbers, does not work. To move or delete text, Block and Move can be used, but not their options for cutting, copying, or retrieving columns (these options are reserved for columns created with Tab, Tab Align, Indent, or hard returns).

Newspaper Columns

A. Defining Newspaper Columns

The first step is to define the columns, including the type (newspaper or parallel), number, spacing between columns, and margins. To try it, follow these steps:

1. Start by pressing the Math/Columns Key (Alt-F7) and you will see this menu:

1 Math On; 2 Math Def; 3 Column On/Off; 4 Column Def; 5 Column Display: 0

2. Select option 4, Column Def. You will then see the Text Column Definition screen, as illustrated in Figure 10.1.

3. The first question on the Text Column Definition screen

Do you wish to have evenly spaced columns? (Y/N)

is there for your convenience. If you reply in the affirmative, the program will automatically calculate the correct margins for each column (although you can override these settings). If you respond in the negative, the program will then skip directly to the third question.

```
Text Column Definition

        Do you wish to have evenly spaced columns? (Y/N) N
        If yes, number of spaces between columns:
        Type of columns: 1
            1 - Newspaper
            2 - Parallel with Block Protect

        Number of text columns (2-24): 0

        Column   Left      Right     Column   Left      Right
          1:                          13:
          2:                          14:
          3:                          15:
          4:                          16:
          5:                          17:
          6:                          18:
          7:                          19:
          8:                          20:
          9:                          21:
         10:                          22:
         11:                          23:
         12:                          24:
```

Figure 10.1: *The Text Column Definition screen*

4. The second question

If yes, number of spaces between columns:

is skipped unless you reply positively to the first one; it allows you to determine the number of blank spaces between columns. The program will then include this variable in its calculations for the margins of your columns. You should consider this carefully, because it affects the appearance of your columns. For example, Figure 10.2 shows two versions of a glossary that was created with the Newspaper Column feature. In the first one, five spaces were left between columns and in the second one, ten spaces were left. As you can see, there is a lot of wasted paper in the second one. Five spaces seem to be just right.

5. The third question

Type of columns:

allows you to specify whether you want to use newspaper columns or parallel columns. To define newspaper columns, reply by typing 1 or pressing Return (1 is the default).

GLOSSARY OF COMPUTER TERMS

Alphanumeric Containing both alphabetic and numeric characters

ASCII American Standard Code for Information Interchange; a standard format for encoding the alphabet, numbers, symbols and functions used by computers. Many word processing programs, for example, read text and data in ASCII format so that they can exchange files with other programs.

Backup A duplicate copy of a database or program stored on separate disk(s) or on tape, as a precaution in case of loss or damage to the original.

Bit Binary digIT, either a "0" or a "1". Bits represent the smallest unit of information used in a computer, and are combined into units including groups of 4 called a "nibble," groups of 8 called a "byte," and groups of 16 called a "word."

Boot In data processing, the term is used to describe turning on a computer.

Byte A set of eight bits, usually used to represent one character or number.

Character set The characters which can be displayed or used for processing on a specific computer, printer, plotter or other peripheral.

Chip A small piece of silicon or other semiconductor material which has been etched with a microscopic pattern of circuits. It is mounted in a package with electrical connections.

Command A directive or instruction such as the "save" command which saves a file from RAM onto a storage disk.

CPU The Central Processing Unit of a computer; it is the brains of the system, controlling all operations such as retrieving, decoding, and executing program instructions. The CPU of a microcomputer is normally contained on a single chip, such as the Intel 8088 in the IBM PC and compatibles.

Crash In data processing, to stop functioning. When a computer system crashes, it can be because of a power loss or other hardware problem or because of a bug in the program.

CRT Cathode Ray Tube; a picture tube used in a video monitor. It is often used to describe the computer display unit which resembles a television screen.

Cursor An electronic marker on the video display screen indicating the position where the next character will be inserted or deleted. It is usually a blinking character such as a rectangle or a flashing underline symbol.

Figure 10.2: *Column spacing*

GLOSSARY OF COMPUTER TERMS

Alphanumeric Containing both alphabetic and numeric characters

ASCII American Standard Code for Information Interchange; a standard format for encoding the alphabet, numbers, symbols and functions used by computers. Many word processing programs, for example, read text and data in ASCII format so that they can exchange files with other programs.

Backup A duplicate copy of a database or program stored on separate disk(s) or on tape, as a precaution in case of loss or damage to the original.

Bit Binary digIT, either a "0" or a "1". Bits represent the smallest unit of information used in a computer, and are combined into units including groups of 4 called a "nibble," groups of 8 called a "byte," and groups of 16 called a "word."

Boot In data processing, the term is used to describe turning on a computer.

Byte A set of eight bits, usually used to represent one character or number.

Character set The characters which can be displayed or used for processing on a specific computer, printer, plotter or other peripheral.

Chip A small piece of silicon or other semiconductor material which has been etched with a microscopic pattern of circuits. It is mounted in a package with electrical connections.

Command A directive or instruction such as the "save" command which saves a file from RAM onto a storage disk.

CPU The Central Processing Unit of a computer; it is the brains of the system, controlling all operations such as retrieving, decoding, and executing program instructions. The CPU of a microcomputer is normally contained on a single chip, such as the Intel 8088 in the IBM PC and compatibles.

Crash In data processing, to stop functioning. When a computer system crashes, it can be because of a power loss or other hardware problem or because of a bug in the program.

CRT Cathode Ray Tube; a picture tube used in a video monitor.It is often used to describe the computer display unit which resembles a television screen.

Cursor An electronic marker on the video display screen indicating the position where the next character will be inserted or deleted. It is usually a blinking character such

Figure 10.2: *Column spacing (continued)*

234 = MASTERING WORDPERFECT

6. The next question allows you to select the number of columns. The glossary shown in Figure 10.2 uses two columns (a total of 24 per page is permitted). If you are using standard size paper, 8½ by 11 inches wide, more than three columns per page may look ridiculous because there won't be enough room in each column for more than a few words. For instance, Figure 10.3 shows the same glossary split into four columns.

7. The final step is to enter the left and right margins for each of your columns. Unless you have changed the margin settings in your document before pressing the Math/Columns Key, the total number of positions available for all your text columns will be 64, equal to the difference between the default margins of 10 and 74, as you can see from Figure 10.4.

If you answered Y to the first question, the correct margin settings will be filled in for you, and you can press Return to accept each of them. For instance, if you define two evenly spaced columns with five blank spaces separating them, the program will enter the margins shown in Figure 10.4.

If WordPerfect's automatic settings are unacceptable, you can override them by typing new ones.

If you choose to use columns that are not evenly spaced, enter the settings, leaving several blank spaces between columns. For instance, to create one narrow column with only 15 positions and one wide one with 44 positions, you would enter these settings:

Column margins	Left	Right
Column 1:	10	25
Column 2:	30	74

If you make a mistake when calculating the margins, an error message such as the following one will appear:

Error: Text columns can't overlap.

and you will have to reenter the numbers. Press Exit (F7) when you have finished entering the margins.

After the columns have been defined, the Reveal Codes screen includes a [Col Def] code and your specifications. The code for the definition shown in Figure 10.4 appears as follows:

[Col Def:2,10,39,45,74,0,0,0,0,0,0,0,0,0,0,0,0,0,0,0,0,0,0,0,0,0,0,0,0,0,0,0,0,0,0,0,0,0,0,0 0,0,0,0,0,0,0,0]

The first number, 2, represents the total number of columns that have been

GLOSSARY OF COMPUTER TERMS

Alphanumeric Containing both alphabetic and numeric characters

ASCII American Standard Code for Information Interchange; a standard format for encoding the alphabet, numbers, symbols and functions used by computers. Many word processing programs, for example, read text and data in ASCII format so that they can exchange files with other programs.

Backup A duplicate copy of a database or program stored on separate disk(s) or on tape, as a precaution in case of loss or damage to the original.

Bit Binary digIT, either a "0" or a "1". Bits represent the smallest unit of information used in a computer, and are combined into units including groups of 4 called a "nibble," groups of 8 called a "byte," and groups of 16 called a "word."

Boot In data processing, the term is used to describe turning on a computer.

Byte A set of eight bits, usually used to represent one character or number.

Character set The characters which can be displayed or used for processing on a specific

computer, printer, plotter or other peripheral.

Chip A small piece of silicon or other semiconductor material which has been etched with a microscopic pattern of circuits. It is mounted in a package with electrical connections.

Command A directive or instruction such as the "save" command which saves a file from RAM onto a storage disk.

CPU The Central Processing Unit of a computer; it is the brains of the system, controlling all operations

such as retrieving, decoding, and executing program instructions. The CPU of a microcomputer is normally contained on a single chip, such as the Intel 8088 in the IBM PC and compatibles.

Crash In data processing, to stop functioning. When a computer system crashes, it can be because of a power loss or other hardware problem or because of a bug in the program.

CRT Cathode Ray Tube; a picture tube used in a video monitor.It is often used to

Figure 10.3: *The glossary with four columns per page*

```
Text Column Definition

       Do you wish to have evenly spaced columns? (Y/N) Y
       If yes, number of spaces between columns: 5
       Type of columns: 1
             1 - Newspaper
             2 - Parallel with Block Protect

       Number of text columns (2-24): 2

       Column    Left    Right     Column    Left     Right
         1:       10       39        13:
         2:       45       74        14:
         3:                          15:
         4:                          16:
         5:                          17:
         6:                          18:
         7:                          19:
         8:                          20:
         9:                          21:
        10:                          22:
        11:                          23:
        12:                          24:

   Press EXIT when done
```

Figure 10.4: *Column margins calculated automatically*

defined. The remaining numbers represent the margin settings, with one pair for each of 24 possible columns. Since only two columns were defined, there are 22 sets of zeroes.

Note that if you define a column in the middle of a line of text, a hard return will automatically be inserted at the cursor location when you turn Columns on using option 3.

B. Turning the Columns Feature On

Once the columns have been defined, the Text Column Definition screen disappears, and you are returned to the Math/Columns Key menu. If you want to start using columns right away, select option 3, Column On/Off. Notice that this is a toggle key, and must be turned off again once you are done working with columns (unless the remainder of the document will be in column format).

It isn't necessary to begin using columns as soon as they are defined; you can turn the Columns feature on whenever you want to enter text into columns. Once you turn it on, a [Col on] code is added to the Reveal Codes screen, and when you turn it off, a [Col off] code is added.

To inform you which column your cursor is in, a column number indicator is added to the Status line. If the cursor is in column two, the Status line will resemble this:

Col 2 Doc 1 Pg 7 Ln 32 Pos 55

C. Entering Text in Columns

When you begin entering text into a newspaper column, it is formatted to fit within the boundaries of the first column until the first column on the first page is full. Then the cursor is moved to the top of the second column on the same page and text is entered there. This process continues until all columns on the first page are full, at which point the cursor is moved to the first column on the second page, along with any text that would have exceeded the page length limit, and the process is continued.

Each column of text is treated by WordPerfect as an independent page and a soft page code is inserted at the bottom of each column. In fact, the cursor will not move to the real second page until the last column is full. Features such as widow and orphan protection operate on a column-by-column basis. For instance, WordPerfect's Delete to End of Line function will only delete lines within a column. However, as you delete them, the entire document will be reformatted, just as it would be in non-column mode, so the text in other columns on the page will be shifted. When you insert words, it may appear as though the text in columns to the right is being pushed aside, but as soon as reformatting occurs, the columns will be realigned correctly.

To keep text from being split between two columns, you can place block protect codes around it, just as you would if you wanted to prevent the text from being split between pages in non-column mode. For instance, in the glossary shown in Figure 10.2, block protect codes were placed around each paragraph. This kept the paragraph about the term Chip intact, otherwise the first two lines would have remained in the first column and the rest of it would have been at the top of column 2.

The Reveal Codes screen will seem to behave oddly in Column mode. For instance, in Figure 10.5 the cursor was positioned on line seven of the second column, as the Status line indicates. However, in the Reveal Codes screen the second column is displayed on the left side and the first column is not visible

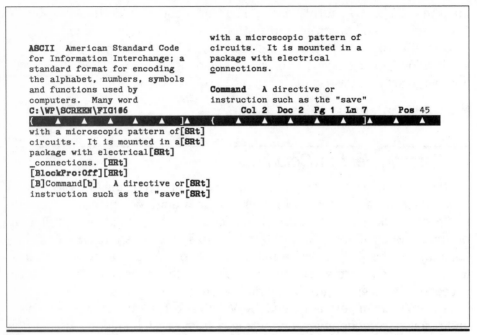

Figure 10.5: *The Reveal Codes screen in Newspaper Column mode*

at all. This happens because WordPerfect treats each column as a separate page, but it is inconsequential, since the columns on your editing screen and printed document will be correctly aligned.

Cursor Movement within Columns

Cursor movement is basically the same in Column mode as in Edit mode, except when moving from one column to another. Pressing the Go To Key (Ctrl-Home) followed by → or ← will move you horizontally to the same line in the next column. If the cursor is located on the last character of a column, pressing → will reposition it to the first character of the next column. If you press ↓, the cursor will move straight down to the same column on the following page. If the cursor is located on the first character of a column, pressing ← will move it to the last character of the previous one. If text (or blank lines) has not yet been entered into a column, you will not be able to move the cursor to it at all.

Block Features

Block and Move Key functions such as cut and copy work normally in Column mode, except that, as mentioned, you cannot use the Cut, Copy, or Retrieve Columns options (option 4 on both Move and Move with Block). If you use Move to cut, copy, or delete a page, all columns on the page will be included, as you would expect. Other functions such as print and save by block work normally also.

When defining a block in Column mode, if you reach the bottom of a column, do not press ↓, because it will immediately block the remaining columns on the page. Instead, use →, which will move the cursor to the top of the next column.

Retrieving Data into a Column

A file can be retrieved into a column using either Retrieve (Shift-F10), option 1 on the List Files Key (F5), or by blocking and copying a section of text from another file in document 2. (Text can be copied between two documents in memory using the Block and Move Keys. See Chapter 4 for more information.) To do this, define the columns, turn on the Column feature, check the Reveal Codes screen to be sure the cursor is positioned after the [Col On] code, then retrieve the file. It will be aligned correctly into the newspaper columns that you have defined.

Erasing Column Formatting

If you change your mind and decide you want to change text from columnar to normal page format, simply use the Reveal Codes screen to erase the [Col on] code. This will format the text as a normal page and maintain the integrity of your work. For instance, Figure 10.6 shows the glossary after the [Col on] code was deleted. As you can see, the text of column 2 is in correct alphabetical order under the text of column 1.

To change your column definition, first use the Reveal Codes screen to delete the [Col Def] code, then proceed to redefine it using the steps described above. When you do this, the [Col on] code will disappear as well and your text will be altered to conform to the currently active page setup (tabs, margins, spacing, and so on). This means the margins will usually be at 10 and 74 and text will be reformatted into them. However,

GLOSSARY OF COMPUTER TERMS

Alphanumeric Containing both alphabetic and numeric characters

ASCII American Standard Code for Information Interchange; a standard format for encoding the alphabet, numbers, symbols and functions used by computers. Many word processing programs, for example, read text and data in ASCII format so that they can exchange files with other programs.

Backup A duplicate copy of a database or program stored on separate disk(s) or on tape, as a precaution in case of loss or damage to the original.

Bit Binary digIT, either a "0" or a "1". Bits represent the smallest unit of information used in a computer, and are combined into units including groups of 4 called a "nibble," groups of 8 called a "byte," and groups of 16 called a "word."

Boot In data processing, the term is used to describe turning on a computer.

Byte A set of eight bits, usually used to represent one character or number.

Character set The characters which can be displayed or used for processing on a specific computer, printer, plotter or other peripheral.

Chip A small piece of silicon or other semiconductor material which has been etched with a microscopic pattern of circuits. It is mounted in a package with electrical connections.

Command A directive or instruction such as the "save" command which saves a file from RAM onto a storage disk.

CPU The Central Processing Unit of a computer; it is the brains of the system, controlling all operations such as retrieving, decoding, and executing program instructions. The CPU of a microcomputer is normally contained on a single chip, such as the Intel 8088 in the IBM PC and compatibles.

Crash In data processing, to stop functioning. When a computer system crashes, it can be because of a power loss or other hardware problem or because of a bug in the program.

CRT Cathode Ray Tube; a picture tube used in a video monitor.It is often used to describe the computer display unit which resembles a television screen.

Cursor An electronic marker on the video display screen indicating the position where the next character will be inserted or deleted. It is usually a blinking character such as a rectangle or a flashing underline symbol.

Figure 10.6: *The glossary after the [Col on] code has been deleted*

once you redefine the columns and turn the feature back on, they will be realigned correctly as you move the cursor through the text.

Column Display

You may have noticed that as the cursor moves through text that is formatted into columns (by using ↑ or ↓, screen up or down, PgUp or PgDn, etc.) it moves a little slower. Also, when you add or delete text, automatic reformatting is not as fast. If you want, you can turn off column display so that these inconveniences are avoided. To do this, press the Math/Columns Key (Alt-F7) and select 5 Column Display, then type N in response to the prompt

Display columns side by side? (Y/N)? Y

This will alter the appearance of both newspaper and parallel columns. If you are using two columns, for example, the first column will appear to be on the left side of the first page and the second column will appear to be on the right side of the following page. Although the columns *appear* to be on separate pages with soft page break indicators (a line of dashes) separating them, if you look at the Status line as you move from the first to the second column, it will show you that they are actually on the same page and they will actually print correctly (side by side) even if you leave Column Display set to No.

Parallel Columns

To create parallel columns, you follow the same steps you did to create newspaper columns, except that when you get to the *Type of columns* prompt, you enter a 2 for Parallel. The only other difference is that you have to insert a hard page break at the end of each column, or text will be wrapped around to the next column, as it is in Newspaper Column mode.

By definition, parallel columns are separate columns of text that always remain next to each other (parallel) on the same page, so that you can read across as in a translation or columnar chart. To achieve this, you insert a hard page break at the end of the first column, which moves the cursor to the beginning of the next column on the same page. Next, you type the second column and then keep following this procedure for each column you have defined. The cursor behaves as though each column were a separate page and will not move to the real second page until after you have filled the last column with text or inserted a hard page break in it.

You should always insert a hard page break before the cursor automatically moves to the next column. If a column is already full and you try to insert text into it, the text at the bottom will spill over into the next column, spoiling the parallel alignment. If the next column is also full, it (the entire next column) will be moved over one more column, and you could be left with a column that has only a few lines of text (because of the hard page breaks). For instance, say you have defined three columns on a page and all three are filled with text. If you try to add several new lines of text to the first column, the text at the bottom (of column 1) will be pushed to column 2. However, since there is a hard page break at the end of column 1, the former contents of column 2 will be moved in their entirety to column 3, and column 2 will only contain a few lines of text. The former contents of column 3 will be moved to column 1 of the next page. Since there is no way around this limitation, parallel columns are only useful on a page by page basis, and major editing changes such as additions and deletions are not possible.

Groups of parallel columns are kept together by WordPerfect's block protection feature. Pressing Ctrl-Return after typing each column except the last one inserts a hard page code [HPg]. When you press Ctrl-Return after typing the last column, it inserts the [BlockPro:Off] [Col off] codes. These terminate block protection and turn the Column feature off, but both features are automatically turned on again and the cursor is placed on the next line at column 1. Columns are permanently turned off by using option 3 on the Math/Columns Key (Alt-F7).

Follow the instructions below to create the parallel columns shown in Figure 10.7.

1. Type the heading (COLUMNS) and first paragraph.
2. To define the columns, press the Math/Columns Key (Alt- F7) and select option 4, Column Def. You will be defining 2 evenly spaced columns (so that the margins are calculated by WordPerfect) with 5 spaces between them. The third question asks what type of columns you want to use; select option 2 for parallel columns. Enter 2 for the

---

COLUMNS

Newspaper columns are used for text that flows up and down through columns, just like in a newspaper, and **parallel** columns are used to keep separate blocks of text next to each other on the same page. Each page can have as many as 24 columns, and they appear next to each other both on screen and in the printed document.

The Math/Columns Key

The Math/Columns Key (Alt-F7) is used to define columns and to turn the column feature on and off. Each column is treated by WordPerfect as a separate page of text, and editing changes only affect the column where the cursor is currently located.

Cursor movement

Cursor movement within columns is basically the same as in edit mode. To move the cursor between columns, you press the Go To Key, which is Ctrl and Home, followed by the Right or Left Arrow Key.

Parallel columns are used to create short charts, tables, and perform other nonnumeric tasks, or to mix columnar and noncolumnar text on the same page. Use newspaper columns, not parallel columns, if the text in columns covers more than one page.

Figure 10.7: *Parallel columns*

number of columns, then press the Return key four times to accept the margin settings.

3. To turn the column feature on, select option 3 (Column On/Off) from the Math/Columns Key. Note the Col 1 indicator on the Status line.

4. Center and type the next heading (The Math/Columns Key). As you see, it is centered over the first column, not the entire page. Type the rest of the paragraph.

5. At the end of the paragraph, press Ctrl-Return. This places the cursor at the top of column 2. Note the Col 2 indicator on the Status line.

6. After you finish typing the second column press Return, then use option 3 on the Math/Columns Key to turn columns off. Finish typing the rest of the text.

If you want, you can add another block of columns by turning column back on again (as in step 3) and repeating steps 4 through 6. You can repeat these steps as long as the columns fit on this page.

Remember, when you want to move the cursor from one column to another after the text has been typed, press Ctrl-Home followed by the → or ← key.

Summary

As you have seen, WordPerfect features two different types of text columns, newspaper and parallel. Parallel columns are useful for short blocks of text that must remain next to each other on a single page, such as side-by-side translations or charts; newspaper columns are used for text in which the words flow from column to column. You can have as many as 24 columns of text on a page, and you can define the margins for each column individually so that they can be uneven in width. WordPerfect's Newspaper Column feature is very flexible, since the program treats columns as separate pages, and editing changes within one column do not affect text on the same line in the adjacent column (except to shift it as the entire document is reformatted).

Newspaper columns are used for text that flows from one column to the next, as in a newspaper. Parallel columns are used to keep blocks of text next to each other on the same page. Each page can have as many as 24 columns, and they appear next to each other both on screen and in the printed document.

The Math/Columns Key (Alt-F7) is used to define both types of columns, and to turn the Column feature on and off. When the Column feature is on, a column number indicator is added to the Status line. Each column is treated by WordPerfect as a separate page of text, and editing changes directly affect only the column in which the cursor is currently located.

Cursor movement within columns is basically the same as in Edit mode, except that you must press → at the bottom of a column to move to the top of the next one, and ← to reverse the action. To move the cursor across to the next column, you press the Go To Key (Ctrl-Home) followed by → or ←.

Parallel columns are useful on a page-by-page basis, to create short charts, tables, side-by-side translations, and anything requiring short groups of text to remain next to each other on the page. A hard page break must be inserted at the end of each parallel column, or text will be wrapped around to the next one, as in the case of newspaper columns.

CHAPTER 11 KEYSTROKE SUMMARY:

The Footnote Key—display options for creating and editing footnotes and endnotes

FOOTNOTES AND ENDNOTES

FOOTNOTES AND ENDNOTES ARE USED in academic work, books, articles, and research reports. The difference between footnotes and endnotes is that footnotes usually appear on the page to which they refer whereas endnotes are grouped together at the end of the document. WordPerfect permits both types of notes in a single document, and numbers them separately. When you create footnotes or endnotes, the program automatically inserts the appropriate numbers into your document and changes them as you add or delete notes. You can change the numbers to letters or make up an identification scheme of your own. As you can see, WordPerfect's Footnote and Endnote features are very flexible.

All footnotes are printed at the bottom of each page if there is enough room. They are separated from the text by two blank lines and a dotted line two inches long, and separated from each other by a single blank line.

These blank lines and the lines used by the footnotes themselves are subtracted from the total number of text lines on the page. (The text lines are reduced by the number of lines in the footnote plus two lines separating them from the text.)

Creating and Editing Footnotes

Creating footnotes is a simple process. First move the cursor to the text you would like to reference with a footnote. Then press the Footnote Key (Ctrl-F7) and select option 1, Create, from the menu that appears as shown below:

1 Create; 2 Edit; 3 New #; 4 Options 5 Create Endnote; 6 Edit Endnote: 0

You will then see the screen illustrated in Figure 11.1. Notice that it resembles the editing screen, but the Status line does not include the document and page indicators. The screen has a number next to the cursor and

```
    1_
```

```
Press EXIT when done                              Ln 1      POS 19
```

Figure 11.1: *The Footnote screen*

a prompt reminding you to press the Exit Key when you are finished typing the note. Press the Spacebar to leave a blank space between the number and the text of your note, then type your note. There is almost no limit to the length of the footnote; a maximum of 16,000 lines are permitted, which is far more than any footnote should ever contain! (Have you ever seen a 300 page footnote?)

When you have finished typing the footnote, press the Exit Key (F7). As you can see, the program automatically enters the footnote number into your document, and it will be printed in superscript if your printer is capable of it.

If you want to see the contents of a footnote, the first fifty characters are visible in the Reveal Codes screen. If it is longer than that, you can view it by selecting option 2, Edit, from the Footnote Key (Ctrl-F7) and typing the number of the note you wish to edit. You can also alter a footnote with this option, which you can select from any location in the document. When you do, you will see the same screen illustrated in Figure 11.1 and you can use all of the familiar WordPerfect commands to insert or delete text.

Creating and Editing Endnotes

Creating endnotes is almost identical to creating footnotes, except that you select option 5, Create Endnote, from the Footnote Key. Endnotes are numbered separately from footnotes, so you can have both types of notes in a single document. The maximum length of an endnote is also 16,000 lines. To edit an endnote, select option 6, Edit Endnote, from the Footnote Key. Your cursor does not have to be positioned on the endnote number to do this, but can be anywhere in the document. (You do have to remember the number of the endnote you wish to edit.)

Changing Footnote and Endnote Options

The Footnote Options screen, shown in Figure 11.2, allows you to change several formatting features such as the spacing within or between notes, the numbering scheme, and the number of lines to be kept together on a page. You should move the cursor to the top of the document before making any changes, to guarantee that all footnote and/or endnote references will be changed.

The first selection, Spacing within notes, can be used to change the spacing within footnotes or endnotes; the default is single spacing. It is unlikely that you will want to change it, since doing so will further reduce the number of lines available for the text of your document. The second selection, Spacing between notes, can be used to change the number of lines between separate footnotes or endnotes; the default is one blank line. To change it, select the option and enter the number you want to use. Note that you can use half lines.

The third selection allows you to alter the number of lines that will remain together on the page containing the reference number in case the footnote or endnote is very long and the reference to it appears near the end of the page. The default is three, meaning that if you have a note of ten lines, at least three of them will remain on the same page with the reference number.

Option 4, Start footnote numbers each page, numbers the footnotes on each page separately, so that the first footnote on each page is number 1. To use this method, type Y. The default is N.

```
Footnote Options

    1 - Spacing within notes              1
    2 - Spacing between notes             1
    3 - Lines to keep together            3
    4 - Start footnote numbers each page  N
    5 - Footnote numbering mode           0
    6 - Endnote numbering mode            0
    7 - Line separating text and footnotes 1
    8 - Footnotes at bottom of page       Y
    9 - Characters for notes              *
    A - String for footnotes in text      [SuprScrpt][Note]
    B - String for endnotes in text       [SuprScrpt][Note]
    C - String for footnotes in note          [SuprScrpt][Note]
    D - String for endnotes in note       [Note].

    For options 5 & 6:              For option 7:
        0 - Numbers                     0 - No line
        1 - Characters                  1 - 2 inch line
        2 - Letters                     2 - Line across entire page
                                        3 - 2 in. line w/continued strings


Selection: 0
```

Figure 11.2: *The Footnote Options screen*

Options 5 and 6 are used to change the numbering style for footnotes and endnotes. As shown at the bottom of the screen, you can select either numbers (0), characters (1), or letters (2). Numbers is the default. Letters are the lowercase alphabetical characters, a through z. Characters can be anything you want, but the default is a single asterisk for the first note, two asterisks for the second note, and so on. To change the asterisk to a different character, such as a number sign (#), use option 9 and enter the new character, then press 5 or 6 and select option 1 Characters. You can use up to five different characters by typing each one, then pressing Return. Figure 11.3 shows how the footnote numbering style was changed to characters.

As you can see, a # will be used to denote the first footnote, an ! will mark the second one, an @ will mark the third, a + will mark the fourth, and a ^ will mark the fifth. The sixth will be marked by ##, the seventh by !!, and so forth.

Option 7 can be used to change the line that separates the footnotes from the text. As you can see in Figure 11.4, the default is a 2-inch line (it is actually a line of tiny dots but they are so small the line appears solid with most printers); it can be changed to no line, a line across the entire

```
Footnote Options

    1 - Spacing within notes                    1
    2 - Spacing between notes                    1
    3 - Lines to keep together                   3
    4 - Start footnote numbers each page         N
    5 - Footnote numbering mode                  1
    6 - Endnote numbering mode                   0
    7 - Line separating text and footnotes       1
    8 - Footnotes at bottom of page              Y
    9 - Characters for notes                     #!@+^_
    A - String for footnotes in text            [SuprScrpt][Note]
    B - String for endnotes in text             [SuprScrpt][Note]
    C - String for footnotes in note               [SuprScrpt][Note]
    D - String for endnotes in note             [Note].

    For options 5 & 6:                  For option 7:
        0 - Numbers                         0 - No line
        1 - Characters                      1 - 2 inch line
        2 - Letters                         2 - Line across entire page
                                            3 - 2 in. line w/continued strings


    Selection: 9
```

Figure 11.3: *Changing option 9, Characters for notes*

page, or a two-inch line with a *continued* message. The *continued* option (#3) is a new feature in WordPerfect 4.2. If the entire text of the footnote does not fit on the page it references, you can use it to print the words "(Continued...)" on the last line of the footnote on the page it references and the first line (of the same footnote) on the next page.

Option 8 will insure that footnotes are always placed all the way at the bottom of the page, even on a page that contains only a few lines of text at the top, by inserting several blank lines between the text and footnotes. The default is Y.

The last four selections, A, B, C, and D, are used to change the appearance of the footnote or endnote number, letter, or character. As you can see from Figure 11.4, footnotes as well as their references in the text are, by default, designated by a superscripted number. You can use options A and C to change this style to anything you want, including underlined numbers, or any combination of characters. Although references to endnotes are also designated in the text by superscripted numbers, the numbers of the endnotes themselves, which appear at the end of the document, are not. Options B and D are used to change endnote numbers.

To insert a code such as [SuprScrpt] or [Note], you have to press the key that generates the code. For instance, to change the footnote numbering style so that the number denoting the text reference will appear without superscript, you select option A, which calls up the following prompt:

Replace with:

Next, you press Ctrl-F7 and this menu will appear:

1 Footnote/Endnote; 2 Set Footnote #; 3 Footnote Options: 0

Press option 1, and the prompt will show that the code for footnote or endnote will be inserted:

Replace with: [Note]

To accept it, press Return. Your screen should now resemble Figure 11.5. Since WordPerfect 4.2 also allows you to edit prompts such as this, you can achieve the same effect by selecting option A and pressing Del once.

The plywood manufacturing process is moderately complex. Logs are peeled into thin strips of veneer, dried in an oven, then pressed and glued into varying thicknesses of plywood. By-products of the peeling process, lumber cores and wood chips, are shipped to the company's beam mill and paper mill, respectively.

The process involves several important decision variables. One is the mixture of logs used in the peeling (veneer producing) process. The company uses their own logs as well as logs purchased on the outside. Currently, this mixture is half of each. Another important variable is the cost of logs. Currently, this cost is $45.00 per MBF[1] for its own logs, and $55.00 per MBF for logs purchased from other sources.

The company's peeling capacity (production of veneer through the peeling process) is 720 MSF[2] of veneer per quarter, and the company's pressing capacity (production of plywood through pressing strips of veneer together) is 288 MSF of plywood per quarter. Both of these could be increased by the purchase of additional equipment.

Since it takes an average of 3 1/3 square feet of veneer to produce one square foot of plywood, the company does not have sufficient peeling capacity to meet its requirements, even

---

[1] Thousand board feet

[2] Million square feet

Figure 11.4: *A 2-inch dotted line separating text and footnotes*

Deleting Footnotes or Endnotes

To delete a footnote or endnote, you have to delete the code that generates it. To do this, position the cursor on the number or character that identifies your note in the document and press the Del key. You will see the following message:

Delete [Note]? (Y/N) N

Press Y to delete it. The notes that follow the deleted one will be renumbered automatically, as soon as the cursor moves past them.

Renumbering Footnotes

You can change the number of a footnote anywhere in your document, and all of the notes that follow it will be renumbered in sequence. To do

```
Footnote Options

     1 - Spacing within notes                 1
     2 - Spacing between notes                 1
     3 - Lines to keep together               3
     4 - Start footnote numbers each page     N
     5 - Footnote numbering mode              0
     6 - Endnote numbering mode               0
     7 - Line separating text and footnotes   1
     8 - Footnotes at bottom of page          Y
     9 - Characters for notes                 *
     A - String for footnotes in text        [Note]
     B - String for endnotes in text         [SuprScrpt][Note]
     C - String for footnotes in note            [SuprScrpt][Note]
     D - String for endnotes in note         [Note].

     For options 5 & 6:           For option 7:
        0 - Numbers                  0 - No line
        1 - Characters               1 - 2 inch line
        2 - Letters                  2 - Line across entire page
                                     3 - 2 in. line w/continued strings


Selection: 0
```

Figure 11.5: *The Footnote screen after changing the string for footnotes in text*

this, use option 3, New #, on the Footnote Key (Ctrl-F7). The following prompt will appear:

Ftn #?

Type the new number for the next footnote, and press Return. When the document is reformatted by pressing ↓, the numbers will be reordered.

How Margin Changes in the Document Affect Footnotes and Endnotes

If you change the margins in your document after entering notes, the margins in the notes will not be automatically adjusted. (You may recall that this also happens with headers and footers.) Instead, you have to force the change by one of two methods. The easiest way is to use the Word-Perfect Speller and perform a word count, which only takes a minute. To do this, press the Spell Key (Ctrl-F2) and select option 6, Count. (If you do not have a hard disk, you will be asked to insert the Spelling Disk into one of the drives.)

The other method is to call up the editing screen for each footnote or endnote in your document, and simply exit from it. To do this, press Ctrl-F7 and option 2 for footnotes or option 6 for endnotes, type the number of the note, and then press Exit to leave the editing screen. This is a slow process if your document includes many notes, so the first method is recommended. (If you understand macros, you can use this feature to automate the process.)

Summary

In this chapter, you have learned how easily WordPerfect creates and numbers footnotes and endnotes, and automatically renumbers them as notes are inserted or deleted. The two types of notes are numbered separately, so both can be used in the same document. Whenever possible, footnotes are printed at the bottom of the page to which they refer, whereas endnotes are all placed in sequential order at the end of the document. These features are very flexible.

Creating footnotes and endnotes is a simple process. To enter a footnote, press the Footnote Key (Ctrl-F7) and select option 1, Create. To enter an endnote, select option 5, Create Endnote. Notes can be as long as 16,000 lines (almost 300 pages).

The program automatically inserts superscripted numbers into your document to cite the notes, and changes them as you add, delete, or renumber notes. The Options selection on the Footnote Key (Ctrl-F7, 4) can be used to change the numbers to lowercase letters, or to any combination of characters you want to use. The Options selection can also be used to further customize the appearance of your footnotes and endnotes. You can use it to change formatting features such as the spacing within or between notes, the numbering scheme, the number of lines to remain together on a page if the footnote or endnote is very long, and the line that separates the footnotes from the text.

To erase a footnote or endnote, you delete the code that generates it by positioning the cursor on the number or character that identifies your note in the document and pressing the Del key. All of the remaining notes will be renumbered in the correct sequential order.

You can renumber the footnotes or endnotes anywhere in your document in case you split it into separate files or want to start the numbering sequence over again in the middle of the document by selecting option 3 on the Footnote Key (Ctrl-F7). All of the notes that follow will be reordered in sequence.

When the margins are changed in a document that already includes footnotes and/or endnotes, the change will not update footnotes and endnotes. To adjust these margins, use the Count option on the Spell Key (Ctrl-F2), or enter and exit the editing screen for each note in the document.

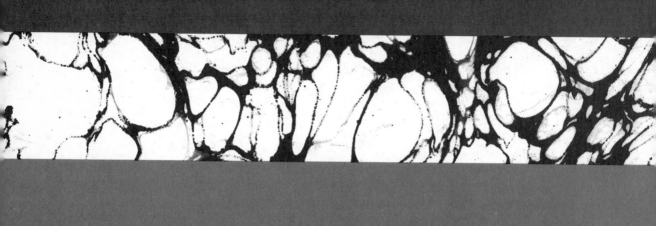

PART III

SUPPLEMENTAL FEATURES

CHAPTER 12 KEYSTROKE SUMMARY:

The List Files Key—retrieve, delete, rename, print, or copy a file; retrieve an ASCII text file; view an unretrieved file's contents; change or make a new directory; or perform a word search

The Text In/Out Key—import or export ASCII text files, add password protection to a file, or document summary and comments.

The Shell Key—temporarily exit to DOS in order to run commands such as FORMAT, DISKCOPY, or DISKCOMP or load and run another program

The Switch Key—simultaneously work on two documents in memory by switching back and forth between their editing screens

The Screen Key—select option 1, Window, to split editing screen in two (for working on two documents at once and keeping both in view)

FILE
MANAGEMENT

YOU HAVE ALREADY USED MANY OF WordPerfect's file management features to save, retrieve, and print files, but you've only scratched the surface of the program's sophisticated filing operations. In addition to being able to run many DOS functions from within WordPerfect, such as delete, rename, copy, and check disk, you can also use WordPerfect to search all files for a word or phrase, convert files to and from ASCII, lock and save documents with a password, temporarily exit to DOS and run another program, split the screen in two, and much more. Users with hard disks will especially appreciate commands that allow you to change default directories, search other directories for files to work with, create a new directory, or delete an empty directory. Since the WordPerfect commands are menu driven, they are much easier to work with than the equivalent DOS commands.

The List Files Key

The List Files Key (F5) is the major file management key. It can be used to retrieve, delete, rename, print, or copy a file, to retrieve a DOS text file, to view the contents of a file without retrieving it for editing from disk, to change the default directory or make a new directory, and to perform a word search. When you press F5 (and Return), a screen similar to the one in Figure 12.1 appears.

At the top of the screen, in the highlighted section, you see the current date and time, the name of the default disk and the path to the directory you are working in, the available space on the default disk (free disk space), and, if you have a document on the editing screen, the size of that document. Underneath is a listing of all files in the directory in alphabetical order, describing their size and the time and date they were last saved. Notice that it resembles the listing you see when you use the DOS DIR command, except that the file names are listed in two columns.

```
03/07/87   22:31              Directory C:\WP2\REVISED\*.*
Document Size:      1349                      Free Disk Space:   1724416

· <CURRENT>    <DIR>                .. <PARENT>    <DIR>
ADD6             633  02/27/87 10:28    CH1      .RV   42570  02/23/87 22:05
CH2      .RV   17530  02/23/87 22:02    CH3      .     32309  02/27/87 14:27
CHANGES  .MWP  31796  02/24/87 18:30    FIG21    .       385  02/23/87 16:42
FIG21A   .       477  02/23/87 17:00    FIG711   .        58  03/01/87 09:18
FIG72    .       340  03/01/87 08:47    FIG74    .       450  03/01/87 09:00
PAGE50   .       410  02/27/87 12:05    PG120    .      1244  02/27/87 13:31
PG155    .       542  03/01/87 10:39    PG169    .       302  03/01/87 11:05
PG187    .       888  03/02/87 10:14    PG188    .      1613  03/02/87 11:56
PG191    .       172  03/02/87 12:20    PG197    .       457  03/04/87 09:00
PG200    .       177  03/04/87 09:09    PG205    .       354  03/04/87 09:37
PG208    .       599  03/04/87 09:49    PG233    .       359  03/06/87 19:38
PG54     .      3151  02/27/87 14:41    PG58     .      1104  03/04/87 08:43
PGXXI    .       472  03/04/87 08:37    SAMPLE2  .      1151  02/24/87 16:27
SCREEN00.CAP    4256  02/23/87 16:16    SCREEN01.CAP    4256  02/23/87 16:16
SCREEN02.CAP    4256  02/23/87 16:17    SCREEN03.CAP    4256  02/23/87 16:17
SCREEN04.CAP    4256  02/23/87 17:02    SCREEN05.CAP    4256  02/23/87 18:04
SCREEN06.CAP    4256  02/24/87 16:13    SCREEN07.CAP    4256  02/24/87 16:17
SCREEN08.CAP    4256  02/24/87 16:17    SCREEN09.CAP    4256  02/24/87 16:19

1 Retrieve; 2 Delete; 3 Rename; 4 Print; 5 Text In;
6 Look; 7 Change Directory; 8 Copy; 9 Word Search; 0 Exit: 6
```

Figure 12.1: *The List Files screen*

If you use a hard disk, you can obtain a listing of the files in a different directory by typing the name (and path if necessary) of that directory, preceded by the DOS backslash symbol (\).

Cursor Movement in the List Files Screen

The highlighted bar at the top left side of the listing represents the cursor. To move this cursor bar, press any of the arrow keys on the numeric keypad or the Screen Up or Screen Down keys. The Page Up or Page Down keys will have the same effect as Screen Up or Down. The Home, Home, ↑ (or ↓) combination moves the cursor to the first (or last) file in the list. If your list is quite long, you can also take advantage of WordPerfect's Name Search option to move the cursor. It works like this: when you type a character, the prompt at the bottom of the screen disappears and is replaced by the character, while the cursor moves to the first file in the list beginning with that character. If there are several files that begin with the same character, narrow the search by typing more characters, as shown in Figure 12.2. To exit from Name Search, press Return, and the List Files menu reappears.

To return to the editing screen, press Cancel, the Spacebar, or option 0.

Selecting Multiple Files

To perform operations such as delete, print, or copy on a group of files, move the cursor to each file and mark it by pressing the Asterisk key. An asterisk will appear next to the file-size statistic in the third column. Then when you select an operation such as delete or copy, you will see a prompt indicating that all of the marked files will be affected. For instance, if you choose to delete several files, this prompt will appear:

Delete Marked Files (Y/N) N

The asterisk mark is a toggle; if you want to remove it from a file, just highlight each file name (one at a time) and press the Asterisk key again.

```
03/07/87   22:37              Directory C:\WP2\REVISED\*.*
Document Size:     1388                      Free Disk Space:   1716224

. <CURRENT>      <DIR>                .. <PARENT>      <DIR>
ADD6    .           633  02/27/87 10:28   CH1    .RV    42570  02/23/87 22:05
CH2     .RV       17530  02/23/87 22:02   CH3    .       32309  02/27/87 14:27
CHANGES .MWP      31796  02/24/87 18:30   FIG21  .         385  02/23/87 16:42
FIG21A  .           477  02/23/87 17:00   FIG711 .          58  03/01/87 09:18
FIG72   .           340  03/01/87 08:47   FIG74  .         450  03/01/87 09:00
PAGE50  .           410  02/27/87 12:05   PG120  .        1244  02/27/87 13:31
PG155   .           542  03/01/87 10:39   PG169  .         302  03/01/87 11:05
PG187   .           888  03/02/87 10:14   PG188  .        1613  03/02/87 11:56
PG191   .           172  03/02/87 12:20   PG197  .         457  03/04/87 09:00
PG200   .           177  03/04/87 09:09   PG205  .         354  03/04/87 09:37
PG208   .           599  03/04/87 09:49   PG233  .         359  03/06/87 19:38
PG54    .          3151  02/27/87 14:41   PG58   .        1104  03/04/87 08:43
PGXXI   .           472  03/04/87 08:37   SAMPLE2 .       1151  02/24/87 16:27
SCREEN00.CAP       4256  02/23/87 16:16   SCREEN01.CAP    4256  02/23/87 16:16
SCREEN02.CAP       4256  02/23/87 16:17   SCREEN03.CAP    4256  02/23/87 16:17
SCREEN04.CAP       4256  02/23/87 17:02   SCREEN05.CAP    4256  02/23/87 18:04
SCREEN06.CAP       4256  02/24/87 16:13   SCREEN07.CAP    4256  02/24/87 16:17
SCREEN08.CAP       4256  02/24/87 16:17   SCREEN09.CAP    4256  02/24/87 16:19


PG               (Name Search;  Use space, enter or arrows to exit name search)
```

Figure 12.2: *Highlighting a specific file with the Name Search option*

Narrowing the Display with Wildcards

You can restrict the directory listing to a specific file by pressing the List Files Key (F5) and typing the file name after the DIR prompt. Notice that as soon as you type the first character, the default directory name will disappear.

If you have forgotten the exact name, or if you want to look up a group of files with similar names, you can use the question mark, which functions as a wildcard character representing any single character. For instance, the chapters for this book are stored in files named ch1, ch2, ch3...ch18. To look them up all at once, I type the following in response to the DIR prompt:

ch??

and my listing appears as in Figure 12.3.

It is often helpful to list a group of files with a common pattern such as the same extension (the three character identifier that follows the file name). To do this, you can use another wildcard character, the asterisk,

```
┌─────────────────────────────────────────────────────────────────────────┐
│ 03/16/87  22:09              Directory C:\WP\BOOK\CH??.*                   │
│ Document Size:        0                        Free Disk Space:   1372160 │
│                                                                           │
│ . <CURRENT>      <DIR>             │  .. <PARENT>      <DIR>               │
│ CH1    .         44672 02/28/86 07:42 │  CH10   .         18716 02/19/86 23:05 │
│ CH11   .         13600 02/19/86 23:06 │  CH12   .         32954 07/30/86 14:05 │
│ CH13   .         24435 03/10/86 17:07 │  CH14   .         23852 03/11/86 19:15 │
│ CH15   .         22520 04/16/86 17:44 │  CH16   .         23814 04/06/86 20:47 │
│ CH17   .         10412 02/19/86 23:08 │  CH18   .         18712 02/19/86 23:08 │
│ CH19   .            65 02/12/86 20:00 │  CH4    .         20480 02/28/86 07:44 │
│ CH8    .         39989 04/20/86 20:39 │  CH9    .         39972 04/20/86 20:34 │
│                                                                           │
│                                                                           │
│                                                                           │
│                                                                           │
│                                                                           │
│                                                                           │
│                                                                           │
│    1 Retrieve; 2 Delete; 3 Rename; 4 Print; 5 Text In;                    │
│    6 Look; 7 Change Directory; 8 Copy; 9 Word Search; 0 Exit: 6           │
│                                                                           │
└─────────────────────────────────────────────────────────────────────────┘
```

Figure 12.3: *Using the wildcard ? in a directory listing*

which represents the character in the position it is located on plus any remaining characters in the file name or extension. For example, to look up the names of all macros, which are always stored with the extension MAC, press F5 and enter *.MAC. (Never try to retrieve a macro.) You could also use the asterisk in place of the two question marks in the example shown in Figure 12.3.

Notice that the designator *.* is automatically used with the DIR command when you press the List Files Key; it means that all files will be shown.

Retrieving Files

You have already used the Retrieve Key (Shift-F10) to retrieve a copy of a file from disk to the editing screen. Option 1 on the List Files Key is another method of doing the same thing. To use it, move the cursor to the file you want to retrieve and press 1. The List Files screen will disappear and the file you requested will replace it on the editing screen. If there is already another document on the screen, the one you are retrieving will be inserted in front of it, pushing it to the end.

Deleting Files

To delete a file, highlight it with the cursor and select option 2, Delete. This prompt will appear on the Status line, double checking to make sure you really want to delete the file:

Delete (*filename*) (Y/N)? N

Needless to say, once you press Y, the file is permanently erased. As mentioned, you can delete several files at once by marking them with asterisks before selecting this option.

Renaming Files

Option 3 can be used to rename a file. To use it, move the cursor to the file you want to rename and press 3; the following prompt will appear:

New Name:

As soon as you type the new name (and press Return), it replaces the old one and appears in the highlighted bar on your screen.

Printing Files

As you learned in Chapter 8, you can print one or more files by selecting option 4, Print, from the List Files menu. The file or files you select will be sent to WordPerfect's print queue and listed on the Printer Control screen.

Importing ASCII Files

When you want to use a file that has been saved as an ASCII file from another program (other than files created under specific programs that can be converted with the WordPerfect Convert utility, such as WordStar, MailMerge, and MultiMate), do not use the Retrieve Key or the Retrieve option on the List Files Key. Instead, use option 5, Text In, on the List Files Key, or option 2 or 3 (Retrieve a DOS text file) on the Text In/Out Key (Ctrl-F5). If you are retrieving text from an ASCII file created using a different word processor, use option 3 on the Text In/Out Key. This will maintain the soft returns found at the end of each line within your paragraphs, and only places hard returns at the end of each paragraph (or wherever two or more carriage return line feed codes are found. The manual suggests resetting the WordPerfect margins before importing a file, to preserve its format (since WordPerfect's margins begin at position 10, while many other programs' margins begin at 0). You can also use either F5, 5 or Ctrl-F5, 2 to import and revise files created from the keyboard, such as batch files created using the DOS COPY command.

Looking at Files

Option 6, Look, is a wonderful utility that you can use to view the contents of any file in the directory listing or to view a listing of all files in another directory. It is helpful when you want to take a quick look at the contents of a file without retrieving it to the editing screen. To use it, move the cursor to the file you want to look at and press 6 or Return. The file will appear on screen without formatting features such as line spacing, as the prompt in the lower portion of the screen reports:

NOTE: This text is not displayed in WordPerfect format.

The file name, path, and size are displayed in the highlighted bar at the top of the screen, as shown in Figure 12.4. Note that you will not be able to edit the document, but you can use ↓, Screen Down, or Page Down to scroll down through it and view sections that are not visible on the screen. If you try to move back up, you will be returned to the List Files screen.

To view a listing of the files in another directory, follow the same procedure, moving the cursor to the directory name and selecting option 6. After pressing Return, you will see the same listing that you see for the current directory when you press the List Files Key and you can use the same options from the menu at the bottom of the screen on these files.

Changing, Creating, or Deleting a Directory

When you press the List Files Key (F5), the DIR command will always show the name of the default directory or disk. You can use option 7 on the List Files screen to change the default directory or to switch from one

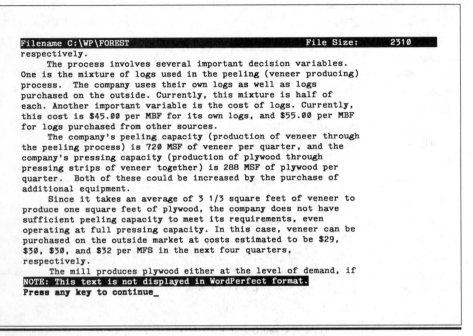

Filename C:\WP\FOREST   File Size: 2310
respectively.
      The process involves several important decision variables.
One is the mixture of logs used in the peeling (veneer producing)
process. The company uses their own logs as well as logs
purchased on the outside. Currently, this mixture is half of
each. Another important variable is the cost of logs. Currently,
this cost is $45.00 per MBF for its own logs, and $55.00 per MBF
for logs purchased from other sources.
      The company's peeling capacity (production of veneer through
the peeling process) is 720 MSF of veneer per quarter, and the
company's pressing capacity (production of plywood through
pressing strips of veneer together) is 288 MSF of plywood per
quarter. Both of these could be increased by the purchase of
additional equipment.
      Since it takes an average of 3 1/3 square feet of veneer to
produce one square feet of plywood, the company does not have
sufficient peeling capacity to meet its requirements, even
operating at full pressing capacity. In this case, veneer can be
purchased on the outside market at costs estimated to be $29,
$30, $30, and $32 per MFS in the next four quarters,
respectively.
      The mill produces plywood either at the level of demand, if
NOTE: This text is not displayed in WordPerfect format.
Press any key to continue_

Figure 12.4: *Viewing a file with the Look option*

disk drive to another. To use option 7, just select it and type the name (and path if needed) of the directory, or the disk drive (A or B) followed by a colon. When you press Return, you will be switched to that directory or subdirectory (it will become the default). Pressing Return again will obtain a listing of the directory just selected. Alternatively, you can move the cursor (the highlighted bar) to the subdirectory name and press 7, and the name will appear after the *New Directory* = prompt (press Return next to switch to it).

For example, I have a subdirectory named *SCREEN* that appears on my List Files screen as follows:

    SCREEN . <DIR>

(The *DIR* appears in place of the file-size statistic.) To switch to that subdirectory, I highlight it, select 7, and press Return. (Note that my WordPerfect directory name is *WP*.) The Status line prompt then changes to:

    Dir C:\WP\SCREEN*.*

and I can press Return once more to obtain a directory listing.

Once you have changed to a different disk, directory, or subdirectory, you can also use option 7 on the List Files Key to go back to the parent directory (which, in my example, is the directory named *WP*). To do this, I press F5 and then press Return to accept the default prompt, which appears on the Status line (such as *Dir C:\WP\SCREEN*.* *). Next, I look for a file in the list named

.. <PARENT> <DIR>

and move the cursor bar to highlight it, then press 7. This prompt appears on the Status line:

New Directory = C:\WP

Pressing Return completes the change. The prompt DIR \WP*.* will then appear, and I can either press Return to get a directory listing, or press the Cancel Key (F1) and Spacebar to get back to the edit screen.

Another way to change the default directory is by pressing the List Files Key and typing an equal sign (=), followed by the name of the directory you want to use. To switch to the SCREEN subdirectory, I press F5, press =, and enter *SCREEN* in response to the prompt *New Directory* = . To change back to my WordPerfect subdirectory, I reverse this action by pressing F5, =, and entering *WP*.

You can also use option 7 on the List Files Key to create a new directory. To do this, press F5, select option 7, and type the name (and path) for the new directory when you see the prompt *New Directory*. If you do not enter a path (using the \), WordPerfect assumes this will be a subdirectory one level under the directory you are presently using, and will enter the path for you. After you press Return, a prompt will ask if you wish to create this directory, and you should type Y. After it has been created, the directory name will show up at the top of your file listing on the screen.

You can use option 2 on the List Files Key to delete a directory on the listing, but it must be empty of all files. To do this, press F5, move the cursor bar to the directory name, select option 2, and type Y in response to the *Delete* prompt. If the directory contains any files, you will get the following message when you try to remove it:

ERROR: Directory not empty

If this happens, you must delete all the files in that directory before proceeding. To be on the safe side, you should follow the procedures outlined above to change to that directory, use option 6 to look at the files to be certain you want to delete them, use option 2 to delete them, then switch back to the parent directory and select option 2 to complete the process of deleting the directory.

Copying Files

You can use option 8 to copy files to another disk drive or directory. To copy a file to another disk, move the cursor to the file and select option 8. The following prompt will appear:

Copy This File To:

Next, type the name of the disk drive (A, B, C) followed by a semicolon. Notice that you do not have to type the file name. When you press Return, it will be copied. If there is another file with the same name on that disk, you will be asked if you want to replace that file. Enter a Y only if you are certain you want to replace it.

To copy the file to another directory on your hard disk, just type the name (path) of the directory (following the DOS rule of preceding it by a \ if necessary), and press Return.

You can also use this option to make an extra copy of a file by assigning a new name to it at this prompt:

Copy This File To:

Because of the new name, the copy will not replace the original.

Searching All Files for a Word or Phrase

Option 9, Word Search, is another practical utility, one that allows you to locate any file or group of files that contain a particular word or phrase. You can use as many as 20 characters in the search, including the wildcard characters ? and *, which you read about earlier in this chapter. The program does not distinguish between uppercase and lowercase during the word search, so the search string can be typed either way. If your phrase includes a space, comma, semicolon, or quotation marks, you must use quotes around the entire phrase.

Only files that are found to contain that word or phrase will be listed, as shown in Figure 12.5. In this example, all files in the subdirectory had similar names: sample1, sample2, sample3, sample4, sample5, and sample6. I knew one of them was a glossary of computer terms, so I searched for the word *glossary,* and after WordPerfect completed its search, the screen was cleared and a new directory listing appeared containing just one file name: sample6. To verify that this was the correct one, I then used option 6, Look.

You can expand or restrict the search by using semicolons, blank spaces, or commas, which serve as *logical operators.* A semicolon or a single blank space between two words stands for AND; it means that you want the program to locate only those files that contain both of the words. A comma between two words stands for OR; it means that you want the program to locate files that contain either (or both) of the words.

Block File Commands

Save

In Chapter 4 you learned how to save a copy of a block of text as a separate file on disk. To review briefly, you use the Block Key (Alt-F4) to mark the text, press the Save Key (F10), then type a name for the new file in which the block will be saved. After it is saved, the Block on prompt will still be visible on the Status line, so you will have to press the Cancel Key (F1) or the Block Key to turn it off.

Append

Instead of saving a block of text in a new file, you can use the Append feature to add it to the end of an existing disk file. To do this, block the text with the Block Key (Alt-F4), then press the Move Key (Ctrl-F4) and select option 3, Append. You will see this prompt:

Append to:

Next, enter the name of the file to which you wish to add the block. The block will still be highlighted but it will disappear once the block has been appended.

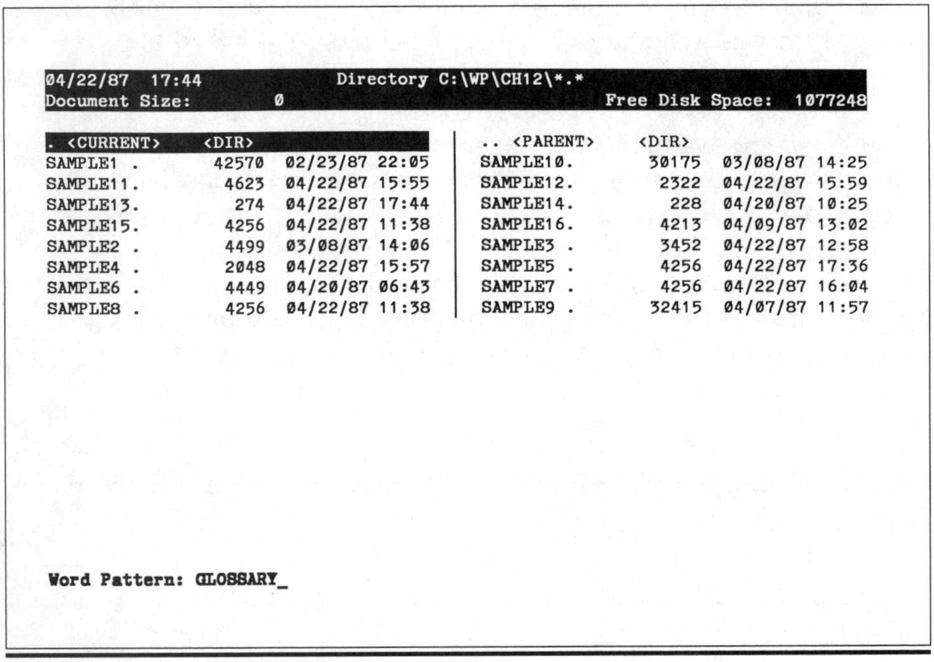

```
04/22/87  17:44              Directory C:\WP\CH12\*.*
Document Size:          0                    Free Disk Space:   1077248

. <CURRENT>    <DIR>              .. <PARENT>    <DIR>
SAMPLE1 .      42570  02/23/87 22:05   SAMPLE10.     30175  03/08/87 14:25
SAMPLE11.       4623  04/22/87 15:55   SAMPLE12.      2322  04/22/87 15:59
SAMPLE13.        274  04/22/87 17:44   SAMPLE14.       228  04/20/87 10:25
SAMPLE15.       4256  04/22/87 11:38   SAMPLE16.      4213  04/09/87 13:02
SAMPLE2 .       4499  03/08/87 14:06   SAMPLE3 .      3452  04/22/87 12:58
SAMPLE4 .       2048  04/22/87 15:57   SAMPLE5 .      4256  04/22/87 17:36
SAMPLE6 .       4449  04/20/87 06:43   SAMPLE7 .      4256  04/22/87 16:04
SAMPLE8 .       4256  04/22/87 11:38   SAMPLE9 .     32415  04/07/87 11:57




Word Pattern: GLOSSARY_
```

Figure 12.5: *Performing a word search*

The Text In/Out Key

You can use WordPerfect's Text In/Out Key (Ctrl-F5) to import and export ASCII files or to add password protection to a file so that unauthorized users cannot read or edit it.

Converting a WordPerfect File to ASCII

Option 1, Save (in DOS Text File Format), can be used to write a file to disk in ASCII format (as a DOS text file), so it can be read by other programs. This action removes all the formatting codes that appear on the Reveal Codes screen, such as line spacing, margin settings, and headers and footers, and also replaces all soft return codes (found at the end of each line within a paragraph if word wrap was used) with hard returns.

When you select this option, the program assumes you want to replace the WordPerfect version of the file with the ASCII version you are about to create.

If you want to keep a copy of the original document in WordPerfect format, you should either make a copy under a different name before the conversion or retrieve the file onto your editing screen and give it a new name when prompted for the name of the file to convert.

Follow these steps to complete the process:

1. Press the Text In/Out Key (Ctrl-F5). You will see the screen illustrated in Figure 12.6 and should then select option 1, Save.

2. You will then see a prompt that asks you to enter the name of the file. If you wish to save the original document and you have retrieved it to the editing screen, enter a new name for it. Otherwise, type the name of the file to be converted (the file can be either on your data disk or editing screen).

3. After you type the file name, you will be asked to confirm that you do want to replace the WordPerfect version of the file with an ASCII version (this prompt won't appear if a new name is used). Press Y and the conversion will then take place. While this is happening, a message will indicate that it is being saved. Do not try to retrieve an ASCII file back into WordPerfect unless you use the second option, as described below.

Importing ASCII Files to WordPerfect

You can use option 2 or 3, Retrieve, on the Document Conversion, Summary, and Comments screen to import a file from other programs that create ASCII files (or that can convert their files to ASCII) or to import and revise files produced at the keyboard, such as batch files created using the DOS COPY command. Note that this feature is the same as option 5, Text In, on the List Files Key. See the section on importing ASCII files earlier in this chapter for an explanation of the difference between options 2 and 3.

Password Protection

Option 4 on the Text In/Out Key lets you save a file with a password, so that nobody else can use it. Once you do this, you will never be able to retrieve it again or even use the Look option on the List Files Key to view its contents unless you remember the password, so be very careful with this option. The easiest way to remember your password is to be consistent; if you always use the same one, chances are you'll never forget it.

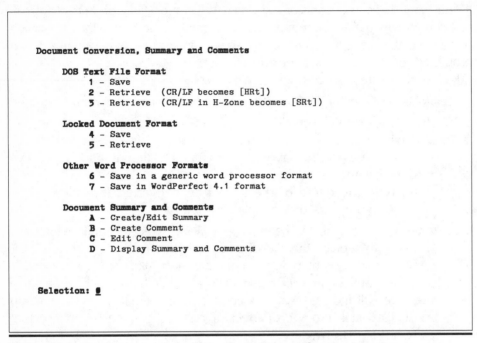

```
Document Conversion, Summary and Comments

       DOS Text File Format
            1 - Save
            2 - Retrieve  (CR/LF becomes [HRt])
            3 - Retrieve  (CR/LF in H-Zone becomes [SRt])

       Locked Document Format
            4 - Save
            5 - Retrieve

       Other Word Processor Formats
            6 - Save in a generic word processor format
            7 - Save in WordPerfect 4.1 format

       Document Summary and Comments
            A - Create/Edit Summary
            B - Create Comment
            C - Edit Comment
            D - Display Summary and Comments



  Selection: █
```

Figure 12.6: *The Document Conversion, Summary, and Comments screen*

Otherwise, it is recommended that you keep a written record of the passwords you have used for each document. There's nothing worse than losing an important document because you can't remember a password you created six months ago.

To protect a document, it is only necessary to lock it once. To do this, press Ctrl-F5, select option 4, and type the password twice, pressing the Return key each time. Next, type the name under which you wish to save the file and press Return. A password can contain as many as 75 characters. For extra security, the password is not visible on the screen as you type it so WordPerfect makes you type it twice to protect against spelling errors. After that, each time you save the file, using the Save or Exit Key, you will be asked to type the password twice.

To retrieve a locked file, be sure that there is not another file which has been retrieved to the screen or created and saved to disk (and still on your edit screen), then proceed as usual by pressing either the Retrieve Key or option 1 on the List Files Key. You will be asked for the password (only once) after you specify the file name. If there is another file on the editing screen, the next time you save the document, it will not be protected. You will know this has happened because you will not be asked for the password when you save it.

The only significant restriction when using password protection is that you cannot print a locked file from disk. Since the password must be entered to retrieve a file before printing, you must use one of the methods that prints the file from the editing screen. This prevents unauthorized users from printing it. It also means that you cannot use option 4 (Print) on the List Files Key, nor can you use the P option on the Printer Control screen. This may become a problem if you are printing a lengthy document and your default disk is almost full, because these methods of printing from the screen create a temporary copy of the file in RAM, or, if there is not enough room in your computer's memory, on the default disk.

You can remove the password protection from a file by retrieving the document with the password, defining the entire document as a block using the Block Key (Alt-F4), and pressing F10 to save the block, using the same file name. Afterward, be sure to clear the screen without saving the old version or it will replace the unprotected version you just saved as a block. Alternatively, you can first type a few characters on the editing screen, save them in a file under a new name, then retrieve your locked file and save it with the same name as the screen file (with only a few characters in it).

Document Summary

Document Summary is a new feature of WordPerfect 4.2 that can be used to create a brief description of the file. It consists of the filename, creation date (of the summary, not necessarily the file), the author, the typist, and a comment section that can contain up to 880 characters. You can create a document summary anytime the document is on the edit screen, even after the file has been saved, and you can choose to turn off the display on the edit screen (the default is to display it). When the summary is displayed, it appears at the beginning of the file surrounded by a box, as shown in Figure 12.7.

The real purpose of the summary is to use it with Look, option 6 on the List Files menu (F5). When you use Look to view your file, the summary is always visible at the top so you can get a quick overview of the file's contents, as shown in Figure 12.8.

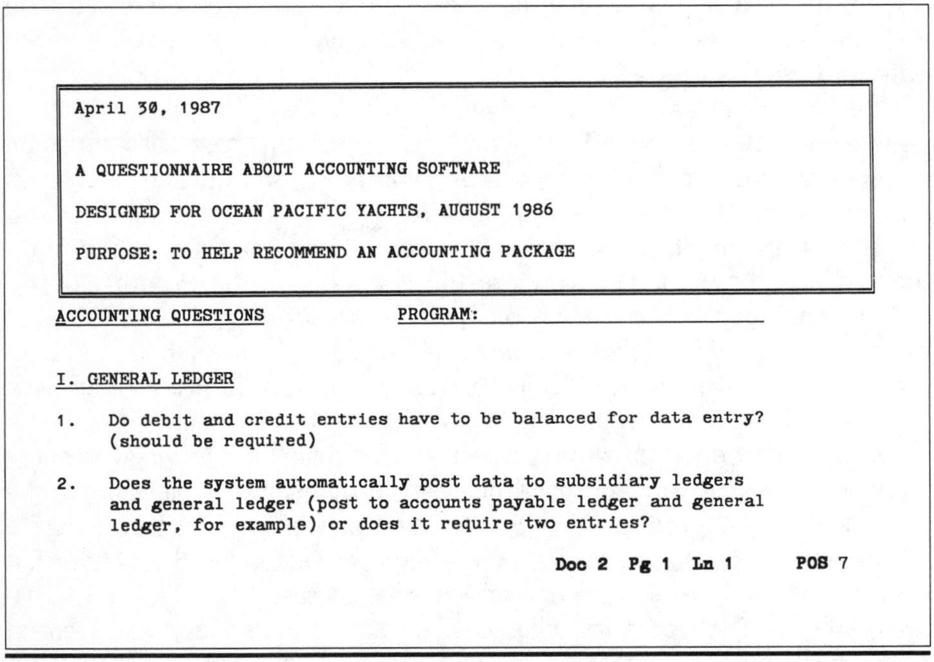

```
April 30, 1987

A QUESTIONNAIRE ABOUT ACCOUNTING SOFTWARE

DESIGNED FOR OCEAN PACIFIC YACHTS, AUGUST 1986

PURPOSE: TO HELP RECOMMEND AN ACCOUNTING PACKAGE

ACCOUNTING QUESTIONS          PROGRAM:

I. GENERAL LEDGER

1.   Do debit and credit entries have to be balanced for data entry?
     (should be required)

2.   Does the system automatically post data to subsidiary ledgers
     and general ledger (post to accounts payable ledger and general
     ledger, for example) or does it require two entries?

                              Doc 2  Pg 1  Ln 1      POS 7
```

Figure 12.7: *A document summary shown on the edit screen*

Consistent and logical use of this feature can be invaluable in keeping track of your files, particularly if you use a hard disk. Through WordPerfect's Set-up screen (see Appendix A) you can make the document summary mandatory so that the Create/Edit Summary screen will automatically appear the first time you save a file. Note that the Word Search feature (9) on the List Files menu includes the text of the document summary in its search.

To create a document summary, press the Text In/Out Key (Ctrl-F5); note that the cursor can be anywhere in the document when you do this. You will see the Document Conversion, Summary and Comments screen illus-trated in Figure 12.6. Press A to select Create/Edit Summary and the screen shown in Figure 12.9 will appear.

The file name appears at the top of the list unless it has not been saved, in which case it will say *(Not named yet)*. The *Date of Creation* line is also filled in for you; note that it corresponds to the date in your computer (if it says January 1, 1980, you forgot to enter the correct date when you turned on your system). If you get in the habit of creating a document

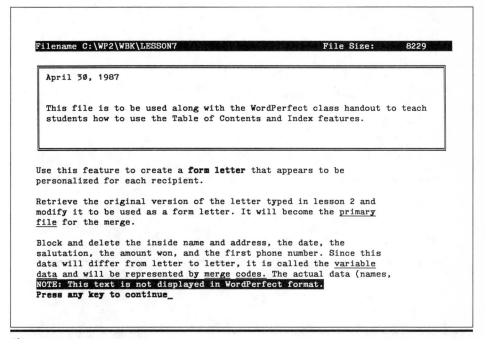

Filename C:\WP2\WBK\LESSON7   File Size: 8229

April 30, 1987

This file is to be used along with the WordPerfect class handout to teach
students how to use the Table of Contents and Index features.

Use this feature to create a **form letter** that appears to be
personalized for each recipient.

Retrieve the original version of the letter typed in lesson 2 and
modify it to be used as a form letter. It will become the <u>primary</u>
<u>file</u> for the merge.

Block and delete the inside name and address, the date, the
salutation, the amount won, and the first phone number. Since this
data will differ from letter to letter, it is called the <u>variable</u>
<u>data</u> and will be represented by <u>merge codes.</u> The actual data (names,
NOTE: This text is not displayed in WordPerfect format.
Press any key to continue_

Figure 12.8: *The document summary viewed with the Look option on the List Files Key*

summary before saving the file for the first time, or if you use the Set-up
screen to make the Document Summary feature mandatory, this date will
always match the original creation date of your file.

You enter the author, typist, and comments. Press Return after typing the
author and typist, and press F7 after you finish entering the comments. To
leave a field blank, just press Return. Press F7 to return to the edit screen
when you are finished.

Document Comments

Document Comments, also a new feature of WordPerfect 4.2, are nonprinting comments you can create anywhere in your document. If Display
Comments is set to yes (the default), they appear on screen where you create them, surrounded by a box. To create a comment at the cursor position, press the Text In/Out Key (Ctrl-F5) and select option B, Create
Comment. The screen illustrated in Figure 12.10 will appear.

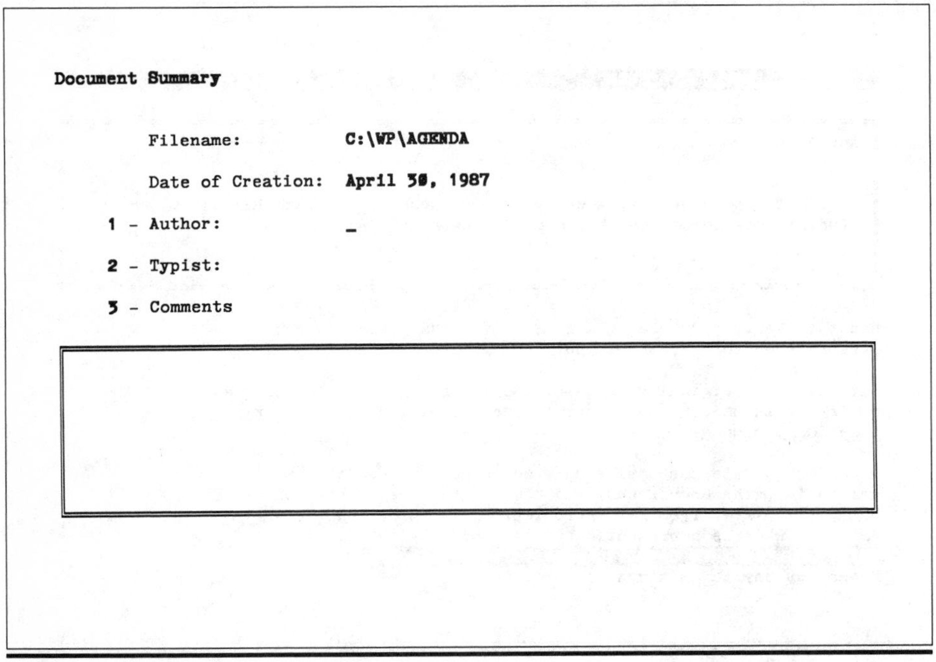

Document Summary

      Filename: **C:\WP\AGENDA**

      Date of Creation: **April 30, 1987**

  1 - Author: _

  2 - Typist:

  3 - Comments

Figure 12.9: *The Document Summary screen*

Type your comment, which can be up to 1,024 characters, then press the Exit Key (F7).

If you have Display Comments set to Y and create a comment in the middle of a line of text, the box will appear to split the text, as shown in Figure 12.11. In reality, the text starts again immediately after the comment, so check the Status line to determine the actual position of the text. If your cursor is at the end of the line, press the → key to jump over the box to the next word.

Displaying the Summary and Comments

WordPerfect normally displays the summary and comments on the edit screen. To turn off the display, select option D from the Text In/Out Key (Ctrl-F5) and enter N in response to the prompts *Display Summary (Y/N)* and/or *Display Comments (Y/N)*. The display stays off during the entire edit

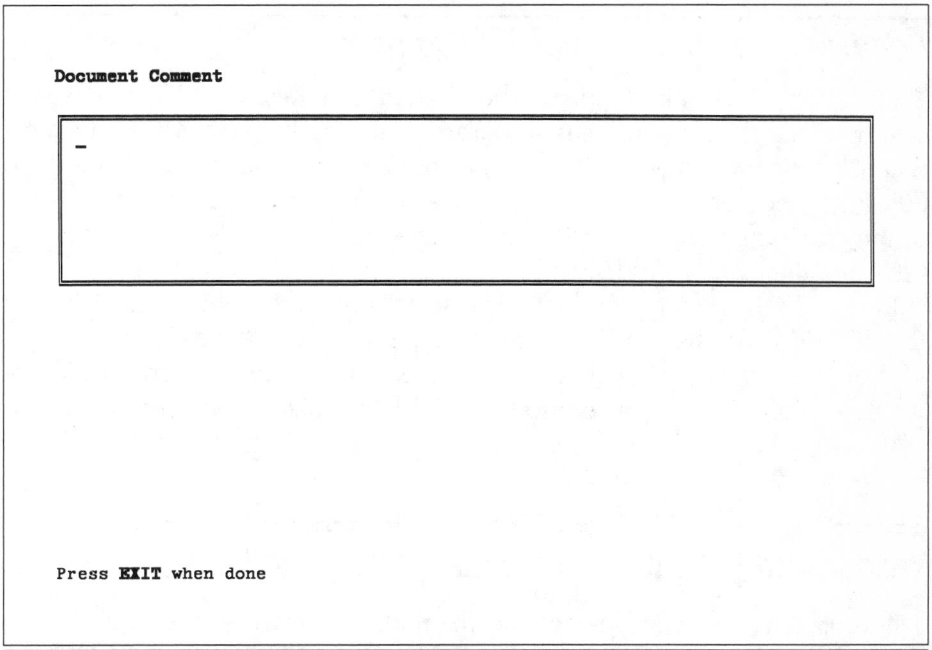

```
┌──────────────────────────────────────────────────────────┐
│                                                            │
│  Document Comment                                          │
│   ┌──────────────────────────────────────────────────┐    │
│   │ _                                                  │    │
│   │                                                    │    │
│   │                                                    │    │
│   │                                                    │    │
│   │                                                    │    │
│   └──────────────────────────────────────────────────┘    │
│                                                            │
│                                                            │
│                                                            │
│                                                            │
│                                                            │
│                                                            │
│                                                            │
│  Press EXIT when done                                      │
│                                                            │
└──────────────────────────────────────────────────────────┘
```

Figure 12.10: *The Document Comment screen*

session, even if you clear the screen and retrieve or create a different document (until you exit from WordPerfect—display will be on the next time you start the program).

When you print the document, neither the summary nor the comments are printed, regardless of whether they are displayed or not.

Deleting the Summary and/or Comments

The Reveal Codes screen shows the first 100 characters of your Document Summary or Comment, along with the code

[Smry/Cmnt:.......]

To delete a document summary or comment, just find the code in the Reveal Codes screen (or use Search, F2, Ctrl-F5 or Shift-F2, Ctrl-F5) and delete it using the Backspace or Del key.

Editing the Summary and/or Comments

To change a comment, press the Text In/Out Key (Ctrl-F5) and select option C, Edit Comment. The program searches backward for the most recent comment and places the cursor inside the box so you can edit it. To edit a specific comment, you must move the cursor to the immediate right of the comment code in the Reveal Codes screen (using Search is the easiest way), then press Ctrl-F5, C.

To edit the document summary, just select option A from the Text In/Out Key (Ctrl-F5) and the Document Summary screen will appear with a *Selection* prompt. Enter 1 to edit Author, 2 to edit Typist, or 3 to edit the Comments section. Press F7 when you are finished making your changes.

Temporarily Exiting to DOS: The Shell Key

If your computer contains enough memory, you can use the Shell Key to exit to DOS in order to run commands such as FORMAT, DISKCOPY, or DISKCOMP (if you have them on your disk), or to load and run another program. To use this feature, press the Shell Key (Ctrl-F1) and select option 1, Go to DOS. You will see the screen, as illustrated in Figure 12.12, which shows the DOS logo and version number.

When you are ready to return to WordPerfect, just type EXIT. The *Enter 'EXIT'* prompt shown in Figure 12.12 will always reappear on the screen after you have run another program, but if you forget and try to return by typing WP, you will receive an error message asking if other copies of WordPerfect are running. If this happens, be sure to press F1 to cancel it, and then type EXIT to return through the Shell command. If you don't, you may destroy the files you were working on before you exited to DOS. When you exit to DOS using the Shell Key, WordPerfect actually creates another copy of the DOS system files. If you try to load WordPerfect from this copy, another copy of WordPerfect will be created. Unless you have a substantial amount of memory (512K), you'll probably receive an error message indicating there is not enough memory to run the program.

Another important warning when using this option is that you should never turn off the computer until you have returned to WordPerfect by typing EXIT and then exiting properly, using the Exit Key (F7).

```
     3.    Does it show who made the transaction entry and when and where
           it was entered (audit)


     4.    Reversing (adjusting) entries: how are they handled?


     5.    Can you go to another accounting period (same year) to post
           transactions or make adjusting entries?  How does this affect
           the audit trail?


     6.    Open vs. closed: can system be modified?


     7.    Statements: balance sheet, income statement, statement of
           changes in financial position are a minimum.  Can they be
           altered?  Exported to their spreadsheet_
   ┌─────────────────────────────────────────────────────────────────┐
   │ Find out which spreadsheet they are using now!                    │
   └─────────────────────────────────────────────────────────────────┘
                                          or a word processor? If
           not, are the formats acceptable?
                                          Doc 1  Pg 1  Ln 38    Pos 51
```

Figure 12.11: *A document comment in the middle of a line of text*

WordPerfect Corporation has recently expanded the Shell into a program manager that can integrate several of their other programs. See Appendix C for more information about the WordPerfect Library.

Working with Two Documents in RAM

WordPerfect provides two methods of maintaining separate documents in your computer's memory, the Switch feature and the Window feature. The main difference is that Switch provides two full editing screens to work with, whereas Window splits a single editing screen into two smaller ones.

To use the first feature, press the Switch Key (Shift-F3). The document indicator on the Status line will change from Doc 1 to Doc 2, and you will have a new editing screen to work on. You can then retrieve a file from the disk, create a new file, or use the Move, or Block and Move Keys to transfer data between the two documents in memory. Press the Switch Key

```
The IBM Personal Computer DOS
Version 3.10 (C)Copyright International Business Machines Corp 1981, 1985
              (C)Copyright Microsoft Corp 1981, 1985

Enter 'EXIT' to return to WordPerfect
C>_
```

Figure 12.12: *The Go to DOS screen*

to move back and forth between the documents. I use this feature constantly to test program features without ruining my manuscript by forgetting to remove formatting codes.

To use Window, press the Screen Key (Ctrl-F3) and select option 1, Window. You will then see a prompt asking how many lines you want in this window. The screen has 24 lines available, so if you want to split it exactly in half, type 12. Alternatively, you can select the number of lines by pressing the ↓ key. When you do so, you will see the Tab Ruler, which you are familiar with from the Reveal Codes screen. Keep pressing ↓ until the Tab Ruler reaches the location where you want to split the screen, then press Return. The document you are currently working on will appear in the top window, and you will see the Tab Ruler in between the windows.

To move the cursor to the second window, press the Switch Key (Shift-F3). Notice how the tab marks change direction when you do this, pointing downward to indicate that you are working in the lower window. You will also see two separate Status lines, one at the bottom of the screen and one just above the Tab Ruler line. Notice that the document number indicators (Doc *n*) are

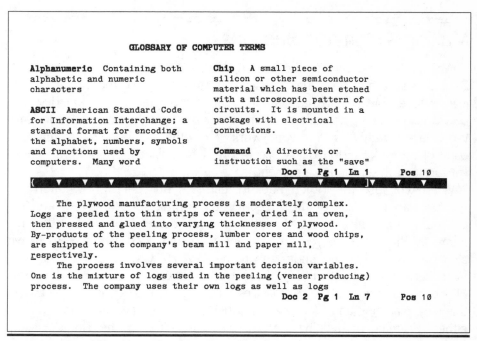

GLOSSARY OF COMPUTER TERMS

Alphanumeric Containing both
alphabetic and numeric
characters

ASCII American Standard Code
for Information Interchange; a
standard format for encoding
the alphabet, numbers, symbols
and functions used by
computers. Many word

Chip A small piece of
silicon or other semiconductor
material which has been etched
with a microscopic pattern of
circuits. It is mounted in a
package with electrical
connections.

Command A directive or
instruction such as the "save"

Doc 1   Pg 1   Ln 1   Pos 10

The plywood manufacturing process is moderately complex.
Logs are peeled into thin strips of veneer, dried in an oven,
then pressed and glued into varying thicknesses of plywood.
By-products of the peeling process, lumber cores and wood chips,
are shipped to the company's beam mill and paper mill,
respectively.
The process involves several important decision variables.
One is the mixture of logs used in the peeling (veneer producing)
process. The company uses their own logs as well as logs

Doc 2   Pg 1   Ln 7   Pos 10

Figure 12.13: *Using windows*

different. You can now retrieve another file into the second window by using the Retrieve Key (Shift-F10), or option 1 on the List Files Key (F5), or use the screen to create a new document. Figure 12.13 shows a screen split in half, with different documents on each half.

To return to a single screen, select the option again (by pressing Ctrl-F3, 1) and enter 25 or any number that exceeds the total number of lines on your screen (0 also works). If you do this from the lower window, you will find yourself in document 2, and will have to press the Switch Key again to return to the first document.

If you like having the Tab Ruler on your screen, you can use the Window option to place it there permanently. To position the ruler at the top of the screen, start with a blank editing screen (otherwise your document will be in the top window, with only one line visible). Select the Window option and enter 2 as the number of lines you want to keep in the window. Then use the Switch Key to move to the lower window, and use that as the editing screen. To place the ruler at the bottom, enter 22. (Two lines is the minimum you can specify for a window.)

Making Automatic Backups

WordPerfect has two methods of making automatic backups, the Timed Backup feature and the Original Backup feature. You use the Timed Backup feature to enable you to recover data that might otherwise be lost due to a power failure, computer failure, or any other problem that forces you to leave WordPerfect without saving your work. The other method makes an extra copy of the disk version of the file before it is replaced by saving an edited version, and this copy is permanent.

When you use the Timed Backup feature, you specify how often you want a backup copy of the file on your editing screen saved, and the program interrupts and saves the file at these intervals under the name {WP}BACK.1. (If you are working with two document screens, it will also save the other file under the name {WP}BACK.2.) When you leave WordPerfect via the Exit Key, these backup files are closed and erased. However, if there is a failure, the files will remain on disk and you can use them by renaming and then retrieving them. If you start WordPerfect without either renaming or deleting them (and continue to use the Timed Backup feature), you will see this message when the program tries to make a new backup copy:

Old backup file exists. 1 rename; 2 delete:

You will have to erase or rename the files. (You can use the List files key to delete it.)

The Original Backup feature creates a permanent copy on the default disk. As you know, when you retrieve a file for editing, you are actually using a copy of it, and after you have made editing changes and have saved the document, the copy on screen replaces the version on the disk. If Original Backup is being used, the original (disk) version will be renamed and saved in a separate file with a different extension (.BK!), instead of being erased by the copy on the edit screen. However, since the extra copy is saved on the same disk, you still should make extra backup copies on separate disks in case of disk failure. If you are in the habit of saving different files under the same name with different extensions, such as sample.1, sample.2, and sample.3, this procedure will only make a backup of the most recently edited document, naming it sample.bk!.

To implement these features, enter the WordPerfect Set-up screen by typing WP/S from the DOS prompt (A> or C>). You will see the screen illustrated in Figure 12.14. Select option 4, Set Backup Options.

```
                              Set-up Menu

      Ø - End Set-up and enter WP

      1 - Set Directories or Drives for Dictionary and Thesaurus Files
      2 - Set Initial Settings
      3 - Set Screen and Beep Options
      4 - Set Backup Options

      Selection: _

      Press Cancel to ignore changes and return to DOS
```

Figure 12.14: *The Set-up screen*

You will then see the screen illustrated in Figure 12.15, which asks first for the number of minutes between backups and then whether you want to backup the original document. To use Timed Backup, enter the number of minutes, and the drive you want the files stored on (and the directory and path if you are using a hard disk), otherwise press the Cancel Key (F1) to move to the second option. To use Original Backup, type Y. Next, type 0 (zero) to enter WordPerfect. Once you select these options, they will always be loaded when you start the program unless you enter the Set-up screen again and change them.

Summary

The List Files Key (F5) is the major key used for file management. Its many functions include options to retrieve, delete, rename, copy, or print files, along with several unusual features such as utilities to change the

```
Set Timed Backup

To safeguard against losing large amounts of text in the event of a power or
machine failure, WordPerfect can automatically backup the document on your
screen at a chosen time interval and to a chosen drive/directory (see Set-up
in the WordPerfect Installation pamphlet).  REMEMBER--THIS IS ONLY IN CASE OF
POWER OR MACHINE FAILURE.  WORDPERFECT DELETES THE TIMED BACKUP FILES WHEN YOU
EXIT NORMALLY FROM WORDPERFECT.  If you want the document saved as a file you
need to say 'yes' when you exit WordPerfect normally.

Number of minutes between each backup: 10


Set Original Backup

WordPerfect can rename the last copy of a document when a new version of the
document is saved.  The old copy has the same file name with an extension of
".BK!".  Take note that the files named "letter.1" and "letter.2" have the
same original backup file name of "letter.bk!".  In this case the latest
file saved will be backed up.

Backup the original document? (Y/N) N
```

Figure 12.15: *Setting the Backup Options*

default directory, create a new directory or erase an empty one, perform a word search, view the contents of a file, and import ASCII files into WordPerfect.

The Delete, Print, and Copy options on the List Files Key can be used with more than one file by marking each file to be included with an asterisk.

The directory listing can be restricted to a specific file by typing its name after pressing the List Files Key. Groups of files can be located using wildcard characters. The question mark substitutes for any one character, and the asterisk substitutes for the character in the position it is located on and any remaining characters in the file name.

A block of text can be saved to a separate file or added to the end of an existing file on disk. To save a block, you mark it with the Block Key (Alt-F4) and press the Save Key (F10). To append a block to another file, you mark it and select option 3, Append, from the Move Key (Ctrl-F4).

The Text In/Out Key (Ctrl-F5) is used to import and export ASCII files to and from WordPerfect or to add password protection to a file to prevent unauthorized users from retrieving or printing it.

Document Summary can be used to create a brief description of the document that includes the date, author, typist, and up to 880 characters of comments. The Summary appears at the begining of the file, surrounded by a box. When you use the Look option on the List Files Key, (F5) the Summary is displayed at the top of the file, providing an overview of the file's contents. Document Comments are notes you can create anywhere in your document and, like the Summary, they are set off by a box on screen. A single comment can contain as many as 1,024 characters. Neither Document Summary nor Comments are printed.

The Shell Key (Ctrl-F1) can be used to exit to DOS temporarily and run DOS commands or other programs, if there is enough memory in your system. When you are done, typing EXIT will return you to WordPerfect.

You can work with two separate documents simultaneously by using the Window option on the Screen Key (Ctrl-F3) or by using the Switch Key (Shift-F3) to switch to a second editing screen. The Window feature splits a single screen in two, whereas the Switch feature provides two full size editing screens to work with. You can permanently place the Tab Ruler on your screen by creating a two line window at the top or bottom of the screen.

To protect your files from power failures or hardware problems, you can use the Timed Backup feature, directing WordPerfect to save the file automatically at regular intervals. It is also wise to use the Original Backup feature, which renames and saves the disk version of a file whenever an edited version of the same file is being saved from the screen. Both of these options are installed by using WordPerfect's Set-up menu.

As you have seen, WordPerfect's file management features are comprehensive and powerful, and the program provides much more than the typical DOS-based commands such as copy, delete, rename, and check disk. Furthermore, they are menu driven and are easier to use than the equivalent DOS commands. Several helpful features accommodate users with hard disks, including commands that allow you to change default directories, search other directories for files to work with, create a new directory, or delete an empty directory. Other interesting features you have explored in this chapter include Word Search, which can search all files for a word or phrase; the Text In/Out Key, which can convert files to and from ASCII, lock and save documents with a password and add a document summary or comments to a file; the Shell Key, which you can use to temporarily exit to DOS and run another program; and the Windows feature, which can split the screen in two so that you can view two documents at once.

The Merge Codes Key—display the merge codes for variable data in the primary file

The Merge Return Key—press after typing each field in a record to insert the ^R code and add a hard return

The Merge End of Record Key—press at the end of each record in the secondary file to insert the ^E code and add a hard return

The Merge/Sort Key—display options for merging the primary and secondary files

MERGES

WORDPERFECT'S MERGE FEATURE IS powerful and versatile, with fourteen merge commands you can combine to generate form letters, reports, lists, mailing labels, contracts, and much more. The easiest and most common application is to create form letters that appear to be personalized. You type the letter only once, inserting special codes in place of data that differs for each letter, such as the name, address, phone number, and salutation and store this letter in a file called the primary file. The variable data (name, address, salutation) is typed in a list that is stored in a file called the secondary file. When they are combined in the merge operation, one letter is produced for each set of variable data.

If you don't need to save the variable data for future use, you have the option of typing it at the keyboard as each letter is

assembled. You can insert messages in the letter to remind yourself what information is needed at each point. (The messages are only visible on screen
when you merge, and won't be printed.) The letters can be produced on
screen and saved in a file or sent directly to the printer. If you store your variable data in a secondary file, you can use it to produce other lists, such as a
list of each name and phone number, or to produce mailing labels, which
exclude phone numbers, salutations, and other extraneous information. A secondary file can also be created using another program such as dBASE and
imported to WordPerfect's merge format through the Convert program.

You can further automate the merge process by using WordPerfect's Sort,
Select, and Macro features. In Chapter 15 you will learn, for example, how
to use sorting to organize your mailing labels by zip code in order to take
advantage of lower postal rates, and in Chapter 16 you will learn how to
use macros with merges.

Form Letters

Suppose the administrator of a national sweepstakes wants to send a letter informing all winners of their prizes and verifying their phone numbers.
Rather than type each recipient's letter individually, he sets up a form letter
with codes for the following variable data: the date, the recipient's name,
address, and phone number, and the dollar amount of the prize he or she
has won. He then merges it with a secondary file containing the specific
data for each winner. Figure 13.1 shows the final letter for one of the
million-dollar winners.

The Primary File

The first step is to create the form letter, using merge codes that direct
the program to insert variable data during the merge. Notice that the first
variable is the date. Although you can use the Date Key to insert a date
function, there is also a merge code for this purpose. To enter it, press the
Merge Codes Key (Alt-F9). The prompt line will list twelve of the special
merge codes, as shown below:

^C; ^D; ^F; ^G; ^N; ^O; ^P; ^Q; ^S; ^T; ^U; ^V:

Most of these codes are mnemonic, and correspond to the first letter of a command. For instance, ^U updates the screen, ^N means next record, ^F means field, and ^D stands for date. To insert the date code, type

    D

and press Return. Note that instead of using the Merge Codes Key, you can press Ctrl and the code letter. This inserts the caret (^) in front of the letter. However, you cannot use the caret sign on the 6 key at the top of the keyboard. (If you use the Merge Codes Key, as shown above, you don't have to press Ctrl.)

Since the date appears at the right margin in the letter, position the cursor to the left of the code and press the Flush Right Key (Alt-F6) to move it there.

The next step is to insert codes for the recipient's name and address. This information is divided into distinct parts called *fields* and the collection of

```
                                                April 13, 1986

Ms. Colleen McDuffy
54 Prince Lane
Salem, GA 32255


Dear Ms. Colleen McDuffy,

     Congratulations!  You are a winner in the $20,000,000
National Sweepstakes and are soon to be the recipient of a check
for $1,000,000, less the appropriate amount of tax required by
the Federal Government.  We will be contacting you soon to
determine this amount.
     Our records show your phone number to be (513) 222-0000.  If
this has changed, please inform us immediately by calling this
toll-free number: (800) 445-0000.
     Please keep this letter for your records.



Yours Truly,



Irwin Kronsky

Sweepstakes Administrator
```

Figure 13.1: *The sweepstakes letter*

all the fields for one recipient is called a *record*. There is no limit to the number of fields a record can contain, but they must be used consistently so that the fields designated by the same number in each record contain the same type of information. For example, in each record in the file field 6 must always contain the check amount. You will learn why later in this chapter.

In this letter there are seven fields per record: the name, street address, city, state, zip code, check amount, and phone number. Although several of these fields could have been combined into a single field, such as the street address, state, and zip code, it is advantageous to place data into separate fields in case you want to sort it by any of these categories or use individual fields separately in a different merge operation.

The first field that appears in the letter is called F1, for field 1. The remaining fields are numbered sequentially in the order they appear. In your letter, field 1 will be the name; field 2 will be the street address; field 3 will be the city; field 4, the state; field 5, the zip code; field 6, the check amount; and field 7, the phone number. To enter the first field, move the cursor down several lines and press the Merge Codes Key (Alt-F9). Type

F

You will see this prompt:

Field Number?

Type

1

and press Return twice, once to enter the ⌃ F1 ⌃ and once to move to the next line for the address. The code will appear as

^F1^

on your screen. (The second caret is inserted for you by WordPerfect.) Repeat this process for fields 2, 3, 4, and 5. Be sure to type a comma and enter a blank space after entering ⌃ F3 in order to separate fields 3 and 4 (the city and state) and be sure to leave a blank space between fields 4 and 5 (the state and zip). Since fields 3, 4, and 5 appear on the same line, you only press Return two times on this line after entering field 5, zip code. (You press it just once after 3 and 4.) Next, move the cursor down a few lines and type the salutation

Dear

and enter the name field code, ^ F1 ^, once again. (Be sure to insert a space after *Dear* and a comma after the field code.) As you can see, a field number can be used more than once in the same primary file. In fact, there is no limit to the number of times it can be used.

When you have entered the first seven codes, your primary file will appear as follows:

```
                                                      ^D
^F1 ^
^F2 ^
^F3 ^,  ^F4 ^  ^F5 ^

Dear ^F1 ^,
```

Type the rest of the letter, inserting the codes for F6 and F7 in place of the check amount and phone number. It will appear as follows:

> Congratulations! You are a winner in the
> $20,000,000 National Sweepstakes and are soon to be the
> recipient of a check for ^F6^, less the appropriate
> amount of tax required by the Federal Government. We
> will be contacting you soon to determine this amount.
>   Our records show your phone number to be ^F7^. If
> this has changed, please inform us immediately by
> calling this toll-free number: (800) 445-0000.
>   Please keep this letter for your records.
>
> Yours Truly,
>
> Irwin Kronsky
>
> Sweepstakes Administrator

Save the file under the name LETTER1.PF and clear the screen. The extension PF stands for primary file (it serves to identify this as a primary merge file). That's all there is to creating a primary file. As you will see, this letter can be used over and over with different variable data inserted to produce a limitless number of form letters.

The Secondary File

The next step is to create the secondary file, which consists of a record for each recipient, each record containing seven fields of variable data separated by merge codes that mark the end of each field and the end of the record. For instance, the record for Colleen McDuffy, which was merged into the letter shown in Figure 13.1, appears as follows:

```
Ms. Colleen McDuffy ^R
54 Prince Lane ^R
Salem ^R
GA ^R
32255 ^R
$1,000,000 ^R
(513) 222-0000 ^R
^E
```

Note the ^R and ^E codes. After typing each field, you press the Merge Return Key (F9), which inserts the ^R code. Since this action also adds a hard return, do not press Return at the end of each line. When you reach the end of a record (after typing the phone number, which is the last field in each letter), press the Merge End of Record Key (Shift-F9), which inserts the ^E code and a hard return. When the form is merged, the ^E also generates a hard page break at the end of each letter, since it marks the end of one form.

Now enter the record shown above, as well as the following two records, and save them in a file named WINNERS.SF. (SF stands for secondary file.) Be very careful not to add any spaces before the ^R and ^E codes, because the spaces will show up in the merged letter. Also, do not use the Return key at all or you will insert extra lines into the merged letter. For example, if you were to press Return after typing the state field, the zip code would appear on its own line instead of on the one with the city and state. If you were to add a hard return after the last ^E, the program might try to create another letter after the last letter was produced from your list.

Here are the next two records:

```
Mr. James Browder ^R
100 Main St. ^R
Mt. Hood ^R
WA ^R
81233 ^R
$10,000 ^R
(802) 331-0000 ^R
^E
```

Mrs. Rhonda Flamestein ^R
233 12th Ave. ^R
San Francisco ^R
CA ^R
91222 ^R
$50,000 ^R
(415) 444-0000 ^R
^E

Merging the Primary and Secondary Files

The final step, merging the files and creating the three letters, is the easiest one. Clear the screen with the Exit Key (F7) and press the Merge/Sort Key (Ctrl-F9). As you see, the prompt provides the following choices:

1 Merge; 2 Sort; 3 Sorting Sequences: 0

Select option 1, Merge. The next prompt will ask for the name of the primary file, and you enter

LETTER1.PF

The last prompt will ask for the name of the secondary file, and you enter

WINNERS.SF

The merge process will begin, and this message will appear in the lower left corner:

∗ Merging ∗

When the merge is complete, you will have three letters on screen, separated by hard page breaks. Scroll through the letters to verify that the correct data was entered in each field. You can then print the letters using the Print Key (Shift-F7) or save them to disk to be printed later.

Stopping a Merge

A merge can be stopped any time by pressing the Cancel Key (F1). If you know in advance where you want to end a merge, you can include the merge code ∧Q (for quit) inside the secondary file. This is especially useful if you are using a secondary file with a large number of records, and don't need to print forms for all of the records. Without the ^Q code, you would either have to create an extra secondary file consisting of just those records to be merged in the current operation, or else delete the ones you don't need. To insert the code in the secondary file, place it on the line following the Merge End code (^E) of the last record you want to include.

Updating the Screen

By including the merge code ^U (update) in your primary file, you can watch each form letter as it is generated. Whenever WordPerfect encounters this code, it rewrites the screen to show the letter with the new set of data and displays it for you. To use it, press the Merge Codes Key (F9) and select U. Be careful where you place the code in the document. In the form letter you just created, if you place the ^U at the beginning, you will see the merge codes, not the variable data, as the letters are generated, because at that point the program has not yet performed the merge. If you place it at the end, you will only see the bottom half of each form letter. The best place to put it is after the phone number, which is the last variable in the form.

Merging to the Printer

As you have seen, the merged letters are created on the screen and are not printed until you issue a print command. If your secondary file is very large, you may not have enough memory in your computer to hold all of the letters being created and the process will stop. Furthermore, you may not want to review them on the screen or save all of them to disk, so WordPerfect provides the option of merging directly to the printer.

To try it, retrieve your primary file, LETTER1.PF, and insert these codes at the end of the document, using the Merge Codes Key (Alt-F9). Save the revised letter as LETTER2.PF.

    ^T ^N ^P ^P

The ^T means *type*, and it causes the program to print (that is, type on the printer) everything that has been merged to that point, then erase it from (RAM) memory. This action occurs after each letter has been merged, which means none of the letters will appear on screen. The ^N means *next,* and it causes WordPerfect to find the next record in the secondary file. If there are no more records, it ends the merge. The two ⌃P codes mean *primary,* and they cause the program to look for a primary file and start the merge process all over again. The file name is normally entered between the two ⌃P codes, but when it is left out, as in this case, the most recently used primary file is automatically used (LETTER2.PF).

The final step is to perform the merge. You follow the same process you used to send merged letters to the screen, except that the name of the altered primary file is different. Be sure the printer is turned on and supplied with paper, and clear the screen. Next, press the Merge/Sort Key (Ctrl-F9) and select option 1, Merge. When you are asked for the name of the primary file, enter

    LETTER2.PF

then enter the name of the secondary file:

    WINNERS.SF

As you will see, the three letters will be sent directly to the printer, and you will not see them on the screen.

Merging from the Keyboard

When you don't have to save the variable data for future use, you can simply enter it from the keyboard, eliminating the lengthy step of creating a secondary file. To do this, you have to change the primary file to eliminate the field codes (⌃F1⌃ through ⌃F7⌃) and replace them with another code, ⌃C, which tells WordPerfect to stop so that you can type the names, addresses, and other variable data for each letter as it is created. (⌃C stands for *console,* which means input from the keyboard.)

Retrieve the LETTER1.PF file to begin this exercise. Next, either move the cursor to each ⌃F code, erase it and enter a ⌃C code in its place, or use Search and Replace to automate the process. To use Search and Replace, press the Replace Key (Alt-F2), press N when asked if you want to use confirm, then press the Merge Codes Key (Alt-F9). The prompt line will appear as follows:

    1 ^C; 2 ^D; 3 ^F; 4 ^G; 5 ^N; 6 ^O; 7 ^P; 8 ^Q; 9 ^S; A ^T; B ^U; C ^V: 0

To select the ＾F code, enter 3. Each of the codes in your primary file has a different number (1 through 7), but you don't have to repeat the operation for each code if you use the wildcard character ＾X as a substitute for the numbers. This will locate all of the field numbers in one operation. To use it, press Ctrl-V (the prompt will say n=), then press Ctrl-X. Press Ctrl-V, Ctrl-X once again to include the second caret sign, which you want to delete since the ＾C code is not followed by a caret as the ＾F code is. The prompt line will appear as follows:

→ Srch: ^F^X^X

Press F2, and you will be asked what to replace it with. Press the Merge Codes Key (Alt-F9) again, and select option 1, the ＾C code (the ＾C code does not require a number). Press F2 once more to begin the search. When it is completed, the pertinent sections of your form letter will appear as follows:

^C
^C
^C, ^C ^C

Dear ^C,

   Congratulations! You are a winner in the
$20,000,000 National Sweepstakes and are soon to be the
recipient of a check for ^C, less the appropriate
amount of tax required by the Federal Government. We
will be contacting you soon to determine this amount.
   Our records show your phone number to be ^C.

Since you are not saving the variable data, reduce the five codes of the address to a single ＾C code by erasing the four extra ＾C's. When the program pauses at this point during the merge, you enter the entire address heading: name, street address, city, state, and zip code, pressing Return to separate the lines.

Now save the file under the name LETTER3.PF and clear the screen. Begin the merge by pressing the Merge/Sort Key (Ctrl-F9) and selecting option 1, Merge. Enter LETTER3.PF as your primary file and press Return to leave the secondary file name blank. When the merge begins, the first ＾C disappears and the cursor is now positioned where the ＾C had been; it is here you type a name. After typing it, press Return to move to the next line and type the street address, then press Return again and type the city, state, and zip code on the following line. Next, press the Merge R Key (F9), (also called the Merge Return key since it inserts a hard return) to move to the next field, which is the name in the salutation (after *Dear*). The second ^C disappears and you type the name, then press F9 again to move to the check amount field. Be sure to press F9 after typing the last field's data (phone number) or the *Merging* message will remain on the screen. When you have entered data in each field, the first form letter will be complete and you can print it. To start over with a new record, either clear the screen or insert a hard page break (by pressing Ctrl-Return), then press Ctrl-F9 again and repeat the process.

Inserting Reminders in the Primary File

If you set up a merge operation that will be used by others, they may need help understanding what is supposed to be entered in each field where a ^C appears. WordPerfect has a special merge code, ^O, which means output a message to the screen. By typing an explanation between a pair of ^Os, you can inform the user exactly what to type at each point in the document.

To try this, retrieve the file named LETTER3.PF and position the cursor on the first ^C code. Press the Merge Codes Key (Alt-F9) and type

O

Next, type this message:

Type the recipient's name and address here

Insert another ^O and the completed sentence will look like this:

^OType the recipient's name and address here^O^C

When you merge this file (using the keyboard for variable data input), this message will appear as a highlighted prompt in the lower left corner of the screen, as shown in Figure 13.2. You can insert similar messages for each field in the primary file.

```
    ▬
    Dear ^C,

         Congratulations! You are a winner in the $20,000,000
    National Sweepstakes and are soon to be the recipient of a check
    for ^C, less the appropriate amount of tax required by the
    Federal Government. We will be contacting you soon to determine
    this amount.
         Our records show your phone number to be ^C. If this has
    changed, please inform us immediately by calling this toll-free
    number: (800) 445-0000.
         Please keep this form for your records.


    Yours Truly,

    Irwin Kronsky
    Sweepstakes Administrator




    Type the recipient's name and address here     Doc 2  Pg 1  Ln 1     Pos 10
```

Figure 13.2: *The customized message*

Producing Mailing Labels and Envelopes from the Secondary File

Creating a list from your secondary file (WINNERS.SF) that can be used to print mailing labels or envelopes is a simple process and it requires running another merge. First, you create a new primary file to merge with the WINNERS.SF file, making use of only five of the original seven fields: name, street address, city, state, and zip code. Your output from this merge must go to the screen. It will be three short forms containing the name and address of each recipient, as shown in Figure 13.3. Next, you change the settings for page (form) length, top margin, and left and right margins to fit your labels, and then you're ready to print.

```
         Mr. James Browder
         100 Main St.
         Mt. Hood, WA
         81233


         ================================================================================
         Mrs. Rhonda Flamestein
         233 12th Ave.
         San Francisco, CA
         91222


         ================================================================================
         Ms. Colleen McDuffy
         54 Prince Lane
         Salem, GA
         32255
         _




                                          Doc 1   Pg 3   Ln 5        Pos 5
```

Figure 13.3: *The mailing label forms*

The first step, then, is to create a new primary file containing fields F1 through F5, arranged in this order:

```
^F1^
^F2^
^F3^, ^F4^
^F5^
```

Use the Merge Codes Key (Alt-F9) to do this, as described above. Next, change the left and right margins to 5,35, the page length to 12, the number of text lines to 9, and the top margin to 6. Save the file under the name LABELS.PF, then clear the screen. Next, begin the merge process by pressing the Merge/Sort Key (Ctrl-F9) and entering LABELS.PF as your primary file and WINNERS.SF as your secondary file. The results are shown in Figure 13.3. Note that each form is considered a separate page, and a hard page break has been inserted after each one.

If data for any of the fields in the secondary file is unavailable, it is impera-tive that you leave a blank field in its place by pressing the Merge R Key (F9). For example, if a zip code is missing in the first record of the secondary file WINNERS.SF and you do not leave a blank field, you will end up with this label:

Mr. James Browder
100 Main St.
Mt. Hood, WA
$10,000

Zip code is the fifth field in the primary file (LABELS.PF) that creates the labels, and when it is missing the program assumes the next field is field 5, and inserts it in place of a zip code. The secondary file that produced this label is shown below:

Mr. James Browder ^R
100 Main St. ^R
Mt. Hood ^R
WA ^R
$10,000 ^R
(802) 331-0000 ^R
^E

To prevent this, retrieve the secondary file and press the Merge R Key (F9) after the state field. This leaves a blank field between the state and check amount, and the secondary file appears as follows:

Mr. James Browder ^R
100 Main St. ^R
Mt. Hood ^R
WA ^R
^R
$10,000 ^R
(802) 331-0000 ^R
^E

When the zip code is missing, leaving an empty field in the secondary file with just a Merge Return code (^ R) produces a blank line in the mail-ing labels. Since it is the last line in the label, this is perfectly acceptable. However, in other cases when data is missing you will want to eliminate the blank line. For example, if we modify our secondary file to include titles and company names, and Rhonda Flamestein's title is missing, the first two labels will look like this:

Mr. James Browder
President
Big Computers, Inc.
100 Main St.
Mt. Hood, WA
81233

Mrs. Rhonda Flamestein
ABC Parts, Inc.

233 12th Ave.
San Francisco, CA
91222

To prevent this, modify the primary file to include a question mark inside of any field number that may be missing data, as shown below:

^F2?^

To do this, just place your cursor on the second ^ and type the question mark. Thus, in both our original letter (LETTER1.PF) and label file (LABELS.PF), we must include the question mark inside of the field containing the title. Rhonda Flamestein's mailing label will then look like this:

Mrs. Rhonda Flamestein
ABC Parts, Inc.
233 12th Ave.
San Francisco, CA
91222

Printing Envelopes and Mailing Labels

The second step is to use the Page Format Key (Alt-F8) and Line Format Key (Shift-F8) to adjust the page length and margins for the labels or envelopes. For continuous feed labels of 2" by 4", use these settings:

Margins (Shift-F8,3):   left margin 5, right margin 35
Page length (Alt-F8,4,3): form length 12 lines, number of text lines 9
Top margin (Alt-F8,5):   6 half-lines

To print the labels, place them in the printer so that the top of the first one is under the print head, and use the Print Key to print the file from the screen (press Shift-F7, 1).

For legal size envelopes that will be inserted manually, use these settings:

Margins (Shift-F8,3):   left margin 40, right margin 80
Top margin (Alt-F8,5):   0 half-lines

To print the envelopes, place the first one in the printer and line it up at the exact spot where you want the first line printed. Next, select the Page option (2) from the Print Key (Shift-F7). Repeat this process for each envelope.

Summary

WordPerfect's merge feature includes fourteen commands that can be used to automate repetitious tasks such as form letters, reports, lists, mailing labels, and contracts. Merged documents can be created on screen and saved in a file to be printed later, or they can be sent directly to the printer.

Form letters are the most common merge application, and they are created in three steps. You type the letter once, using the Merge Codes Key (Alt-F9) to insert special codes that represent variable data (data that changes in each letter, such as the name, address, and phone number). This master letter is stored in a file called the primary file. Next you type a list of the variable data (name, address, and so on). The fields are separated by ^R codes inserted by pressing the Merge R Key (F9), and the records are separated by ^E codes inserted by pressing the Merge E Key (Shift-F6). This list is saved in a file called the secondary file. The final step is to use the Merge/Sort Key (Ctrl-F9) to initiate the merge operation, which produces one letter for each set (record) of variable data.

Instead of creating a secondary file, you have the option of typing the variable data at the keyboard as each letter is assembled. This is useful if you do not have to save and reuse the data. When you use this method, another WordPerfect merge command, ^O, can be inserted into the document along with messages that guide the user in the data entry process. The messages appear as highlighted prompts in the lower left corner of the screen and disappear after Merge R is pressed.

A merge in process can be stopped by pressing the Cancel Key (F1). Also, by placing the merge code ∧Q in a secondary file, you can end the merge at any point. This is useful if you have a large secondary file, and do not need all of the records merged.

You can use Merge to extract names and addresses from a secondary file in order to print them on envelopes or mailing labels. To do this, you create a new primary file that includes only the name and address fields from each record, then run the merge. The last step is to adjust the left, right, and top margins and page length to match the labels or envelopes.

CHAPTER 14 KEYSTROKE SUMMARY:

The Math/Columns Key—press to display Math options

With Math on, press to invoke the Alignment Character prompt

The Block Key—mark math columns for cutting, copying, or moving

The Move Key—use to cut and move columns of numbers

MATH

MATHEMATICAL OPERATIONS ARE VITAL in business, and it's unrealistic to confine them to the realm of the spreadsheet. Although WordPerfect does not purport to replace this type of software for complex analytical operations, its Math feature is adequate to handle common calculations such as those used in financial statements, so that you can incorporate them into your documents. Like a simple calculator, the program can add, subtract, multiply, and divide, as well as calculate subtotals, totals, grand totals, and averages. You can also use parentheses to change the order of calculation in a formula.

Math formulas are entered in structured columnar format, with columns located at each tab stop. You can define up to 24 columns containing either text, numbers, calculations, or totals, but only four of them can contain calculations (formulas). Using math formulas requires six steps: setting tabs, defining the columns, turning on the Math feature, entering data, calculating, and turning off the Math feature. Calculations are performed across rows, except for subtotals, totals, and grand totals, which can be computed down columns. Each column is limited to one formula. If your calculations only require subtotals, totals, and grand totals, you may skip the most complex step, defining math columns, but you can only calculate down the columns, not across the row. WordPerfect's Tab Align feature is the foundation for both methods.

Totalling Numbers

The simplest method of performing mathematical operations is to total numbers down a column, without predefining the column. You must change the tab settings before doing this, because the default settings (every 5 positions) are so close together that the numbers you enter may overlap, in which case your calculations will not be accurate. You can use four operators: the plus sign (+) for subtotals, the equal sign (=) for totals, the asterisk (*) for grand totals, and N for subtraction.

Begin this exercise by changing the tab settings so that a tab appears every 20 positions beginning with position 45. Press the Line Format Key (Shift-F8), select option 1 or 2 (Tabs), press Ctrl-End to clear all tabs, and enter

    45,20

for the new settings, then press Exit (F7). Next, turn the Math feature on by pressing the Math/Columns Key (Alt-F7) and selecting 1 Math On from this menu:

    1 Math On; 2 Math Def; 3 Column On/Off; 4 Column Def; 5 Column Display: 0

The following message will appear in the lower left corner of your screen:

    Math

It will remain there until you press Alt-F7, 1 again to turn Math off (it is a toggle). Turning Math on and off inserts a pair of codes into your document, [Math On] and [Math Off]. In editing, whenever the cursor is moved into the area between these codes, the Math prompt will again appear.

You will be entering the left side of a balance sheet, as shown in Figure 14.1. Begin by typing the first heading, Cash. Next, press the Tab key and you will see this message in the lower left corner of the screen:

Align Char = .

With Math on, the Tab key invokes the Alignment Character prompt, which lines up the numbers at the tab setting, against or around a character such as a decimal point or asterisk, or a blank space inserted using the Spacebar. The default is the decimal point, as shown above, but you can change it anytime. Chapter 7 included a detailed section about the alignment character as it is used with text columns, and most of that information is relevant to this chapter. To summarize it, after you press the Tab key, numbers that you type are inserted to the left of the cursor and the cursor remains stationary at the tab stop, until the alignment character (a decimal point) is entered. After that the prompt disappears, indicating that the Alignment feature has been turned off, and the cursor moves normally again, advancing to the right of the remaining digits as you type them. As

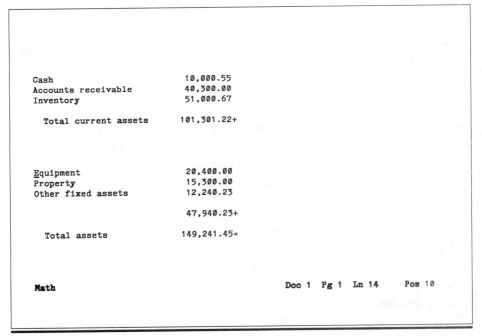

```
Cash                        10,000.55
Accounts receivable         40,300.00
Inventory                   51,000.67

   Total current assets    101,301.22+



Equipment                   20,400.00
Property                    15,300.00
Other fixed assets          12,240.23

                            47,940.23+

   Total assets            149,241.45=



Math                              Doc 1  Pg 1  Ln 14    Pos 10
```

Figure 14.1: *The asset side of a balance sheet*

you can see in Figure 14.1, the result is that the column of numbers is ver-tically aligned around the decimal points, which are located in position 45 on each line (the first tab stop).

One warning: never enter numbers that are to be calculated unless you see the Align Char = prompt. This means that numbers cannot be entered at the left margin.

Now type this number, including the comma:

    10,000.55

Press Return to move the cursor down a line and then repeat the process described above, typing the next two headings (Accounts receivable and Inventory) and the accompanying figures.

The first calculation in your column will be the subtotal, Total current assets, so press the Spacebar twice to indent and type this heading. Next, press the Tab key to move to the math column and press the plus (+) key (with Num Lock on if you use the plus key on the numeric keypad). (The plus key is the Subtotal operator.) This will be the only character appearing in the column on that line until you perform the calculation. Now press the Math/Columns Key (Alt-F7) and select option 2, Calculate. Notice how the menu differs when Math is turned on:

    1 Math Off; 2 Calculate; 3 Column On/Off; 4 Column Def; 5 Column Display: 0

The correct subtotal, 101,301.22, should now appear in front of the plus sign. Notice that although the plus sign remains at the right of the figure on the screen, it will not appear in the printed document, because the pro-gram considers it a code. If you look at it on the Reveal Codes screen, you will see that it is bold, like all the other codes.

Now enter the next three headings and figures, then type another plus sign to calculate the second subtotal, 47,940.23. The last entry, Total assets, adds the two subtotals created with the plus sign. To enter it, type an equal sign (=), which is the Total operator, and select the Calculate option from the Math/Columns Key (Alt-F7) again. The last step in this process is to turn Math off, by selecting 1 Math Off from the Math/Columns Key.

You can experiment with the figures. Change a few of the fixed numbers (not the calculated ones) and use the Calculate option on the Math/Columns Key to recalculate them. The cursor must be in between the pertinent Math on/off codes or you won't be able to select the Calculate option. The Math indicator will appear on the Status line to inform you.

Try changing a figure to a negative number by either entering a minus sign or N in front of it, or surrounding it with parentheses. For example, Figure 14.2 shows an income statement in which all of the expenses were entered in negative numbers. If they had been entered without an N, parentheses, or a minus sign, they would have been added to the total income figure to produce an incorrect net income of $822,310.86. Once you have performed the calculation and are sure you won't need to recalculate it, you can erase the parentheses or minus signs so that it will look like a standard income statement. If you use the N operator, you will not have to erase it because, like the subtotal and total operators (the plus and equal signs), it will not show up when the document is printed.

The only operator you have not used in this exercise is the asterisk, which calculates grand totals. You use it to add two totals (the figures computed with an equal sign), and it works exactly the same way as the other operators.

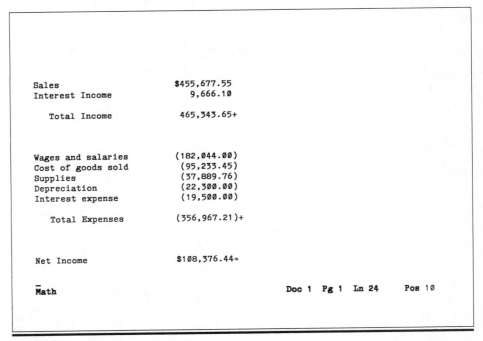

Figure 14.2: An income statement

Math Columns

A more formal and flexible approach to mathematical operations is to define columns and set up formulas to do the calculations. You can create four types of columns: numeric, text, calculation, and total. Out of 24 possible columns, only 4 can be calculation columns. The formulas in your calculation columns can include operators for addition, subtraction, multiplication, and division, and there are four special operators to add or average numbers in numeric columns (+, +/) and add or average numbers in the columns of the "total" type (=, =/).

As always, the best way to learn these operations is through exercises, so let's begin with an easy one. You will be creating the table in Figure 14.3, which shows budgeted vs. actual expenditures and calculates the dollar variance and percentage variance.

The first step is to change the tab settings to every 10 positions beginning at position 35. Select option 1 or 2 (Tabs) on the Line Format Key (Shift-F8),

	Budgeted vs. actual expenses			
	Budgeted	Actual	Variance	%
Expense A	1000.00	1555.25	555.25!	55.5!
Expense B	2000.00	1900.75	-99.25!	-5.0!
Expense C	3000.00	3500.50	500.50!	16.7!
Total	6,000.00+	6,956.50+	956.50!	15.9!

Math   Doc 1 Pg 1 Ln 24   Pos 10

Figure 14.3: *Budgeted vs. actual expenses*

press Ctrl-End to delete the old settings, and enter

35,10

for the new settings, then press Exit (F7). Next, use the Line Format Key to switch to double spacing.

Defining the Columns

The second step is to define the math columns. Select option 2 (Math Def) from the Math/Columns Key (Alt-F7) and the screen shown in Figure 14.4 will appear.

The columns are labelled A through X, and the row below that, which is full of 2s, represents the type of data each column contains: 0 for calculation, 1 for text, 2 for numeric, and 3 for total. The third row is used to define the symbol that will appear with negative numbers, either a minus sign (−) or a set of parentheses. As you can see, the default is parentheses.

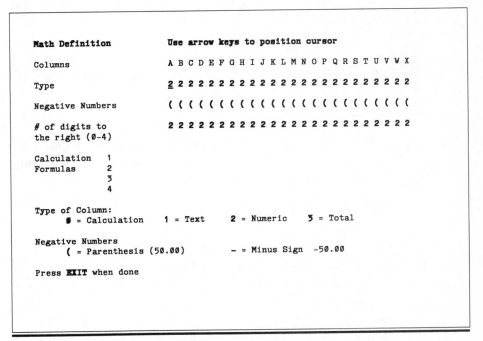

Figure 14.4: *The Math Definition screen*

In the fourth row, you specify how many numbers will appear after the decimal point (the default is 2).

The first two columns in Figure 14.3, Budgeted and Actual expenses, are numeric columns, so press → to accept the default of 2 (for numeric). The cursor will then move to Column C, which will be the first calculation column, so enter

    0

and the cursor will jump to the calculation definition area. Notice that a C will appear to the left of the cursor, reminding you that you are creating a formula for Column C.

The Variance column (C) is the difference (in each row) between the numbers in the column labelled Actual (Column B) and those in the column labelled Budgeted (Column A). Now enter this formula (in either lowercase or uppercase and with no spaces):

    B – A

After you press Return, the cursor will move back to the top row, under Column D. This column is also a formula: the variance divided by the budgeted amount, multiplied by 100. Enter

    0

for a calculation column. This will place the cursor back in the calculation definition area. Then enter the formula

    C/A∗100

Next, you will change the symbol for negative numbers to a minus sign. Press ↓ to move the cursor to the second row (the one with the parentheses), use ← to move it to Column A, then enter

    –

in Columns A through D.

To see how it works, your last step in the definition process is to change the number of digits to the right of the decimal point in Column D to 1. To do this, use the arrow keys to move the cursor to the third row under Column D, then enter

    1

The Math Definition screen should now resemble Figure 14.5.

```
Math Definition              Use arrow keys to position cursor

Columns                      A B C D E F G H I J K L M N O P Q R S T U V W X

Type                         2 2 ▓ ▓ 2 2 2 2 2 2 2 2 2 2 2 2 2 2 2 2 2 2 2 2

Negative Numbers             - - - - ( ( ( ( ( ( ( ( ( ( ( ( ( ( ( ( ( ( ( (

# of digits to               2 2 2 1 2 2 2 2 2 2 2 2 2 2 2 2 2 2 2 2 2 2 2 2
the right (0-4)

Calculation    1     C       B-A
Formulas       2     D       C/A*100
               3
               4

Type of Column:
        ▓ = Calculation    1 = Text      2 = Numeric    3 = Total

Negative Numbers
        ( = Parenthesis (50.00)        - = Minus Sign  -50.00

Press EXIT when done
```

Figure 14.5: *The completed Math Definition screen*

Entering the Data

Since you have finished defining the columns, press Exit (F7). This will bring back the Math/Columns menu, so select option 1, Math On. The rest of the steps in this exercise are similar to the ones you followed in the first exercise. Notice the Math message in the lower left corner of your screen.

Using the Reveal Codes screen, move the cursor to the left of the [Math On] and [Tab Set] codes, so that you can use the Tab key in its standard mode and settings to enter the column titles on the first row:

Budgeted Actual Variance %

Budgeted will start at position 30, *Actual* will start at 40, *Variance* will start at 50, and % will be at 63. Move the cursor down a few lines so that the Math prompt appears, and enter the title of the first row:

Expense A

Press the Tab key to move to the first column and the Align Char = . message will appear. As was explained earlier in this chapter, you should never enter numbers that are to be calculated unless you see the Alignment Character prompt (so they can't be entered at the left margin). Next, enter the budgeted amount for expense A:

1000.00

Press the Tab key again and enter the amount in the Actual column:

1555.25

Press the Tab key again to move to Column C. You will see an exclamation point (!), which indicates that this is a predefined calculation column, and your screen will resemble Figure 14.6. *Do not enter anything in this column,* because it will be disregarded when the program calculates the number. Column D is also a calculation column, so press the Tab key to move the cursor there and you will see another exclamation point. Again, enter nothing else and press Return to move to the next row.

To calculate the last two columns, press the Math/Columns Key (Alt-F7) and select option 2, Calculate. Your variance should now be 555.25 and the percent variance should be 55.5. Although the exclamation points

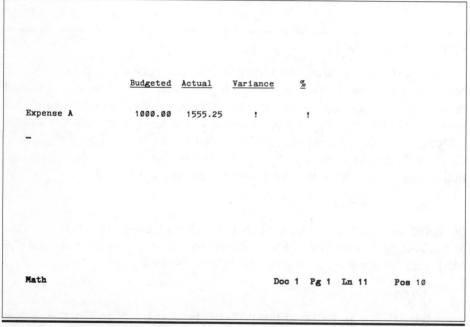

Figure 14.6: *Exclamation points in the calculation columns*

remain at the right of the numbers on the screen, they will not show up when the document is printed.

Repeat the steps outlined above to enter the headings and figures for the next two rows, Expense B and Expense C. The calculated variance and percent figures for Expense B will be negative. After that, skip a line, enter the line separating the totals, and enter this row name beneath it:

Total

Press the Tab key and enter the subtotal operator:

+

Repeat this for Column B, and press the Tab key twice to enter the exclamation point in Columns C and D. When you are finished, the last row will contain no numbers, and it will look like this:

Total   +   +   !   !

Now select the Calculate option from the Math/Columns Key and your work will be complete. When you print it, it should look just like Figure 14.3, except that the printed version won't have the exclamations and pluses.

Changing the Math Definition

You may not always be pleased with the appearance of your math document, or you may find that your formulas were incorrect and need to be reentered. For instance, the last column in Figure 14.3 contains only one digit after the decimal point, whereas the others contain two, so let's be consistent and change the % column to match the others.

The first step is to position the cursor after the [Math Def] code, using the Reveal Codes screen to help you. Note that the cursor must be placed before the [Math On] code or you will not be able to call up the Math Definition screen (shown in Figure 14.5) to make the changes. Next, select option 2 (Math Def) from the Math/Columns Key (Alt-F7). Move the cursor to column D, row 3 and change the 1 to a 2, then press F7 to exit. Next, use the Backspace key to delete the first math definition code (it helps to use the Reveal Codes screen to locate it). The last step is to move the cursor to the right of the [Math On] code, so that the Math message appears in the lower left corner of the screen, and recalculate the formulas (using option 2 on the Math/Columns Key). The result is that the fourth column now contains two digits after the decimals, just like the other three.

Using Total Columns

Instead of placing a subtotal, total, or grand total at the bottom of a column, you can set it apart by creating a total column in the next column to the right. For instance, Figure 14.7 shows a balance sheet in which subtotals and totals for assets, liabilities, owners' equity, and total equities are calculated in a separate column (Column B).

This example will demonstrate one of the limitations of WordPerfect's Math feature when compared to a spreadsheet: the formulas in a column calculate all figures in a column, and cannot be used selectively to add figures such as the total liabilities and total owners' equity in this example. As a result, it was necessary to turn Math off after calculating the subtotal for

```
ASSETS

  Current                $ 2432
  Other investments         448
  Property                 3648
  Prepaid expenses          128
                         _____

     TOTAL ASSETS                          $ 6,656.00
                                           ============


EQUITIES

  Current                $ 1024
  Long-term debt            576
                         _____
     Total liabilities                     $ 1,600.00

  Common stock             1024
  Capital surplus           960
  Retained earnings        2816
  Reserves                  256
                         _____
     Total owners equity                     5,056.00

                                           _____

  TOTAL EQUITIES                           $ 6,656.00
                                           ============
```

Figure 14.7: *Using a total column*

total assets, then turn Math on again so that the last total calculation, total equities, would include only the subtotals for total liabilities and total owners' equity. If Math had not been turned off and on again, the figure for total equities would equal the sum of assets, liabilities, and owners' equity, 13,312.00, and the balance sheet would appear to be out of balance! Follow these steps to see how it was done:

1. Set the tabs so that there are tab stops at positions 40 and 55 (Shift-F8,1).

2. Use the Math Definition screen (Alt-F7,2) to change Column B to a total column by selecting 3 for Type.

3. Exit from the Math Definition screen and turn Math on (Alt-F7, 1).

4. Enter the headings and numbers for each of the assets, using the Tab key to align the numbers. Type the line under the last entry in the group, *prepaid expenses.*

5. After you type the heading, TOTAL ASSETS, press the Tab key twice and enter the subtotal operator + in Column B.

6. Calculate the subtotal by pressing Alt-F7, 2.

7. Turn Math off (Alt-F7,1) and press Return. Then turn Math on again (Alt-F7,1).

8. Type the headings and numbers for the liabilities and owners' equities, and enter the subtotal operators in Column B for total liabilities and total owners' equity. Type the lines under the last entries in each group.

9. Enter the last heading, TOTAL EQUITIES, then press the Tab key twice and enter the equals sign (the totals operator).

10. Select 2 Calculate from the Math/Columns Key.

That's all there is to it.

Copying, Deleting, and Moving Columns

In Chapter 4 you learned how to cut, copy, and move blocks of text, but we saved the subject of rearranging columns for this chapter. The following exercise will teach you how to move a math column. The same steps can be used to move columns (both text and math) that have been defined by Tabs, Tab Aligns, Indents, or Hard Returns (but not parallel or newspaper columns). You will be using the table shown in Figure 14.3, *Budgeted vs. actual expenses,* and switching the Budgeted and Actual columns. The process is similar to moving a block of text: you mark the column with the Block Key (Alt-F4), select the Cut/Copy Column option from the Move Key (Ctrl-F4) to cut the column, move the cursor to the new location, then select Retrieve Column from the Move Key. The only difficult step is the first one, blocking the column.

1. To block and highlight the column, move the cursor to any character in the column title, Budgeted, and press the Block Key (Alt F4). (The titles in this row must have been positioned with the Tab key or this will not work. To be sure, check the Reveal Codes screen for a [Tab] in front of each title.) You must begin this process with the cursor on the first row of the column to be moved.

2. Move the cursor to the last row in the column, so that it is located anywhere on the number 6,000.00. At that point, all of the columns will be highlighted, as shown in Figure 14.8. Don't worry. The next

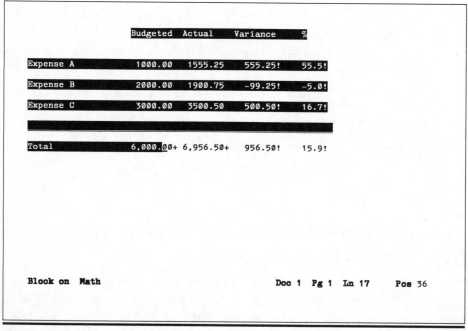

Figure 14.8: *The blocked columns*

step will narrow down the highlighting so that it covers only the column that you want to move.

3. Press the Move Key (Ctrl-F4) and select 4 Cut/Copy Column. This will reduce the block so that only the column under the title Budgeted is highlighted, as shown in Figure 14.9.

   Next, press 1 to cut the column. Do not use option 3 Delete or you will not be able to retrieve it again. As you can see, the other three columns will be moved to the left to fill in the empty column.

4. Place the cursor on the V in the heading Variance, which is where you will be inserting the column you just cut. Press the Move Key and select option 4 to retrieve the column. The results will be as follows:

	Actual	Budgeted	Variance	%
Expense A	1555.25	1000.00	555.25!	55.53!
Expense B	1900.75	2000.00	–99.25!	–4.96!
Expense C	3500.50	3000.00	500.50!	16.68!
Total	6,956.50+	6,000.00+	956.50!	15.94!

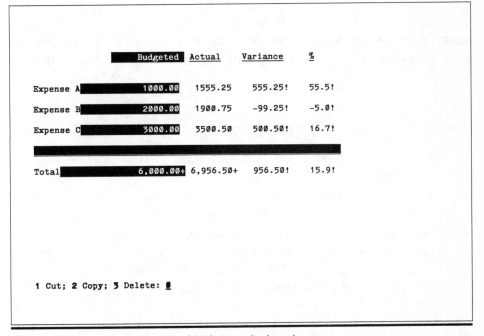

Figure 14.9: *After narrowing the block to a single column*

5. The final step is to recalculate the figures (use option 2 on the Math/ Columns Key) since the calculation is now reversed (so that the Variance column equals the budgeted figures less the actual ones, instead of actual minus budgeted, and the percentage column is variance divided by actual). The new results for the last two columns will be:

	Variance	%
Expense A	−555.25!	−35.70!
Expense B	99.25!	5.22!
Expense C	−500.50!	−14.30!
Total	−956.50!	−13.75!

Using Averages in Math Columns

You can also use the Math Columns feature to calculate averages. For example, Figure 14.10 shows expenses A, B, and C for the years 1984 and 1985, with averages for the two years in the third column. The steps used to create this chart are similar to the ones you used to create the budgeted vs. actual expenses chart shown in Figure 14.3, except that the formula in Column 3 is as follows:

+/

To create the chart, follow these steps:

1. Enter the headings: 1984 at position 32, 1985 at position 42, and Average at position 52.
2. Press Return twice to add the blank lines, then change the tab settings to every 10 positions beginning at position 35.
3. Press Return again, and then press Alt-F7, 2 to define the math columns. Press → twice to leave the default of 2 (for numeric columns) in Columns A and B, and enter 0 to create a calculation in Column C. The cursor will move down to the Calculation Formulas area, where you enter

+/

and press Return. Change the number of digits to the right of the decimal point to 0 for all three columns. Press Exit to leave the Math Definition screen.

4. You will see the Math/Columns menu, so press 1 to turn Math on.

5. In each of the three rows corresponding to the individual expenses (A, B, and C), enter the heading, press Tab and enter the figure for 1984, press Tab and enter the figure for 1985, then press Tab and Return. The last column in each row will have only an !. Press Return to leave a blank line between each row.

6. Press Return, type the separating line after the row for Expense C, then press Return twice and enter the heading *Total*. Press Tab and enter a + in Columns A and B. Press Tab and the ! will appear in Column C, then press Return.

7. Press option 2, Calculate from the Math/Columns Key (Alt-F7).

Your work should now resemble Figure 14.10 with the correct averages.

	1984	1985	Average
Expense A	2000	1500	1,750
Expense B	1000	1250	1,125
Expense C	3100	2400	2,750
Total	6,100	5,150	5,625

Figure 14.10: *Averages in math columns*

Summary

WordPerfect's Math feature can be used to calculate subtotals, totals, and grand totals, as well as to add, subtract, multiply, divide, and average in predefined columns of numbers. You can define up to 24 columns, using a maximum of 4 for calculations. To use the columns, follow six steps: set the tab stops, define the columns, turn on the Math feature, enter the data, calculate it, and turn off the Math feature.

To add or subtract numbers down a column (in subtotals, totals, and grand totals), you can skip the math definition step and just turn on the Math feature. This converts the Tab Key into a Tab Alignment Key, and permits you to use four special operators in the columns: the plus sign (+) for subtotals, the equal sign (=) for totals, the N for subtracting, and the asterisk (*) for grand totals.

To perform more complex mathematical operations, use the Math Definition option on the Math/Columns Key. With it you can establish columns for text, numbers, calculations, or totals, and in the calculation columns you can create formulas using fixed numbers, numbers in the same row in other columns, or a combination of the two. You can also define totals columns for subtotals, totals, or grand totals so that the figures appear in the column to the right rather than at the bottom of the column of numbers being added. When you use math columns, calculations are performed across the rows.

Individual columns of numbers or text that have been defined using the Tab, Tab Align, Indent or Hard Return Keys can be cut, copied, or moved by marking them with the Block Key and selecting option 4 Cut/Copy Column from the Move Key. To block the column, you place the cursor inside the column on the first row, then move it to a position within the column on the last row. Although all of the text will then be highlighted, once you select the Cut/Copy Columns option on the Move Key, it will reduce the highlighting to include only the column where the cursor is positioned. To retrieve the cut column, move the cursor to the location where it is to be placed, press the Move Key (Ctrl-F4) and use option 4, Retrieve Column.

CHAPTER 15 KEYSTROKE SUMMARY:

The Merge/Sort Key—select option 2, Sort, to begin any sort operations, including line sorts, paragraph sorts, merge sorts, and the Select feature

SORT AND SELECT

WORDPERFECT'S SORT AND SELECT features are easy, fast, and useful. You can perform a sort or select operation on an entire file, regardless of size, or you can mark a block and limit the sort or select to a specific area. The sorter can perform three different types of sorts: *line sorts, paragraph sorts,* and *merge sorts.* If data is arranged in rows and columns, as in a spreadsheet, you use line sort. If data is arranged in paragraphs so that one or more paragraphs exceed one line in length, you use the paragraph sort. The third type is the merge sort, which you use to sort data stored in secondary merge files. You define the key words that will be used in the sort order; you can specify up to nine different keys per sort.

The Select feature can be used alone or in conjunction with the Sort feature. With it, you can isolate records from a list that meet conditions you define, such as those of customers who live in the state of California or who have a line of credit exceeding a specified amount. Operators such as *equals, greater than, less than,* or *greater than or equal to* help you define the selection conditions.

Line Sort

Line sorts are the easiest type of sort to perform in WordPerfect. To use line sort, the data must be arranged in rows and columns, as in a spread-sheet. Figure 15.1 shows a list of names that were entered in no particular order. You can see that the names are arranged in rows (lines) and columns. Each row contains an individual's first and last names, and consti-tutes one record. In this exercise, you will use a line sort to rearrange the list by last name.

The first step in creating the list is to set the tab stops. As you can see in Figure 15.1, the name file consists of two columns of text separated by tabs. Each row is a *record,* and each column in a record is called a *field.* Each field should contain the same type of data down the column, such as last name or first name, as in this example. In a line sort, fields are always separated by one tab setting (using either Tab or Indent). You are going to set the tabs at 10 and 25, so that there will be only one tab stop between your fields in each of the rows. Field 1 will be the first-name column while field 2 will be the last-name column. If you were to retain the default tab

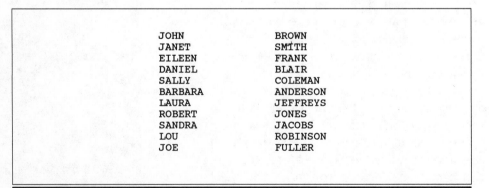

```
        JOHN            BROWN
        JANET           SMITH
        EILEEN          FRANK
        DANIEL          BLAIR
        SALLY           COLEMAN
        BARBARA         ANDERSON
        LAURA           JEFFREYS
        ROBERT          JONES
        SANDRA          JACOBS
        LOU             ROBINSON
        JOE             FULLER
```

Figure 15.1: *A list of names to be sorted*

settings (every 5 positions), yet place the first column of data (first names) at position 10 and the second column (last names) at the tab stop at position 25, the sort would not work correctly. It is important that you understand why. You type field 1, the first name, at the margin (the tab stop at position 10). If the first name contains more than five characters, the cursor passes the tab setting at position 15, so you must press Tab twice to get to position 25, where you type the last name. Since two tab stops separate it from field 1, the last name is field 4. This leaves two empty columns (where Tab was pressed), and these are fields 2 and 3.

If the first name contains fewer than five characters (JOHN BROWN, LOU ROBINSON, and JOE FULLER), you press Tab three times before typing the last name at position 25. In these three rows, the last name is field 5 and fields 2, 3, and 4 are empty. Even though there is no data in these empty fields, the program counts them when it performs the sort.

If you were to sort on field 2 or 3, which are empty in all the rows, there would be no data to sort by so the file would remain in the same order after you perform the sort. Also, since some of the last names would be in field 4 and some in field 5, sorting on 4 or 5 should not work either.

Now that you know why, use the Tabs option on the Line Format Key (Shift-F8, 1), to delete the default tab settings and set tab stops at positions 10 and 25. Next, enter your text, separating the fields by a tab.

Now press the Merge/Sort Key (Ctrl-F9) and select option 2, Sort. Your cursor can be located anywhere in the list when you begin this process. When you press Ctrl-F9, 2, you will see the prompt

Input file to sort: (Screen)

asking for the name of the input file. Although the file to be sorted can be either on screen or on the disk, the default is the document on screen. The *(Screen)* message will appear even if you have an empty screen at the time.

Press Return to accept the default (Screen). You will then see this prompt:

Output file for sort: (Screen)

WordPerfect assumes that you want to sort the file to the screen, replacing the current version. However, you can also sort it to disk by typing a name for the output file. If you do sort to a disk file, your screen will remain unchanged after the procedure. To see the sorted list, you will have to retrieve it from the disk.

Press Return to accept the default (Screen). The screen will then be split in half by the tab ruler and the Sort by Line screen will replace the bottom half, as illustrated in Figure 15.2.

If a different screen appears—either Sort Secondary Merge File or Sort by Paragraph—select option 7, Type, from the menu, then select option 2, Line.

Next, specify the field (or fields) to be sorted by using option 3, Keys. In this example, you will be sorting the file on just one field, last name, but you can sort on as many as nine. Each field you choose to sort on is called a *key*. The first field you select (last name in this example) is called the *primary key;* it will be the first sort order.

Let's digress for a minute so you will understand how sort ordering with keys works. Let's say your list were expanded to include these fields: last name, first name, street, city, state, and zip. You want to send out a mass mailing sorted by zip code, so zip code will be your first key. Within each zip code category you want the fields alphabetized by last name, so this will be the second key. In case there are multiple occurrences of common last names such as Smith, Jones, and Brown, you want them arranged by first name so

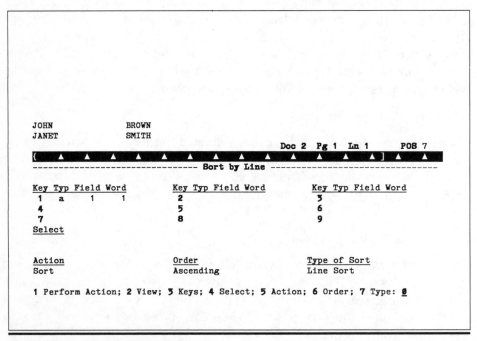

Figure 15.2: *The Sort by Line screen*

you include a third key: first name. After you perform the sort, your list will be arranged by zip code, and within each zip code it will be sorted by last name. Finally, if more than one recipient in the same zip code has the same last name, the first name will determine which appears first on the sorted list. The output would be similar to Figure 15.3. Notice the order of the first two names, Barbara Anderson and Mary Anderson.

Select option 3, Keys, now. Your cursor will then be moved into position to select the first key, under the heading *Typ*. Here you specify whether the key field is alphanumeric (A) or numeric (N). Alphanumeric fields can consist of letters or numbers, but the numbers must be equal in length, such as zip codes. Numeric fields contain only numbers, which may be of unequal length and may contain dollar signs, commas, and periods. Since your name field is alphanumeric, press Return to accept the default. Next, your cursor moves to the position under the heading *Field* and you must specify the field number of your primary-sort key. Since last name is the second field in your list, replace the default of 1 by entering

2

Next, specify which word in the field is to be used for the sort. Words within a field are separated by blank spaces, and are counted from left to right. Since your key field consists of a single word, accept the default of 1. After you press Return, the cursor will be moved into position to select the

```
BARBARA    ANDERSON   67 KIRKHAM          SAN FRANCISCO  CA   94112
MARY       ANDERSON   320 34TH AVE.       SAN FRANCSICO  CA   94112
JOE        FULLER     9431 CAMINO CORTO   SAN FRANCISCO  CA   94112
SANDRA     JACOBS     567 12TH AVE.       SAN FRANCISCO  CA   94112
LOU        ROBINSON   12 ADMIRALITY WAY   SAUSALITO      CA   94112

DANIEL     BLAIR      43 BRUCE CT.        SAN FRANCISCO  CA   94911

SALLY      COLEMAN    89 CAMINO WEST      TIBURON        CA   94920
EILEEN     FRANK      565 SPRING AVE      SAUSALITO      CA   94920
LAURA      JEFFREYS   13425 LOS OLIVOS    TIBURON        CA   94920
JANET      SMITH      1934 VINTAGE ST.    TIBURON        CA   94920

JOHN       BROWN      100 MAIN ST.        SAUSALITO      CA   94965
ROBERT     JONES      25 2ND ST.          SAUSALITO      CA   94965
```

Figure 15.3: *A sorted list with three keys*

specifications for key 2. Since you are only using one key, press Exit (F7) to return the cursor to the menu.

The other two options on the menu can be used to change the order of the sort or to move the cursor into the text and look at it. You can use option 6, Order, to change the sort order to descending. As you can see from the screen under the heading *Order,* the default is ascending, which you will be using in this exercise, so don't change it. When you sort a numeric field in ascending order, it is arranged with the lowest numbers at the beginning (1, 2, 3, 4, 5, and so on). When you sort an alphanumeric field in ascending order, it is arranged from A to Z (with A at the beginning). If both numbers and characters are contained in an alphanumeric field, the numbers will be sorted first, then the characters. When you select 2 for View, the cursor moves out of the Sort by Line screen and into the text, which you can scroll through and look at. However, you cannot make any editing changes.

Now you are ready to perform the sort. Select option 1, Perform Action. You will see messages (very briefly, since your file is so small) listing the number of records examined, records selected, and records retrieved and then the sorted file will appear. It should resemble Figure 15.4.

Select

Let's use the same list to perform another simple task, selecting those whose last names begin with characters between *A* and *J*. To do this, press

```
BARBARA      ANDERSON
DANIEL       BLAIR
JOHN         BROWN
SALLY        COLEMAN
EILEEN       FRANK
JOE          FULLER
SANDRA       JACOBS
LAURA        JEFFREYS
ROBERT       JONES
LOU          ROBINSON
JANET        SMITH
```

Figure 15.4: *The sorted list*

option 2 on the Merge/Sort Key (Ctrl-F9) and direct both input and output to the screen. When the Sort by Line screen appears, choose option 4, Select. The cursor will be positioned under Select on the screen; here you specify the conditions that must be met. The prompt line changes and appears as follows:

+(OR), *(AND), =, < >, >, <, > =, < =; Press EXIT when done

As you can see, you set up selection conditions using the operators *equal to, not equal to, greater than, less than, greater than or equal to,* and *less than or equal to,* as well as the connectors *or* and *and,* which are symbolized by + and *. Using the file shown in Figure 15.3, for example, you could use *equal to* to select only those whose zip codes are 94920. You can use +(OR) to specify an *either/or* condition, such as last name equals either Anderson or Jones. You can use *(AND) to specify two conditions, both of which must be met, such as those who both live in San Francisco and have the zip code 94112. (Daniel Blair would be the only San Francisco resident who would be excluded from the resulting list.)

Our condition is going to be that the last name starts with a character between A and J. To enter it, you specify the key and the operator and condition to be met. Our key is last name, and it is already established as key 1. Our operator and condition is *less than or equal to JX.* To enter it, type

Key1 < = JX

and press Return (case is irrelevant). Note that JX will include all last names starting with A through J and with the second character between A and X. If you enter *Key1<=J,* WordPerfect excludes all the last names beginning with J. If you use *JE,* it will include Jacobs but not Jeffreys.

Your screen should now resemble Figure 15.5. Notice that the Action is Select and Sort and the Order is Ascending.

If you did not want the list to be sorted, you could use option 5, Action, to limit the action to select only. If you did, you would see this prompt:

Action 1 Select and Sort; 2 Select Only: 0

If you then selected option 2, the message under Action would change to

Select

to verify that you were performing only a select.

However, since this will be a sort and select, do not change it. Now generate your sorted and selected list by choosing option 1, Perform Action.

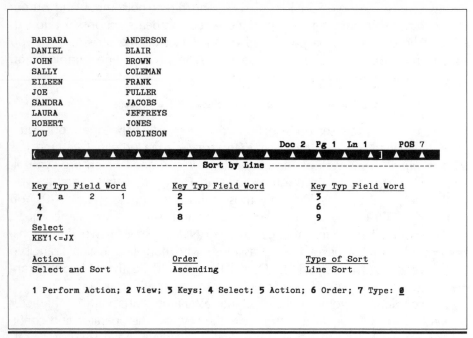

Figure 15.5: *Selection conditions on the Sort by Line screen*

The results will be as follows:

```
BARBARA        ANDERSON
DANIEL         BLAIR
JOHN           BROWN
SALLY          COLEMAN
EILEEN         FRANK
JOE            FULLER
SANDRA         JACOBS
LAURA          JEFFREYS
ROBERT         JONES
```

Now let's try a sort with two conditions. You will need one more tab stop so that you can add a third field, age, to your original list. Retrieve the original list and reset the tabs to 10, 25, and 40 (be sure to place the cursor after the previous tab setting before doing so, using the Reveal Codes screen if necessary). Enter the data for the age field:

```
JOHN           BROWN          32
JANET          SMITH          20
```

EILEEN	FRANK	45
DANIEL	BLAIR	56
SALLY	COLEMAN	29
BARBARA	ANDERSON	31
LAURA	JEFFREYS	52
ROBERT	JONES	36
SANDRA	JACOBS	37
LOU	ROBINSON	24
JOE	FULLER	30

The first step is to use option 3, Keys, to add Key 2, Age. Note that the new key definition can be either alphanumeric or numeric. Now select those whose last names range between A and JX and who are over 30 years old. The condition will be

Key1 < = JX * Key2>30

Finally, select option 1, Perform Action, to begin selecting the records. Your results will be as follows:

BARBARA	ANDERSON	31
DANIEL	BLAIR	56
JOHN	BROWN	32
EILEEN	FRANK	45
SANDRA	JACOBS	37
LAURA	JEFFREYS	52
ROBERT	JONES	36

Notice that Joe Fuller was excluded; he was not *over* 30 years old.

Paragraph Sort

A paragraph sort is used to alphabetize paragraphs by first word, as in a glossary. WordPerfect defines a paragraph as a group of text ending in two or more hard returns or a page break, and each paragraph can be as small as a single line or as large as a page. Figure 15.6 shows the first page of a document describing the WordPerfect function keys and their various commands, arranged in ascending function-key order. Note that the longest paragraph is five lines, and that there is only one tab setting, at position 20.

F1	Cancel Key: undelete when used alone; cancel when pressed after other key combinations
Alt-F1	Thesaurus Key: lists synonyms
Ctrl-F1	Shell Key: temporary exit to DOS
Shift-F1	Super/Subscript Key: Superscript; Subscript, Overstrike, Advance Up, Advance Down, Advance Line
F2	Forward Search Key: search forward for characters or function codes
Alt-F2	Replace Key: search and replace
Ctrl-F2	Speller Key: Check spelling of current word, page or document; change dictionaries; look up words phonetically; look up words that match a pattern; word count
Shift-F2	Reverse Search Key: search backwards for characters or function codes
F3	Help Key; provides alphabetical list of features; info on any key combination; keyboard template when pressed twice
Alt-F3	Reveal Codes Key: displays a screen with hidden function codes
Ctrl-F3	Screen Key : 1) rewrite screen 2) split screen into windows 3) line draw 4) reassign Ctrl/Alt and A-Z keys 5) change colors 6) auto rewrite - reformats screen after down arrow pressed
Shift-F3	Switch Key: switch to document 2; case conversion with Block key on
F4	Indent Key: temporary left margin
Alt-F4	Block Key: defines a block of text
Ctrl-F4	Move Key: copy or cut 1) sentence or 2) paragraph or 3) page; 4) retrieve column 5) retrieve text 6) retrieve rectangle. When pressed after Alt-F4 (Block on): 1) cut block 2) copy block 3) append block; 4) cut or copy a column 5) cut or copy a rectangle
Shift-F4	Left/Right Indent Key: indents left and right margin one tab stop

Figure 15.6: *The WordPerfect Function Keys*

I used paragraph sort to rearrange the document in alphabetical order by keyname using these steps:

1. Press The Merge/Sort Key and select option 2, Sort.

2. Press Return twice to accept the defaults for input and output to the screen.

3. Select option 7, Type, for the sort type.

4. Select option 3, Paragraph, for paragraph sort. You will then see the Sort by Paragraph screen, illustrated in Figure 15.7. Note that there is one more option under key definition: you are asked for the line number of the key in addition to the type, field, and word. The only other difference between this and the Sort by Line screen is that under the heading *Type of Sort,* the type is Paragraph Sort.

5. Select option 3, Keys, to define the key. Key 1 will be alphanumeric, line 1, field 2, word 1. Be sure to delete any other keys that you defined in the previous exercise (use the Del key). Press F7 when you are finished.

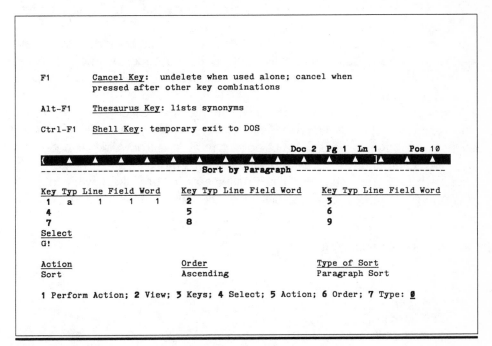

Figure 15.7: *The Sort by Paragraph screen*

6. If the selection condition remains from the previous exercise, use option 4 to enter the specification area and delete it with the Del key.

7. Press 1 Perform Action.

The results of this sort are shown in Figure 15.8.

Secondary Merge Sort

Once you have worked with WordPerfect's Merge feature, the merge sort operation is easy because you are already familiar with the concepts of field and record. To review, data that changes for each form (such as the recipient's name and address in a form letter) is divided into fields, and the collection of all fields for each form (each individual getting the form letter) is called a record. The records are stored in a file called a secondary file (unless the merge is performed from the keyboard), and merged with a master file called a primary file. The primary file contains codes such as F1, F2, and F3 (fields 1,2, and 3), which tell WordPerfect where to place the actual data for these fields when it is merged with the secondary file.

The merge sort can enhance your merge operations by sorting your secondary merge records numerically, such as by zip code, or in alphabetical order, such as by last name. In this exercise, you are going to rearrange a file by last name.

In Chapter 13 you created a secondary merge file named *Winners.sf,* which you used to produce several form letters from a single primary file. If you still have it, use it for this exercise (but do not retrieve it from disk). If not, enter the names and addresses shown below and remember to press Merge R (F9) after each field, and Merge E (Shift-F9) after each record. (Review Chapter 13 if you forget the steps.) Save the file under the name Winners.sf and clear the screen using the Exit Key (F7).

```
Ms. Colleen McDuffy ^ R
54 Prince Lane ^ R
Salem ^ R
GA ^ R
32255 ^ R
$1,000,000 ^ R
(513) 222-0000 ^ R
 ^ E
```

Alt-F4	<u>Block Key</u>: defines a block of text
F1	<u>Cancel Key</u>: undelete when used alone; cancel when pressed after other key combinations
F2	<u>Forward Search Key</u>: search forward for characters or function codes
F3	<u>Help Key</u>; provides alphabetical list of features; info on any key combination; keyboard template when pressed twice
F4	<u>Indent Key</u>: temporary left margin
Shift-F4	<u>Left/Right Indent Key</u>: indents left and right margin one tab stop
Ctrl-F4	<u>Move Key</u>: copy or cut 1) sentence or 2) paragraph or 3) page; 4) retrieve column 5) retrieve text 6) retrieve rectangle. When pressed after Alt-F4 (Block on): 1) cut block 2) copy block 3) append block; 4) cut or copy a column 5) cut or copy a rectangle
Alt-F2	<u>Replace Key</u>: search and replace
Alt-F3	<u>Reveal Codes Key</u>: displays a screen with hidden function codes
Shift-F2	<u>Reverse Search Key</u>: search backwards for characters or function codes
Ctrl-F3	<u>Screen Key</u> : 1) rewrite screen 2) split screen into windows 3) line draw 4) reassign Ctrl/Alt and A-Z keys 5) change colors 6) auto rewrite - reformats screen after down arrow pressed
Ctrl-F1	<u>Shell Key</u>: temporary exit to DOS
Ctrl-F2	<u>Speller Key</u>: Check spelling of current word, page or document; change dictionaries; look up words phonetically; look up words that match a pattern; word count
Shift-F1	<u>Super/Subscript Key</u>: Superscript; Subscript, Overstrike, Advance Up, Advance Down, Advance Line
Shift-F3	<u>Switch Key</u>: switch to document 2; case conversion with Block key on
Alt-F1	<u>Thesaurus Key</u>: lists synonyms

Figure 15.8: *The WordPerfect Function Keys list after paragraph sort*

Mr. James Browder ^ R
100 Main St. ^ R
Mt. Hood ^ R
WA ^ R
81233 ^ R
$10,000 ^ R
(802) 331-0000 ^ R
 ^ E

Mrs. Rhonda Flamestein ^ R
233 12th Ave. ^ R
San Francisco ^ R
CA ^ R
91222 ^ R
$50,000 ^ R
(415) 444-0000 ^ R
 ^ E

Press Ctrl-F9, 2 to begin the sort. When asked for the name of the input file, enter

Winners.sf

For the output file, press Return to accept the default, the screen.

One of the sort screens will then appear, and some of the records from your disk file will also appear above it. (The Sort by Paragraph screen will appear if you just completed the last exercise, and the Sort by Line screen will appear if you have not performed another type of sort since turning on the computer. Be sure to delete any keys or selection conditions that may remain on the screen from previous exercises before you proceed.) In either case, your first step is to use option 7, Type, to select the merge sort. When you do, the screen illustrated in Figure 15.9 will appear.

Like the Sort by Paragraph screen, this screen is slightly different from the Sort by Line screen because the keys are defined by type, field, line, and word, whereas the Sort by Line screen does not include the line specification. Also, the heading *Type of Sort* indicates that this is a merge sort.

The next step is to define the key WordPerfect will use to perform the sort. Since the records are to be sorted alphabetically by last name, you will be using the first field, name, as key 1. There is only one line within this field, so leave the default (1) for line. Since you want to sort by last name, which is the third word in each record, enter 3 for the word. Press F7 after making these entries.

Now you are ready to run the sort, so press 1 Perform Action. Your three records will then be rearranged (on screen) so that the record for

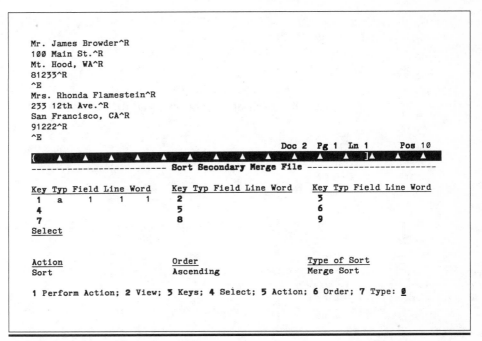

Figure 15.9: *The Sort Secondary Merge File screen*

Mr. James Browder is the first on the list, Mrs. Rhonda Flamestein is the second, and Ms. Colleen McDuffy is the last.

You may want to try it again using one of the numeric fields such as zip code or check amount as your primary key. To do this, just repeat the steps and replace the original primary key. To sort by zip code, in key 1 you would enter either alphanumeric or numeric as the type, 5 as the field, and 1 as the line and word. To sort by check amount, you would have to enter N for numeric type, since there is a dollar sign in the field and since the numbers are not even in length. Then enter field 6, line 1, and word 1 as the other options. Note that the list will be sorted in ascending order (unless you change this default), so the largest check amount ($1,000,000) will be at the bottom.

Sorting a Block

If you don't want to sort the entire file on screen, use the Block key to designate the text you want sorted, then proceed in the standard manner by pressing Merge/Sort (Ctrl-F9) and choosing your options. Using this method, you won't have to designate the input and output files. To try it, block the first five names in the original list (shown in Figure 15.1) and sort them in first name order by changing key 1 to field 1. (Be sure to change the Type of Sort back to Line.) I also separated the block from the other six names with a blank line. When you finish, the list will appear as follows:

```
DANIEL      BLAIR
EILEEN      FRANK
JANET       SMITH
JOHN        BROWN
SALLY       COLEMAN

BARBARA     ANDERSON
LAURA       JEFFREYS
ROBERT      JONES
SANDRA      JACOBS
LOU         ROBINSON
JOE         FULLER
```

Summary

WordPerfect's Sort and Select features are fast and powerful. There are three types of sorts: line sorts for data in rows and columns, paragraph sorts for paragraphs, and merge sorts for secondary merge files. Each type can rearrange alphanumeric or numeric data in ascending or descending order, using one to nine key words. The data to be sorted can be on screen or in a disk file, and the results can be directed to the screen or to a disk file. You can sort an entire file, or use the Block Key to mark and sort just a section. With WordPerfect's Select feature, you can isolate information that meets the exact conditions you define with the help of operators such as *equals, greater than,* and *less than or equal to,* and so on.

Line sorts are used to rearrange information that is stored in rows and columns, as in a spreadsheet. Each row is a record, and the data at each tab stop in a row is a field. Each field in each record must contain the same category of information, such as zip code or telephone number. You choose one or more fields to sort the records by, and each is called a key. Up to 9 keys can be selected in one sort. For example, you may choose to sort a customer file by state, and within each state by city, and within each city by zip code. The state field would be key 1, the city field would be key 2, and the zip code field would be key 3.

You select the keys by pressing Ctrl-F9, 2 (the Merge/Sort Key) directing the input and output to the screen or files, and using option 3 on the menu that appears. When you define each key you also specify the type of data it contains (numeric or alphanumeric), its field number in the file (this corresponds to the tab setting), and the word number to be used in the sort if there are more than one in the field. Other options on the Sort by Line screen are used to change the sort order, which can be either ascending or descending, or to move the cursor into the text of your file, which appears on the top half of the screen, where you can scroll through it.

The final step in performing the sort is to select option 1, Perform Action, on the Sort by Line screen.

The other two types of sorts are paragraph and merge sorts. WordPerfect defines a paragraph as a group of text ending in two or more hard returns or a page break; it can be as short as one line or as long as one page. A merge sort is used to rearrange data stored in a secondary merge file.

The steps used for paragraph and merge sorts are almost identical to those used for line sorts. Once you press the Merge/Sort Key and direct your input and output, you use option 7 from the menu to choose the sort type: merge, line, or paragraph. Each type of sort has a unique screen. Unlike line sorts, fields are not limited to a single row, so when you define the key(s) for a merge or paragraph sort, you must enter one additional specification, the line number.

The Select feature is useful when you want to separate certain records from the rest of the file, such as those of all customers who live in the state of California. To use it, choose the Sort option from the Merge/Sort Key (Ctrl-F9, 2), direct the input and output, and choose option 4, Select, from the menu. Next, define the conditions that must be met for a record to be included in your new list by designating one or more keys and using them in combination with operators such as *equal to* or *greater than*. To select only customers in

California, for example, define KEY1 as the state field and enter *KEY1 = California* as the selection condition. You can also specify either/or conditions, such as residence in either California or Nevada, as well as conditions in which two or more prerequisites must be met, such as residence in California *and* ownership of real estate.

CHAPTER 16 KEYSTROKE SUMMARY

The Macro Definiton Key—press to name and define a macro

The Invoke Macro Key—to use any macro, press and type the macro's name

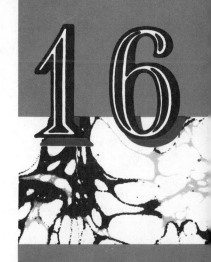

MACROS

A MACRO IS SIMPLY A SEQUENCE OF keystrokes that you record and save in a file so that it can be used again whenever you wish, just by typing a name that you assign to stand for the sequence. Think of a macro as a shortcut for entering frequently used data or commands, or a combination of the two. Some macros will save you a few keystrokes, others will save many. Macros can range from very short, simple entries to very elaborate chains. However, it is often the shortest ones that prove the most valuable because you use them the most often.

WordPerfect's macros are almost effortless to create. You just press the Macro Definition Key (Ctrl-F10), assign a name to your macro, type the keystrokes to record them in the file, then press Ctrl-F10 again. When you want to use the macro, you press the Invoke Macro Key (Alt-F10) and type the macro's name. Try creating a simple macro now to see how easy it can be. This macro will type *Sincerely yours* whenever you use it.

Press Ctrl-F10 and you will see this message on the Status line in the lower left corner of the screen:

Define Macro:

Enter this name for your first macro:

CLOSE

Be sure to press Return after entering the name. Note that a macro name must contain two to eight characters (with one exception that you will study shortly). You will then see a blinking message on the Status line: *Macro Def*.

Next, type the following:

Sincerely yours,

If you make a typing error, just backspace and type the correct characters.

The final step is to press Ctrl-F10 again. Now your macro is stored on the default disk and can be executed anytime you need it. Notice that the contents of the macro (*Sincerely yours,*) remain on screen; to clear it, press F7, N, N. Now try using the macro by pressing Alt-F10, the Invoke Macro Key. This prompt will appear in the lower left corner of the screen:

Macro:

Enter the name of your macro, CLOSE.

The message

* Please wait *

will appear very briefly (so quickly that you may miss it), and then the words you stored will appear on your screen at the cursor position.

WordPerfect automatically assigns the extension MAC to all macros, so you can always view them in your directory by pressing the List Files Key (F5) and typing

*.MAC

in response to the DIR prompt. Figure 16.1 shows a listing of the macros in my default directory.

If you are using a system with floppy drives, you have room to store several macros on the system disk, since macros do not use up much space (my longest one is 117 bytes). When you first name the macro (after pressing Ctrl-F10), be sure to type the drive designator (A:) first. However, when you invoke the macro (by pressing Alt-F10) you do not have to type *A:* before the macro name, because WordPerfect always searches both the default disk and the WordPerfect System disk for a macro (assuming you are starting WordPerfect from drive B, otherwise it will only search the System disk).

If you prefer to store macros on the data disk in drive B, it is a good idea to keep a master macro disk that contains your most frequently used macros. Each time you format a new data disk you simply copy all of the macros from the master onto the new data disk.

Hard disk users who store data files in more than one subdirectory can store all macros (except Alt key macros, which you will study in the next section) in a separate subdirectory and create a macro to help start them. This macro "presses" the Invoke Macro Key and enters the path to the subdirectory, then waits for you to enter the name of the macro you want to use. To do this, name your subdirectory containing the macros *MAC*, and follow these steps:

1. Press Ctrl-F10 and name the macro.
2. Press Alt-F10, then enter \MAC\
3. Press Ctrl-F10 to end macro definition.
4. Press F1 to get rid of the prompt.

It is even faster if you store this as an Alt macro, since you will only have to press two keys to start it.

A word of warning: macros cannot be edited in WordPerfect, and you should not try to retrieve a macro to the editing screen or you may damage your document. Macros can be deleted or renamed with the List Files Key, but if you want to change them, you must retype them. See Appendix C for information about a macro editor, which you can purchase from WordPerfect Corp. as part of the Library Program.

Alt Macros

As you can see, four of the macros in the directory listing shown in Figure 16.1 have names that start with ALT. These are macros that were assigned

```
04/29/87  08:01              Directory C:\WP2\*.MAC
Document Size:          0                    Free Disk Space:      761856

 . <CURRENT>    <DIR>                  .. <PARENT>     <DIR>
ALTB    .MAC        6  10/17/86 15:55  ALTC    .MAC       26  04/22/87 10:03
ALTF    .MAC        7  02/16/87 22:28  ALTI    .MAC        8  03/29/87 17:16
ALTN    .MAC        8  03/29/87 17:17  ALTP    .MAC        2  09/29/86 11:15
ALTQ    .MAC        5  02/16/87 22:27  ALTR    .MAC        7  02/16/87 22:33
ALTU    .MAC        4  02/14/87 16:15  ALTW    .MAC       12  09/26/86 15:29
ALTX    .MAC        4  09/26/86 15:30  ALTZ    .MAC        4  09/26/86 15:30
FNTTEST1.MAC      169  10/28/86 14:47  FONTTEST.MAC     3811  10/28/86 14:47
TEN     .MAC       29  04/24/87 11:16  UB      .MAC       10  02/14/87 15:45




1 Retrieve; 2 Delete; 3 Rename; 4 Print; 5 Text In;
6 Look; 7 Change Directory; 8 Copy; 9 Word Search; 0 Exit: 6
```

Figure 16.1: *Macro names shown in the file directory*

to the Alt key in combination with one of the characters A through Z. To use one of them, you press the Alt key along with the character key. Since you do not have to press the Invoke Macro Key or enter a name, these Alt macros are real time-savers. The macro ALTW in my listing enters the word *Word-Perfect,* which I use frequently. The program does the typing with just two keystrokes, saving me a total of 11 keystrokes (including pressing the Shift key twice) every time I use it. Since Alt macros are quite easy to invoke accidentally, you should never use them to perform such tasks as deleting text or clearing the screen, which may have a detrimental effect on your document if the macro is invoked unintentionally.

A Line-Spacing Macro

Two other Alt macros that I use constantly alter the line spacing by executing a series of commands: Shift-F8 (the Line Format Key), 4 (spacing),

and 1 or 2 for single or double spacing. Try following these steps to create
an Alt macro for double spacing:

1. Press Ctrl-F10 to define the macro.
2. Assign the name by pressing Alt together with the S key.
3. Type Shift-F8, 4, 2, Return.
4. Press Ctrl-F10 to end macro definition.

Now press Alt-S to invoke the macro. If you check the Reveal Codes
screen, you will see the code for double spacing:

[Spacing Set:2]

In fact, you will see it twice because when you create a macro, the keystrokes are executed in your document at the same time they are being
recorded in the file. If you don't want this to happen, switch to the Doc 2
work area before creating the macro. After you save the macro, exit without saving from Doc 2 (press F7, N, Y).

Temporary Macros

The first two methods you studied create permanent macros, but Word-
Perfect also lets you establish temporary macros to use just in one editing session. Temporary macros are deleted when you exit from WordPerfect. The
advantage in using them is that they do not consume valuable space on your
disk or clutter up your directory with macros you'll never use again.

To create a temporary macro, you follow the same steps used to create
your first macro, CLOSE, except that you assign a name that consists of
only one letter, or you press the Return key and that becomes its name.
(Note that the manual uses the term *Enter key*, which is the same as the
Return key. I will refer to it as the *Return* key for consistency.) To invoke a
macro with a single-letter name, you press Alt-F10 and enter the letter; to
invoke one stored on the Return key, press Alt-F10, Return. You can only
store one macro on the Return key, so if you create another in the same
editing session, it will replace the first.

A Macro to Underline a Word

To try this, create a temporary macro that will underline a single word. Move the cursor to the beginning of the word *Sincerely,* which you typed earlier, and follow these steps:

1. Press Ctrl-F10.
2. Enter U as the name of your temporary macro, and press Return.
3. Enter these keystrokes: Alt-F4, Ctrl-→, ← (to exclude the blank space after the word), F8.
4. Press Ctrl-F10 to end macro definition.

Since your keystrokes are executed while being recorded in the file, the word *Sincerely* will be underlined on the screen. Now move the cursor to the word *yours,* and use the temporary macro by typing Alt-F10, U, and pressing Return. The entire word including punctuation should be underlined.

A Macro to Convert a Character to Uppercase

Now create a macro using the Return key as the name. This one will convert the first character of a word to uppercase, and is useful when you rearrange a sentence in a way that causes the first word to be deleted or moved.

1. Press Ctrl-F10.
2. Press Return.
3. Enter these keystrokes: Alt-F4, →, Shift-F3, 1, Alt-F4.
4. Press Ctrl-F10 to end macro definition.

To execute the macro, move the cursor to the letter you want capitalized, then press Alt-F10 and Return.

Both the underline and uppercase conversion macros are quite useful, and you may want to save them as permanent macros. The uppercase conversion macro can be expanded into a macro that will convert the first word in each sentence of your document to uppercase, so that you can type the entire document in lowercase and fix it later. You'll learn how to create such a macro in the section below on chained macros.

Repeating a Macro

If you want to use your uppercase conversion macro to convert an entire word to uppercase, you can use the Esc key to repeat the macro. To do this, press Esc, enter the number of times you wish to repeat the macro, which is the length of the word, but do not press Return. Next, press Alt-F10 and Return (which, as you recall, is the macro name unless you saved it as a permanent macro). Your entire word will then appear in capital letters.

User Input in a Macro

WordPerfect allows you to insert a pause in a macro so that you can enter data from the keyboard while the macro is being executed. To insert the pause, you press Ctrl-PgUp, then press Return twice. After that, continue entering the keystrokes for your macro, then save it.

As an example, you could create a macro that begins a standard thank-you letter and eliminates much of the formatting work. It enters the current date at the top of the letter, pauses while you type the recipient's name and address, then moves down a few lines and types *Dear*. It then pauses while you enter the name, types a comma and moves down two lines, inserts a tab, then types the beginning of the first sentence. After it is invoked, the results will be similar to Figure 16.2.

To try it, follow these steps:

1. Press Ctrl-F10 and name the macro LTR.
2. Press Shift-F5, 1 (the Date Key), and press Return three times to leave three blank lines.
3. Insert the first pause by pressing Ctrl-PgUp, Return, Return. Press Return a third time to end the line with the name.
4. Repeat step 3 twice for the second and third line (the address).
5. Press Return three times to move to the salutation line. Type

   Dear

```
                      April 29, 1987

                   Mr. John Doe
                   100 Main St.
                   Sausalito, CA 94965


                   Dear Mr. Doe,

                      Thank you so much
```

Figure 16.2: *Using a macro to begin a letter*

6. Insert another pause by pressing Ctrl-PgUp, Return, Return.

7. Type a comma, then press Return twice.

8. Press Tab, then type

   Thank you so much

9. Press Ctrl-F10 to end macro definition.

Now clear the screen, press Alt-F10, enter the name of the macro, LTR, and press Return. The date will be entered, and the cursor will move down three lines. Next type the name and address, pressing Return after each of the three lines. After you type the last one and press Return, the cursor moves down four lines and *Dear* is typed. Press the Spacebar and type the name, press Return, and a comma is entered. The macro finishes by moving down two more lines, inserting a tab, and typing the beginning of the sentence.

This procedure could also be entered as a primary merge file to be merged with data from the keyboard. This topic is covered in Chapter 13, "Merges." I find it easier to use the macro.

Making Your Macros Visible

As you've seen, macros are executed so fast you can't tell what they are doing until they are finished. If this bothers you, add a pause and a number for a delay value. This will slow down the macro so that you can watch the keystrokes as they are executed. The number for the delay value can range from 0 to 254, but 10 to 20 should be sufficient. I tried using 150 and had to leave and have a cup of coffee while I waited for the macro to finish.

To see how this works, let's recreate the line spacing macro.

1. Press Ctrl-F10 to define the macro.
2. Enter the name by pressing Alt-S. (You will be asked to confirm that you want to replace the earlier version, so answer Y.)
3. For the pause, enter Ctrl-PgUp, then 10 for the delay value. Press Return.
4. Type Shift-F8, 4, 2, Return.
5. Press Ctrl-F10 to end the macro definition.

Now start the macro by pressing Alt-S and watch as it completes its task.

Macros with Search and Replace

When combined with other features such as Search and Replace, macros become especially powerful. For example, I have a macro that inserts a special place marker for me and two other macros that locate it (with forward and reverse searches). This makes it easy, after moving around in the document, to return to the last place I was working (which isn't necessarily the end of the document). For your place marker, use an unusual combination of characters that will never appear under normal circumstances in your documents. I use QQQQQ and store it as the macro Alt-Q. By adding a number to the end, I can easily create sequential place markers. Since the Search feature does not look for an exact match unless you surround the search string with spaces (or the punctuation that surrounds it in the document), the combination will always be found. I store the forward search macro under the name Alt-F and the reverse search macro under the name Alt-R.

To create the macros, follow these steps:

The Place Marker Macro

1. Press Ctrl-F10 and enter Alt-Q for the macro name.

2. Type QQQQQ.

3. Press Ctrl-F10 to end the macro.

The Forward Search Macro

1. Press Ctrl-F10 and enter Alt-F for the macro name.

2. Press the Search Key (F2) and enter QQQQQ as the search string.

3. Press F2 to begin the search.

4. Press Ctrl-F10 to end the macro.

The Reverse Search Macro

1. Press Ctrl-F10 and enter Alt-R for the macro name.

2. Press the Reverse Search Key (Shift-F2) and enter QQQQQ as the search string.

3. Press F2 to begin the search.

4. Press Ctrl-F10 to end the macro.

Now use Alt-Q to enter the place marker several times, separating the markers with blank lines, and test your Alt-R macro.

Once you execute the Alt-R macro, you can repeat your search by pressing Shift-F2, F2, or by starting the macro again. However, it would be easier to set up the macro so that it repeats itself until there are no more occurrences of the search string (QQQQQ). To try it, add one more step to the Alt-R macro. After step 3, press Alt-F10 and enter the name of the macro, Alt-R. The complete new sequence is shown below.

1. Press Ctrl-F10 and enter Alt-R for the macro name, then press Y to replace the original version.

2. Press the Reverse Search Key (Shift-F2) and enter QQQQQ as the search string.

3. Press F2 to begin the search.

4. Press Alt-F10 (Invoke Macro) and enter Alt-R for the macro name.

5. Press Ctrl-F10 to end the macro.

Now try the Alt-R macro and watch what happens. Although you know the search string appears several times on your screen, the macro seems to ignore all but the last one. In reality, the search macro did stop at each occurrence of the search string but it happened so fast you didn't see it. To prevent this, redefine the macro and enter a pause of 20 before step 4. (Press Ctrl-PgUp, 20, Return.)

Press Alt-R again to invoke the macro. This time, you can see the * *Please wait* * prompt as the macro is performing its keystrokes, and it stops at each instance of the QQQQQ search string. Now when you find the one you want you can press the Cancel Key (F1) to stop the macro and remain there.

Macro Chaining

The macro you just finished running is called a repeating chain. As you have seen, this is not nearly as complex as it sounds. Chained macros are two macros strung together, with one macro invoking the other. When a search is included and a macro invokes itself, as in the example above, it is called a repeating chain. The conversion macro, that changes the first character of each sentence to uppercase, mentioned earlier in this chapter, is also a repeating chain. Be sure you have a sentence or two on your screen or you won't be able to create this macro. The steps to create it follow:

1. Press Ctrl-F10 and name the macro *Caps.*
2. Press F2 (the Search Key).
3. For the search string, type

   .

   (period) and press the Spacebar.
4. Press F2 (to start the search).
5. Press Alt-F4 (Block on).
6. Press → (to highlight the character).
7. Press Shift-F3, 1 (uppercase conversion).
8. Press Alt-F4 (to turn Block off again).

9. Press Alt-F10 and type the macro name *(Caps)* and press Return (this repeats the macro).

10. Press Ctrl-F10 (to end macro definition).

The only flaw in this macro is that it does not convert the first character in each paragraph because those characters do not follow the period and Spacebar combination, which is used to locate the first word of each sentence. To overcome this deficiency, you can create another macro that will uppercase the first character of each paragraph. Since each paragraph starts with a tab, you just direct the macro to search for tab codes, then follow the same steps to block and convert the character to the right, and repeat the macro. Since a macro ends when the search string cannot be found anymore, you cannot chain this macro to the Caps macro.

Macros with Merges

Macros and merges can be combined in many ways. One of the most useful combinations is a macro that starts a merge and enters the name of the primary and secondary file for you. This is particularly useful for merges from the keyboard. So that you don't start the merge as you define the macro, which can be confusing, the easiest way to set it up is to include only the steps up to the point where you enter the name of the secondary file. Here are the steps:

A Macro for Keyboard Merges

1. Press Ctrl-F10 and name the macro KMERGE.
2. Press Ctrl-F9 (the Merge/Sort Key) and 1 (for Merge).
3. Enter the primary file name and press Return.
4. Press Ctrl-F10 to end the macro.
5. Press the Cancel Key (F1) to get rid of the prompt: *Secondary file.*

After you start the macro, it will run through the first 3 steps and ask you for the name of the secondary file. Once you press Return, the merge will begin.

If you enter a pause (Ctrl-PgUp, Return, Return) in step 3 instead of the primary file name as described below, the macro will prompt you for both the primary and secondary file:

A Macro That Prompts for Primary and Secondary File Names

1. Press Ctrl-F10 and name the macro.
2. Press Ctrl-F9, 1.
3. Press Ctrl-PgUp, Return, Return, Return.
4. Press Ctrl-F10 to end the macro.

Another useful macro is one that automatically creates mailing labels by running a merge that extracts the name and address fields from a secondary file. The macro then sets up the correct margins and page length for the labels that are produced. This merge process was explained in Chapter 13; all you have to do is combine the steps into a macro.

Starting a Macro from within a Merge

WordPerfect has a special merge code, ^G, which starts a macro from within a merge. The macro begins as soon as the merge ends. To use it, you add it to your primary document by pressing the Merge Codes Key (Alt-F9), entering G, typing the name of the macro, then pressing Alt-F9, G again. For example, you can include a macro in a primary file used with a keyboard merge that will save the file, clear the screen, and start the merge again. For the next exercise, you will have to use the file LETTER3.PF, which you created in Chapter 13, or create a different primary file for keyboard merging.

This macro will chain the macro KMERGE to the end so that the merge will automatically begin again after the save. Also, it will type the letters LTR as the first characters of the filename, and pause for you to enter the remaining characters. You can then name the letters in sequence: LTR1, LTR2, LTR3, etc. When you want to stop the macro, press the Cancel Key (F1).

Note that you must have a file on screen in order to include the Save operation in your macro. (If you don't, nothing will happen when you press F10.) A file can consist of a single letter, so just type A. After you create the macro you will have a file named LTR and you should delete it from your disk. Here are the steps to create the Save macro:

1. Press Ctrl-F10 and name the macro SAVEIT.

2. Press F10 to save the merged document.

3. Type LTR and enter a pause by pressing Ctrl-PgUp, Return, Return. Press Return a third time to begin the Save operation. (This will also save the document on screen under the name LTR.)

4. Press F7, N, N to clear the screen.

5. Press Alt-F10, and enter the name of the macro to be chained, KMERGE.

6. Press Ctrl-F10 to end the macro.

Now retrieve your primary merge document (LETTER3.PF) and add the macro to the end using these steps:

1. Press the Merge Codes Key (Alt-F9), G.

2. Type the macro name, SAVEIT.

3. Press Alt-F9, G again.

4. Save the primary file.

When you finish, the code that adds the macro will look like this:

```
^GSAVEIT^G
```

Now try merging the document (press Ctrl-F9, 1, enter the primary file name, and press Return twice). After the first document is complete, you will be prompted for a file name (starting with LTR), and then the document will be saved, the screen cleared, and the merge will begin again.

Summary

A macro is a sequence of keystrokes that has been saved in a file for repeated use. It is one of WordPerfect's most useful features, yet it is easy to set up and use. Anytime you find yourself repeatedly typing a sequence of commands or a word, phrase, or paragraph, consider recording the keystrokes in a macro file so that you can save yourself extra typing the next time you need them.

The Macro Definition Key (Ctrl-F10) is used to create and store a macro. Each macro is assigned a name, which can be from 2 to 8 characters or a combination of the Alt key with one of the characters A through Z. To create a temporary macro to use until you exit from WordPerfect, assign a name consisting of a single character or press Enter when prompted for the name.

To use a macro, press the Invoke Macro Key (Alt-F10) and enter the name. If the macro was named with the Alt key and one of the characters A through Z, start it by pressing the Alt key and the character. Since you don't have to press Alt-F10 and type a name, the Alt macros are the easiest and fastest to start. If you did not assign a name but pressed Return instead, start the macro by pressing Alt-F10, Return.

You can insert a pause in a macro so that keyboard entries can be made while it is executing, or so that the macro will run at a speed that permits you to watch the keystrokes. To insert the pause, press Ctrl-PgUp, then press Return twice.

A macro can be started from within another macro; this feature is called macro chaining. When the chained macro includes a forward search, reverse search, or search and replace, it is called a repeating chain. An example of a repeating chain is a macro that searches for a place marker, and repeats the search until all occurrences of the marker have been located.

Macros are all stored with the extension .MAC, so you can get a listing of them by pressing the List Files Key (F5) and entering *.MAC. Although macros can be deleted or renamed, they cannot be edited in Word-Perfect. To change a macro, it must be retyped. (A macro editor can be purchased separately. See Appendix C for details.) Pressing the Cancel Key (F1) stops the execution of a macro. The Esc key followed by a number can be used to repeat a macro several times.

A macro can be used to start a merge; it is especially helpful for starting merges from the keyboard. In addition, a macro can be stored in a primary file and started from within a merge.

CHAPTER 17 KEYSTROKE SUMMARY:

The Screen Key—press and select option 2, Line Draw, to display the Line Draw prompt

The Block Key—mark a drawing as a rectangle for cutting, copying, and moving operations

The Move Key—press for options to cut or move a rectangle

LINE
DRAWING

LINE DRAW IS AN INTERESTING FEATURE that can be used to draw lines, boxes, graphs, and simple illustrations such as flow charts and organization charts. The characters can be seen on a standard IBM monochrome monitor, but a printer with graphics capability (such as many of the dot matrix and laser printers) is required to print them as they appear on the screen. If you ever used an Etch-a-Sketch when you were a kid, you'll have just as much fun with this feature!

Using Line Draw

Line Draw works in Typeover mode, replacing other characters on the screen with your drawing. To add text after creating a drawing, you also have to be in Typeover mode (press the Ins key). Also, you can't press the Return key on a line that includes a drawing or you will disfigure the drawing. In case you do press Return, use Backspace to realign the drawing.

To learn how this feature works, start by drawing a small box. Begin with a clear screen to make sure no formatting codes have been entered, such as line spacing. (If there is anything on your editing screen, use the Exit Key to save it.) Position the cursor on line 1, position 10. Press the Screen Key (Ctrl-F3), and select option 2, Line Draw. You will see the prompt illustrated in Figure 17.1.

As you can see, there are three standard characters you can select from: a single line, a double line, or asterisks. There is also a fourth option, Change, which you will study later. Asterisks can be printed by most

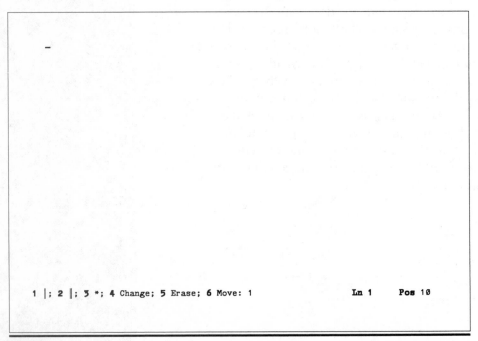

Figure 17.1: *The Line Draw prompt*

printers, including letter-quality ones, but the other characters cannot. Select option 2 to create a box with a double line. (If you don't select 1, 2, or 3, option 1, a single line, will be used to draw the line.)

Press → and a horizontal double line will appear. Press it nine more times, then press ↓ ten times. As you can see, you are starting to create a rectangle, not a square as you might have expected, because moving the cursor 10 positions in the vertical direction is not the equivalent of moving 10 positions in the horizontal direction. To complete the rectangle, press ← ten times, then press ↑ ten times. Press Exit (F7) or Cancel (F1) to end line drawing, and press Return to move the rectangle down a line.

Now take a look at the Reveal Codes screen (by pressing Alt-F3) to see what WordPerfect has actually done. (Make sure the cursor is on line 1, outside of the rectangle.) As you can see, there is a hard return code at the end of each line, which the program inserted automatically when you pressed ↓. If you tried to draw a line in Edit mode (using the hyphen key, for example) you would also have to press the Return key at the corner, and insert several blank spaces on line 2 until you reached position 20, where the first vertical character would be entered. As you can see, using Line Draw differs little from Edit mode, except in the types of characters that can be used.

Move your cursor to line 3, position 11, which is inside the rectangle, and type

hello

Notice that the character that forms the right border on line 3 has been pushed to the right five spaces. To correct it, use Backspace to delete the word *hello,* which will move the border back into position. Next, press the Ins key to turn on Typeover mode. Now try typing *hello* again; the border remains in the correct position. As you have seen, text must be added to a drawing in Typeover mode. You can also wait and draw the figure around text that has already been entered, which is the easiest method.

Using the Escape Key to Speed Up Drawing

As you learned in Chapter 7, you can use the Escape key to repeat an operation as many times as you want. This can really speed up line drawing. To try it, select Line Draw from the Screen Key (Ctrl-F3, 2), and then select option 1 to draw a single line. Press the Esc key, and you will see the following prompt:

    n = 8

This tells you the number of times your action will be repeated; eight is the default. Type 35 in its place, then press →. A line of 35 characters will automatically be drawn for you.

    Notice that if you press Esc again, you will again see the original prompt (n = 8). To replace the default number (8), press Esc, type the number you want to use, such as 35, then press Return. The next time you press Esc, that number will appear.

Using Option 4 to Change the Character

    You can draw an asterisk by selecting option 3 on the Line Draw menu, or use option 4 to change this asterisk to one of eight other characters, as shown in Figure 17.2.

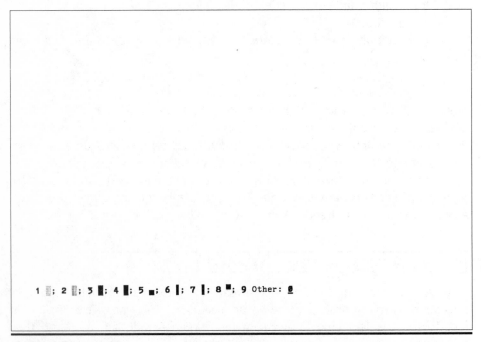

1 ░; 2 ▓; 3 █; 4 █; 5 ▄; 6 │; 7 │; 8 ■; 9 Other: 0

Figure 17.2: *The Change prompt on the Line Draw menu*

If you want to use a character that is not on this list, select option 9 and type any character on the keyboard, or enter the decimal code for the ASCII character. For instance, entering 1 will produce a smiling face, 3 will produce a heart, and 30 will produce a triangle. If you like to doodle, you can really have fun with these characters, as I did in Figure 17.3.

On a more serious note, I drew the keyboard shown in Figure 17.4.

Moving the Cursor

Option 6 can be used to move the cursor without disturbing the drawing or exiting from Line Draw. To use it, select option 6 and move the cursor with any of the arrow keys. To return to drawing line characters when you are finished moving the cursor, select option 1, 2, or 3 again.

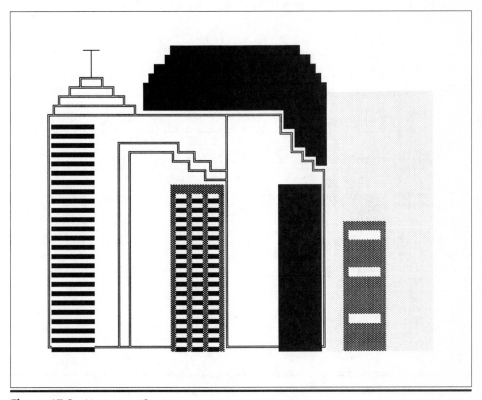

Figure 17.3: *Abstract art?*

Erasing a Line

Option 5 allows you to erase a line that has been drawn. To use it, move the cursor to the position where you want to start erasing and press 5. As you move your cursor with one of the arrow keys, the line will be deleted.

Cutting, Copying, or Moving a Line Drawing

You can use WordPerfect's Block and Move Keys to cut, copy, or move a line drawing; the process is the same as moving text except that you must mark two opposite corners and use the Rectangle option on the Move Key. You use the Block Key (Alt-F4) to mark the section as a rectangle (you must use ↓ and →, not just ↓), then press Move (Ctrl-F4) and select option 5, Cut/Copy Rectangle. If you are copying it, move the cursor to the new location, press Move again and select option 6, Move Rectangle.

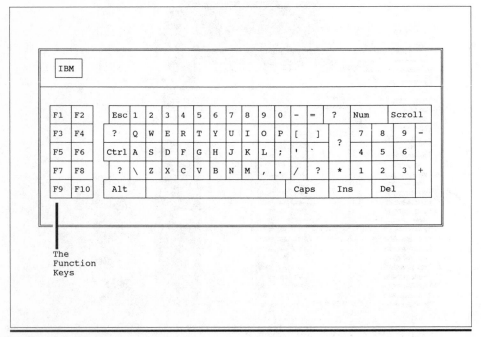

Figure 17.4: *The PC keyboard*

Printing

Printing your drawings may present problems. In fact, you should test your printer before drawing anything elaborate. To do this, draw a few characters using each of the options on the Line Draw menu, and use the Print Key (Shift-F7) to print the page. You may also try using different printer definitions. For instance, I was able to print all of the characters after redefining my Epson printer, which is actually an RX-80, as an FX-85. See Appendix A for help with this process.

If your printer cannot print all the characters you want to use, the manual suggests using Search and Replace to redefine the graphics characters with characters that can be printed by all printers, such as the plus and minus sign. However, this alters the appearance so much that it is hardly worth the considerable effort involved. You have to enter the decimal value of each ASCII graphics character in the search string, by pressing Num Lock, then the Alt key with the number from the numeric keypad.

For instance, to replace the horizontal lines drawn using option 1, press the Replace Key (Alt-F2), N or Y, Num Lock, then hold down Alt while typing 196. As soon as you let go of these keys, the graphics character will appear in the search string. Next, press F2, then press the minus sign as the replacement. To replace a vertical line drawn with the same option, you must search for the decimal code 179 and replace it with a different

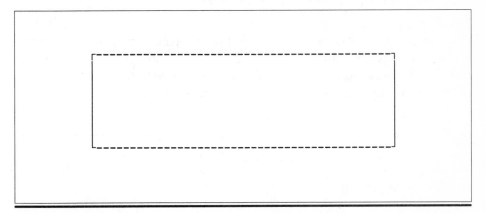

Figure 17.5: *A rectangle after replacing the graphics characters*

character: ⌐. A rectangle drawn with single lines will end up looking like Figure 17.5.

Summary

Line drawing is another one of WordPerfect's many extras: it can be used to enhance the appearance of your documents by adding charts, boxes, and similar figures. As you have learned, it is easy to use, as long as you remember that it works in Typeover mode. Also, you should be careful not to insert extra hard returns, since WordPerfect automatically inserts them at the end of each line when you draw with ↓.

The Line Draw feature on the Screen Key (Ctrl-F3) can be used to draw lines, boxes, charts, and other simple illustrations using characters such as a single or double line, asterisks, a solid box, or a box of dots. You can choose from among eleven different characters, or change the characters using the decimal equivalents of ASCII characters. The characters can be seen on any monitor, but many printers are incapable of printing them.

Line Draw works in Typeover mode, so the Ins key must be pressed before typing text inside of a drawing. To create drawings such as organizational charts, it's easier to type the text first (in Edit mode), then draw the boxes around the titles.

Since many printers, including most daisy wheel printers, cannot print graphics characters, it is advisable to test your printer before creating drawings for your documents. Changing printer definitions may correct the output. If all else fails, you can redefine the graphics characters using WordPerfect's Search and Replace feature.

CHAPTER 18 KEYSTROKE SUMMARY:

The Spell Key—display options for the Speller. You can check for misspellings in small units (option 1, Word; option 2, Page) or throughout a document

The Block Key—to check for misspellings within a specific block of text, mark the block before starting the Speller.

The Thesaurus Key—display synonyms for a specified word

THE SPELLER AND THESAURUS

WORDPERFECT'S SPELLING CHECKER contains over 100,000 words, about as many as the average desktop dictionary. However, the Speller does much more than automatically find and correct your spelling mistakes. Think about how you use a dictionary: if you forget how to spell a word, you usually look it up before typing it, or else just after typing it. WordPerfect can do both. If you're really uncertain about how to spell it, you can have the program check the dictionary for a pattern or phonetic match, and have it enter the correct word into your document. The program can also check a page, block, or the entire document, provide you with a count of the total number of words, and catch double occurrences of a word. To customize the dictionary, you can direct the program to add words to the list as they are found, or you can add an entire file of your own words to the dictionary. The Speller is definitely one of WordPerfect's most valuable utilities, and one of the easiest to use.

The WordPerfect Speller actually contains three dictionaries: a common word list, a main word list, and a supplemental list that is created when you add words of your own. The common word list contains about 1,550 of the most frequently used words in the language; the Speller always checks these first. Since it is the smallest one, the program can check this list very quickly. If the word is not found there, the main word list is searched. The last list to be checked is the supplemental one. If the word is not found, you can add it to the supplemental list for future reference. This list can later be incorporated into the main one using the Speller Utility.

The WordPerfect Thesaurus is another wonderful tool for writers, but it can be useful for everyday applications as well, especially if you aren't sure of the exact meaning of a word. If a word is found in the Thesaurus, a list of synonyms appears on the screen, classified into groups of nouns, adjectives, and verbs, and subdivided into groups with the same connotation. There are over 10,000 *headwords* in the Thesaurus, comparable to the average desktop version.

The Speller

Checking a Word, Page, Block, or Document

In Chapter 3 you learned how to check a document for spelling, so this will be a review of that process. Remember that you can interrupt the operation anytime by pressing the Cancel Key (F1).

Retrieve the file you want to check to the editing screen. If you want to check a block, mark it with the Block Key (Alt-F4). Next, press the Spell Key (Ctrl-F2). If you do not have a hard disk, insert the Speller diskette into your B drive, then press Ctrl-F2. The following menu will appear on the Status line, unless you are checking a blocked section, in which case the speller will begin searching:

Check: 1 Word; 2 Page; 3 Document; 4 Change Dictionary; 5 Look Up; 6 Count

To check the entire document, press 3. To limit the operation to the page where your cursor is located, press 2. To check just the word your cursor is located on, press 1. Using option 2 or 3 will also check any headers, footers, footnotes, or endnotes you have placed in your document, when it reaches the header/footer definition code. After you select the option you want, you will know that the Speller is looking for misspelled words because the * *Please wait* * message will appear on the Status line.

If you are checking a single word and the cursor moves to the next word after you select option 1, it means that the word is correctly spelled. You can then press any key to exit from the Speller menu or continue checking other words or the page or document.

If the Speller locates a word that is not in the dictionary, it will stop and highlight the word in reverse video, and you will see this prompt at the bottom of the screen:

Not Found! Select Word or Menu Option (0 = Continue): 0
1 Skip once; 2 Skip; 3 Add Word; 4 Edit; 5 Look Up; 6 Phonetic

A double line of dashes will appear on the screen, and a list of suggested replacements the program has found in its dictionary will appear, as shown in Figure 18.1. To replace the misspelled word with one of the suggestions,

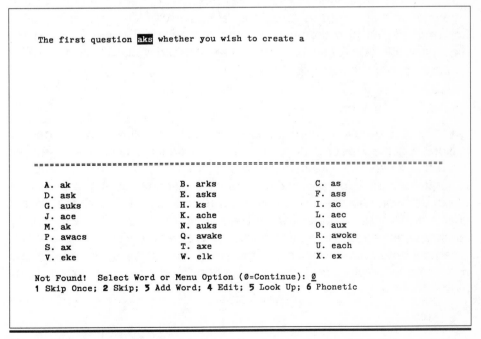

Figure 18.1: *Suggested replacements*

just type the letter appearing next to the correct suggestion. If the word in your document was capitalized, the replacement will be too.

Skipping or Adding a Word

If, however, the word is not in the list of suggested replacements, you have several choices. If you select option 1, the Speller will accept this occurrence of the word, but if it finds it anywhere else (on the page if you are checking the page, or in the document if you are checking the document), it will stop once again. If you select option 2, the Speller will accept the word and skip it wherever it is found on this page or this document. Use these options to skip words such as names, cities, and other proper nouns that are not in the dictionary, unless you want to add them to the dictionary. If the Speller stops on a correctly spelled word you use frequently, you can add it to the supplementary dictionary by selecting option 3, Add Word.

Editing

Option 4, Edit, allows you to leave the Speller menu temporarily and enter the editing screen to revise the text yourself. After you finish, press Return to get back to the Speller. If the revised word is not found in the dictionary, the *Not Found* prompt will remain and you will have to select another option, such as Skip, to continue.

Looking Up a Word

The Look Up option (5) on the *Not Found!* menu allows you to look up a word that the Speller cannot find in the dictionary, such as a misspelled word that differs by more than one letter, or two or more letters typed out of sequence. You can use this option to try a different spelling to locate the word, and you can use a question mark (?) and/or asterisk (*) as wildcard characters to help with the search. The question mark stands for any single letter, and an asterisk stands for a sequence of letters. For example, if you type *concientous,* a misspelling of the word *conscientious,* the Speller will not locate the replacement. To find the correct word, select option 5 and type this sequence:

cons*

and you will see the list, as shown in Figure 18.2.

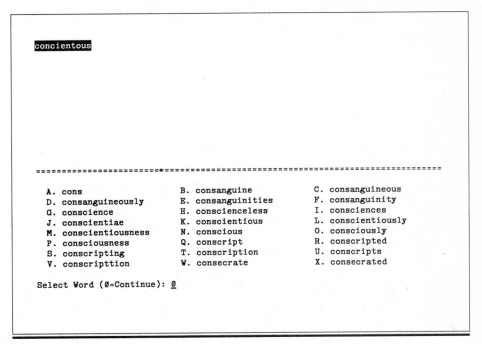

Figure 18.2: *Looking up a word*

As you can see, the word next to the letter K is the correct one, so press K to insert it into your text. If the word you want is not on the list, press the Cancel Key (F1) and try another pattern.

Question marks are helpful to find the correct spelling for words such as *apparent,* which is often misspelled as *apparant.* To locate it, enter this sequence:

app?r?nt

The Look Up option on the main Speller menu (also option 5) allows you to look up a word in the dictionary and determine the correct spelling before typing the word, but it cannot be used to substitute the word into your document. To use this option, you press the Spell Key (Ctrl-F2), select option 5, then type the word or word pattern using asterisks and/or question marks. For example, when you use this method to look up the word *cons** from this menu, you see the screen illustrated in Figure 18.3.

Note that there are letters next to the words, but you can't use them to enter the word into your document.. As the prompt *Press any key to continue* suggests, as soon as you press a key you see the next screenful of

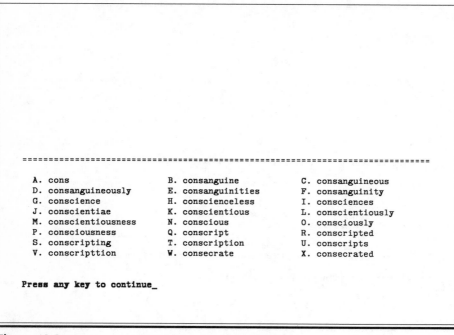

```
================================================================================

     A. cons              B. consanguine       C. consanguineous
     D. consanguineously  E. consanguinities   F. consanguinity
     G. conscience        H. conscienceless    I. consciences
     J. conscientiae      K. conscientious     L. conscientiously
     M. conscientiousness N. conscious         O. consciously
     P. consciousness     Q. conscript         R. conscripted
     S. conscripting      T. conscription      U. conscripts
     V. conscripttion     W. consecrate        X. consecrated


  Press any key to continue_
```

Figure 18.3: *Looking up a word from the main menu*

words in the dictionary. When you come to the last screenful that matches your word pattern, you are asked to enter another word or word pattern.

If you want to use the Look Up option to replace a word, type the word first (don't worry about the spelling) then place your cursor anywhere in it and use option 2, Word, from the main Speller menu. Next, select option 5 from the Not Found! menu and enter your word pattern.

Looking Up a Word Phonetically

WordPerfect always uses a phonetic method to look up words that can't otherwise be found, searching for words that sound like the misspelled word. For example, if you type *fone* instead of *phone*, the Speller finds a screenful of words that begin with *f*, and one word beginning with *p*, *phone*, as shown in Figure 18.4.

Occasionally, users of WordPerfect 4.1 and earlier versions will find that the Speller cannot find a word. If this happens, try using the phonetic option

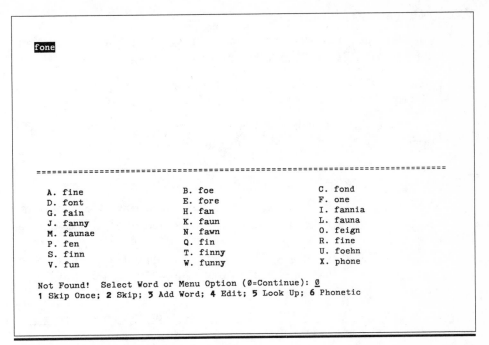

Figure 18.4: *A phonetic lookup*

(6 on the Not Found! menu) to locate it before using Edit. WordPerfect 4.2 users rarely need this option because the Speller automatically includes it.

Word Count

When the Speller is finished it displays a count of the total number of words and this message:

Press any key to continue

If you have checked only a page or a word, pressing any key will bring back the Speller menu. Then, to return to the document, press any key except one of the menu selections. However, if you have checked the entire document, the Speller menu will not reappear.

To obtain a count of the total number of words in your document without going through the spelling check process, select option 6, Count, from the Speller menu.

Words Containing Numbers

The Speller skips numbers, but it stops on words that contain numbers and letters, such as F3, and the following prompt appears:

> Not Found! Select Word or Menu Option (0 = Continue): 0
> 1 2 Skip; 3 Ignore words containing numbers; 4 Edit

To skip all other words with numbers in them, choose option 3. If you select option 1 or 2, it will just skip this particular word.

Double-Word Occurrences

If the Speller locates a word that occurs twice in a row, it will stop and highlight both of them. Pressing option 3 will delete the second one, as shown in Figure 18.5.

If deleting the word is not the solution, you can either skip it (1 or 2) or edit it (4). Option 5 allows you to turn this feature off, so that the Speller will not stop at double words.

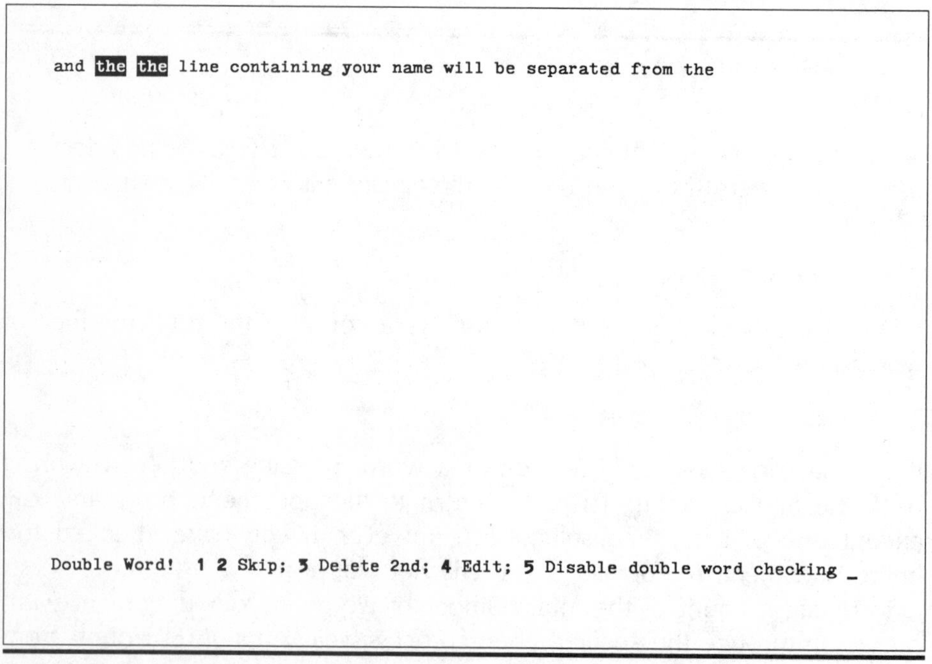

```
     and the the line containing your name will be separated from the

















     Double Word!  1 2 Skip; 3 Delete 2nd; 4 Edit; 5 Disable double word checking _
```

Figure 18.5: *Double-word checking*

The Speller Utility

The Speller Utility is an independent program that can be used to create a new dictionary, change dictionaries, add a list of words to the dictionary, delete words, display the common word list, check to see if a word is in the dictionary, or perform a look-up. Don't use this program casually, or you may end up erasing the WordPerfect dictionary. Also, it is not a practical method of adding or deleting a small number of words, since the process takes up to twenty minutes. When you add or delete words with this utility, the entire dictionary has to be resorted, to place each word in the proper alphabetical order.

As you know, when you add words to the dictionary using option 3 on the Speller Not Found menu, they are added to a supplemental dictionary. If you add enough words during one session, you may run out of room in your computer's memory (RAM), and you will see this message:

Dictionary Full.

If this happens, you should add the supplemental dictionary to the main one, then delete the supplemental one from your disk. To do this, exit to DOS and load the Speller Utility by typing

SPELL

If you do not have a hard disk, insert the Speller disk into drive A and type

A:SPELL

to start it. You will see the Speller Utility's main menu, as shown in Figure 18.6.

Select option 2, Add words to dictionary, from the Speller Utility's main menu. Next, select option 4, Add to main word list (from a file). Type the name of the supplemental file, {WP}LEX.SUP, as shown in Figure 18.7 (be sure to include the braces), then press Return and select option 5, Exit.

You will then see a message indicating that the dictionary is being updated, as shown below:

Updating the dictionary
Writing the a's

This process can take several minutes, so take a coffee break or find some

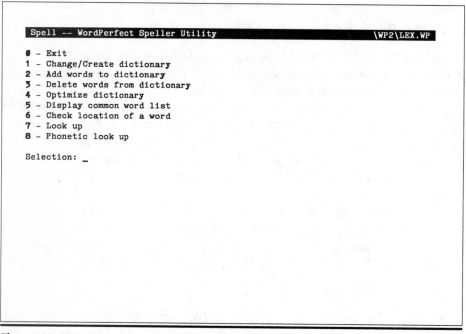

```
Spell -- WordPerfect Speller Utility                    \WP2\LEX.WP

 0 - Exit
 1 - Change/Create dictionary
 2 - Add words to dictionary
 3 - Delete words from dictionary
 4 - Optimize dictionary
 5 - Display common word list
 6 - Check location of a word
 7 - Look up
 8 - Phonetic look up

Selection: _
```

Figure 18.6: *The Speller Utility's main menu*

other work to do in the meantime. When it is finished, the Main menu will reappear and you can press 0 to exit to DOS.

You can also use the Speller Utility to find out if a word is contained in the Speller dictionary, and if so, which list it is in, the common or the main one. To check a word, select option 6 from the Speller Utility's main menu, Check location of a word. In response to the prompt

> Word to check

enter your word. If it is found, you will see one of these messages:

> Found in main dictionary

or

> Found in common word list

If it is not found, you will see

> Not found

In all cases, you will be returned to the *Word to check* prompt and can

```
┌─────────────────────────────────────────────────────────────────────┐
│                                                                       │
│  Spell -- Add Words                                        \WP2\LEX.WP│
│                                                                       │
│  0 - Cancel - do not add words                                        │
│  1 - Add to common word list (from keyboard)                          │
│  2 - Add to common word list (from a file)                            │
│  3 - Add to main word list (from keyboard)                            │
│  4 - Add to main word list (from a file)                              │
│  5 - Exit                                                             │
│                                                                       │
│  Selection: 4                                                         │
│  Enter file name: {WP}LEX.SUP_                                        │
│                                                                       │
│                                                                       │
│                                                                       │
│                                                                       │
│                                                                       │
│                                                                       │
│                                                                       │
│                                                                       │
└─────────────────────────────────────────────────────────────────────┘
```

Figure 18.7: *Using the Speller Utility to add words from the supplemental dictionary to the main dictionary*

either enter another word or press Return or F1 to return to the Speller Utility menu.

You can use option 5 to display the entire common word list. When you do, it will be displayed in alphabetical order, one screen at a time. You can exit from it anytime by pressing the Cancel Key (F1).

Option 7 and 8 (Look up and Phonetic look up) work just as they do on the Not Found menu in the Speller itself.

The Thesaurus

The WordPerfect Thesaurus is useful as a supplement to the Speller and as an independent tool for writers. If you don't understand the exact meaning of a word, use the Thesaurus instead of the Speller.

To use it, move the cursor to the word you want to look up and press the Thesaurus Key (Alt-F1). Alternatively, you can place the cursor on a blank space and press Alt-F1, then enter a word you want to look up. If you don't have a hard disk, you'll have to insert the Thesaurus disk in drive B before pressing Alt-F1. If the word that you were looking for is not found, you will see a *Word not found* prompt, which will soon change to this prompt:

Word:

At this point, you can either press F1 twice to cancel the Thesaurus, or enter another similar word to look up.

If the word is found, four lines of your document (or two lines if it's double spaced) will remain at the top of the screen, and the synonyms, which are called references, will appear in columns surrounded by boxes, as shown in Figure 18.8.

The screen you see when looking up the word *top* (Figure 18.8) is divided into groups of nouns, adjectives, antonyms, and verbs, and each group is separated by a solid line. The first 12 references (in column 1) are

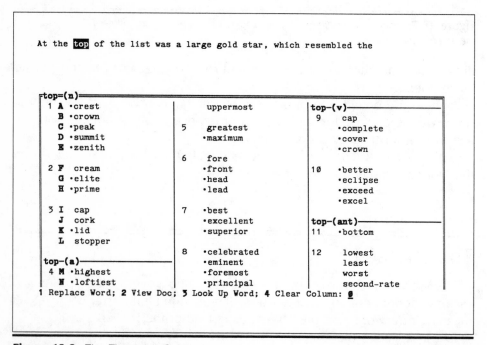

Figure 18.8: *The Thesaurus Screen*

nouns. The numbers to the left represent subgroups of words that have similar connotations such as group 2: cream, elite, and prime.

Notice that the word *top* is highlighted in the text, since it represents the word being looked up in the Thesaurus. Any word that can be found in the Thesaurus is called a headword. The references that are preceded by dots are also headwords, and if you press the letter next to them, a list of their synonyms will replace whatever is in the second column. For instance, pressing C will yield a list of words under the headword *peak,* as shown in Figure 18.9.

If the headword you want to look up is in column 2 or 3, such as *head* or *cover,* it will not have a letter in front of it. However, if you use → to move the cursor to that column, the letters will follow the cursor. Likewise, pressing ↑ or ↓ will display words that do not fit on the screen, if there are any. The Page Up, Page Down, Screen Up, and Screen Down keys can be used to move the column up or down.

To replace the word in your text with one of the words in the list, select option 1, Replace Word, and type the letter next to it (A, B, C, and so on).

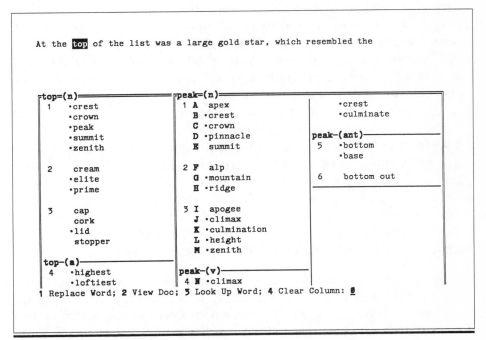

Figure 18.9: *Looking up another headword*

If you decide not to replace the word, you can exit from the Thesaurus screen by pressing the Spacebar, Return, Exit (F7), or Cancel (F1).

Option 2, View Doc, can be used to leave the Thesaurus temporarily and move the cursor around in the document. You cannot perform any editing tasks in this mode, but you can press the Thesaurus Key to look up another word. To return to the Thesaurus without looking up another word, press Return, Exit, or Cancel.

If the word that you were looking for is not on the list, you can use option 3, Look Up Word, to enter it. If you want to start with a clean slate, use option 4, Clear Column, to erase the other references.

Summary

WordPerfect's spelling checker is comprehensive, consisting of three dictionaries with over 100,000 words. It can look up individual words, or check the spelling of a block, page, or document that is on the screen. Words can be found by matching patterns that include the wildcard characters * or ?, or they can be found using the phonetic method, which matches words that sound alike. The Speller provides a count of all the words it checks; it can also perform this count without checking the spelling. If you use specialized terminology, as in the legal or medical professions, you can add words to the dictionary as the Speller finds them, or you can create a file with a list of the words you use most often and append it to the dictionary with the Speller Utility.

The Thesaurus is another helpful tool you can use to find a list of synonyms for approximately 10,000 different headwords. When a word is found, it is shown on screen with one or more columns of synonyms, classified according to whether they are nouns, verbs, adjectives, or antonyms, and subdivided into groups of words with the same connotations. Both the Thesaurus and the Speller are easy to use, and if you get into the habit of using them often, your writing will improve significantly.

To check the spelling of the entire document you are working on, press the Spell Key (F2) and select option 3, document. To check just the page where your cursor is positioned, select option 2. To verify a single word, select option 1. To check a section of text, mark it with the Block Key (Alt-F4), then press the Spell Key. The Speller will flag double word occurrences so that you can eliminate them. Although it will skip numbers, it will stop on words that contain both numbers and letters and you can direct it to skip these as well.

If a word is not found in the dictionary, the Speller will stop to highlight it and show a list of possible replacements. If one of them is the correct spelling, press the letter appearing next to it to replace the incorrect one in your text.

If the Speller does not find the word, you can either skip it, have it look up another possible spelling using pattern matches, or use the phonetic method to locate words that sound like the one you have misspelled. You can also exit temporarily from the Speller menu and edit the word in your document.

If the Speller stops at a word such as a proper noun or specialized term you use frequently, you may choose to add it to the dictionary so that it will not question the spelling in the future. You can even add a whole list of words to the dictionary by using the Speller Utility.

When the Speller finishes checking a page, block, or document, it provides you with a count of the total number of words. By selecting option 6 on the Speller menu, you can obtain this count without checking the spelling.

The Speller Utility is a separate program that can be used to make a new dictionary, change the dictionary, add or delete words from it, add the supplemental list to the main list, verify whether a specific word is in the dictionary, display the common word list, or perform a look up.

The Thesaurus is invoked by pressing the Thesaurus Key (Alt-F1). It locates lists of synonyms for about 10,000 different entries, and helps you figure out the the best substitute.

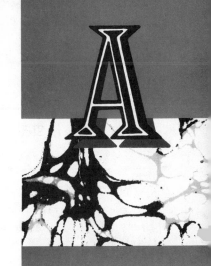

INSTALLATION

WORDPERFECT 4.2 REQUIRES AN IBM OR compatible computer with a minimum of 256k, either two double-sided disk drives or one hard disk and one double-sided disk drive, and DOS 2.0 (or later version). Separate versions of the program are available for a number of other MS-DOS based computers.

Program Installation

Floppy Drive System

To install WordPerfect on a system with floppy disk drives, you format six new disks to use as your working copies of the program (and one for a data disk), copy the DOS system files onto the disk that will be the working copy of the WordPerfect System disk, copy the files from the five original Word-Perfect disks onto the newly formatted disks, then store the originals in a safe place. The steps are as follows.

Label the first new disk *WordPerfect System* and place it in drive B. You will be formatting the disk and copying certain DOS files that are needed on the WordPerfect system disk. A word of warning: this procedure completely destroys any data on the disk in drive B, so you must be sure that you are using a new disk (or one that contains nothing you want to keep). If you are unsure, check the disk for files by entering

DIR B:

If the disk is unformatted, the DIR command will not list any files and you will be asked to abort, retry, or ignore. This means that the disk is new and you can type

A

(for abort) and proceed with formatting.

Place your DOS disk in drive A. With the A> prompt on the screen, enter

FORMAT B:/S

The /S option copies certain DOS files onto your disk so that this disk will be self-booting (that is, you can place it in drive A, turn on the computer, and DOS will be loaded). You will see a message telling you to insert a new disk into drive B and press any key to continue. It will take a minute or so to format the disk and then you will be asked if you want to format another disk. Enter N.

The next step is to place another new disk in drive B. This one will be formatted without the /S option, since the DOS files aren't needed on the backup copies of the Speller, Thesaurus, Printer, and Learning disks. From the A> prompt, enter

FORMAT B:

then press any key to begin the process. After the disk is formatted you will be asked if you want to format another. This time, enter Y. You will then be asked to place a new disk in drive B, so insert another new one and press any key to begin formatting. Repeat this procedure to format each of the remaining new disks.

The next step is to copy the files from the original WordPerfect disks. Place the original WordPerfect System disk in drive A and the one you formatted and labelled *WordPerfect System* in drive B. To copy the files, at the A> prompt enter

COPY A:*.* B:

Next, label each of the four remaining disks and repeat the process to make copies of the original versions of the Speller, Thesaurus, Printer, and Learning disks.

To start the program, place a blank formatted disk in drive B (this will be your *data disk*) and your copy of the WordPerfect System disk in drive A. Log on to drive B by entering

B:

then enter

A:WP

to start WordPerfect. Refer to the instructions in Chapter 1 for more details.

Hard Disk System

If you have a hard disk, it is still a good idea to follow the steps outlined above to make backup copies of the original WordPerfect disks. However, it is not necessary for installation.

The first step is to make a new directory for your WordPerfect files. You can name the directory WP or WORD or anything you want, but try to make it mnemonic. The main text of this book assumes you named the

directory WP. To create a directory with the name WP from the root directory, enter

    MD WP

Next, log onto the subdirectory by entering

    CD WP

Now insert the original WordPerfect System disk into drive A. With the C>
prompt on your screen, enter

    COPY A:∗.∗

This will copy all of the files from the original WordPerfect disk onto your
hard disk, showing you the names of the files as they are copied. When the
files are all copied, a message will appear telling you how many were copied. Repeat this process to copy the Speller disk and the Thesaurus disk.

    The last step is to copy the Help files from the original WordPerfect
Learning disk. If you wish to copy all of the files from this disk, repeat the
procedure described above. However, there are quite a few tutorial files
on this disk and if you don't use them, cluttering up your directory this
way is not recommended. To copy just the Help files, place the Learning
disk in drive A and enter

    COPY A:WPHELP∗.FIL

    To start WordPerfect, make sure you are in the subdirectory you created
for the WordPerfect files and enter

    WP

You can also use several start up options to enter WordPerfect, as
described in the options section of this appendix.

The PC-DOS Tree Command

    If the WordPerfect program is already installed on your hard disk but
you are unsure of the directory name, you can locate it by checking the
entire hard disk using the DOS Tree command. You will be looking for
the file WP.EXE.

    If your disk contains a large number of files and subdirectories, when you
issue the Tree command you will see many names disappear off of the top
of the screen before you get a chance to read them. To stop this scrolling

action so that you can view an entire screenful, press the Ctrl key and con-tinue holding it down while pressing the Num Lock key. To start scrolling again, press any key except Num Lock. If you wish to terminate the Tree command altogether, press the Ctrl and Break (Scroll Lock) keys, and you will see the C prompt again. Alternatively, you can view a screen at a time by issuing the Tree command in combination with the More command.

Issue the Tree command by entering

    TREE/F

or by entering it with the More command.

    TREE/F ¦ MORE

If you see the file named WP.EXE listed under one of the subdirectories, press Ctrl-Break and at the C> prompt, change to that subdirectory by typing

    CD

followed by a space and the name of the subdirectory containing the file (preceded by a \ and, if necessary, a path), then press Return.

Next, start the WordPerfect program by typing

    WP

and pressing the Return key.

If you do not find the WP.EXE file, it has not been installed on your hard disk.

Options for Entering WordPerfect

When you start WordPerfect, you can use one or more options to per-form tasks such as starting a macro, retrieving a file, starting the automatic backup feature, and much more. You do this by entering the option(s) after typing WP to start the program.

Automatic Backup

If you start the program by typing

    WP/B-*n*

where *n* is a number such as 10, the automatic backup feature will save the file you are working on every *n* minutes. This feature can also be installed permanently using the Set-up menu, as described in the next section.

Redirecting Overflow Files, Buffers, and Temporary Macros

If you start the program by typing

WP/D-

followed by the letter corresponding to the drive (A,B, or C) and the path and directory name if appropriate, the overflow files, buffers, and temporary macros will be redirected to that disk. When you use this and the /R option described below, you can take the System disk out after loading WordPerfect and use drive A for other files such as macros or the help files. If you simply enter WP/D-, these files will be created on the disk and directory where your WordPerfect System disk is located.

Start Up with a Document File

If you start the program by typing

WP *filename*

the named file will be retrieved as soon as WordPerfect is loaded.

Uninstalled or Copied Versions of the Original

If you install WordPerfect from a copy, such as when using a RAM drive, or if you have a hard disk but have not copied the program onto your hard disk, start the program from the A drive by entering

WP/I

Start Up with a Macro

If you want to start a macro as soon as the program is loaded, enter

WP/M-*macroname*

where *macroname* is one of your macros.

Non-Flash Version

Some IBM compatible computers and windowing programs will not run correctly unless you start the program with the non-flash option. If your screen goes blank from time to time or if you are using one of the window programs such as Microsoft Windows or Topview, start the program by entering

    WP/NF

so that WordPerfect will not override these programs with its own screen calls.

Non-Synch Version for Hyperion Machines and Color Monitors

If you are using a Hyperion computer, you must use the non-synch option to run the non-synch version of the program. In addition, some color monitors will run faster if you use this option, although it also may cause "snow" on some. To use it, start WordPerfect by entering

    WP/NS

Speeding Up the Program

If you have enough RAM, you can make WordPerfect run faster by starting it with this option:

    WP/R

This loads menus, error messages, and overlays from the System disk into your computer's memory.

Starting WordPerfect with the Set-Up Menu

To run the Set-up menu, you start WordPerfect by entering

    WP/S

This is the only start-up option that cannot be combined with one of the others. The others can be combined in any sequence by typing them without any spaces in between, such as WP/d-/r/b-10, which is my start-up sequence. The options available on this menu are described in the next section.

The WordPerfect Set-Up Menu

You can use the Set-up menu to change several of WordPerfect's options on a permanent basis, including the defaults for line spacing, tabs, margins, and justification, as well as to change the screen size, load the Speller or Thesaurus from a drive and/or directory other than the default one, set the backup options and set the beep options.

To run the set-up menu, you enter WordPerfect by typing WP/S, as described above. You will then see a menu with the following five selections:

1. Set Directories or Drives for Dictionary and Thesaurus Files
2. Set Initial Settings
3. Set Screen Size
4. Set Backup Options
5. Set Beep Options

Use option 1 if you wish to store your Thesaurus (TH.WP), Speller dictionary (LEX.WP), and/or the supplementary dictionary in a different drive or directory (other than the default). You will be asked where you want to store each of the three files, and to enter the full pathname for each one. Do not enter the file name itself. For example, if your WordPerfect system files are on drive C in a directory named *WP* and your LEX.WP file (the Speller dictionary) is located in a subdirectory named *SPELL,* when asked

> Where do you plan to keep the dictionary (LEX.WP)?
> Enter full path name:

you enter

> C:\WP\SPELL

Option 2, Set Initial Settings, is used to change formatting defaults on a permanent basis. These settings are changed within the program on a temporary basis by using the Line Format, Page Format, Print Format,

Print, Date, Mark Text, Footnote, Escape, Screen, and Insert Keys, and the process is similar in the Set-up menu. When you select 2, a menu will appear listing the keys and the initial settings that can be changed. To change one, you press the function key combination and select the feature. For example, if you want to turn off right justification and use a ragged right margin, you press the Print Format Key (Ctrl-F8); this brings up the same menu you see when you press it from within WordPerfect. Enter option 3 to turn off justification, then press Return to leave the Set Initial Settings menu. To make the Document Summary feature mandatory so that the Create/Edit Summary screen will automatically appear the first time you save a file, use Set Initial Settings (option 2) and press Ctrl-F5, then Y in response to the prompt

Enter Document Summary on Save/Exit? (Y/N)

then press Return. The last step is to enter 0 (zero) to start WordPerfect.

If your monitor is capable of displaying a wider or longer screen than the default settings of 25 rows and 80 columns, you can use option 3, Set Screen Size, to alter these settings. To use it, you press 3, enter the new settings, then press Return and 0 (zero) to enter WordPerfect.

Use option 4 if you want to use one or both of WordPerfect's backup features, Timed Backup and Original Backup. Please see Chapter 12 for details about these options.

In Chapter 6 you studied Search and Replace and learned that the Set-up menu could be used to make your computer beep when the search string isn't found in the document. You can also have the computer beep when an error occurs. To install this feature, press 5, Set Beep Options, and enter Y when asked

Beep when search fails? (Y/N) N

and/or when asked

Beep on error? (Y/N) N

If you make a mistake in the set-up process, press the Cancel Key (F1) to return to DOS without installing the modifications. Otherwise, make the change(s) and then type 0 (zero) to enter WordPerfect. The new defaults will remain in effect permanently and you can only change them by entering the Set-up menu again and repeating the process.

Printer Installation

To install your printer(s) for use with WordPerfect, use the Select Printers option on the Printer Control menu. As of this writing, the program was able to fully support 179 printers, and partially support 69 others. You can install up to 6 printers at once.

When you direct WordPerfect to install one or more printers, it copies specific instructions for those printers (called printer definitions) from the WordPerfect Printer disk and creates three new files on your system disk: WPRINTER.FIL, WPFEED.FIL, and WPFONT.FIL. If you ever want to delete the printer definitions and start over, simply erase these three files and begin the process again. Some versions of the WordPerfect Installation booklet suggest that you recopy the WPRINTER.FIL file from the Word-Perfect printer disk and start over, but this does not work. If you try this procedure, when you select option 2 from the Printer Control menu to see which printers and fonts are installed (as described in Chapter 8), you will see this message:

Bad or missing WPRINTER.FIL or WPFONT.FIL or WPFEED.FIL

To install your printer(s), the first step is to press the Print Key (Shift-F7) and select option 4, Printer Control. From the Printer Control menu, select option 3, Select Printers. You will then see a menu that you will use to install new printers. The cursor will be located after the line: Printer 1, Using Definition 1. If there are any printer definitions already installed, you will see them listed at the top of the screen.

Press PgDn and you will see a message telling you the program can't find the printer files, and directing you to place a WordPerfect Printer Disk-ette into any floppy drive and press the drive letter when ready. Note that there are two Printer disks: Printer 1 and Printer 2. Find your WordPerfect Printer 1 disk and insert it in drive B, then type *B*.

A list of printers will then appear; you will be selecting your printer defini-tion from this list or a similar list on the Printer 2 disk. Note that it is arranged in alphabetical order and fills several screens. If your printer is not shown on the first screen, press the PgDn key to view the next one. Continue pressing PgDn until you come to the last screen. You will know you have reached the last screen because the next time you press PgDn you will be back at the first printer definition file (and the printer name will begin with the letter A). Press-ing the PgUp key takes you back one screen.

If your printer is not on any of the screens, press the Cancel Key (F1), remove the Printer 1 disk from drive B and replace it with the Printer 2 disk. Next, start over by pressing 3 (Select Printers), PgDn to see the list, and B to specify that the Printer 2 disk is in drive B. Note that some of the printer files on this disk are marked with an asterisk in between the number and printer name. The asterisk indicates that the printer is only partially supported, so certain formatting features such as superscript, subscript, redline, strikeout, bold, or underline may be unavailable to you.

When you do find your printer on the list, type the number that appears to the left of it and this number will then appear after the words *Using Definition:*. As soon as you press Return, the program copies the definition file from the Printer disk onto your default disk.

You will then see a screen that asks you to select the printer port. Most IBM compatible printers use a parallel port (either LPT1, LPT2, or LPT3), but a few, including some laser printers, use a serial port (COM1, COM2, COM3, or COM4). If you are using only one printer and you know that it is parallel, you will probably use the first parallel port, LPT1. If you are using a serial printer, you will select COM1, COM2, COM3, or COM4, depending on how many other devices (such as modems) are connected to your computer with a serial interface. When you choose a serial port, you will also have to specify several other parameters such as the baud rate, parity, number of stop bits, and character length, so consult your printer manual for this information.

After you select the printer port, you will be asked to select from three different methods of feeding the paper into your printer: continuous, hand fed, or sheet feeder. Select 1, Continuous, if you are using a printer with a tractor or feed the paper continuously. Select 2, Hand Fed, if you insert each sheet individually (as you do with a typewriter) or 3, Sheet Feeder, if you have a sheet feeder installed on your printer.

After these selections are made, you will be returned to the Printer Definition screen and the name of the printer definition you just installed will now appear at the top of the screen. If you want to install another printer at this point, press ↓ to change the printer number (in the lower left corner of the screen) to 2, 3, 4, 5, or 6, then press PgDn and repeat the process of selecting a printer definition from the list of available ones. On the other hand, if you want to use the same printer with a different form-feed option or with a different printer interface than the ones you selected for printer 1, select another printer number (2, 3, 4, 5, or 6) by pressing ↓ and (next to the Using Definition prompt) type the definition number (1) appearing at the top of the screen next to the printer you just installed. It should look like this:

Printer 2
Using Definition: 1

This time, you will not see the long list of printer definitions (since you have already selected definition 1). Instead, you will go straight to the screen that asks for the printer port and type of form you wish to use; you should select a different one(s) for this "printer." Now you will have two "printers" installed, both of which use the same definition (as copied from the Printer disk) but different interfaces and/or form feed methods. When you return to the Printer Definitions screen, you will see only one definition listed at the top.

As you have seen, each printer definition that is copied from the Printer disk appears at the top of the Printer Definitions screen with a number next to it. Note that these numbers refer to the number following the Using Definition prompt, not the printer number of the printer you have installed. This can be confusing since, in the previous step, you entered an entirely different number (such as 82) for your definition, and that number then appeared after the Using Definition prompt. In case this is unclear, look again at the prompt in the lower left corner of the Printer Definition screen:

Printer
Using Definition:

The number that follows the words *Using Definition* is the one that corresponds to the number next to each printer definition on the list at the top of the screen. The number that follows the word *Printer* is the number you have established to install printers 1 through 6 by going through the definition process explained above. The use of the term *Printer* can be misleading here, because it implies that each "printer" is a separate piece of equipment. In reality, they can all be the same printer used in a variety of ways, with different form-feed options and/or printer-port options. Also, if you use a laser printer you will have to copy a different file definition for each font (soft font or cartridge) that you want to use. Each font will be set up as a separate printer number.

Since printer 1 is the default, it will always be used to print a document unless you select another. Chapter 8 explains how to use one of the other printers you have installed, either for a single print job or for everything you print during the current editing session. If you want to permanently change the printer number, use the Set-up screen when you enter WordPerfect, as described in the preceding section.

COMMANDS, FUNCTIONS, AND CODES

Commands and Functions
—Listed Alphabetically

COMMAND OR FUNCTION	KEY SEQUENCE
Advance to specified line	Shift-F1 6
Advance up (or down) half line	Shift-F1 4 (*or* 5)
Alignment character definition	Shift-F8 6
Append marked block to end of disk file	Alt-F4 Ctrl-F4 3
Auto rewrite	Ctrl-F3 5
Binding width	Shift-F7 3 3
Block cut/copy	Alt-F4 Ctrl-F4
Block Key	Alt-F4
Block protection	Alt-F4 Alt-F8
Bold Key	F6

COMMAND OR FUNCTION	KEY SEQUENCE
Calculate (with Math on)	Alt-F7 2
Cancel Key	F1
Cancel a print job	Shift-F7 4 C
Case conversion	Alt-F4 Shift-F3
Center Key	Shift-F6
Center page between top and bottom margins	Alt-F8 3
Change default drive	F5
Characters per inch (pitch)	Ctrl-F8 1
Colors	Ctrl-F3 4
Column cut or copy	Alt-F4 Ctrl-F4 4
Columns (define as newspaper or parallel)	Alt-F7 4
Comment	Ctrl-F5 B (or C)
Conditional end of page	Alt-F8 9
Copy files	F5 Return 8
Ctrl/Alt key reassign	Ctrl-F3 3
Cut or copy sentence, paragraph, or page	Ctrl-F4 1 (or 2 or 3)
Cut or copy rectangle	Alt-F4 Ctrl-F4 5
Cut, copy, append a marked block	Alt-F4 Ctrl-F4
Date Key	Shift-F5
Define lists, index, table of authorities, table of contents, paragraph/outline numbering	Alt-F5 6
Define macro	Ctrl-F10
Delete character at cursor	Del
Delete character left of cursor	Backspace
Delete characters to left of cursor within word	Home Backspace

COMMAND OR FUNCTION	KEY SEQUENCE
Delete characters to right of cursor within word	Home Del
Delete to end of line	Ctrl-End
Delete to end of page	Ctrl-PgDn
Delete file(s)	F5 Return 2
Delete word	Ctrl-Backspace
Disk directory (change)	F5 Return 7
Display printers and fonts	Shift-F7 4 2
Display disk space	F5 Return
Display columns side by side	Alt-F7 5
Display all print jobs	Shift-F7 4 D
Document summary (create)	Ctrl-F5 A
Document summary (display)	Ctrl-F5 D
Edit a comment	Ctrl-F5 C
Edit two documents (switch)	Shift-F3
End of field	F9
End of record	Shift-F9
Endnote (edit)	Ctrl-F7 6
Endnote (create)	Ctrl-F7 5
Execute merge	Ctrl-F9
Exit Key (exit from WordPerfect)	F7
Exit to DOS temporarily	Ctrl-F1
Extended characters	Alt <ASCII code, using numbers centered from numeric keypad>
Extended search	Home-F2
File management	F5
Flush Right Key	Alt-F6

COMMAND OR FUNCTION	KEY SEQUENCE
Fonts (change)	Ctrl-F8 1
Footnote Key	Ctrl-F7
Forward Search Key	F2
Generate list, index, and tables	Alt-F5 6 8
Go To Key	Ctrl-Home
Go to DOS	Ctrl-F1 1
Hard page break	Ctrl-Return
Hard space	Home-Spacebar
Headers or footers	Alt-F8 6
Help Key	F3
Hyphen character (hard)	Home-(hyphen)
Hyphenation on/off	Shift-F8 5
Hyphenation zone (set)	Shift-F8 5 3
Import DOS text file	Ctrl-F5 2 (or F5 Return 5)
Indent Key	F4
Index (mark word for)	Alt-F5 5
Justification off (on)	Ctrl-F8 3 (or 4)
Left/Right Indent Key	Shift-F4
Line drawing	Ctrl-F3 2
Line Format Key	Shift-F8
Line numbering	Ctrl-F8 B 2
Line spacing	Shift-F8 4
Lines per inch	Ctrl-F8 2
List Files Key	F5
List (mark text for list)	Alt-F4 Alt-F5 2
Lock a file	Ctrl-F5 4
Look at contents of a disk file	F5 Return 6

COMMAND OR FUNCTION	KEY SEQUENCE
Lowercase conversion	Shift-F3 2 (Block on)
Macro Define Key	Ctrl-F10
Macro Key (invoke)	Alt-F10
Margin release	Shift-Tab
Margins (set)	Shift-F8 3
Mark Text Key	Alt-F5
Math columns on	Alt-F7 1
Math column definition	Alt-F7 2
Math/Columns Key	Alt-F7
Merge (run)	Ctrl-F9 1
Merge Codes Key (insert codes)	Alt-F9
Merge End Key (insert end of record code)	Shift-F9
Merge Return Key (insert end of field code)	F9
Merge/Sort Key	Ctrl-F9
Move Key	Ctrl-F4
Name search (file name)	F5 Return <characters>
Outline mode toggle	Alt-F5 1
Overstrike	Shift-F1 3
Page break	Ctrl-Return
Page Format Key	Alt-F8
Page length	Alt-F8 4
Page number position	Alt-F8 1
Page number (new)	Alt-F8 2
Paragraph numbering	Alt-F5 2
Password protection	Ctrl-F5 4
Pitch	Ctrl-F8 1
Preview a document	Shift-F7 6
Print defined block	Alt-F4 Shift-F7

COMMAND OR FUNCTION	KEY SEQUENCE
Print Format Key	Ctrl-F8
Print from disk	Shift-F7 4 P (*or* F5 Return 4)
Print full text	Shift-F7 1
Print Key	Shift-F7
Print multiple copies for current job	Shift-F7 3 2
Print multiple copies for current session	Shift-F7 4 1 2
Print a page	Shift-F7 2
Print selected pages (from file on disk)	Shift-F7 4 P <*page numbers*>
Printer number (select for current job)	Shift-F7 3 1
Printer number (select for current session)	Shift-F7 4 1 1
Printer status and control	Shift-F7 4
Printers and fonts (display)	Shift-F7 4 2
Proportional spacing	Ctrl-F8 1
Protect a document	Ctrl-F5 4
Redline	Alt-F5 3
Release left margin	Shift-Tab
Remove redline and strikeout text	Alt-F5 6 6
Rename file	F5 Return 3
Repeat a command *n* number of times	Esc <*n*><*command*>
Replace Key (search and replace)	Alt-F2
Retrieve column, text, or rectangle	Ctrl-F4 4 (*or* 5 *or* 6)
Retrieve copied or cut text	Ctrl-F4 5
Retrieve DOS text file	Ctrl-F5 2 (*or* 3) (*or* F5 5)
Retrieve file from disk	Shift-F10 (*or* F5 Return 1)

COMMAND OR FUNCTION	KEY SEQUENCE
Retrieve locked document	Ctrl-F5 5
Retrieve Text Key	Shift-F10
Reveal Codes Key	Alt-F3
Reverse Search Key	Shift-F2
Rewrite screen	Ctrl-F3 0
Rush print job	Shift-F7 4 R
Save DOS text file	Ctrl-F5 1
Save file in WordPerfect 4.1 format	Ctrl-F5 7
Save Key	F10
Screen Key	Ctrl-F3
Search (extended)	Home F2
Search for text in files	F5 Return 9
Search and Replace Key	Alt-F2
Search Key (forward search)	F2
Select print options	Shift-F7 4 1
Set line spacing	Shift-F8 4
Set margins	Shift-F8 3
Set tabs	Shift-F8 1 (or 2)
Sheet feeder bin number	Ctrl-F8 9
Shell Key	Ctrl-F1
Short form (enter)	Alt-F5 4
Soft hyphen	Ctrl-(hyphen)
Sort (select)	Ctrl-F9 2
Sorting sequence (select)	Ctrl-F9 3
Space (hard space)	Home-Spacebar
Speller Key	Ctrl-F2
Split screen into windows	Ctrl-F3 1
Start a macro	Alt-F10

COMMAND OR FUNCTION	KEY SEQUENCE
Stop printing	Shift-F7 4 S
Strikeout	Alt-F4 Alt-F5 4
Super/Subscript Key	Shift-F1
Suppress formatting for current page	Alt-F8 8
Switch Key (switch to Doc 2)	Shift-F3
Tab Align Key	Ctrl-F6
Tab ruler	Ctrl-F3 1 1
Table of authorities (define)	Alt-F5 6 4
Table of authorities (edit full form)	Alt-F5 6 7
Table of authorities (mark text for)	Alt-F4 Alt-F5 6
Table of contents (mark text for)	Alt-F4 Alt-F5 1
Tabs (set)	Shift-F8 1 (or 2)
Text column definition (newspaper, parallel)	Alt-F7 4
Text column on/off toggle	Alt-F7 3
Text In/Out Key	Ctrl-F5
Thesaurus Key	Alt-F1
Time Format	Shift-F5 2
Top margin setting	Alt-F8 5
Type-thru	Shift-F7 5
Typeover mode	Ins
Undelete Key	F1
Underline Key	F8
Underline style	Ctrl-F8 5 (or 6 or 7 or 8)
Uppercase conversion	Shift-F3 1 (Block on)
Widow/orphan protection	Alt-F8 A
Windows	Ctrl-F3 1
Word count	Ctrl-F2 6
Word search	F5 Return 9

Commands and Functions—Listed by Key

KEY SEQUENCE	COMMAND

F1   *Cancel Key:* Undelete when used alone; cancel when pressed after other key combinations.

Alt-F1   *Thesaurus Key:* List synonyms.

Ctrl-F1   *Shell Key:* Temporarily exit to DOS.

Shift-F1   *Super/Subscript Key:* Enter superscript or subscript, overstrike, advance up, advance down, advance line.

F2   *Forward Search Key:* Search forward for characters or function codes.

Alt-F2   *Replace Key:* Search and replace.

Ctrl-F2   *Speller Key:* Check spelling of current word, page, or document; change dictionaries; look up words phonetically; look up words that match a pattern; perform word count.

Shift-F2   *Reverse Search Key:* Search backward for characters or function codes.

F3   *Help Key:* Display alphabetical list of features or information about any key combination; display keyboard template (when pressed twice).

Alt-F3   *Reveal Codes Key:* Display a screen with hidden function codes.

Ctrl-F3   *Screen Key:* (0) Rewrite screen, (1) split screen into windows, (2) line draw, (3) reassign Ctrl/Alt and A–Z keys, (4) change colors, (5) auto rewrite—reformat screen after down arrow is pressed.

Shift-F3   *Switch Key:* Switch to document 2; case conversion with Block on.

KEY SEQUENCE	COMMAND
F4	*Indent Key:* Set temporary left margin.
Alt-F4	*Block Key:* Define a block of text.
Ctrl-F4	*Move Key:* Cut, copy, or delete (1) sentence, (2) paragraph, or (3) page; retrieve (4) column, (5) text, or (6) rectangle. When pressed after Alt-F4 (Block on): (1) cut block, (2) copy block, (3) append block, (4) cut or copy a column, (5) cut or copy a rectangle.
Shift-F4	*Left/Right Indent Key:* Indent left and right margin one tab stop.
F5	*List Files Key:* (1) Retrieve file, (2) delete file, (3) rename file, (4) print file, (5) retrieve DOS text file, (6) look at file contents, (7) change directory, (8) copy file, (9) search all files for a word, (0) exit.
Alt-F5	*Mark Text Key:* (1) Toggle outline mode, (2) mark paragraph number, (3) mark text for redline, (4) enter short form for table of authorities, (5) mark word for index, (6) select other options (Other Options 1–5 are define formats for paragraph/outline numbering, lists, table of contents, table of authorities, and index; Other Options 6 is remove redline markings and strikeout text, Other option 7 is edit table of authorities full form, other option 8 is generate tables and index. When pressed after Alt- F4 (Block on), mark blocked text for (1) table of contents, (2) list, (3) redline, (4) strikeout, (5) index entries, (6) table of authorities.
Ctrl-F5	*Text In/Out Key:* (1) Save document as DOS text file, (2)–(3) retrieve DOS text file, (4) lock and save document, (5) retrieve locked document, (6) save in generic word processor format, (7) save in WordPerfect 4.1 format, (A) create or edit document summary, (B) create comment, (C) edit comment, (D) display summary and comments.
Shift-F5	*Date Key:* (1) Insert date, (2) change date format, (3) insert date as function.

F4

F5

KEY
SEQUENCE   **COMMAND**

F6   *Bold Key:* Toggle bold on/off.
Alt-F6   *Flush Right Key:* Align text at the right margin.
Ctrl-F6   *Tab Align Key:* Align text on tab setting.
Shift-F6   *Center Key:* Center a line of text between margins or on a tab setting; with Block on, center a block.

F7   *Exit Key:* Save and clear screen; save and exit; clear screen without saving; exit WordPerfect.
Alt-F7   *Math/Columns Key:* With Math on: (1) toggle Math on/off, (2) calculate, (3) toggle Column on/off, (4) define newspaper or parallel columns, (5) display columns side by side. With Math off, option 2 becomes define math columns.
Ctrl-F7   *Footnote Key:* (1) Create footnote, (2) edit footnote, (3) renumber footnotes, (4) options, (5) create endnote, (6) edit endnote.
Shift-F7   *Print Key:* (1) Print full text, (2) print page, (3) change print options temporarily, (4) printer control screen, (5) Type-thru (typewriter mode), (6) preview document.

F8   *Underline Key:* Toggle Underline on/off; with Block on, underline defined block.
Alt-F8   *Page Format Key:* (1) Page-number position, (2) new page number, (3) center page top to bottom, (4) page length, (5) top margin, (6) headers or footers, (7) page-number column position, (8) suppress for current page only, (9) conditional end of page, (A) widow/orphan protection. With Block on, prevent block from being split by a page break.
Ctrl-F8   *Print Format Key:* (1) Pitch, font, (2) lines per inch, (3) right justification off, (4) right justification on; (5–8) change underline style; (9) sheet feeder bin number; (A) insert printer command; (B) line numbering on/off.

KEY
SEQUENCE   **COMMAND**

Shift-F8   *Line Format Key:* (1), (2) Tabs, (3) margins, (4) line spacing, (5) hyphenation, (6) alignment character.

F9   *Merge Return Key:* Designate end of a field in a secondary merge file and end of text input for a field in a merge operation from the keyboard.

Alt-F9   *Merge Codes Key:* Display menu of 12 merge codes.

Ctrl-F9   *Merge/Sort Key:* (1) Merge, (2) sort and select, (3) sorting sequences.

Shift-F9   *Merge End Key:* Designate the end of a record in a secondary merge file.

F10   *Save Key:* Save document on screen to disk and continue working on it.

Shift-F10   *Retrieve Key:* Retrieve file from disk and copy it to the screen.

Ctrl-F10   *Macro Define Key:* Record all keystrokes in a macro file.

Alt-F10   *Invoke Macro Key:* Start a previously defined macro.

Cursor Movement

KEY SEQUENCE	COMMAND
↓	Move one line down.
↑	Move one line up.
←	Move one position left.
→	Move one position right.
Ctrl-←	Move one word left.
Ctrl-→	Move one word right.
PgDn	Move one page down (top of next page).
PgUp	Move one page up (top of previous page).
+ (numeric keypad)	Move one screen down.
− (numeric keypad)	Move one screen up.
Home-↓	Move one screen down.
Home-↑	Move one screen up.
Home Home ↑	Move to beginning of file.
Home Home ↓	Move to end of file.
Home Home Home ←	Move to left edge of screen before codes.
Home Home Home →	Move to right edge of screen before codes.
Home-←	Move to left edge of screen.
Home-→	Move to right edge of screen.

Go To Key: Ctrl-Home

Ctrl-Home ↑	Move to top of current page.
Ctrl-Home ↓	Move to bottom of current page.
Ctrl-Home *n*	Go to page *n*.
Ctrl-Home <*character*>	Go to next occurrence of *character*.

Esc key:

Esc <*n*> ↑ (or ↓)	Move up or down *n* lines.
Esc <*n*> → (or ←)	Move right or left *n* spaces.
Esc *n* <*command*>	Repeat *command n* number of times.

Codes

CODE	MEANING
_ (blinking)	Cursor Position
[ ]	Hard Space
[-]	Hyphen
-	Soft Hyphen
/	Cancel Hyphenation
[A][a]	Tab Align or Flush Right (begin and end)
[Adv▲]	Advance Up ½ Line
[Adv▼]	Advance Down ½ Line
[AdvLn:n]	Advance to Specified Line Number (n = line number)
[Align Char:]	Alignment Character
[B][b]	Bold (begin and end)
[Bin#:n]	Sheet Feeder Bin Number (n = bin number)
[Block]	Beginning of Block
[BlockPro:Off]	Block Protection off
[BlockPro:On]	Block Protection on
[C][c]	Centering (begin and end)
[Center Pg]	Center Current Page Top to Bottom
[Cmnd:]	Embedded Printer Command
[CndlEOP:n]	Conditional End of Page (n = number of lines)
[Col Def:]	Column Definition
[Col Off]	End of Text Columns
[Col On]	Beginning of Text Columns
[Date:n]	Date/Time Function (n = format)
[DefMark:Index, n]	Index Definition (n = format)
[DefMark:List, n]	List Definition (n = list number)
[DefMark:ToA, n]	Table of Authorities (n = section number)
[DefMark:ToC, n]	Table of Contents Definition n = ToC level)

CODE	MEANING
[EInd]	End of → Indent or → Indent ←
[EndDef]	End of Index, List, or Table of Contents
[EndMark:List, n]	End Marked Text (n = list number)
[EndMark:ToC, n]	End Marked Text (n = ToC level)
[Font Change:n, n]	Specify New Font or Print Wheel n = pitch, font)
[FtnOpt]	Footnote/Endnote Options
[Hdr/Ftr:n, n;text]	Header or Footer Definition (n = type, occurrence)
[HPg]	Hard Page Break
[HRt]	Hard Return
[Hyph on]	Hyphenation On
[Hyph off]	Hyphenation Off
[HZone Set:n, n]	Reset Size of Hyphenation Zone (n = left, right)
[→ Indent]	Beginning of Indent
[→ Indent ←]	Beginning of Left/Right Indent
[Index:heading; subheading]	Index Mark
[LnNum:On]	Line Numbering On
[LnNum:Off]	Line Numbering Off
[LPI:n]	Lines per Inch (n = number of lines)
[← Mar Rel:n]	Left Margin Release (n = positions moved)
[Margin Set:n, n]	Left and Right Margin Reset (n = left, right margin setting)
[Mark:List, n]	Begin Marked Text for List (n = list number)
[Mark:ToC, n]	Begin Marked Text for ToC (n = ToC level)
[Math Def]	Definition of Math Columns
[Math Off]	End of Math
[Math On]	Beginning of Math
!	Formula Calculation
t	Subtotal Entry

CODE	MEANING
+	Calculate Subtotal
T	Total Entry
=	Calculate Total
*	Calculate Grand Total
[Note:End, *n*; [*note#*]*text*]	Endnote (*n* = endnote number)
[Note:Foot, *n*; [*note#*]*text*]	Footnote (*n* = footnote number)
[Ovrstk]	Overstrike preceding Character
[Par#:Auto]	Automatic Paragraph/Outline Number
[Par#:*n*]	Permanent Paragraph Number (*n* = level number)
[Par#Def]	Paragraph Numbering Definition
[Pg#:*n*]	New Page Number (*n* = page number)
[Pg# Col:*n*, *n*, *n*]	Column Position for Page Numbers (*n* = left, center, right)
[Pg Lnth:*n*, *n*]	Set Page Length (*n* = form lines, text lines)
[Pos Pg#:*n*]	Set Position for Page Numbers
[RedLn][r]	Redline (begin and end)
[Rt Just Off]	Right Justification Off
[Rt Just On]	Right Justification On
[Set Ftn#:*n*]	New Footnote Number (*n* = note number)
[Spacing Set:*n*]	Spacing Set (*n* = spacing increment)
[SPg]	Soft Page Break
[SRt]	Soft Return
[StrkOut][s]	Strikeout (begin and end)
[SubScrpt]	Subscript
[Sumry/Cmnt:*text*]	Document Summary or Comment
[SuprScrpt]	Superscript
[Suppress:*n*]	Suppress Page Format Options (*n* = format(s))
[TAB]	Move to Next Tab Stop
[Tab Set:]	Tab Reset

CODE	MEANING
[ToA:*n*; [*short form*];]	Short Form for Table of Authorities (*n* = section number)
[ToA:*n*;*short form*;<*Full Form*>]	Full Form for Table of Authorities (*n* = section number)
[Top Mar:*n*]	Set Top Margin in Half Lines (*n* = margin setting)
[U][u]	Underlining (begin and end)
[Undrl Style:*n*]	Underlining Style (*n* = underlining style option number)
[W/O Off]	Widow/Orphan Protection Off
[W/O On]	Widow/Orphan Protection On

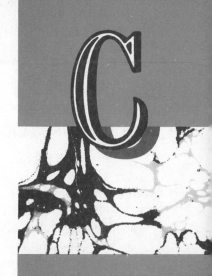

WORDPERFECT CORPORATION'S OTHER PRODUCTS

WORDPERFECT CORPORATION PRODUCES several other programs that are compatible with WordPerfect, including WordPerfect Library, DataPerfect, and PlanPerfect. Word-Perfect is available in several foreign-language versions, including French, German, Spanish, Finnish, Swedish, Norwegian, Dutch, and Danish. In addition, a network version is available that is compatible with Novell NetWare, AST-PCnet, 3Com Etherseries, and the IBM PC Network.

WordPerfect Library

WordPerfect Library, released in 1986, is a collection of programs that were designed to supplement and integrate the company's other software, and it includes a shell, a calculator, an appointment calendar/alarm clock, a notebook, a file manager, a program editor/macro editor, and a game called Beast. The shell can be used to create a customized menu of up to 20 applications programs, DOS commands, and batch files, as well as any number of subordinate menus. Some or all of them can be loaded into memory simultaneously, depending on the capacity of your system. (The program supports up to 8 megabytes using expanded memory boards.) Switching back and forth between the programs requires a single key-stroke, and data can be transferred between applications using the Clipboard feature.

When you use WordPerfect with the shell, the menu that appears when you press the Shell Key (Ctrl-F1) provides different choices. Instead of *Go to DOS,* you can select between *Go to Shell* and *Retrieve Clipboard.* From the shell menu you can then exit temporarily to DOS, just as you do when using the WordPerfect Shell Key without the WordPerfect Library, or you can run one of the other programs on the menu. You can also switch programs from within WordPerfect (or whichever program you're running) by pressing Alt-Shift and typing the character corresponding to the program. The Retrieve Clipboard option allows you to retrieve data from another program that has been defined as a block and saved to the Clipboard. The contents of the clipboard can be viewed from the shell menu.

The desktop utilities include a calculator/alarm clock, notebook, and appointment calendar. The calculator has scientific, financial, programming, and statistical functions, and its display modes include decimal (fixed or floating decimal point), octal, hexadecimal, exponential notation, and Radian/Degree conversions. It displays a "tape" on screen that can be saved, printed, or sent to another program through the Clipboard. The appointment calendar can keep appointments, memos, and to-do lists, and an alarm can be set to remind you about appointments. The to-do lists can be sorted according to priority, and if items are not marked as completed they are carried forward to the next day's agenda. Lists or appointments can be printed or sent to other programs through the clipboard. A Date Search feature lets you move quickly to a specific date, and a Word Search feature lets you find appointments, lists, or memos containing a certain word or words.

The Notebook is a list manager that stores records in rows and columns and saves them in a WordPerfect merge file. It can be used to create Forms Fill-In screens, and records can be sorted and/or selected with WordPerfect's Sort and Select features. If you have a modem, the Notebook can be set up to automatically dial phone numbers for you.

The File Manager is an expanded version of the menu (and screen) that appears when you press the WordPerfect List Files Key (F5). It includes all of the List Files utilities and more. With it you can sort files by either file name, extension, or date and time; select only files that were modified before, on, or after a certain date; lock files with a password; find the directory in which a file is located; and print the list of files.

The program editor is designed to create and edit ASCII files, batch files, object files, binary encoded files, and program files. It has many of the same features found in WordPerfect, including undelete for the last three deletions, search and replace in a forward or reverse direction with optional wildcards, block cut, copy, and move, split-screen windows, and on-screen help. The macro editor is an extension of the program editor, and you can use it to edit and create macros that will run under any of the programs you have installed through your shell menu.

PlanPerfect

PlanPerfect is WordPerfect Corporation's spreadsheet package, and it also includes graphics and data management. The program has over 60 functions, including arithmetic, financial, date, logical, text, and special functions. Other features include WordPerfect-type macros as well as cell macros, on-screen help, password protection, windows, sort, search, select, and locate capabilities, a transpose function to switch rows with columns, and linking and overlaying of worksheets. Graphics can be produced on a monochrome screen, and they can be saved as text files to be used with WordPerfect. PlanPerfect features a virtual memory design so that when the computer's memory is full, worksheet data (empty cells) are temporarily moved to the disk, freeing up RAM for cells that contain data. Files can be imported and exported in several formats, including ASCII DIF files, and Lotus 1-2-3 version 1A. PlanPerfect is completely compatible with WordPerfect, and many of the commands and keys are the same for both programs.

DataPerfect

DataPerfect is a relational database-management program that will be released in August of 1987.

Repeat Performance

Repeat Performance is a keyboard enhancer that features several utilities that can be used with WordPerfect, the Library, PlanPerfect, and many other programs (except a few of the memory-resident utilities available from other companies). One of the program's most important functions is to change the speed at which the cursor moves on the screen; you can vary it between 11 and 1000 characters per second to match your typing skills. You can also use the "panic button" to temporarily increase the speed to a preselected level. Fast typists can set the keyboard buffer to "remember" up to 10,000 keystrokes typed in advance. This is useful when you load WordPerfect from the DOS prompt, and are anxious to start typing before the edit screen appears. Another feature clears the keyboard buffer so that the auto repeat feature is disabled as soon as you take your finger off a key. If you type with "heavy fingers" you can adjust the repeat delay so that as you press and hold a key, it doesn't repeat as frequently. Finally, you can use Repeat Performance to disable the reverse Caps Lock so that if Caps Lock is turned on and you press the Shift key and type a letter, it will still be entered in uppercase, not lowercase.

For more information about these WordPerfect Corporation products, you can write the company at this address:

> 288 West Center Street
> Orem, Utah 84057

Their telephone number is (801) 225-5000.

The WordPerfect Support Group

The WordPerfect Support Group publishes a newsletter called *The WordPerfectionist*, which is full of useful advice and information for users of WordPerfect and other products by WordPerfect Corporation. The group also runs a bulletin board where members can exchange ideas and assist each other with questions. Back issues of the newsletter are available, as well as disks containing monthly messages from the electronic mail system and software utilities from the online library. You can also purchase a disk with conversion utilities to translate dBASE III PLUS files into WordPerfect merge format and to translate WordPerfect files to and from other word processors not included in the WordPerfect Convert utility. Annual membership in the support group is $36.00. You can join the group by writing to them at this address:

> The WordPerfect Support Group
> P.O. Box 1577, Dept. 205
> Baltimore, MD 21203

The WordPerfect Support Group is independent of WordPerfect Corporation.

INDEX

A

Advance Line, 146–147, 156
Advance Up/Down, 144–146, 156
Alt key, 6–7, 23
Alt macros, 351–353
AND, 271, 335
Append marked block, 66, 271, 286
Arrow keys, 15–16, 24. *See also* Cursor movement
ASCII characters, line drawing, 369, 371
ASCII file
conversion/importation, 266–267, 272–273, 286
Asterisk, 156, 270, 310, 326, 335, 401
AST-PCnet, 423
Automatic backup, 284, 395–396
Automatic rewrite, xxiv
Auto-repeat feature, 15
Averaging, 324–325. *See also* Math

B

Backslash (\\), 263, 270
Backspace key, 11–12, 24, 68
Backup disks, 393–395
Backup options, 284, 395–396
Backward search, 112
Beep options, 112, 399
Binding width, 172, 184
Block Key (Alt-F4), 63–76
Blocks
activating/deactivating, 64
appending to disk file, 66, 271, 286
centering, 88
of columns, 65, 239, 321–324, 326
cursor movement in, 64
deleting, 65–68
printing, 70, 164
protecting, 100–102, 106, 275
of rectangles, 65, 370
retrieving, 66–67, 71–72, 75
saving, 71–72, 271, 286
sorting, 343–344
of text, 65–68, 74
underlining/boldfacing, 63, 74
see also Mark Text Key
Bold Key (F6), 45–46, 60, 74–75
Booting WordPerfect, 2–3, 23, 395–398
Boxes/rectangles, 367, 370. *See also* Line drawing
Buffers, 396

C

Calculations. *See* Math
Canceling
another Key's operation, 14
Block Key, 64
with Exit Key, 35
hyphenation, 55, 125, 139
line drawing, 367
merge, 297–298
printing, 167–168
spell checking, 376
Tab menu, 47
Thesaurus, 388
Undelete operation, 13–14
Cancel Key (F1), 13–14, 24
Capitalization. *See* Caps Lock; Case conversion
Caps Lock
indicator, 11, 23, 46
key, 10, 23, 45–46

Caret (^), 293
Carriage return. *See* Return key
Case conversion, 72–73, 75, 354, 359–360
Center Key (Shift-F6), 45, 59
Clearing
screen, 23, 35, 37
tabs, 46–47
Codes
deleting, 12, 17–18
finding/replacing/deleting, 118–120, 194–195
hidden, 17
list of, 418–421
Reveal Codes Key, 56–60
Columns
activating/deactivating text, 236–238, 241
blocking, 65, 239, 321–324, 326
cutting/copying/moving, 65, 321–324
math, 314–326
newspaper, xxiv, 229–241, 244
parallel, xxiv, 229, 241–245
sorting by, 330–334, 343–344
see also Alignment character
Concordances, 201, 204–207, 226
Conditional end of page, 100, 106
Copy/Cut
block, 65–66
columns, 65, 321–324
files, 270, 393–394
line drawings, 65, 370
sentence/page/paragraph, 68–70
see also Blocks; File management; Move operations

COPY (DOS command), 393–394
Ctrl key, 6–7, 23
Cursor movement
  backspacing, 11, 24
  to beginning/end of line, 16, 24
  in Block mode, 64
  by character, 14–15, 24
  in columns, 238
  with Esc key, 417
  over hidden codes, 17, 44, 136
  keys described, 4, 417
  by line, 15, 24
  in line drawings, 369
  in List Files screen, 263
  by page, 16–17, 24
  in Reveal Codes screen, 58, 136
  in Search mode, 112
  in Type-thru mode, 165–166
  by word, 16, 24
Cursor position indicator, 5, 23
Cut. See Copy/cut; Deleting

D

Dash (double hyphen), 127, 154
DataPerfect, 426
Date
  entering with Date Key (Shift-F5), 28, 37, 139–142, 155
  entering in merge operations, 292–293
Decimal point, 311
Decimal tabs, 129–130, 154
Default drive, 3, 163, 262
Default settings
  changing permanently, 398–399
  for justifying margins, 179
  for line spacing, 53, 60
  for lines per inch, 179

for margins, 5, 43, 59, 91–92
for page length, 85, 90
for page numbering, 84–88
for pitch and font, 176–177
for repetition of commands, 368
for tabs, 46–47, 60
Defining a Printer Driver, 183
Deleting
  with Backspace key, 11, 24, 68
  blocks, 65–68
  characters, 11, 32
  codes, 12, 17–18, 118–120
  directories, 267–270
  to end of line, 21, 24
  to end of page, 21, 24
  files, 266
  page breaks, 18
  sentences, 32
  and undeleting, 13–14, 24
  words, 21, 24, 32
  see also Copy/cut
Del key, 11, 24, 32
Dictionaries, 376, 383–384
DIR (DOS directory command), 10, 162, 392
Directories, 3, 262, 267–270, 394, 396, 398. See also List Files Key
Disks
  backup, 393–395
  checking space on, 262
Document indicator, 4–5
Documents, switching, 5
Document Summary/Comments, 275–280, 287
DOS (Disk Operating System)
  COPY command, 393–394
  DIR (directory) command, 10, 162, 392
  files, converting to/from, 266–267, 272–273
  FORMAT command, 392–393

MD/CD (directory) commands, 394–395
  temporary exit to, 280–281
  Tree command, 394–395
Double hyphen (dash), 127, 154
Double spacing, 53, 352–353
Double word occurrence, 382
Drawing. See Line Drawing
Drive, default, 3, 163, 262

E

Edit screen, 4–5, 95–97
Embedded codes. See under Codes
End key, 16
Endnotes. See Footnotes/Endnotes
Enter key. See Return key
Envelopes/labels, 302–307
Equal sign, 310, 326
Erase. See Deleting
Error messages
  Bad command or file name, 4
  Directory not empty, 269
  Disk Full, 160
  Invalid directory, 4
  Printer is not accepting characters, 167
  Text columns can't overlap, 234
Esc key, 134–135, 355, 367
Exclamation point, 318
Exiting
  to DOS temporarily, 280–281, 287
  from Help menu, 18, 20
  from List Files operations, 163
  from overflow files, 22
  from Reveal Codes screen, 58
  and saving file, 34–35, 37
  from Tab menu, 130

from WordPerfect, 21–22, 25, 33–35, 280
without saving file, 22, 34
Exit Key (F7), 20–22, 37, 280

F

Fields, 293–294, 330. *See also* Merging; Sorting
Files
backup for, 284
managing, 22–23, 272–273
naming, 33, 266
overflow, 22, 396
primary/secondary files for merging, 292–297, 306–307
see also List Files Key
Fixed paragraph numbers, 217
Floppy disk systems
installation of WordPerfect on, 2, 23, 392–393
saving files on, 33–34
saving macros on, 350–351
using Speller on, 49, 376
using Thesaurus on, 386
Flush Right Key (Alt-F6), 44, 59, 93
Fonts, 169–170, 176–179
FONT.TST file, 177–178
Footers, 90, 93–98, 105
Footnotes/Endnotes, 247–256
Foreign characters, 147, 156
Foreign language versions of WordPerfect, 423
FORMAT (DOS command), 392–393
Formatting codes, 17–18, 56. *See also* Page formatting
Form letters, 292–297, 306
Forms, 92, 165. *See also* Page formatting
Formulas. *See* Math
Forward Search Key (F2), 110, 121. *See also* Searching
Forward Search macro, 358
Full form, 209–214, 227
Function keys, 7, 23

G

Get files/documents. *See* Retrieving
Go to DOS, 280
Go To Key, 112

H

Hanging paragraphs, 142–143, 155
Hard disk systems
installation of WordPerfect on, 393–394
saving files on, 33–34
saving macros on, 351
Speller on, 49
starting WordPerfect on, 3–4, 23
Tree command on, 394–395
viewing directories on, 261, 263
Hard page breaks, 18, 242
Hard returns, 57, 121. *See also* Word wrap
Hard spaces, 137–139, 155
Headers/footers, 90, 93–98, 105, 377
Headword, 387. *See also* Thesaurus Key
Help Key (F3), 18–20, 24
Hidden codes, 17
Home key, 16, 90
Hyperion computer, 397
Hyphenation
activating, 54, 60
canceling, 55, 125, 139
with double hyphen (dash), 127, 154
in equations (minus signs), 127, 154
and hard spaces, 138–139
with soft hyphens, 54, 126–127, 154
zone, 55, 124, 127–128, 154
H-zone. *See* Hyphenation

I

Indent Key (F4), 48, 60, 218
Indexes, 201–208, 226
Insert Printer command, 166, 176–181
Ins key, 12, 24
Installing
printers, 400–402
WordPerfect, 391–395
Invoke Macro Key (Alt-F10), 349, 363

J

Justification, 179, 365. *See also* Margins

K

Keyboard
described, 1, 6–14, 413–416
merges, 299–301, 306–307
template for, 8
toggle key, 46
Keys, Sort/Select, 329, 344–345

L

Labels/envelopes, 302–307
Leading characters (leaders), 131–132, 154, 191
Letterhead, 92, 181
Line Advance, 144–147, 156
Line Drawing
ASCII characters, 369, 371
boxes/rectangles, 367, 370
canceling, 367
characters, 369
copying/cutting/moving, 65, 370
erasing, 370
moving cursor in, 369
options for, 366–367
printing, 371–372
speeding up, 367–368

Line Format Key (Shift-F8)
  and alignment character,
    132–137, 155, 311
  for hyphenation, 54–55, 60,
    154
  for line spacing, 53, 60
  for margins, 43, 52, 59
  for tabs, 46–49, 60, 130
  see also Page formatting
Line indicator, 5
Line numbering, 150–154, 156
Line spacing, 53, 60
Lines per inch, 89, 179
Lines per page, 85, 90–93, 97,
  100–102. See also Margins
List Files Key (F5)
  for copying files, 270
  for deleting files, 263, 266
  for directory handling,
    267–270
  for importing ASCII files,
    266–267
  for name search, 263–264
  for printing files, 159, 162,
    183–184, 266, 275
  for renaming files, 266
  for retrieving files, 265–266
  for viewing file/directory
    contents, 267
  for word search, 270–271
  see also Printing
Lists, 189–196, 225
Locking documents, 273–275
Logged disk drive. See Default
  drive
Logical operators, 271, 335
Lowercase conversion, 72–73,
  75

M

MAC file extension, 350, 363
Macro Definition Key
  (Ctrl-F10), 349, 362–363
Macros
  for case conversion, 354,
    359–360
  chaining, 359–360, 363

creating, 349–351
described, 349
for double spacing, 352–353
editing, 351, 363
for forward/reverse search,
  358–359
and Invoke Macro Key
  (Alt-F10), 349, 363
invoking, 349–350, 352, 396
with merges, 360–363
pausing for user input,
  355–356
for place marking, 357–359
to prompt for
  primary/secondary file
  names, 361
repeating, 355, 363
with search and replace,
  357–359
starting with, 396
stopping, 363
storing, 350–351
for underlining, 354
viewing in directory, 350,
  363
visible (slowed), 356–357
Mailing labels/envelopes,
  302–306
Margin Release Key (Shift-Tab),
  44
Margins
  bottom, 90–92, 105
  for footnotes/endnotes, 255
  for headers/footers, 97
  with pitch/font changes, 178
  releasing, 44
  right justifying, 54, 179
  ruler line for, 56, 129
  setting, 43, 52, 59
  top, 88, 90–93, 105
Mark Text Key (Alt-F5)
  for concordances, 201,
    204–207, 226
  for indexes, 201–208, 226
  for lists, 189–196, 225
  for outlines/paragraph
    numbering, 216–226

for redlining, 148–150
for tables of authorities,
  208–216, 227
for tables of contents,
  196–201, 226
see also Blocks
Math
  averaging, 324–325
  column activation, 314–315,
    317–319, 326
  column copy/delete/move
    operations, 321–324, 326
  column definition, 315–327,
    319, 326
  columns for totals, 320–321,
    326
  formulas, 310, 314
  with negative numbers, 313
  totalling, 310–313
Math/Columns Key (Alt-F7),
  310–321
MD/CD (DOS directory
  commands), 394–395
Memory. See RAM
Menus
  Not Found!, 377–378
  Page Format, 82
  Printer Control, 37
  Set-up, 285
  Speller Utility, 384
  Tab, 47, 130–131
Merge Codes Key (Alt-F9),
  292, 298
Merge End of Record Key
  (Shift-F9), 296
Merge Return Key (F9), 296
Merge/Sort Key (Ctrl-F9), 297,
  331. See also Merging;
  Sorting
Merging
  data entered from keyboard,
    299–301, 306–307, 360
  entering date for, 292–293
  envelopes/labels, 302–307
  form letters, 292–297, 306
  primary/secondary files for,
    292–297, 306–307

to printer, 298–299
with reminder messages on
  screen, 301–302, 306–307
with screen updating, 298
stopping, 297–298, 307
see also Sorting
Microsoft Windows, 397
Minus signs, 127, 313, 315
Move Key (Ctrl-F4)
  for relocating sentences, 70
  for retrieving columns,
    66–67, 239
  for retrieving line drawings,
    67, 370
  for retrieving previous line,
    166
  for retrieving text, 66–69, 75
  see also Copy/Cut; Blocks

N

Negative numbers, 313. *See
  also* Math
Network (IBM PC), 423
Networks, 423
Newspaper columns. *See
  under* Columns
Non-flash option, 397
Non-synch option, 397
Novell NetWare, 423
Numeric columns. *See*
  Columns
Numeric keypad, 10–11. *See
  also* Keyboard
Num Lock
  indicator, 11
  key, 10, 23, 99

O

Open files. *See* Retrieving
Operators, logical, 271, 335
OR, 335
Orphan/Widow protection,
  102–104, 106, 237
Outlines, 216–226

Overflow files, 22, 396
Overstrike, 147–148, 156

P

Page Down/Up Key, 16, 24
Page Format Key (Alt-F8), 82,
  104
Page formatting
  with automatic rewrite, xxvi
  block protection, 100–102,
    106, 237
  centering, 88–90, 105
  conditional end of page,
    100, 106
  headers/footers, 90, 93–98,
    105
  lines per inch, 89, 179
  lines per page, 85, 90–93,
    97, 100–102
  menu for, 82
  page breaks, 18, 98–104
  page length, 90–93, 105
  previewing before printing,
    181–182
  reformatting, 31, 48
  soft page, 99–100
  widow/orphan protection,
    102–104, 106, 237
  see also Line Format Key;
    Margins; Page numbers
Page indicator, 5
Page numbers
  column position of, 85–87,
    104
  in headers/footers, 97–99
  new, 86–87, 105
  position of, 82–85, 104
  style of, 87–88
  suppressing, 84, 98, 105
Page Up/Down Key, 16, 24
Paper
  and binding width, 172, 184
  continuous feed, 173, 401
  hand-feed option, 36, 173,
    401
  letterhead, 92, 181

numbering wide sizes of, 85
sheet-feeder, 36, 180–181,
  401
varying size of, 90, 181
Paragraphs
  hanging, 142–143, 155
  numbering, 216–226, 216,
    217, 220, 224–226
Parallel columns, xxiv, 229,
  241–245
Parallel printers, 401
Parentheses, 309, 315
Password protection, 273–275
Pitch, 84, 176–179
Place-marker macro, 357–359
PlanPerfect, 425–426
Plus sign, 310, 326, 335
Ports, 401
Position indicator, 5, 23
Primary merge files, 291–295,
  306–307
PRINTER2.TST file, 177–178
Printer
  control menu, 37
  definition, 402
  display fonts, 169–170
  font/pitch on, 177–178
  inserting commands for, 166,
    176–181
  installation of, 169, 400–402
  number, 171–172, 184, 402
  paper continuous feed, 173,
    401
  paper hand-feed option, 36,
    173, 401
  paper sheet-feeder, 36,
    180–181, 401
  parallel, 401
  serial, 401
  status and control, 36,
    168–176
  test files for, 178
  troubleshooting, 36
PRINTER.TST file, 177–178
Print Format Key (Ctrl-F8),
  176–181, 183–184
Printing

adjusting for binding width, 172, 184
blocks, 70, 75, 164, 184
canceling/pausing, 174, 184
characters/lines, 164–167, 184
displaying all jobs awaiting, 175–176
envelopes/labels, 302–307
from disk, 161–163, 183–184
job list for, 162, 175–176, 184
line drawings, 371–372
multiple copies, 172, 184
multiple documents, 162–163, 172–174
queue for, 159, 172–174
rush jobs, 174–175, 184
saving prior to, 160–161
screen/page/document, 35–36, 38, 70, 160–162, 164
select print options for, 169–172
in Type-thru (typewriter) mode, 164–167, 184
viewing before, 181–182, 185
see also List Files Key
Print Key (Shift-F7), 38, 70, 159–165, 168–176, 182–185
Print screen key, 157–160
Prompt line, 7
Proportional spacing, 177–178, 180
PS.TST file, 177–178

Q

Question mark, 378
Queue, 159, 172–174
Quit. See Exiting

R

RAM, 22, 160, 201, 362–363
Records, 294, 330

Rectangles, 367, 370
Redlining, 148–150, 156
Reformatting text, 31, 48
Repeating commands, 134–135
Repeat Performance, 426
Replace Key (Alt-F2), 115–119, 121. See also Searching
Required page break, 18, 242
Required space, 137–139, 155
Retrieving
  blocks, 66–67, 71–72, 75
  columns, 67, 239
  files, 60, 71, 265–266, 283
  rectangles, 370
Retrieving Text Key (Shift-F10), 53, 60, 71
Return key
  in block mode, 64, 101
  to end paragraphs, 9, 23, 30
  as Enter key, 10
  and [HRt] code, 111
  in outline mode, 216–217
Reveal Codes Key (Alt-F3)
  in column mode, 237–238
  described, 56–60
  in line draw mode, 367
  screen, 56–60, 135–137
  see also Codes
Reveal codes. See Codes
Reverse Search Key (Shift-F2), 112, 121. See also Searching
Reverse search macro, 358–359. See also Searching
Right justification, 54, 179
Roman numeral page numbering, 87–88
Ruler, tab, 56, 129, 283, 287

S

Save Key (F10), 33–34, 37
Saving
  blocks, 71–72, 271, 286

files/documents, 22–23, 32–35
password-protected documents, 274
prior to printing, 160–161
Screen, clearing, 23, 35, 37
Screen Down/Up, 16–17, 24
Screen Key (Ctrl-F3), for line drawing, 366–372
Screen Key (Ctrl-F3) for split screen, 281–283, 287
Screen messages
  Align Char=, 132–134
  Block on, 64
  Cancel all print jobs?, 174
  Cmnd:, 166, 181
  Confirm?, 115
  Define Macro:, 350
  Delete Block?, 68
  Delete (filename)?, 266
  Delete Marked Files, 263
  Delete Redline Markings and Strikeout Text?, 150
  Delete Remainder of page?, 21
  Delete [Undrline]?, 12, 18
  Dictionary Full, 383
  Document to be Retrieved:, 53
  Document to be Saved, 14, 33–34
  Existing tables, lists, and indexes will be replaced. Continue? 193
  201, 208, 216
  Exit WP?, 23, 35
  Fix Printer – Reset top of form, 174
  NOTE: This text is not displayed in WordPerfect format., 267
  Not Found, 111, 377–378
  Old backup file exists., 284
  Position hyphen, 124
  Press EXIT when done, 130
  Print Block?, 71
  Replace (filename)?, 34

Replace with:, 115
Save Document?, 22–23, 34, 36
Saving (filename), 34
Typeover, 12
Waiting for a "Go", 36
WPHELP.FIL not found, 20
see also Error messages
Screens
    Change Print Options Temporarily, 171
    Character Type-thru, 167–168
    Date Format, 139–140
    Document Conversion, Summary, and Comments, 274, 278–279
    Editing, 4–5, 4, 95–97
    Footnote, 248
    Footnote Options, 250
    Header-Footer Specification, 93–94
    Help, 19–20
    Line Numbering, 151
    Line Type-thru, 165–166
    List Definition, 191
    List Files, 163, 262
    Math Definition, 315
    Other Mark Text Options, 190
    Page length, 91
    Page Number Column Position, 86
    Paragraph Numbering Definition, 223
    Printer Control, 161–162, 173, 184
    reminder messages on during merges, 301–302, 306–307
    Reveal Codes, 56–60, 238
    selecting, 7
    Select Print Options, 169–172
    Sort by Line, 332
    Sort by Paragraph, 339

Suppress Page Format, 98–99
Screen size, 399
Scrolling. See Cursor movement
Searching
    for Cancel Hyphenation codes, 125
    and case considerations, 116
    cautions on, 116–117, 120
    extended, 120
    for hidden codes, 118–120, 194
    macros for, 358–359
    repeating, 111–112
    and replacing, 115–121
    in reverse, 112
    strings for, 111–115, 121, 358
    for whole words, 113, 121
    with wildcard characters, 113, 121, 300
Secondary merge files, 291, 295–297, 306–307
Select, 329–330, 334–337
Serial printers, 401
Set-up Menu, 397–399
Sheet-feeder, 36, 180–181, 401
Shell Key (Ctrl-F1), 280, 287, 424
Shift key, 6
Short form, 209–214, 227
Single spacing, 53, 60
Slash (/), 125
Soft hyphens, 54, 126
Soft page breaks, 18, 99, 106
Sorting
    by block, 343–344
    columns, 330–334, 343–344
    by line, 329–334, 344–345
    by paragraph, 329, 337–340, 345
    keys, 329, 344–345
    with merge, 329, 340–343, 345
    with Select feature, 329–330, 334–337, 344–345

Spaces. See also Hard spaces
Spell checking
    adding words, 50, 60, 378, 389
    canceling, 376
    dictionaries for, 376, 383–384
    double words, 382
    editing while, 378
    headers/footers/endnotes, 377
    and looking up words, 378–381, 384–385
    phonetic, 373, 380–381
    and replacing words, 49, 377–378, 389
    and skipping words, 49–50, 378
    with Thesaurus, 376, 385–389
    with wildcard characters, 378
    word/block/page/document, 49–51, 60, 376–378, 388
    and word count, 51, 60, 381, 389
    words with numbers, 50–51, 382
Speller Key (Ctrl-F2), 49, 376–382, 388
Speller Utility, 383–385, 389
Starting
    macros (Invoke Macro), 349, 363
    WordPerfect, 2–3, 23, 395–398
Status line, 4–5, 23, 85, 237
Strikeout, 148–150, 156
Subdirectories. See Directories
Subtotal operator, 312. See also Math
Super/Subscript Key (Shift-F1), 143–144, 155. See also Advance Line; Overstrike
Switch Key (Shift-F3)
    and case conversion, 72–73, 75

to switch documents, xxiv, 5, 281–283, 287
Synonyms, 386, 388

T

Tab, ruler, 56, 129, 283, 287
Tab Align Key (Ctrl-F6), 130, 132–137, 155, 310
Tables of authorities, 208–216, 227
Tables of contents, 196–201, 226
Tab settings
  changing, 46–47, 59
  clearing, 46–47
  left/right/center/decimal, 129–131
  in math calculations, 310–311
  in outline mode, 218
  for sorts, 330–331
  in text columns, 230
  vs. indenting, 48–49
Template, 8
Text
  editing aligned, 135–137
  inserting, 30–31
  reformatting, 31, 48
  relocating, 65–70
  restoring deleted, 14, 66, 68, 75
  see also Columns; Marking Text; Move Key
Text In/Out Key (Ctrl-F5), 272–275, 286

Thesaurus Key (Alt-F1), 376, 385–389
3Com Etherseries, 423
Time, 140–141, 155
Toggle keys, 46
TopView, 397
Totals operator, 312. See also Math
Totals/subtotals, 310–313
Tree command, 394–395
Typeover, 13
Type-thru, 164–167, 184
Typewriter mode, 164–167, 184

U

Undelete, 13–14, 24. See also Canceling
Underline Key (F8), 12, 45–46, 56–58, 60, 74–75
Underline macro, 354
Underline style, 180
Uppercase
  conversion to, 72–74
  macro for conversion to, 354, 359–360

V

Viewing, See List Files Key; Screens

W

Widow/orphan protection, 102–104, 106, 237

Wildcard characters
  in filename search (List Files Key), 163, 263–265, 286
  in Speller, 378
  in word search, 270–271, 378
Windows, xxiv, 281–283, 287
Word count, 51, 60, 381, 389
Wordperfect, exiting from, 21–22, 25, 33–35, 280
WordPerfect, starting, 2–3, 23, 395–398
WordPerfect Corporation, xxiv, 423, 426
WordPerfectionist, 427
WordPerfect Library, 424–425
WordPerfect Support Group, 427
Word search, 270–271, 287–288
WP.EXE file, 394
WPHELP.FIL, 394
{WP}BACK.1 file, 284
{WP}BACK.2 file, 284
{WP}.BV1 file, 22
{WP}.BV2 file, 22
{WP}LEX.SUP file, 383
{WP}.TV1 file, 22
{WP}.TV2 file, 22
Wrapped format, 199–200

Z

Zip code sorts, 332, 343

Selections from The SYBEX Library

WORD PROCESSING

MASTERING PAGEMAKER ON THE IBM PC
by Antonia Stacy Jolles
300 pp., illustr., Ref. 393-7
A guide to every aspect of desktop publishing with PageMaker: the vocabulary and basics of Page design, layout, graphics and typography, plus instructions for creating finished typeset publications of all kinds.

INTRODUCTION TO WORDSTAR (3rd Edition)
by Arthur Naiman
208 pp., illustr., Ref. 134-9
A bestselling SYBEX classic. "WordStar is complicated enough to need a book to get you into it comfortably. Naiman's **Introduction to WordStar** is the best."
—*Whole Earth Software Catalog*

" . . . an indespensable fingertip guide, highly recommended for beginners and experienced users."
—*TypeWorld*

PRACTICAL WORDSTAR USES
by Julie Anne Arca
303 pp., illustr. Ref. 107-1
Pick your most time-consuming wordprocessing tasks and this book will show you how to streamline them with WordStar.

MASTERING WORDSTAR ON THE IBM PC
by Arthur Naiman
200 pp., illustr., Ref. 250-7
The classic Introduction to WordStar is now specially presented for the IBM PC, complete with margin-flagged keys and other valuable quick-reference tools.

WORDSTAR TIPS AND TRAPS
by Dick Andersen, Cynthia Cooper, and Janet McBeen
300 pp., illustr., Ref. 261-2
The handbook every WordStar user has been waiting for: a goldmine of expert techniques for speed, efficiency, and easy troubleshooting. Arranged by topic for fast reference.

THE COMPLETE GUIDE TO MULTIMATE
by Carol Holcomb Dreger
250 pp., illustr. Ref. 229-9
A concise introduction to the many applications of this powerful word processing program, arranged in tutorial form.

PRACTICAL MULTIMATE USES
by Chris Gilbert
275 pp., illustr., Ref. 276-0
Includes an overview followed by practical business techniques, this covers documentation, formatting, tables, and Key Procedures.

MASTERING DISPLAYWRITE 3
by Michael McCarthy
447 pp., illustr., Ref. 340-6
A complete introduction to full-featured word processing, from first start-up to advanced applications—designed with the corporate user in mind. Includes complete appendices for quick reference and troubleshooting.

WORDPERFECT TIPS AND TRICKS
by Alan R. Neibauer
350pp., illustr., Ref. 360-0
A practical companion for users of WordPerfect versions through 4.1—packed with clear explanations and "recipes" for creative uses, including outline processing, graphics, spreadsheet and data management.

MASTERING SAMNA
by Ann McFarland Draper
425 pp., illustr., Ref. 376-7
Learn the power of SAMNA Word and the SAMNA spreadsheet from an expert user and teacher. This comprehensive tutorial lets you build on the basics to get the most from the software's unique features.

MASTERING MS WORD
by Mathew Holtz
365 pp., illustr., Ref. 285-X
This clearly-written guide to MS WORD begins by teaching fundamentals quickly and then putting them to use right away. Covers material useful to new and experienced word processors.

PRACTICAL TECHNIQUES IN MS WORD
by Alan R. Neibauer
300 pp., illustr., Ref. 316-3
This book expands into the full power of MS WORD, stressing techniques and procedures to streamline document preparation, including specialized uses such as financial documents and even graphics.

INTRODUCTION TO WORDSTAR 2000
by David Kolodnay
and Thomas Blackadar
292 pp., illustr., Ref. 270-1
This book covers all the essential features of WordStar 2000 for both beginners and former WordStar users.

PRACTICAL TECHNIQUES IN WORDSTAR 2000
by John Donovan
250 pp., illustr., Ref. 272-8
Featuring WordStar 2000 Release 2, this book presents task-oriented tutorials that get to the heart of practical business solutions.

MASTERING THINKTANK ON THE 512K MACINTOSH
by Jonathan Kamin
264 pp., illustr., Ref. 305-8
Idea-processing at your fingertips: from basic to advanced applications, including answers to the technical question most frequently asked by users.

Software Specific

SPREADSHEETS

UNDERSTANDING JAVELIN
by John R. Levine, Margaret H. Young, and Jordan M. Young
350 pp., illustr., Ref. 358-9
A complete guide to Javelin, including an introduction to the theory of modeling. Business-minded examples show Javelin at work on budgets, graphs, forecasts, flow charts, and much more.

MASTERING SUPERCALC 3
by Greg Harvey
300 pp., illustr., Ref. 312-0
Featuring Version 2.1, this title offers full coverage of all the sophisticated features of this third generation spreadsheet, including spreadsheet, graphics, database and advanced techniques.

DOING BUSINESS WITH MULTIPLAN
by Richard Allen King
and Stanley R. Trost
250 pp., illustr., Ref. 148-9
This book will show you how using Multiplan can be nearly as easy as learning to use a pocket calculator. It presents a collection of templates for business applications.

MULTIPLAN ON THE COMMODORE 64
by Richard Allen King
250 pp., illustr. Ref. 231-0
This clear, straightforward guide will give you a firm grasp on Multiplan's function, as well as provide a collection of useful template programs.

DATABASE MANAGEMENT SYSTEMS

UNDERSTANDING dBASE III PLUS
by Alan Simpson
415 pp., illustr., Ref. 349-X
Emphasizing the new PLUS features, this

extensive volume gives the database terminology, program management, techniques, and applications. There are hints on file-handling, debugging, avoiding syntax errors.

ADVANCED TECHNIQUES IN dBASE III PLUS
by Alan Simpson
500 pp., illustr., Ref. 369-4

The latest version of what *Databased Advisor* called "the best choice for experienced dBASE III programmers." Stressing design and structured programming for quality custom systems, it includes practical examples and full details on PLUS features.

MASTERING dBASE III PLUS: A STRUCTURED APPROACH
by Carl Townsend
350 pp., illustr., Ref. 372-4

This new edition adds the power of PLUS to Townsend's highly successful structured approach to dBASE III programming. Useful examples from business illustrate system design techniques for superior custom applications.

ABC'S OF dBASE III PLUS
by Robert Cowart
225 pp., illustr., Ref. 379-1

Complete introduction to dBASE III PLUS for first-time users who want to get up and running with dBASE fast. With step-by-step exercises covering the essential functions as well as many useful tips and business applications.

UNDERSTANDING dBASE III
by Alan Simpson
250 pp., illustr., Ref. 267-1

The basics and more, for beginners and intermediate users of dBASEIII. This presents mailing label systems, bookkeeping and data management at your fingertips.

ADVANCED TECHNIQUES IN dBASE III
by Alan Simpson
505 pp., illustr., Ref. 282-5

Intermediate to experienced users are given the best database design techniques, the primary focus being the development of user-friendly, customized programs.

MASTERING dBASE III: A STRUCTURED APPROACH
by Carl Townsend
338 pp., illustr., Ref. 301-5

SIMPSON'S dBASE III LIBRARY
by Alan Simpson
362 pp., illustr., Ref. 300-7

Our bestselling dBASE author shares his personal library of custom dBASE III routines for finance, graphics, statistics, expanded databases, housekeeping, screen management and more.

UNDERSTANDING dBASE II
by Alan Simpson
260 pp., illustr., Ref. 147-0

Learn programming techniques for mailing label systems, bookkeeping, and data management, as well as ways to interface dBASE II with other software systems.

ADVANCED TECHNIQUES IN dBASE II
by Alan Simpson
395 pp., illustr. Ref., 228-0

Learn to use dBASE II for accounts receivable, recording business income and expenses, keeping personal records and mailing lists, and much more.

MASTERING Q&A
by Greg Harvey
350 pp., illustr., Ref. 356-2

An experienced consultant gives you straight answers on every aspect of Q&A, with easy-to-follow tutorials on the write, file, and report modules, using the Intelligent Assistant, and hundreds of expert tips.

MASTERING REFLEX
by Robert Ericson and Ann Moskol
336 pp., illustr., Ref. 348-1

The complete resource for users of Borland's Reflex: The Analyst, with extensive examples and templates for practical applications.

POWER USER'S GUIDE TO R:base 5000

by Alan Simpson

350 pp., illustr., Ref. 354-6

For R:base 5000 users who want to go beyond the basics, here is an in-depth look at design and structured programming techniques for R:base 5000—packed with expert tips and practical, usable examples.

UNDERSTANDING R:base 5000

by Alan Simpson

413 pp., illustr., Ref. 302-3

This comprehensive tutorial is for database novices and experienced R:base newcomers alike. Topics range from elementary concepts to managing multiple databases and creating custom applications.

Integrated Software

MASTERING 1-2-3

by Carolyn Jorgensen

466 pp., illustr., Ref. 337-6

Here is a thorough, lucid treatment of 1-2-3, including Release 2, with emphasis on intermediate to advanced uses—complex functions, graphics and database power, macro writing, and the latest add-on products.

SIMPSON'S 1-2-3 MACRO LIBRARY

by Alan Simpson

298 pp., illustr., Ref. 314-7

Share this goldmine of ready-made 1-2-3 macros for custom menus, complex plotting and graphics, consolidating worksheets, interfacing with mainframes and more. Plus explanations of Release 2 macro commands.

ADVANCED BUSINESS MODELS WITH 1-2-3

by Stanley R. Trost

250 pp., illustr., Ref. 159-4

If you are a business professional using the 1-2-3 software package, you will find the spreadsheet and graphics models provided in this book easy to use "as is" in everyday business situations.

THE ABC'S OF 1-2-3 (2nd Ed)

by Chris Gilbert and Laurie Williams

245 pp., illustr., Ref. 355-4

A complete introduction to 1-2-3, featuring Release 2—for first-time users who want to master the basics in a hurry. With comprehensive tutorials on spreadsheets, databases, and graphics.

" . . . an easy and comfortable way to get started on the program."

—*Online Today*

MASTERING SYMPHONY (2nd Edition)

by Douglas Cobb

817 pp., illustr., Ref. 341-4

"*Mastering Symphony* is beautifully organized and presented . . . I recommend it," says *Online Today. IPCO Info* calls it "the bible for every Symphony user . . . If you can buy only one book, this is definitely the one to buy." This new edition includes the latest on Version 1.1

ANDERSEN'S SYMPHONY TIPS AND TRICKS

by Dick Andersen

321 pp., illustr. Ref. 342-2

Hundreds of concise, self-contained entries cover everything from software pitfalls to time-saving macros—to make working with Symphony easy, efficient and productive. Includes version 1.1 and new Add-in programs.

FOCUS ON SYMPHONY DATABASES

by Alan Simpson

350 pp., illustr., Ref. 336-8

An expert guide to creating and managing databases in Symphony—including version 1.1—with complete sample systems for mailing lists, inventory and accounts receivable. A wealth of advanced tips and techniques.

FOCUS ON SYMPHONY MACROS

by Alan Simpson

350 pp., illustr., Ref. 351-1

Share Symphony expert Alan Simpson's approach to planning, creating, and using Symphony macros—including advanced techniques, a goldmine of ready-made macros, and complete menu-driven systems. For all versions through 1.1.

BETTER SYMPHONY SPREADSHEETS
by Carl Townsend
287 pp., illustr., Ref. 339-2
For Symphony users who want to gain real expertise in the use of the spreadsheet features, this has hundreds of tips and techniques. There are also instructions on how to implement some of the special features of Excel on Symphony.

MASTERING FRAMEWORK
by Doug Hergert
450 pp., illustr. Ref. 248-5
This tutorial guides the beginning user through all the functions and features of this integrated software package, geared to the business environment.

ADVANCED TECHNIQUES IN FRAMEWORK
by Alan Simpson
250 pp., illustr. Ref. 257-4
In order to begin customizing your own models with Framework, you'll need a thorough knowledge of Fred programming language, and this book provides this information in a complete, well-organized form.

MASTERING THE IBM ASSISTANT SERIES
by Jeff Lea and Ted Leonsis
249 pp., illustr., Ref. 284-1
Each section of this book takes the reader through the features, screens, and capabilities of each module of the series. Special emphasis is placed on how the programs work together.

DATA SHARING WITH 1-2-3 AND SYMPHONY: INCLUDING MAINFRAME LINKS
by Dick Andersen
262 pp., illustr., Ref. 283-3
This book focuses on an area of increasing importance to business users: exchanging data between Lotus software and other micro and mainframe software.

Special emphasis is given to dBASE II and III.

MASTERING PARADOX (2nd Edition)
by Alan Simpson
463 pp., illustr., Ref. 375-9
Total training in Paradox from out bestselling database author: everything from basic functions to custom programming in PAL, organized for easy reference and illustrated with useful business-oriented examples.

JAZZ ON THE MACINTOSH
by Joseph Caggiano and Michael McCarthy
431 pp., illustr., Ref. 265-5
Each chapter features as an example a business report which is built on throughout the book in the first section of each chapter. Chapters then go on to detail each application and special effects in depth.

MASTERING EXCEL
by Carl Townsend
454 pp., illustr., Ref. 306-6
This hands-on tutorial covers all basic operations of Excel plus in-depth coverage of special features, including extensive coverage of macros.

MASTERING APPLEWORKS
by Elna Tymes
201 pp., illustr., Ref. 240-X
This bestseller presents business solutions which are used to introduce AppleWorks and then develop mastery of the program. Includes examples of balance sheet, income statement, inventory control system, cash-flow projection, and accounts receivable summary.

PRACTICAL APPLEWORKS USES
by David K. Simerly
313 pp., illustr., Ref. 274-4
This book covers a breadth of home and business uses, including combined-function applications, complicated tasks, and even a large section on interfacing AppleWorks with external hardware and software.

APPLEWORKS: TIPS & TECHNIQUES
by Robert Ericson
373 pp., illustr., Ref. 303-1
Designed to improve AppleWorks skills, this is a great book that gives utility information illustrated with every-day management examples.

Computer Specific

AMIGA

AMIGA PROGRAMMER'S HANDBOOK Volume 1
by Eugene Mortimore
575 pp., illustr., Ref. 367-8
All the Amiga's power at your fingertips! Organized for working programmers, this is an A to Z compendium of Amiga system facilities, including ROM-BIOS exec calls, the Graphics Library, Animation Library, Layers Library, Intuition calls, and the Workbench.

APPLE II - MACINTOSH

THE PRO-DOS HANDBOOK
by Timothy Rice and Karen Rice
225 pp., illustr. Ref. 230-2
All Pro-DOS users, from beginning to advanced, will find this book packed with vital information. The book covers the basics, and then addresses itself to the Apple II user who needs to interface with Pro-DOS when programming in BASIC. Learn how Pro-DOS uses memory, and how it handles text files, binary files, graphics and sound. Includes a chapter on machine language programming.

PROGRAMMING THE MACINTOSH IN ASSEMBLY LANGUAGE
by Steve Williams
400 pp., illustr. Ref. 263-9
Information, examples, and guidelines for programming the 68000 microprocessor are given, including details of its entire instruction set.

USING THE MACINTOSH TOOLBOX WITH C
by Fred A. Huxham, David Burnard and Jim Takatsuka
559 pp., illustr., Ref. 249-3
In one place, all you need to get applications runnning on the Macintosh, given clearly, completely, and understandably. Featuring the C language.

MASTERING Pro-DOS
by Timothy Rice and Karen Rice
250 pp., illustr., Ref. 315-5
This companion volume to The ProDOS Handbook contains numerous examples of programming techniques and utilities that will be valuable to intermediate and advanced users.

THE EASY GUIDE TO YOUR MACINTOSH
By Joseph Caggiano
214 pp., illustr., Ref. 216-7
Simple and quick to use, this tells first time users how to set up their Macintosh computers and how to use the major features and software.

MACINTOSH FOR COLLEGE STUDENTS
by Bryan Pfaffenberger
250 pp., illustr., Ref. 227-2
Find out how to give yourself an edge in the race to get papers in on time and prepare for exams. This book covers everything you need to know about how to use the Macintosh for college study.

ATARI

UNDERSTANDING ATARI ST BASIC PROGRAMMING
by Tim Knight
300 pp., illustr., Ref. 344-9
Here is a comprehensive tutorial and reference guide for ATARI ST BASIC programming, including graphics, sound and GEM windows. With a complete ST BASIC command summary.

CP/M SYSTEMS

THE CP/M HANDBOOK
by Rodnay Zaks
320 pp., illustr., Ref 048-2
An indispensable reference and guide to
CP/M – complete in reference form.
"An excellent reference guide . . ."
Dr. Dobbs Journal

MASTERING CP/M
by Alan Miller
398 pp., illustr., Ref. 068-7
For advanced CP/M users or systems
programmers who want maximum use of
the CP/M operating system: this book
takes up where the CP/M Handbook
leaves off.

THE CP/M PLUS HANDBOOK
by Alan Miller
250 pp., illustr., Ref. 158-6
This guide is easy for beginners to understand, yet contains valuable information
for advanced users of CP/M Plus.

MASTERING DISK OPERATIONS ON THE COMMODORE 128
by Alan R. Miller
f238 pp., illustr., Ref. 357-0
This guide to using CP/M Plus on the
Commodore 128 is essential for users at
all levels, offering introductory tutorials, in-
depth treatment of major topics, a look
inside the operating system, and a CP/M
Plus command summary.

IBM PC AND COMPATIBLES

OPERATING THE IBM PC NETWORKS
Token Ring and Broadband
by Paul Berry
363 pp., illustr., Ref. 307-4
This tells you how to plan, install, and use
either the Token Ring Network or the PC
Network. Focusing on the hardware-
independent PCN software, this book
gives readers who need to plan, set-up,
operate, and administrate such networks
the head start they need to see their way
clearly right from the beginning.

THE ABC'S OF THE IBM PC
**by Joan Lasselle and Carol Ramsay
(2nd Edition)**
200 pp., illustr., Ref. 370-8
Complete hands-on training for first-time
users—in clear, understandable terms.
With step-by-step tutorials on everything
from handling disks, to running programs, to using the PC's special capabilities.

MS-DOS POWER USER'S GUIDE
by Jonathan Kamin
400 pp., illustr., Ref. 345-7
A guide to the advanced and subtle features of DOS. Contains a goldmine of
techniques to streamline operations by
automating complex tasks and repeated
operations. Includes a review of the
basics, plus tutorials on less familiar DOS
functions. For version 2.1 through 3.1

THE MS-DOS HANDBOOK
by Richard Allen King (2nd Ed)
320 pp., illustr., Ref. 185-3
The differences between the various versions and manufacturer's implementa-
tions of MS-DOS are covered in a clear
straightforward manner. Tables, maps,
and numerous examples make this
the most complete book on MS-DOS
available.

ESSENTIAL PC-DOS
by Myril and Susan Shaw
300 pp., illustr., Ref. 176-4
Whether you work with the IBM PC, XT,
PC jr. or the portable PC, this book will be
invaluable both for learning PC DOS and
for later reference.

THE IBM PC-DOS HANDBOOK
by Richard Allen King
296 pp., Ref. 103-9
Explains the PC disk operating system.
Get the most out of your PC by adapting
its capabilities to your specific needs with
confidence. Includes both the PC-DOS
features and functions, and also the
advanced capabilities.

BUSINESS GRAPHICS FOR THE IBM PC
by Nelson Ford
259 pp., illustr. Ref. 124-1
Ready-to-run programs for creating line graphs, multiple bar graphs, pie charts and more. An ideal way to use your PC's business capabilities!

MASTERING THINKTANK ON THE IBM PC
by Jonathan Kamin
350 pp., illustr, Ref. 327-9
This comprehensive guide to idea processing with ThinkTank takes you from starting a first outline to mastering advanced features. It includes undocumented tips and tricks and an introduction to *Ready!*, the RAM-resident outline processor.

THE IBM PC CONNECTION
by James Coffron
264 pp., illustr., Ref. 127-6
Teaches elementary interfacing and BASIC programming of the IBM PC for connection to external devices and household appliances.

DATA FILE PROGRAMMING ON YOUR IBM PC
by Alan Simpson
219 pp., illustr., Ref. 146-2
This book provides instructions and examples for managing data files in BASIC Programming. Design and development are extensively discussed.

Introduction to Computers

THE SYBEX PERSONAL COMPUTER DICTIONARY
120 pp. Ref. 199-3
All the definitions and acronyms of micro computer jargon defined in a handy pocket-sized edition. Includes translations of the most popular terms into ten languages.

FROM CHIPS TO SYSTEMS: AN INTRODUCTION TO MICROPROCESSORS
by Rodnay Zaks
552 pp., 400 illustr., Ref. 063-6
A comprehensive introduction to microprocessors from both a hardware and software standpoint: what they are, how they operate, how to assemble them into a complete system.

Special Interest

CELESTIAL BASIC
by Eric Burgess
300 pp. 65 illustr. Ref. 087-3
A collection of BASIC programs that rapidly complete the chores of typical astronomical computations. It's like having a planetarium in your own home! Displays apparent movement of stars, planets and meteor showers.

PERSONAL COMPUTERS AND SPECIAL NEEDS
by Frank G. Bowe
175 pp., illustr. Ref. 193-4
Learn how people are overcoming problems with hearing, vision, mobility, and learning, through the use of computer technology.

Languages

BASIC

BASIC PROGRAMS FOR SCIENTISTS AND ENGINEERS
by Alan R. Miller
318 pp., illustr., Ref. 073-8
A course in mathematical problem-solving and BASIC programming techniques, as well as a sourcebook of practical, ready-to-use programs for statistical analysis, linear and non-linear curve-fitting, numerical integration and more.

SYBEX Computer Books
are different.

Here is why . . .

At SYBEX, each book is designed with you in mind. Every manuscript is carefully selected and supervised by our editors, who are themselves computer experts. We publish the best authors, whose technical expertise is matched by an ability to write clearly and to communicate effectively. Programs are thoroughly tested for accuracy by our technical staff. Our computerized production department goes to great lengths to make sure that each book is well-designed.

In the pursuit of timeliness, SYBEX has achieved many publishing firsts. SYBEX was among the first to integrate personal computers used by authors and staff into the publishing process. SYBEX was the first to publish books on the CP/M operating system, microprocessor interfacing techniques, word processing, and many more topics.

Expertise in computers and dedication to the highest quality product have made SYBEX a world leader in computer book publishing. Translated into fourteen languages, SYBEX books have helped millions of people around the world to get the most from their computers. We hope we have helped you, too.

For a complete catalog of our publications:

SYBEX, Inc. 2021 Challenger Drive, #100, Alameda, CA 94501
Tel: (415) 523-8233/(800) 227-2346   Telex: 336311

ANNOUNCING:

SYBEX WORDPERFECT STUDY GUIDE
Duane R. Milano, Dianne Jennings, John C. Copeland
$10.95   150 pp.   7½" × 9"   ISBN 0-89588-434-8

SYBEX WORDPERFECT INSTRUCTOR'S MANUAL
Duane R. Milano, Dianne Jennings, John C. Copeland
Price: Not for Resale   50 pp.   7½" × 9"   ISBN 0-89588-435-6

The SYBEX *WordPerfect Study Guide* and *Instructor's Manual* are
supplements to *Mastering WordPerfect*. These are ideal for high school,
college, and university classes.

Each chapter contains a synopsis of the corresponding chapters in
Mastering WordPerfect.

The SYBEX *WordPerfect Study Guide* includes

- a chapter summary for review of material covered
- a summary of key words to focus on important concepts
- a multiple-choice test of about 20 questions to help assess
  progress and identify problem areas
- a series of supplemental exercises for extra hands-on practice
  with specific features and techniques
- answers to multiple-choice questions for instant feedback

The SYBEX *WordPerfect Instructor's Manual* includes an instructor's
outline of the corresponding chapter in *Mastering WordPerfect*, and also
an introduction which details suggested course syllabi.

ABOUT THE AUTHORS

Duane R. Milano received his B.A. from Saginaw Valley State College,
his M.B.A. and Ph.D. from Michigan State University. He is an associate
professor of accounting at East Texas State University. He has published
numerous books and articles in the accounting and microcomputer
disciplines. Dianne Jennings received her B.B.A. from East Texas State
University. She is a cost analyst at Serv-Air, Inc., Greenville, Texas.
John C. Copeland is a cost accountant at Walker-McDonald, Mfg.,
Greenville, Texas.

Call SYBEX Academic Sales Department at 800-227-2346 or
415-523-8233

MASTERING
WORDPERFECT

SAMPLE FILES AVAILABLE ON DISK

If you'd like to use the examples in this book without typing them yourself, you can send for a disk containing all the files used in Chapters 2-18, and several extra macro files along with explanations of what they do. To obtain this disk, complete the order form below and return it along with a check or money order for $20.00 per copy, made out to Susan B. Kelly.

Susan B. Kelly
P.O. Box 617
Sausalito, CA 94965

Name:_____

Address:_____

City:_____

State:_____ Zip:_____

Quantity:_____

WordPerfect version (4.0, 4.1, 4.2):_____